Exiles from a Future Time

from a Future Time

# Exiles from a Future Time

The Forging of the Mid-Twentieth-Century Literary Left

Alan M. Wald

Exiles

The University of North Carolina Press : Chapel Hill and London

Designed by Richard Eckersley
Set in Trinité
by Tseng Information Systems, Inc.

Manufactured in the United States of America

The paper in this book meets the guidelines for
permanence and durability of the Committee
on Production Guidelines for Book Longevity of
the Council on Library Resources.

Publication of this book was partially supported
by the William Rand Kenan Jr. Fund of the University of North Carolina Press.

Library of Congress Cataloging-in-Publication Data
Wald, Alan M., 1946–
Exiles from a future time: the forging of the mid-
twentieth-century literary left / Alan M. Wald.
    p. cm.
Includes bibliographical references and index.
ISBN 0-8078-2683-9 (alk. paper) –
ISBN 0-8078-5349-6 (pbk.: alk. paper)
1. American literature – 20th century – History
and criticism.    2. Communism and literature –
United States – History – 20th century.
3. Socialism and literature – United States –
History – 20th century.    4. Right and left
(Political science) in literature.    I. Title.
PS228.C6 W35    2002
810.9′358 – dc21    2001053069

Cloth     06  05  04  03  02      5  4  3  2  1
Paper     06  05  04  03  02      5  4  3  2  1

To my daughters, Sarah and Hannah,

in hopes of a better world

I am that exile
from a future time,
from shores of freedom
I may never know,
who hears, sounding in the surf,
tidings from the lips of waves
that meet and kiss
in the submarine gardens
of a new Atlantis . . .

— From "The Bellbuoy," by Sol Funaroff


In the Johannesburg mines
There are 240,000 natives working.

What kind of poem
Would you make out of that?

240,000 natives working
In the Johannesburg mines.

— "Johannesburg Mines," by Langston Hughes

# CONTENTS

# ILLUSTRATIONS

*Exiles from a Future Time* is the inaugural volume in a sequence treating the Literary Left in the United States as an undammed stream running from the time a Communist-led tradition was first forged in the early 1930s, through the tradition's various permutations and crises, until it was supplanted by a "New Left" cultural upheaval in the 1960s. In this and subsequent books I will reconfigure the themes, chronology, and personnel of our indigenous Marxist cultural movement, progressing in each volume from topics such as the creation of a proletarian avant-garde in poetry to radical regionalism in fiction, and then to the Left presence in mass culture and the cultural criticism produced by blacklisted literature professors in the McCarthy era.

The structure of the order of themes from *Exiles* to subsequent books in the series will not be stringently chronological, nor will it correspond to decades. Rather, a succession of leitmotifs, originating with romantic-utopian impulses in *Exiles* and shifting to militant antifascism followed by resistance to domestic repression in successor studies, will distinguish the prevalent trend of the particular books. Some cultural developments very much rooted in the 1930s (the evolution of the Workers Theater movement, the rise of the proletarian novel, the founding of the journal *Science & Society*, the attraction of Jews to the Left) will only be approached in later volumes, while careers surveyed in this first book will not be broken off precipitously but pursued to encompass episodes as late as the 1960s. In reconstructing careers and trajectories, *Exiles* and its successors grant unique accentuation to the 1940s–50s "bridge" between the 1930s and the 1960s, which are relatively neglected decades for the study of Left writing.

Moreover, in the various volumes, women authors, writers of color, gay and lesbian cultural workers, along with divers genres, will be contemplated in the general narrative as well as in discrete chapters. The design is to acknowledge the patterns of particular cultural strains associated with collective experiences, while also contesting customary compartmentalization of Left cultural workers (as "Writers of the 1930s," "Black Radicals," "Political Poets") and reassembling the intricate lacework of overlapping and interfacing that constitutes the actuality of the Left community.

While the aim of this project is not to demonstrate any particular pet theory, my contemplation of the material in this first volume has caused me to revisit, and finally to introduce, six conceptual approaches to cultural practice that in assorted, serrated, and overhanging fashions apprehend central (and memorable) aspects of the lives and works of my subjects:

1. The "elective affinity" that impelled them into a common project.
2. The "revolutionary romanticism" that bedeviled even the most modern of their cultural endeavors.
3. The "force fields" of publications, networks of cultural activists, and writers' organizations that partly shaped cultural work within the framework of national and international events.
4. The "gender ideology" with which women writers grappled as they sought to negotiate personal experience and political loyalties.
5. The "Afro-cosmopolitanism" championed by Black Marxists in white America.
6. The avant-garde quality of the poetry ensuing from the Left's equivocal quarrel with High Modernism.

Some chapters give extended stress to one concept over another; for example, Chapters 3 through 5 are apportioned to exploring creative personalities within the force fields of Left institutional infrastructures, while Chapters 2, 6, and the conclusion speak to modernism and the avant-garde. Yet the concepts also accrue particular attention in parts of other chapters; for example, gender ideology and Afro-cosmopolitanism are somewhat addressed in Chapter 3, and then both are investigated more exhaustively in Chapters 7 and 8. In some other areas — sexual orientation, connections with the film industry — some particulars are given in *Exiles*, but extensive analysis is projected for a later volume. In order to avoid bogging down the narrative with excessive theoretical discourse, these six approaches and other concepts (such as Walter Benjamin's "living in a state of emergency") will be elaborated, albeit briefly, in the most appropriate chapter.

*Exiles* carries forward the exertions of other scholars to speak to cultural commitment in terms of political affiliations, stances, and activities, as well as in respect to the aesthetics and forms of cultural production itself.[1] I put my chief accent, however, on individualized research into matters such as the writer's intimate life, friendships, occupation, and precise political activities, as a prerequisite to reckoning the "value" of artistic work. Thus, in a sharp departure from earlier studies, including several of my own, the focus of literary analysis is not restricted to works of literature intended to explicitly dramatize political ideas, as in the depiction of a strike or an account of a conversion to socialism. Rather, I pose the question: What kinds of texts did writers with radical commitments, ascertained by their having substantial ideological and organizational ties to the Communist Left, actually yield? Readers may be surprised by the answers.

My motivation to produce such a "revisionist" work about the mid-twentieth-century Literary Left stems first of all from my sustained encounters as a reader with the fiction and poetry generated by several hundred imaginative writers who identified with Marxist movements in mid-century. (By this I mean writers who either openly proclaimed their political affiliation or else demonstrated an association with the Communist Party and Left-led organizations over a protracted period of years, thereby indicating that the connection was not merely an accident or the result of a misunderstanding.)[2] While probing the range of possible relations between creative practice and radical political commitment, I found that many lesser-known authors were as intriguing and meaningful as the twenty or so "canonical" radical writers who have dominated earlier studies.

Most significant, my method of evaluating cultural and political practice that incorporates subjective dimensions and quotidian activities is rooted in first-hand primary research into personal biography and the circumstances (networks, writers' organizations, mentor relationships) involved in literary production. Consequently, judgments are not derived by looking at experiences and writings restrictively through the prism of Communist Party positions or theoretical estimates of Stalinism, although, of course, such policies and assessments are significant factors. Where befitting, I have also tried to evaluate individual writers by adhering to a stance suggested by the late Black activist and minister Adam Clayton Powell. Reverend Powell avowed that Harlemites neither demonized Communists nor "fell over backwards in admiration," but judged them "individually" on the basis of their commitment to Black equality.[3] I, too, strive to judge the writers individually on the basis of the merits of their cultural and political practice. When I furthermore identify writers as having been pro-Communist in various fashions, I am not intending to offer that affiliation as a simple explanation for their values or their writing, or to translate psychological and artistic affairs into the language of politics. To the contrary, such a political identification serves to render their lives and work as much more intricately problematic by adding yet another feature – and a vexing one at that – to lives already plentiful in personal and cultural experiences.

Second, my decision to strike out in a new direction was reinforced by more than two decades of teaching mid-twentieth-century radical poetry, fiction, drama, film, and criticism. My students responded to the literature variously. Their contemporary preoccupations led them to preferences for novels and poems that I hardly anticipated. Frequently evidenced by undergraduates was a difficulty in grasping apparent contradictions raised by the professed ideals of the writers and the sometimes sensational charges of their anti-Communist literary and political opponents. As a result, I have also tried to produce a study that will address the concerns of young cultural and political activists today who might profit from knowing more about the attainments and inadequacies of their predecessors.

It is also important to note that a number of my findings, such as those recapitulated in the conclusion to this volume, are intimately tied to the methodology of this study. For example, one of my aims in Exiles is to compensate for the deficiencies of many earlier cultural histories to fully appreciate the subtleties and contradictions of the avant-garde aspects of pro-Communist poets, diversely evident in the "proletarian" as well as post-1935 "People's Front" eras. My suspicion is that the limitations of such outlooks were bolstered by approaches downgrading the biographically idiosyncratic elements of the artists (sexual orientation, regional background, ethnicity, details about precise political commitments), partly due to the absence of information, which made it more tempting to conceive of pro-Communist authors primarily as bearers of a general "Left" ideological position. To re-introduce the individualized *habitus* (in Pierre Bourdieu's sense)[4] of the writer's singular being and consciousness is not to become a biographer but to restore the self-activity of Left cultural workers as well as to supply some of the neglected mediations in the creative act – especially the mentality of the artist and the force field of the institutions within which he or she worked.

The final version of this first volume on the forging of a Left tradition is the result of wrenching negotiations among all sorts of contending claims in determining scope and structure, as well as the limitations of my own areas of expertise. These are some of the reasons why, even though I designed this overall project to dramatically advance our knowledge of mid-twentieth-century literary history and, more specifically, the Literary Left, there is no claim to have written a "definitive" study, least of all a work that in any way precludes further exploration of the field. For example, it is crucial to recognize the "linguistic limits" of my project. Beyond the scope of this study are the novels, poetry, drama, and criticism created by u.s. socialists who wrote in languages besides English; in particular, that of the thriving Left-wing movement of Yiddish authors that lasted from the 1890s through the Cold War, including the "Sweatshop Poets," and the "Prolet-pen" contributors to Der Hammer, Signal, and Yiddishe Kultur.[5] Interrelations between literary practice and painting, cartooning, sculpting, dance, music (including composing, choral singing, and folk singing), acting, and directing are slighted as well, although references to extant scholarship will be cited where pertinent.

Instead, I will count this and subsequent volumes successful to the extent that they open up novel areas of inquiry for students, scholars, and cultural workers; facilitate the rediscovery of long-neglected writers; promote the rethinking of familiar texts and episodes, and the rectification of mistakes that I have made; and expedite the unearthing of original information about the many literary figures who are of necessity mentioned only in passing. My conclusions are meant as hypotheses, although some are obviously far more strongly held than others.

As I conducted the early phases of the research for this multivolume study, my beloved wife of seventeen years, Celia Stodola Wald (1946–1992), suffered from the onset and fatal effects of the pernicious disease scleroderma. Our intense relationship began with the rise of the New Left in the mid-1960s, which imparted a shared purpose to our lives. *Exiles from a Future Time* is dedicated to our extraordinary daughters, Sarah and Hannah.

## A Note on Terminology and Illustrations

In order to tackle complex and often misunderstood political-literary relationships, I have adopted methods of capitalization in this book that may deviate from editorial norms practiced at certain journals and publishing houses. In particular, I capitalize "Communist" and "Communism" when referring to official parties of the Third International, but not when pertaining to other adherents of Bolshevism or revolutionary Marxism (which encompasses small-"c" communists such as Trotskyists, Bukharinists, council communists, and so forth). Moreover, I capitalize "Party" when the word is part of an organization's name, such as Communist Party, Socialist Party, Socialist Workers Party, Democratic Party, and Progressive Party. When used by itself, however, the capitalized term "Party" designates the Communist Party, the dominant political organization in this study. Finally, I capitalize the term "Left" in respect to political movements and individuals more radical than New Deal liberalism, even if they may have been pro-FDR at times.

In addition, I follow the practice of capitalizing "Black" when referring to populations of the African Diaspora. The reason is to underscore that my concern in this study is the national culture of African Americans, not skin color or any other alleged mark of "race."

I must note that there is extraordinary inconsistency in the history of the Left in regard to the use of an apostrophe in names of organizations such as New Playwrights Theater, Workers Theater, American Writers' (or Writers) Congress, and so forth. Where possible, I have tried to follow the predominant style used by key participants.

Photographs are crucial to any narrative seeking to humanize literary and political activity, but are limited by availability, cost, and the amount of space that can be allocated in a book already quite long. Moreover, after forty or fifty years, it is sometimes difficult to identify the exact year in which the photograph was taken or the name of the photographer. In the captions to the photographs I have attempted to give the fullest information available at this time.

In the Notes, the citation style for issues of the New Masses will vary according to whether the publication is on a weekly or monthly schedule.

# Strange Communists I Have Known

On 9 July 1945, Guy Endore, a popular novelist and Hollywood screenwriter, awoke as usual before dawn. Of wiry build with brownish blond hair and blue eyes, Endore weighed a trim 145 pounds and stood five feet seven-and-a-half inches tall, looking at least a decade younger than his forty-five years. As he reached for the pad and pencil that always rested near his bedside to record his waking thoughts, a characteristically gentle yet enigmatic smile spread across his face.

Politically, Endore was what historians of the Literary Left would regard as an orthodox "Stalinist." In 1934, even before formally joining the Communist Party, he wrote the *New Republic* to criticize an editorial that condemned the violent disruption by Communists of a Socialist Party meeting in Madison Square Garden, which was called to defend the armed struggle of Social Democrats in Austria against the dictatorship of Engelbert Dollfuss. The Communists' thuggish seizure of the Socialists' platform was one of the manifestations of the disruptive "United Front from Below" strategy of the Communist International that drove one-time Party sympathizers such as John Dos Passos (1896–1970), Edmund Wilson (1895–1972), and Lionel Trilling (1905–1975) to publicly oppose the Party. Endore, however, insisted that the Socialists, not the Communists, were responsible for creating the divisive provocation; he accused them of excluding Communists from the speakers' list, confiscating a Communist banner, and inviting a conservative to address the rally.[1]

During the early 1930s, Endore had read everything by Marx and Engels available in English, French, and German, as well as Werner Sombart's multivolume history of capitalism. Sometime between 1936 and 1938, at the height of the infamous Moscow Purge Trials, when philosopher John Dewey (1859–1952) led a campaign to expose their frame-up character, Endore took out Communist Party membership after moving from New York to Hollywood. In the fall of 1939, as the news of the Hitler-Stalin Pact drove a number of disaffected intellectuals from the League of American Writers and other Communist-led organizations, Endore extolled the pact as evidence of Stalin's tactical genius, and he concurred in the Party's disbanding of its extremely successful Hollywood Anti-Nazi League. A year and a half later, when the pact was repudiated in the wake of Hitler's attack on the Soviet Union, Endore wrote his friends: "Everyone is now laughing at the Communists. Personally, I still think that the Pact was fine: It turned Hitler's fury in every other direction but Russia for two years."[2]

In May 1945, official Communist criticism from abroad began, which led to the expulsion of Communist Party general secretary Earl Browder in February 1946 for "social imperialism"; Endore, however, waxed enthusiastic that the comrades were once more returning to their principled politics. Thus he decided, on 9 July 1945, to dash off a letter to New Masses literary editor Isidor Schneider (1896–1977), praising the public statement by French Communist Jacques Duclos that signaled the eventual end of Browderism: "Nothing so hopeful has struck us as this recent French detergent."[3]

According to recollections of friends, family, and his own private correspondence, a typical morning in the summer month when Endore sent this letter might begin with Endore jotting down his waking thoughts, after which he would return his pad of paper to the table. He would then place it alongside the Gideon Bible that was always near at hand, although he was quick to reassure all friends who inquired that, while a Jew by birth (his father had changed the family name from Goldstein), he was actually a lifelong mystic sympathetic to theosophy. Next Endore might consult Genesis, chapter 9, on which he had been meditating the night before. More than twenty years earlier, that passage had convinced him that he must convert humankind to vegetarianism or the species would destroy itself.

From the corner of his eye, Endore might note with satisfaction the bookshelf that held his masterpiece on the Paris Commune, the 1933 best-selling horror classic The Werewolf of Paris. Next to it was his new novel, which would create much excitement in the review and letters column of the Communist weekly New Masses, the psychoanalytical mystery thriller Methinks the Lady (1945).[4] Endore would then bounce energetically to his feet and walk toward the wall, where he stood on his head for at least half an hour twice a day. He maintained this practice despite once having been the subject of a hostile interrogation by local Communist Party leaders based on the circulation of nasty rumors about his study and practice of Yoga.[5] Next he would enjoy his morning repast of fruit and nuts, which, together with a special health bread that he carried with him to restaurants and dinner parties, was virtually the only kind of food he ate since he had begun the research for his gruesome werewolf novel in the early 1930s.[6]

This was reportedly the daily regimen in the mid-1940s of the rare genius, impish personality, devout Stalinist, and militant antivivisectionist born Samuel Guy Endore in New York City in 1900. He died in Los Angeles in 1970. During a career in which he shuttled between New York publishers and the Hollywood film industry, he wrote best-selling novels including the Book-of-the-Month-Club selection *King of Paris* (a 1956 biography of Alexander Dumas), coauthored influential films such as *The Story of G.I. Joe* (1945), and produced a series of pamphlets and books on controversial causes.[7] These ranged from *The Crime at Scottsboro* (1938), which defended a group of African American youth framed on rape charges in 1931 in Alabama; to *The Sleepy Lagoon Mystery* (1944), which supported a group of Mexican American young people falsely charged with murder in Los Angeles; and finally to *Synanon* (1968), an exposition of the philosophy of the drug rehabilitation center and utopian community founded in 1958 in Los Angeles, of which Endore, by then a former Communist, was the intellectual guru.

By all reasonable criteria Endore was an exceptionally loyal Communist for nearly two decades, yet his personality and literary output bear scant resemblance to the popular conception of canonical Communist writers held by most students and scholars of literature, and others concerned with literary history. This is partly because only a handful of books, aside from a few biographies, treat the personalities and private lives of Left-wing writers; even then, the focus is too often on a few prominent writers who departed from the movement in abject bitterness. Of the dozen representative Euro-American male writers profiled in Daniel Aaron's distinguished study *Writers on the Left: Episodes in American Literary Communism* (1961), only three held membership in the Communist Party when the Depression began; by 1939, two of them had left the Party on bad terms. As Aaron's subtitle recognizes, the "episodes" convey a pivotal component but scarcely the comprehensive narrative. Endore, for example, is cited only as the author of a "violent story of the Santo Domingo slave insurrection."[8]

It is useful to recall that in the early spring of 1960, Joseph Freeman (1897–1965), a sixty-three-year-old veteran leader of the Literary Left, offered Aaron, a forty-eight-year-old Smith College professor, some words of advice for his book-in-progress:

> As the story of the literary Left is told nowadays it involves only Big Shots, men and women of Distinction, award winners. But one important key to the literary Left . . . was that it was trying to develop writers from The Lower Depths, people who would write from a revolutionary viewpoint not out of abstract fantasies or for the sake of a career, but because such was their life and their hope.[9]

When Aaron's *Writers on the Left* appeared, Freeman was gratified, as he was among the dozen writers featured in the narrative.[10] Yet when novelist Josephine Herbst (1892–1969) saw Aaron's book, she reacted bitterly: "His heroes were the entrepreneurs of writing, the head-boys who have been mostly re-sponsible for the re-hashes. . . . The entrepreneurs whom Dan Aaron wrote about were all stuck in the claustrophobia of New York City."[11] Herbst came from the West and frequently traveled in the 1930s; she is barely mentioned in Aaron's 500-page tome, and her novels are not among those described.

Other writers of the era griped with equal fervor about the limitations of *Writers on the Left*. In a 1974 interview, novelist Albert Maltz (1908–1985) declared it "A book without a heart" on the grounds that Aaron focused on "polemic," but not "creative work." Maltz asserted that this was due to Aaron's fear of "taking a stand," of saying that "this has merit and this didn't," lest he be tarred with the Communist brush.[12] But it is just as likely that Maltz's criticism was motivated by his awareness that his own record as a polemicist was embarrassing – due to his public recantation of his criti-cisms of Communist cultural policy in 1946 – which is the only time Maltz is discussed in Aaron's study.[13] Likewise, Walter Snow (1905–1973), for many years a pro-Communist writer who strongly identified with William Z. Fos-ter's brand of political leadership, scornfully denounced Aaron's "distor-tions" in a series of letters in the early 1970s that he sent to his stepson, the historian Maurice Isserman, which Snow attributes to Aaron's "major reliance [for information] on embittered renegades, especially Joseph Free-man."[14] In each of the aforementioned grievances, there is the customary merging of transparent self-promotion with legitimate concern.

Nonetheless, much as one might belabor Aaron for his limitations,[15] it is no easy task to narrate the story of a cultural movement engaging hun-dreds of writers, and influencing thousands more, over several decades. In the forty years since the publication of *Writers on the Left*, no other scholarly book on the Communist cultural movement has brought as many writers to life.[16] Moreover, while various kinds of attractions to Marxism may bind together several hundred writers in an identifiable tradition, their lives and work can hardly be adequately explained by such ideological and organiza-tional loyalties.

In the instance of Guy Endore, with whose idiosyncratic morning rou-tine this introduction began, one has a writer whose literary value has a comparatively indirect and elusive correlation with his commitment to the Communist Party. His most explicitly revolutionary work, *Babouk* (1934), a masterful narrative set in the early period of the Haitian slave revolution, appeared while he was ideologically and emotionally drawn to the Party but

4

not yet a member.[17] After joining and teaching novel writing at the Party-sponsored People's Educational Center in Los Angeles, he wrote his psycho-sexual thriller, *Methinks the Lady* (1945). His most successful novel, *King of Paris* (1956), appeared as he was severing from the Party organization, but it was written while he was still friendly to Communism's basic principles and active mainly in the anti-blacklisting campaign although no longer a member of the Hollywood branch. Did Party membership ever directly curtail the content of his literary output? Endore later claimed that certain members of the Party discouraged him from completing a nonfiction "History of Human Skill" that he had planned to publish, due to doctrinal disagreements. Yet the work he valued most, an autobiographical work called "The Gordon Family," was suppressed not by the Communist Party but initially by his own family members and then by publishers who considered it unsellable.[18]

To what extent is Endore an anomaly in the Communist literary movement, a poor example for understanding its cultural work? A close look at Endore's early life discloses many unique features that might usefully be deployed to assist in explaining assorted aspects of his wide-ranging creative life. Yet there are no serious reasons for declaring Endore altogether atypical, thereby discounting him from consideration as a bona fide example of the Communist Literary Left. His work cannot be set aside, for instance, on the grounds that his status as a Columbia University graduate means that he experienced a more secure or privileged youth than typical Left writers usually identified with the proletarian genre. Like several of the canonical pro-Communist writers whose experiences with colleges were minimal or nonexistent (Mike Gold and Jack Conroy, for example), Endore came from a background of financial and personal instability. His mercurial father had worked as a coal miner in Pennsylvania, although occasionally he sold an invention or made an investment that did extraordinarily well, momentarily precipitating a phase of prosperity that never lasted. His mother, unable to cope with extreme poverty, committed suicide at a young age, after which Endore was shunted to an orphanage.

Unlike Conroy's and Gold's writing, however, the backbone of Endore's literary reputation never rested on a working-class or strike setting, a narrative of "bottom dog" life, or a "socialist conversion" story. Endore's forté was and would remain a remarkable series of rich, subtle, and elegant—but often violent and erotic—fictionalized biographies of Casanova, Joan of Arc, Rousseau, Voltaire, the Marquis De Sade, and Alexander Dumas.[19] "Most Endore" was a phrase coined by Marxist theater and film director Herbert Biberman (1900-1971), one of the "Hollywood Ten," to refer to a style characterized by neat scholarship, fervent devotion to material, and a "respect for a reader's willingness to adventure."[20] The New York critic Alexander Wolcott, struck by the discrepancy between the diminutive Endore's mild personality and the bloody horrifics of *The Werewolf of Paris*, dubbed Endore "the weremouse."[21]

I contend that Endore's career as a novelist, which continued long after the Depression, is as legitimate a part of the Communist Literary Left as were the careers of Gold and Conroy. Yet nowhere are achievements such as Endore's featured in studies of Left-wing fiction. To reestablish the full scope and trajectory of the Communist Cultural Left, I have embarked on a project that will return to memory dozens of extraordinarily talented writers of unique and pioneering texts who have "disappeared" from cultural history, while reassessing scores of others who have been appraised out of context (that is, without taking into account the author's Left commitments) due to the still existing secrecy about activities of the Literary Left during the Cold War.

As the example of Endore dramatizes, I have also found that a project such as this cannot be merely a literary study but needs to be partly a collective biography. In some cases I have been able to ascertain a density of detail about a writer's background; in others, selective anecdotes that may give the reader a feeling of the lived complexity of radical commitment. Although I have tried to remain factually grounded in verifiable claims, this project is somewhat akin to the writing of narrative poetry or prose fiction; I mean this in the sense of the distinction between poetry and criticism that one-time Marxist Kenneth Burke (1897–1993) noted at the 1937 American Writers' Congress: "the poet's way is necessarily more cumbersome. It is the longer way round. It has not got there until it has humanized, personalized."[22] Veteran radical poet Norman MacLeod (1906–1985) put it in like fashion in a letter to novelist Jack Conroy in which he contemplated the early 1930s from the vantage point of the late 1960s: "The older I get the more I see that it was and is the human stuff that gives or gave flesh and blood and meaning to the ideas and the spirit of the times."[23] Josephine Herbst, in particular, resisted the notion of interpellating writers into a construct of "The Thirties"; rather, the era was a "humanscape – the setting of my loves and discoveries."[24]

Fashioning a "humanscape," of course, means going beyond the official published record to more intimate sources. As Freeman observed in a communication to Herbst, "The letters of writers are the only way we have to know how writers lived in any given time and place."[25] Oral history is a precious tool as well, although a small quantity may be hazardous if it lacks the controls of historical context and a breadth of other accounts.[26] Yet the pitfalls of oral history need to be poised against the considerable perspicuity of journalist Murray Kemptom's 1957 apology to blacklisted screenwriter and former Communist Dalton Trumbo (1905-1976), acknowledging that a personal interview might have mitigated the unfair portrait of Trumbo that appeared in *Part of Our Time: Some Ruins and Monuments of the Thirties* (1955): "I can only plead, pompous as it sounds, that I have come to believe it is the greatest of crimes to write about a man whose face you have never seen."[27] Although face-to-face meetings with elderly, and sometimes ornery, writers can be emotionally grueling and physically exhausting, they have been indispensable to the historically contextualized humanscape I have endeavored to sculpt in this narrative. How else other than by humanizing and personalizing can one tell the important story of "engaged" or "committed" writers in a way that acknowledges their sacrifices as well as their very human mistakes?

Their mistakes, of course, are so infamous that one historian justifiably remarked, "For most Americans, intellectuals included, few tasks are easier than deriding Communists."[28] But for those seeking to more fairly explore this United States version of *Littérature Engagée*, more needs to be said about the writers' sacrifices, their loss of jobs, relocation under duress to other countries, serving of prison terms, risking of their own lives in violent confrontations with right-wing mobs, and, in some cases, dying on the battlefields in Spain and in World War II — fighting for a new world that they would never see.

In the narrative that follows I will acquaint the reader with a range of cultural workers who both shaped, and were shaped by, the Communist cultural movement in mid-century. Some names may be well known from earlier studies — Mike Gold, Joseph Freeman, Meridel Le Sueur, Langston Hughes, Richard Wright — but many more have been brought up only in passing, if at all. The heart of this inaugural volume, *Exiles from a Future Time*, lies in the formation of the tradition and organization of the cultural Left, especially in association with the antinomies affecting its avant-garde poets, the fashioning of a Black radical literary movement, the unease between feminist concerns and class identity, and the role of dissimilar personalities in the force field of Party-led publications and institutions. Some of the same cultural workers will reappear in later volumes where I address more fully the production of fiction, drama, film, and criticism, as well as gay Left writers, Jewish American writers, and writers of color in addition to African Americans. Moreover, the volume's leitmotif of an aura of a melancholic romanticism — haunting the very utopian longings birthed by the spirit of revolutionary romanticism discussed in Chapter 1 – shall return as well in new forms as the tradition wends its way to a kind of tragic "reconciliation with reality" after 1956.

Since dates of publication, and dates of life spans, are indispensable to this cultural history, my general practice has been to date a pertinent author, event, or book in parentheses at first mention, unless the dates themselves are part of the narrative. However, this is violated on certain occasions, such as when there are lists of individuals contributing to a publication, or when the date seems relatively inconsequential. Often dates will be repeated when the publication or individual is considered in dissimilar contexts, or at distant points in the narrative. For individuals still alive as the book goes to press, I furnish only a birthdate. In a few cases I provide a question mark where I have been unable to definitively determine the date of birth or death of an individual, or else I indicate "dates unknown" where I have been incapable of discovering them.

There are many cultural workers who appear in cameo, or as part of lists of names, in this volume; they will be more fully fleshed out in subsequent ones, and their cultural legacies will likewise be appraised at that time. Still, I recognize that of the hundreds of individuals named throughout the narrative, some will be quite familiar to specialists of various kinds, while many more will be entirely unknown to the general reader. Therefore, at first mention of a person, I have provided brief biographical "tags" to help bring the name to life in some significant way (usually by identifying a person's field of work but also by sometimes indicating nationality, color, sexual orientation, political background, and so forth), and I have also provided an insert with photographs to reinforce the sense of the writers' individualities. Still, the use of tags can be hazardous if the reader employs them narrowly, and, of course, readers may wonder why certain tags are employed in some cases and not in others. The explanation for decisions as to whom to tag, and how, partly flows from the author's surmise that, at this point in the recovery of literary history, a general reader is likely to assume a writer to be Euro-American and heterosexual unless otherwise identified; Jewish only if the name is identifiably such; and so forth. I regret any poor judgment calls that I have made in the use of both tags and dates.

## CHAPTER 1

# American Jeremiad

## Recording Angel

On the afternoon of 28 June 1961, the former New Masses editor Joseph Free-man (1897-1965) lugubriously trudged over to the old red-brick Baptist-Congregationalist church on Washington Square South in New York City to attend the memorial service for the writer Kenneth Fearing (1902-1961), dead of lung cancer at age fifty-nine. The next day, Freeman mailed a seven-page report on the event to poet Horace Gregory (1898-1982), the friend and political associate of both Freeman and Fearing since the Depression era, when Fearing's verse seemed a beacon for the cultural Left.[1]

The death of Fearing, the premier poet of the Communist cultural movement who turned maverick mystery writer, thirty-two years after the stock market crash of 1929, occurred at perhaps the nadir in the history of Left-wing poetry. Just five years earlier, the old Communist Literary Left, which had inspired and then disappointed all three men, was dealt a near-death blow by Khrushchev's revelations of Stalin's crimes, coming in the wake of nearly a decade of Cold War witch hunting. The only poets of national reputation who called themselves large "C" Communists after that date were Walter Lowenfels (1897-1976) and Thomas McGrath (1916-1990). As Fearing died in 1961, a nascent New Left was birthing beneath the placid surface of U.S. society evidenced by the burgeoning civil rights demonstrations in the South and elements of "Beat" culture in the urban North and West. Within three or four years this new radicalism would burst forth as a powerful and transformative social and cultural force encompassing the Free Speech, anti-Vietnam War, Black Power, and Women's Liberation movements.

Fearing, whose sensibilities were formed during the 1920s and who reached maturity in the 1930s, who lived on as a lonely Left-wing fighter on the cultural front in the 1940s and 1950s, and who anticipated New Left cultural and political attitudes in his Kafkaesque view of modern bureaucracy and neo-Luddite themes,[2] died on the eve of the emergence of the New Left. Freeman, who was a genuine bridge from the old Masses (1911-17) to the New Masses (1926-48) until forced out of the Communist movement for alleged undisciplined behavior in 1939 to become a chastened but un-repentant "post-Communist," succumbed to cancer four years later. Only Gregory, who in the early Depression published subtle and well-crafted volumes of revolutionary verse such *Chelsea Rooming House* (1930), *No Retreat* (1933), and *Chorus for Survival* (1935), lived into the era of the new radicalism, dying in poverty and near obscurity in 1982. Ironically, as a poet of the Left, Gregory had already given up the ghost four decades earlier, even before reports began to circulate of his red-baiting attacks on his pro-Communist colleague at Sarah Lawrence College, poet Genevieve Taggard (1894-1948), a harassment that many on the Left believed hastened her death due to complications of hypertension at the onset of the Cold War.[3]

Nevertheless, Joseph Freeman, consummate in the role he played during his last few years of forgiving almost all those who had earlier shunned him, both from the Left and the Right, wrote with an open heart to Gregory about Fearing's memorial. Exuding that irrepressible and irresistible charm for which he was famous – Gregory would remember Freeman as "a wonderfully radiant human being"[4] – Freeman described himself to Gregory as modestly sitting alone in the last row under a high dome and beneath stained glass windows of the Romanesque Judson Memorial Church. Like an invisible recording angel, Freeman silently observed the Fearing mourners as they entered. Then, Freeman's imagination began "to spin a funeral discourse of its own" as he conjured up a memory of the first time he met Fearing.

It was the summer of 1927. Floyd Dell (1887-1969), Freeman's comrade from the original *Masses* and *Liberator*, had asked him for an introduction to several members of the "Younger Generation" so that Dell might use the resulting material for a novel in progress. The ever-accommodating Freeman organized a party and asked his sister, Ruth, and brother, Harry, to invite their friends.

Harry Freeman (1906-1978), a recent Cornell graduate embarking on a life-long career at TASS (the Soviet News Agency), brought Fearing, already known as a published poet, to the party at the East 16th Street Manhattan penthouse of Egmont Arens (1899-1966), the industrial designer and *New Masses* editor. Following introductions, Dell turned to Fearing and asked him to recite verse. To Dell, this was a traditional activity at radical literary parties in the 1920s. Indeed, only a few weeks earlier, Dell and Freeman had attended a party in Croton, New York, where they stood and performed together for two hours – Dell reciting Byron, Shelley, Keats, Wordsworth, and Millay; Freeman declaiming Eliot, Pound, Cummings, and Yeats. But

Fearing responded to Dell's request with the profane groan, "O shit!" Then he stumbled into the kitchen for another slug of gin.

After an interlude, Freeman turned to Dell and said: " 'If you are going to do a novel about the Younger Generation you ought to give careful consideration to what Kenneth Fearing said.' 'O shit?' 'O shit,' I said. 'It's the end of one era and the beginning of another.' " Freeman concluded his letter to Gregory with the observation, "[T]hat summer night, Kenneth had revealed the break with romanticism that was to mark not only his own poetry but the poetry of others in our time."[5]

To what extent was it merely hyperbole for Freeman to assert that a rupture with romanticism marked the poetry rising to center stage among the 1930s generation? The "O shit!" response makes a good story, but one that scarcely proves that the advent of a new phase in Left poetry began with Fearing's blunt refusal to carry on the performative tradition of public recitation. Such a decision may well have been idiosyncratic to the man and the moment.

It is one of the contentions of this book that Freeman misperceived the genuine character of Left poetic practice in his 1961 observation, just as twenty-five years earlier he unduly simplified his own "representative" trajectory toward Communism in his autobiography, *An American Testament*:

> If I have ventured to recount certain personal experiences, it has been on the assumption that they might be of interest to those who want to know how an American writer, starting from one set of social, moral and literary values, may arrive at another; how he may develop from romanticism toward reality.[6]

The narrative of Left poets moving beyond romanticism on the road to "reality" may seem opportune to conveying the hands-on engagement of Marxist writers, especially motivated by the pressure of mutating historical conditions, and their efforts to embrace, and often immerse themselves in, working-class life, experiences, and battles. Yet it also bolsters conventional figurations of "Great Depression Literature," "Proletarian Writers," "Socialist Realism," and other hackneyed images used to conflate the Literary Left into "The Thirties" as a rather dreary interlude; the effect can be to close off the Left from earlier and later decades, along with the more diversified cultural advances associated with the 1920s and 1940s. The literary term "realism," more than "romanticism," also appears merited by the direct language, colloquial (and sometimes dialect) speech, and antibourgeois themes of Left-wing poetic strophes. Yet these attributes are not specific to realism, having been traits of avant-garde and much romantic verse since the time of Rimbaud and Whitman.[7] Moreover, if we turn from literary style to epistemology, the Communist Left's "realism" in regard to the race and class inequalities of capitalism and the rise of fascism was offset by illusions in the Soviet Union and the future of the American working class that might most generously be designated as "romantic idealism." One of the uncommon books about U.S. Communism that manages to humanize a sweep of actors is Vivian Gornick's justly titled *The Romance of American Communism* (1977).

In more rigorously cultural terms, Freeman's contention might seem persuasive in that Marxist poets customarily esteem but ultimately discard romanticism, due to the historic links between Marxism and the Enlightenment's secularism, rationality grounded on empiricism, and convictions about material progress producing widening democratization. Moreover, the common kinship of the term "romantic" with the gothic, erotic, adventurous, and individualistic, along with romanticism's cults of nature and of genius, do not resonate with the predominant practice of Marxist poets. Yet there are other significant strains within romanticism that seem appurtenant to the modern Left; in particular, romanticism's mode of vision and imagination organized about the goal of a social utopia; the Wordsworthian demand for simplicity in language; the desire to regenerate humanity by returning to some essential qualities deformed by contemporary values and social organization; and specific styles such as the meditative voice of the romantic lyric. This last quality informs the three volumes of verse, published between 1933 and 1955, of the Communist poet Edwin Rolfe (born Solomon Fishman, 1909–1954), remembered by a friend decades later as "a Jewish replica of Keats."[8] If adapted to contemporary urban life, and tempered by the brutality of modern racism and fascism, the category of romanticism remains beneficial to apprehending the evolution of the Left tradition.

Nonetheless, despite Freeman's hyperbole, there was legitimacy to his avowal that a cultural break or rupture was in progress between the 1920s and the early 1930s. The national and international political emergencies of the Depression era, combined with the dynamism of publications and organizations led by Communist Party members and sympathizers, did forge a unique cultural crucible that would mix older romantic and more recent modernist legacies in unprecedented ways. What ensued, in terms of appraising poetic practice on a particular as well as an accumulated basis, must be apprehended as the result of distinctive temperaments finding their subjects and forms in affiliation with an increasingly organized political movement — one that variously gained their confidence and became the repository for their hopes. The coalescence of a distinct Communist-led Left tradition in the pre-World War II years was demonstrated on the "policy" level in two definite stages documented by resolutions of writers' groups and statements of Party leaders assigned to the cultural field.

First, there was the revolutionary, proletarian poetry retrospectively embraced as well as freshly produced in the early 1930s – poetry that seemed most befitting to the longing that one's art might serve as a "weapon" in the "class struggle." This phase was followed by the democratic and "people's poetry" appearing under the aegis of the post-1935 Popular Front, then theorized as an instrument in the "anti-fascist struggle."[9] In poetic practice, of course, nothing quite so clearly bifurcated and monodimensional occurred. A substantial number of poets in the 1930s, mostly younger ones, produced verse amidst the contradictory terrain forged by their early education in conventional romantic poetry, their attraction to the new modernism, and by the competing emotional claims of the evolving Left-wing orientations. There is no doubt that writers who migrated to the Left in the early 1930s were amply alert to the 1935 policy change and not infrequently made accommodations; Rolfe, for example, after the Popular Front, voluntarily revised an earlier poem, "Cheliuskin," concerning the Soviet polar expedition, so that the less sectarian phrase "socialist will" was exchanged for "Soviet will," and "the people of Leningrad" replaced "the proletariat of Leningrad."[10] Conversely, all through the Popular Front a number of writers, especially those who felt most attached to the Party, persisted in demarcating their verse as "proletarian," and Party publications continued to exercise the idiom as well.[11]

In both the early and late 1930s, the Party's orientations, magazines, and institutions were as emancipating as they were constricting. They furnished a focus and theme, a potential audience and venues of publication for writers who might otherwise have gone unpublished, and a set of technical problems around which diverse individuals could hold discussions and debates. Yet such alignments could also be turned into cudgels with which to beat literary or political or even personal rivals who might be imputed with deviations. Some leading Communists even used the requisiteness of political commitment to suggest that literary work be abandoned, a view reflected by Party leader William Z. Foster in his correspondence with V. F. Calverton.[12] Equally problematic is the origin of these priorities in political, rather than literary, strategies, strategies significantly generated by the Communist Party membership's faith in the Soviet Union as the vanguard of freedom and justice.

The USSR connection was reinforced by the subject matter of certain poems (as in Rolfe's "Cheliuskin") and parallel campaigns in U.S. and Soviet publications against writing regarded as too "negative." Thus an erroneous view took root outside Party circles that Left poetry was primarily driven by "foreign" ideology rather than, first of all, the complexity of a poet's creative drive. Soviet critics certainly wrote long essays urging U.S. writers to cleave to priorities generated by international literary conferences organized under Comintern auspices; yet there were admitted contradictions in regard to national situations. One example is that Soviet literary officials abandoned the idea of "proletarian literature" after 1932 in favor of "socialist realism," yet the latter doctrine presupposed a successful socialist revolution – hardly the state of affairs in countries to which Comintern policies were exported.[13] Moreover, even if Soviet critics urged U.S. writers to dramatize the Stalinist version of Marxist eschatology, most indigenous pro-Communist poetry equally shared in the millenarian vision of a signal destiny for the United States characteristic of mainstream writers. The omnipresent obsession with discouraging allegedly "decadent" and "passive" writing appears to have generated independently from U.S. as well as Soviet sources.[14]

Furthermore, the impact of the Communist cultural tradition is more consequential than just a Depression "moment." Writers drawn to the Communist Left exhibited impressive coherency, albeit with diverse strains that persevered over the years, the maturing of particular poets over decades, and the appearance of newer trends in the atmosphere of the postwar era. What was necessary for this coherency was that the poets perpetuate their general loyalties to the Left and persevere in publishing in collaborative journals and volumes. The tradition first forged in the early Depression vigorously endured during the World War II and the Cold War decades, and can be traced through a series of anthologies and special issues of journals that include *We Gather Strength* (1933), with an introduction by Michael Gold; *Proletarian Literature in the United States: An Anthology* (1935), edited by Granville Hicks and others; the "Social Poets Number" of *Poetry* (May 1936), edited by Horace Gregory; *American Stuff: An Anthology of Prose and Verse by Members of the Federal Writers' Project* (1937); *New Letters in America* (1937), edited by Horace Gregory; *Salud! Poems, Stories and Sketches of Spain by American Writers*, edited by Alan Calmer; *Get Organized* (1939), edited by Alan Calmer; *This Generation* (1939), edited by George K. Anderson and Eda Lou Walton; *War Poems of the United Nations* (1943), edited by Joy Davidman; *Seven Poets in Search of an Answer* (1944), edited by Thomas Yoseloff; and *The Rosenbergs: Poems of the United States* (1957), edited by Martha Millet. Surviving participants from this tradition who remained engaged with the Left – most famously, Walter Lowenfels, Aaron Kramer, Thomas McGrath, Muriel Rukeyser, and Langston Hughes (despite his hiatus in the McCarthy era) – subsequently helped create the climate for the politically committed poetry of the 1960s. Lowenfels and Kramer expressly memorialized the tradition in their anthologies, *The Writing on the Wall: 108 American Poems of Protest* (1969) and *On Freedom's Side: An Anthology of American Poems of Protest* (1972). But how did that tradition begin?

## Shakespeare in Overalls

In the early 1930s, the literary organs, institutions, and circles associated with the Communist movement were aflame with a new kind of poetry that expressed a novel and extraordinary stage in the age-old aesthetic tension between the form and content of poetic communication. This intense, stimulating, and heterogeneous cultural conflagration was sparked by the atmosphere of crisis engendered by the depths of the first years of the Depression. As a result, writers whose sensibilities were formed simultaneously by the romantic traditions of the nineteenth century and the modernist experimentation of the 1920s were dramatically impelled to beget intensified moods of compassion, fear, and anger. These poets of dual sensibility – some embarking on their first publication, others a bit older and further along in their careers – wondered, as did the Bohemian-radical poet and playwright Alfred Kreymborg (1883-1966) in his "American Jeremiad" (1935), how the poet should respond when faced with mass suffering:

> What shall a lover sing when half the land
> Is driven cold and lives on dank despair?[15]

Others went even further in trying to reformulate not just "what" but "how" such a poem should be sung.

The proletarian version of the "American Jeremiad" that became the driving theme of much radical verse in the United States in the early 1930s, and which would create the foundation for mid-twentieth-century Left poetry, was forged by divergent pressures. On the one hand, poets felt the need to express the practical-utilitarian class consciousness that comes from making a commitment to an organized Marxist movement. On the other, they could not abandon entirely the semi-autonomous "craft consciousness" championed most recently by expatriates in the 1920s; such technical skill was still seen as crucial to the poetic process of reworking experience into stirring images, rhythms, and language. The end product was initially envisioned by political radicals of Freeman's and Dell's preceding generation as less a revolution in literary form or technique, and more the production of verse structurally similar to classics from Elizabethan to late romantic poetry.

However, there emerged a post-1929 sentiment that the new poetry would be increasingly penned by workers and reflect working-class experience from a Marxist perspective, and would eventually produce "a Shakespeare in overalls."[16]

Such a tension was implicit, but far less pronounced, in the first years of literary activity associated with Communism in the United States after it emerged from its illegal underground existence under the name "Workers Party" in 1922. Drawn to Communist literary circles at that time were poets of *The Liberator* such as Max Eastman (1883-1969), Joseph Freeman, Michael Gold (a pseudonym for Irwin Granich, 1893-1967), and the Caribbean-born Claude McKay (1890-1948), all of whom voted that year to affiliate the journal with the Workers Party. The riddle encountered in harnessing a literary project to a Marxist party – how to reconcile political commitment with poetic craft – would be cast and recast in the late 1920s, the post-1935 Popular Front years, the World War II period, and the Cold War era.

One of the most arresting and exhilarating features of the early post-1929 phase of the new radical poetry, inaugurated by the collision of the experimental impulses of the 1920s with the political urgency of the Depression, was the highly self-conscious, almost "theoretical," quality of the resulting literary activity. Poets wrangled in meetings and in the pages of journals about their responsibilities regarding antiracist, pro-union, and antifascist struggles.[17] Another conspicuous feature was the way in which the literary eruption of the Depression years engaged such a broad range of poets beyond the traditional elite poetry circles.

Compared with the non-Left literary circles – the Fugitives and the Algonquin Wits come to mind – the pro-Communist poets were drawn more markedly from different classes, ethnic groups, regions, traditions, and generations, and, to some extent, more equally from both genders. Most poets in the revolutionary milieu remained relatively conscious of their different cultures, even as they sought common ground in an overriding identity as partisans of the international proletariat. Nevertheless, there endured, implicitly as well as explicitly, an embryonic version of "identity politics" in their writings, often marking the poets not only by class but by gender, color, and ethnicity. These attainments are sufficient to link aspects of the early 1930s radical poetic tradition thematically and even stylistically with the 1960s upheavals in poetic themes and conventions that emerged among women poets and writers of color.[18]

Prior to the 1930s, modern poetry had been already developing for several decades in tandem with a socialist-inflected rebellion against the dehumanizing and inequitable features of U.S. capitalism. During and after World

War I, writers advanced cultural and political dissidence through a variety of publications and causes (such as the defense of anarchists Sacco and Vanzetti), and by gravitating to the Bohemian cultural ghettos of many cities, most notably New York City's Greenwich Village.[19] In the atmosphere of national crisis following the 1929 stock market crash, however, the organizational coherence, fierce utopian vision, and courageous militancy of the Communists in the United States proved unique in their ability to attract men and women of proven or developing literary talent to an extent never again replicated by any Left political organization.

The Communist movement, which had fewer than 20,000 members in the early Depression years, managed to telescope, crystallize, and articulate concerns felt by a far greater number of individuals, becoming for many an institutionalized conscience. The process, of course, was variegated, because Communist ideology and activism struck a chord among writers with diverse literary sensibilities who were at disparate stages in their careers. Conversely, implementation of the Communist Party's organizational practices was sometimes shaped by the opinions expressed by writers drawn toward the Party's institutions and activities. The poets felt obliged to make contributions through their writing, by collaborating on cultural projects, or, in a few instances, by abandoning poetry for full-time Party activities, as was the case for many years with Walter Lowenfels, George Oppen (1908–84), and A. B. Magil (b. 1905).

No single factor accounted for the writers being attracted by the Communist Party, although it was common at some point for a writer to come into personal contact with a charismatic advocate of Communist views, most often a Left-wing teacher, fellow student, coworker, relative, or effective public speaker. Between 1929 and 1935, when the Party was in its ultra-revolutionary "Third Period" phase, more than forty small literary publications and hundreds of writers showed demonstrable evidence of being attracted to Communist ideas and activities, but the manifestations of this sympathy within a coherent Left tradition followed no predictable schema in either the literary art produced by the writers or the subsequent course of their lives.[20]

Most noteworthy for the relationship between poetic form and content is that, coincident with the onslaught of unemployment and hunger during the Depression, the cultural activity surrounding the Communist movement was significantly informed by a wave of modernist sensibility and experimentalism that related to old traditions of romantic worker-poetry in complex ways. In particular, a dramatic increase in self-conscious technical innovation by Left poets rendered even more intricate the longstanding tension between the claims of practical politics and literary craft. Left poets and critics fell out along a spectrum as to their notions regarding the degree of difficulty permissible in socialist verse; they were equally diverse in their beliefs about the degree of proximity a poem's content had to have to the exigencies of the class struggle. Then, as now, the conceptual problem of combining an experimental and difficult form with a non-elitist content remained a conundrum without general resolution.

It is not surprising, then, that from the zenith of the Communist Party's cultural influence in the mid-1930s to the various stages of its demise in the post–World War II era, the Party-led cultural effort would episodically erupt in feuds and factions, sometimes resulting in the antagonizing of an individual writer and in a few instances small groups of writers. Usually disputes arose when writers objected to unfair political judgments made about their work.[21] Moreover, while the Communist movement's self-willed dependency on the Soviet Union for cultural as well as political leadership at times exacerbated the problem of developing appropriate forms for Marxist poetic expression, many of the attitudes precipitating disputes were indigenous to the cultural Left in the United States, and some issues were simply inherent in the very nature of literary practice. Hostility to difficult modern literature, for example, yoked certain Communist writers firmly to one of their arch political enemies, Max Eastman, who was Leon Trotsky's U.S. translator.

## Poems for Workers

When the Communist movement was founded in 1919, only two years after the Russian Revolution, the form of poetry favored by U.S. Left activists and political leaders was very much in the tradition of workers' songs, ballads, and folk culture, partly homegrown and partly the product of class-conscious immigrant workers. This literary heritage distinguished turn-of-the-century socialist publications such as the *Comrade*, which featured poetry by Edwin Markham (1852–1940), Mary Wilkins Freeman (1852–1930), and Horace Traubel (1858–1919).[22] Before World War I, such styles and themes had been championed by worker-bards of the Industrial Workers of the World such as Ralph Chaplin (1888–1961), Arturo Giovannitti (1884–1959), and Joe Hill (1892–1915).[23] In the first decade of the Communist Party's activity, popular anthologies such as *Poems of Justice* (1929), edited by Thomas Curtis Clark, with a foreword by Zona Gale (1874–1938), and *An Anthology of Revolutionary Poetry* (1929), edited by Marcus Graham, a pseudonym for anarchist Shmuel Marcus, preserved this working-class literary legacy alongside more broadly radical poetry that often had been written by British romantics or Transcendentalists in the United States. It was also not exceptional for Left poets to appropriate the images and metrics of biblical passages and Christian hymns.[24]

Poetry published in the Communist movement's *Daily Worker, Young Worker,* and *Workers Monthly* (which replaced *The Liberator* in 1924), was mostly in this vein. To some extent this orientation received official imprimatur when the Communist Party issued the volume *Poems For Workers* (1927), edited and introduced by Manuel Gomez. "Gomez" was a pseudonym for the Jewish Communist activist Charles Francis Phillips (1895–1989), who, despite his *nom de plume* (he also used "J. Ramirez" when he collaborated with Michael Gold on a 1923 *Proletarian Song Book*), was neither a Latino nor a Spaniard. He later became a Wall Street financier.[25] In a flamboyant gesture, Gomez announced that his edition of worker-poetry was counterposed to all other such collections, including Upton Sinclair's *The Cry for Justice: An Anthology of the Literature of Social Protest* (1915). Gomez's profession to originality was his belief that he had assembled the only volume in the English language truly written for the working class. In his preface there were no references to literary form, other than an implicit assumption that the language and style of the poetry must be accessible to his mental picture of the working-class audience to whom the poems were addressed. As for content, Gomez explained:

> Workers will see in these poems an earnest [sic] of the invincible sweep, the elemental necessity, the suffering and heroism, the sacrifice and courage, the bitterness and devotion, the steady persistence, the already dawning triumph, of the class struggle of the proletarians of all nations for the overthrow of wage-slavery and the establishment of a new society.[26]

Despite the sentimentalized view of the class struggle, Gomez's outlook is in the tradition of literary "utility" championed by Whitman – especially in Whitman's non-hierarchical and democratic poetry of the open road, and his aspiration to create a public language demonstrating its power in public speech.

The zeal to promote working-class literature sprang from genuinely generous motives but also embodied a temptation to indulge in anti-intellectual, subjective, and partisan simplicities. On the generous side, the impulse to use art to draw attention to socioeconomic oppression usually produces poetry that tries to render clear and more concrete the relations of domination in society. The resulting themes are often premised on a belief in the persuasive power of poetry, which means that the poetry aims to inculcate readers with an understanding of class oppression, a sense of working-class solidarity, and an eagerness to fight for change. Poets may also try to commemorate events and delineate heroic figures with the purpose of creating a cultural memory and heritage distinct from what they perceive as a "dominant culture" that explicitly or implicitly ratifies the status quo and elides sites of effective struggle. A popular strategy is to use poetry to create images of the rulers and the ruled that can be counterpoised to those that appear in writing advanced by the governing class as well as by the mass-culture industry.[27] Humor was also a serviceable stratagem for debunking the pretensions of elite culture; for a workshop at the Fourth American Writers' Congress in 1941, twenty-one-year-old Martha Millet contributed "The Love Song of J. Anonymous Proletariat," which had as its refrain: "About us people come and go / Talking of the C.I.O."[28]

More troubling, however, is a familiar tendency of poets who align themselves with specific political movements to increasingly prioritize relatively narrow and sometimes immediate political objectives. They, along with influential political activists who take an interest in cultural affairs, understandably end up promoting a literature compatible with the politics and visions of these movements; in effect, the poets increasingly become the cultural "arm" of the political movement. But efforts to appraise cultural works in light of their degree of service to a political movement is complicated because interpretations of the entire range of possible meanings generated by a text vary considerably according to the subjective premises of the interpreter and the contexts in which works are received. Such ambiguity allows for bigoted and unfair complaints about the political intentions of verse, sometimes motivated by genuine misunderstanding but also by political fervor, rivalry, and even malice.

Moreover, poetic symbols and allusions are difficult to translate into precise political strategies. Even more vexing is the puzzle of conceiving and addressing working-class audiences. Those who work for a living are divided by ethnicity, color, region, class fraction, gender, and so many other elements of personal life that it is hard to achieve agreement about which vocabularies, allusions, metaphors, and other poetic devices would be most suitable to reach them. Moreover, whose experience can stand for a larger group or class? Should radical poets attempt to reproduce all cultural facets of the working class, including those antithetical to class consciousness and class unity; or should they emphasize only elements that the poets deem to be "in the objective interests" of the workers?

Edwin Rolfe agonized over this dilemma in "Catalogue of I," a late poem in which he reworks themes from Whitman. He initially affirms that, as an artist, he transcends his own identity to speak for revolutionaries and the oppressed of all times and nations:

> ... I am the pilgrim of every race,
> of every age, landing on every shore:
> he of the slant eyes, blond hair black face ...

He thereupon adds the victims of war, but excludes "he who causes war or welcomes, profits by it." The viewpoint seems categorical until a detached coda:

> Who fears inclusion in this catalogue of I
> Is useless, valueless, deserves to die.
> Yet he, my doomed and unloved brother,
> Is also I, is also I.[29]

While Rolfe never details in verse the behavior of those who, while not exploiters and profiteers, still fail to share his antiracism, internationalism, and class solidarity, he confesses a puzzlement that has haunted and to some degree compromised an important strain within Left culture.

Most often, efforts to appeal to the general category of "workers" prompted poets to selectively depict working-class culture by employing primarily radical elements aimed at a popular common-denominator choice of language and style. Accordingly, simplicity became a primary aesthetic criterion, especially among editors of daily and weekly publications of the movement.[30] This is a stance much in contrast to the view, espoused most famously by poets such as Eliot but attractive to some Leftists as well, that poetry must be difficult if it is to perform its function in the modern world.

The Communist Party-sponsored *Poems for Workers* presented only literary forms that were conventional and rarely difficult. Fragmentation, discontinuous form, erudite allusions, word surprises, and other defamiliarization techniques of modernism are virtually absent. Still, the volume's poems vary considerably in terms of direct and indirect methods of communicating meaning and emotion. It is likely that Gomez meant to suggest a tradition of working-class literature by his decision to open the collection with a poem by the Chartist leader Ernest Jones (1819-1869), "The Song of the Classes," which begins:

> We plough and sow – we're so very, very low
>    That we delve in the dirty clay,
> Till we bless the plain – with the golden grain,
>    And the vale with the fragrant hay.

Our place we know – we're so very low.
　'Tis down at the landlord's feet:
We're not too low – the bread to grow,
　But too low the bread to eat.[31]

Jones's poem presents the poet as the voice of the workers' aspirations, putting class unity between the workers and the writer in the foreground (Jones himself was a barrister from an aristocratic family). The stanza's political lesson corresponds to basic Marxist teachings: farm workers produce value, most of which is then expropriated by the landlord as the consequence of a perverted social order. Conventional religious and romantic associations are used to describe the plains as "blessed" and the products of nature as "golden" and "fragrant." Social relations are depicted as an ignominious manmade system of domination, a distortion of what the natural order should be. As the poem progresses to subsequent stanzas, the refrain of those kept on the bottom, "we're so very, very low," becomes increasingly sardonic. The bitterness of the poet's voice builds to an ironic climax at the point where the exploitative economic relations divulge their true political significance. The result is that the workers are mobilized to overthrow the monarchy but they are kept from enjoying the fruits of their rebellion.

"Caliban in the Coal Mines," by Louis Untermeyer (1885–1977), offers a divergent approach, one befitting his reputation as a popular parodist and anthologist. Together with his wife, Jean Starr Untermeyer (1886–1970),[32] he was often close to the Communist movement. Untermeyer was a member of the Communist-led John Reed Clubs, an endorser of the call for the 1939 American Writers' Congress, and the chair of a session at the 1949 Communist-led "Cultural and Scientific Conference for World Peace" held at the Waldorf Hotel in New York City.[33] As a result of these associations, he was fired as a panelist on the television show "What's My Line" in the early 1950s.

The newspapers often referred to Untermeyer as "the millionaire poet," not only because he seemed rather well fed, and was always neatly and tastefully attired, but also because he had inherited his father's prosperous jewelry business. Moreover, with his acquiline nose and intense eyes peering through pince-nez glasses under a high forehead with hair brushed straight back, he always maintained a donnish demeanor.[34] In poetry, though, he was a rebel against Victorian gentility, and a bit of a Luddite in response to the ills of industrialization. Parts of "Caliban in the Coal Mines" employ a gentle mockery as he toys with familiar cultural tropes and symbols:

God, we don't like to complain –
We know that the mine is no lark –

But – there's the pools from the rain;
But – there's the cold and the dark.

God, You don't know what it is –
You, in your well-lighted sky,
Watching the meteors whizz;
Warm, with the sun always by. . . .[35]

Untermeyer's tone is more suggestive of the playful verses of Emily Dickinson than the dirge-like drone of Ernest Jones's lines. He also relies on popular references, such as the Job-like plea to God, and a borrowing from Shakespeare's *The Tempest*, where he refigures Caliban (a name intended by Shakespeare as an anagram for "cannibal") into a symbol of the proletariat.

Moreover, Untermeyer's attitude toward nature seems to invert the romantic tradition. The rain accumulates in the mine in dirty pools, and the atmosphere is cold and dark. Nature is only pleasant in the privileged world of God, for which Untermeyer employs adjectives that depict nature as a modern technological achievement to the advantage of the powerful: the benefits of a "well-lighted sky" provide a ringside seat to the entertainment of the whizzing meteors, during which time the sun serves as a heating device that warms God. While hardly modernist, the sensibility is mischievously modern.

"To France," by the IWW poet and artist Ralph Chaplin, memorializes revolutionary history to create an archive of memory as well as a usable past. Chaplin's first stanza invokes the Paris Commune as an inspiration and model for the coming class struggle:

Mother of revolutions, stern and sweet,
Thou of the red Commune's heroic days;
Unsheathe thy sword, let thy pent lightning blaze
Until these new bastilles fall at thy feet.
Once more thy sons march down the ancient street
Led by pale men from silent Père la Chaise;
Once more La Carmagnole – La Marseillaise
Blend with the war drum's quick and angry beat.[36]

Using a tightly controlled ABBAABBA rhyme scheme to reinvigorate images from the past, Chaplin fuses religious and revolutionary figures of speech. He conjures up a scene of rebellion in heroically biblical dimensions, establishing transcendent symbols of oppression (such as the Bastille of the 1789 French Revolution), and elevating revolutionary songs to mythic stature. The stanza that closes the poem identifies the Parisian Communards with Christ.

Another selection from *Poems for Workers*, Joseph Freeman's "Slaves," suffuses conventional rhyming quatrains with a modern perspective to dramatize the psychological consequences of the tyranny of industrial society:

> Again the grinding of the iron gods,
> The old familiar fury of the wheels;
> Again the accustomed clamor of the rods,
> The giddy belting, and the room that reels;
>
> The dim light dancing, and the shadows shaking,
> The little sudden pains, the mute despairs,
> The patient and the weary hands; till, waking,
> At dusk, we tumble down the crazy stairs.

Freeman does not lecture the reader about wage slavery's similarity to chattel and ancient slavery; instead, suggestive synecdoche and claustrophobic atmosphere evoke the emotions one associates with alienated labor. Machinery becomes reified into brutal gods, while the workings of capitalism are likened to Sisyphean labor. The diminishment of nature (dim light, shaking shadows) combines with machinery to cause the workers' physical and emotional debilitation, pain, and despair. The poem's climax is a reverse epiphany with the worker "waking" at the end of day to stumble down the "shaky" old factory stairs additionally made "crazy" by the distortions wreaked upon the senses due to his exhaustion.

*Poems for Workers* probably represents the zenith of the indigenous working-class poetic tradition in the United States prior to the 1930s; the temptation to engage in proletarian didacticism evidenced here is mild compared to that found in the pages of the Communist journal *Young Worker* throughout the 1920s. "Clarity and Action" by S. Max Kitzes (dates unknown) is typical of the juvenilia published therein:

> Clear your road through Education;
> Fight the Night: its dread and fear.
> Kill all Hate and Superstition;
> Greet the Dawn with hope and cheer.
>
> Dawn is Red. And so's our Banner.
> Rise Young Worker: main and might!
> Close up the Ranks! Concert your Power!
> And change your force and plute-planned plight.[37]

Other verses by aspiring young poets in the Communist movement bore titles such as "The Red Dawn," "Song of Youth," "Freedom," and "Hail, Young

Workers!"[38] On occasion, established poets contributed in this vein to the *Young Worker*, such as Sara Bard Field (1882–1974) and John G. Neihardt (1881–1973).[39] The latter's "Cry of the Workers" begins:

> Tremble before your chattels,
>> Lords of the scheme of things!
> Fights of all earth's battles
>> Ours is the might of kings!
> Guided by seers and sages,
>> The world's heart beat for a drum,
> Snapping the chains of the ages,
>> Out of the night we come![40]

Simultaneously, the *Young Worker* published short essays explicitly defending a functional approach to poetry. For example, "The Poetry of Revolution," by Virgil Geddes (1897–1989), later famous for his taboo-breaking plays in the areas of incest and adultery such as *Native Ground* (1932), declared:

> What we need is an immediate poetry, whose every word and song has been dictated by an unrestrained impulse, that is seeking the light of a new day in its cry for liberation. A poetry that is born out of the despair of our smoky and grimy existence, yet the ardour of which helps us to rise and escape momentarily from our predicament. And this verse should have a purpose, or rather, it should be sufficiently intentional and clearly inspired as to be an encouragement to surmount our present conditions by the vision of a new order. It should be like the joy of a streak of pure blue sky shining through, and apart from, the Depression of sooty smoke-stacks.[41]

This direct fusion of romanticism and proletarianism for didactic purposes, so prevalent in the 1920s, would remain a part of the Communist cultural tradition, especially in poetry of young activists, novice poets, worker-poets, and midwestern and southern regional poets. What is noteworthy is that there appear to be no references to Soviet cultural policy to justify such an orientation; the extreme, reductive utilitarianism sometimes decried as a "Stalinist" aberration of overpoliticized art had its own indigenous roots in U.S. radical culture.

Of course, there still remained in the 1920s the poetic tradition of Greenwich Village Bohemianism typified by the *Masses* and the early *Liberator*. This cultural milieu stood somewhat at arm's length from Communist Party organs and institutions, and to some extent blended in with the liberal magazines of the pre- and post-WWI period.[42] *May Days: An Anthology of Verse from the Masses-Liberator,* chosen and edited by Genevieve Taggard, was published in 1925, preserving much of the poetry featured in the publications. Taggard's preface argued that the demise of the *Liberator,* successor to the *New Masses* that had been folded into the Party-sponsored *Workers Monthly* in 1924, brought to an end the coexistence between the free-wheeling *Masses-Liberator* tradition and the organized Communist movement:

> [T]he *Masses-Liberator* spirit was gone – not so much dead as dispersed and divided. The magazine, until the war, was like a self-fertilizing tree. Social passion and creative beauty grew from the same branches. Now there had been pruning and grafting, – we have in consequence two trees – the air is sultry – there is no cross pollenizing. The artists who were attracted to the *Masses* for its art have gone one way; the revolutionists another. The two factions regard each other with hostility and suspicion. They consider themselves mutually exclusive and try their best to remain so.[43]

It is probable that the disunion of art and politics observed by Taggard in this passage expresses an exaggeration of trends and inclinations. Quite a few poets appear in both the Gomez and Taggard anthologies.

Besides, one year after publication of this volume, proletarian and Bohemian writers, including many of the original contributors to the *Masses* and *Liberator,* regrouped to create the *New Masses* in a spirit not so different, at least at the outset, from its predecessors. Correspondingly, throughout the 1920s the *Modern Quarterly,* under the editorship of V. F. Calverton (born George Goetz, 1900–1940), maintained a link between Communist Party politics, to which Calverton was sympathetic, and modern (especially Freudian) intellectual developments, recalling the original *Masses.*[44] Moreover, modern-oriented publications of the 1920s such as the early volumes of *The American Caravan* included writers variously associated with the Communist Left. Finally, even though Mike Gold himself steered the *New Masses* aggressively toward worker-poets between 1928 and 1930, when he was voted into editorial power and some of his rivals departed, the broader Bohemian tradition reasserted itself in the magazine rather quickly after the formation of the Communist-led John Reed Clubs at about the same time.[45]

A survey of the plethora of independent Left and John Reed Club magazines that blossomed in the years just after the 1929 stock market crash shows a contentious marriage of proletarian didacticism with romantic and increasingly modernist modes and themes. Among those who wrote in styles close to the older, premodernist tradition were many contributors to *The Rebel Poet* (1931–32), the organ of a loose network of writers that united anarchists, socialists, and pro-Communists under its inspiring and apt banner,

"Art for Humanity's Sake."[46] The inaugural issue of *The Rebel Poet* carried an obituary of the expatriate-modernist Harry Crosby (1898–1929), who was among the charter members of the Rebel Poets Society and whose poetry was included in the society's annual volumes *Unrest 1929* and *Unrest 1930*. Jack Conroy (1899–1990), one of the editors, eulogized Crosby without reference to his literary experimentalism as "A rare and delicate spirit, his clear eyes unblinded by wealth, his Muse untarnished by the fool's gold of commercialism."[47]

More characteristic of *The Rebel Poet* were paeans to the imagined state of poetry in the Soviet Union, such as "Poetry and Revolution: A Study of Poetry in the U.S.S.R.," by Morris Spiegel (dates unknown) and Ralph Cheyney (1897–1941), which declares: "the toilers' poets stand by to inspire and strengthen the masses marching to the new dawn. They did not forsake the people in the critical moment of rebirth. A new poetic art looms on the Soviet frontier; its rays are already visible."[48] Mainly the magazine leaned toward the proletarian-didactic pole of the Left literary tradition. Editor Jack Conroy had no hesitation about dictating themes and moods, as in a rather feckless letter he sent to African American poet Sterling Brown: "The material we desire must, of course, deal with Negro proletarian life, and we'd rather see the Negro getting militant and willing to fight for his rights, than the traditional 'spiritual' and 'blues' type moaning that he's unable to cross Jordan by himself."[49] The liveliest verse published by Conroy was probably the witty doggerel sort such as the rhymed couplets by Henry George Weiss (1898–1946), "To a Fat Bourgeois," which begins:

O you are hog-fat and your clothing is fine.
So strike down your fodder and lap up your wine,
Let the paunch of your plenty protrude from your vest,
And the jowls of contentment fold down on your breast.
For we lean and hungry are supple and strong,
With thin lips that murmur, Not Long Now, Not Long.[50]

The vein is classic satire, lyrically mocking, comically polemical and moralistic in a standard verse form that recalls some of Stephen Crane's stanzas. *The Rebel Poet*'s freshest contributions were stark, grim lines delineating class oppression and rebellion such as the opening descriptive verses of "Picket Lines on a Coal Mine," by W. S. Stacy (dates unknown):

Gaunt faces and tense bodies
knit by hunger's bond
into a solid chain
indissolvable—

> weaves into a threatening lash
> with a thousand smashing thongs
> striking deep into the dark chambers
> bringing up men to walk the earth
> of a hundred coal towns.[51]

Here the techniques of imagism, especially non-ornamental diction devoted to clarity and compression, are deftly adapted to deliver poetry closer to the realities of place and the dynamics of class conflict.

## "Write It Plain"

Although worker-poetry of *The Rebel Poet* sort was most aggressively recommended by the Left mainly in the early 1930s, it endured as a constituent of the tradition thereafter. For the most part, during and after the Popular Front, it comprised a minor poetic stream, especially in northern urban centers. Yet even in official Communist publications, the prominence of such verse decreased as opportunities for attracting better-known and more influential poets increased, especially following the achievement of the 1932 Communist Party presidential election campaign in drawing to the Party an imposing array of intellectuals.[52] Of the poems selected for inclusion in the Party's 1935 collection *Proletarian Literature in the United States*, appearing at an odd juncture due to the announcement of the Popular Front that year,[53] only a handful were clearly in the worker-poet vein. The most outstanding was "Papermill," by Joseph Kalar (1906–1972). A worker in saw and lumber mills during his most prolific years, Kalar simply stopped publishing poetry at the time of the Popular Front.[54] Two other worker-poets whose verse appeared in the volume, Jim Waters (dates unknown), who had been published earlier in *Poems for Workers*, and H. H. Lewis (1901–1985), also disappeared poetically after the Depression.[55]

In the poetry of one southern writer whose work appeared in the volume, however, the vitality of the worker-poet tradition continued for five decades. Donald Lee West (1906–92) was a Communist poet, ordained Christian minister in the Congregationalist church, and life-long labor activist who helped found the Highlander Folk School in the early 1930s and the Appalachian Folk Life Center in the 1950s.[56] West was the eldest son of Scots-Irish sharecroppers, growing up in isolation between the Blue Ridge and Smoky Mountains. He was nurtured on the Southern Appalachian ballad form, and a view of Appalachia as a unique environment—one untainted by a history of slavery, and conducive to the spiritual qualities that abet a social-gospel interpretation of Christianity.

West attended a mountain missionary high school but was so provoked by a campus showing of the racist film *Birth of a Nation* (1915) that he organized a protest that brought about his expulsion. From there he enrolled in Lincoln Memorial University near Knoxville, Tennessee, where he took writing classes taught by a nonconformist professor named Harry Harrison Kroll. Thereupon he joined a literary circle with Kroll's protégés, Jessie Stuart and James Still. Already showing signs of talent as a poet, West soon issued *Crab-Grass* (1929), comprised of dialect verse and rhymes of Appalachian origin. At one point West led a student strike against the disrespectful treatment of Appalachian culture at Lincoln, as well as the inferior food and facilities made available for students. West orated his militant speeches in the form of sermons. Expelled by the administration, he arranged to return and graduate in 1929.

West and his circle moved on to do graduate work at Vanderbilt University but soon parted ways when Stuart and Still inclined toward poet Donald Davidson and the Southern Agrarians. West, in contrast, fell under the spell of the social-gospel advocate Alva Taylor, who urged West to get involved in the 1929 Gastonia textile strike. There West met Ella Mae Wiggins, whose ballads fused radical politics with the native culture; it was at that time that West first cast eyes on real live Communists. He was further transfigured by the poverty, suffering, and violence – including the murder of Wiggins – that occurred during the strike. Soon West signed up to join the Socialist Party and then won a scholarship to Denmark to study the Danish Folk School system. He returned to collaborate with Myles Horton (1905-1990) in founding Highlander Folk School in Monteagle, Tennessee. Unfortunately, these two men with strong egos were soon locked in conflict, with the result that West would depart after only a few years. In late 1933, following a trip by motorcycle to New York City to learn how he might help in defending the Scottsboro Boys, West attended Communist Party classes and became a formal member; a year later he studied at the Party's national training school. Sometimes using the Party name "Jim Weaver," and occasionally "Frank Shipman," West returned to the South to serve as district and state Party organizer in diverse areas, including Georgia and Kentucky. For the next several decades he led a rough and tumble life, sporadically fleeing from vigilantes in the middle of the night, occasionally carrying a pistol for self-protection, and losing almost every job he managed to secure. Occasionally he won scholarships for graduate study at different institutions in the North, although he never finished the doctorate or the novel on which he worked for many years.

West's poems appeared in the *Daily Worker*, *Harlem Liberator* and *New*

*Masses.* His books include *Between the Plow Handles* (1932), *Toil and Hunger* (1940), *Broadside to the Sun* (1946) *Clods of Southern Earth* (1946), *The Road Is Rocky* (1951), and *O Mountaineers!* (1974). The publication in 1982 of a substantial collection of his work, *In a Land of Plenty,* convincingly presents West as a faithful expression of the worker-poet tradition of the early 1930s adapted to regional conditions. Furthermore, his assimilation of Marxism to his outlook of "Applied Christianity" – a designation that means the interpretation of scripture so as to recognize social and political realities – remained nearly seamless.

The images of simplicity and innocence promoted in *Land of Plenty,* inaugurated by the cover photo of West in his overalls looking like the salt of the earth, should not deceive one into missing the clever design of West's project; the self-created aura recalls that of folksinger Woody Guthrie (1912–1967).[57] Like Guthrie, West's work aimed to modify consciousness by drawing upon many sources of the national and folk culture in the United States for the purpose of "Americanizing" the fundamentals of class struggle. In a 1943 correspondence with Langston Hughes, West affirms that he intends to reclaim the original meaning of the term "cracker," which he insists refers to the first settlers of Georgia who were actually antislavery.[58] The 1982 retrospective volume, *In a Land of Plenty,* also discloses West's stratagem, during his fifty-year literary career, of dedicating himself to creating authentic working-class poetry as proto-socialist culture through the creation of myths about himself and a new history of his region.

From the statements on the first page – "No Grants" and "No Copyright" – the book defines itself as a countertext to anthologies of poetry that, by West's implication, rather than by any direct labeling or strident accusation, appear to be "bourgeois" commodities. Moreover, the introductions to the various sections of *Land of Plenty* are not written by professional scholars but by workers who insist that their main qualification for writing the introductions is that they have dirty fingernails and calluses on their hands. The poem serving as a frontispiece, "In a Land of Plenty," effectively conveys much of West's method:

Up, up mountain toilers
And hear what I tell
In a land of plenty
There's hunger and hell!

We dig and we shovel
We weave and we sweat

But when comes the harvest
It's little we get . . .

O this is the story
Of you and the rest
And if I am lying
My name's not Don West.[59]

In his verse, West presents himself as a working-class version of the prophet of old, who comes to preach the truth about capitalism in biblical metaphors. He employs the national myth of a "Land of Plenty" without the sarcasm that one might expect from a radical. As a speaker, he identifies unconditionally with the poor and the oppressed. Turning to his intended audience, he embraces the manual worker of both genders – those who dig, and those who weave. Like them, he knows the exploited firsthand, and his job is to reveal the truth of their condition.

The last two lines of the poem, "And if I am lying / My name's not Don West," underscore the significant role of the promotion of his own self-made legend in his poetry. Various stanzas of his verse disclose that he is a mountain boy, six foot two inches tall, strong as an ox, and part Cherokee, who seems to have lived everywhere – the South, Chicago, Baltimore, New York, Europe. He also seems to have had every occupation: coal miner in Kentucky, deck hand on a Mississippi steamboat, sailor, school superintendent, radio commentator in Georgia, preacher, union organizer, farmer, and college professor. Moreover, he avows to have been a student at Vanderbilt University, the University of Chicago, Columbia University, Oglethorpe University, the University of Georgia, Johns Hopkins University, the University of Maryland, and several universities in Western Europe. Omitted, however, is mention of his service as a central leader of the Communist Party in the South.[60] Moreover, he battled heroically against the odds – he fought the Klan, served in jail, suffered beatings from gun thugs, and experienced McCarthyite persecution.[61]

Besides creating a larger-than-life persona who blends a mountain man-Paul Bunyanesque figure with a working-class revolutionary, West's poems also depict a mythological world of characters. Some of the inhabitants are genuine relatives such as Grandpa Kim Mulkey, a bitter foe of the Confederacy; West's father, who died young from overwork; and West's mother, who endured acute poverty. Fictitious, perhaps, are some of the victims of oppression and fighters against exploitation who most likely are composites or meant to typify workers in characteristic situations.[62]

Strategically, Don West as a poet is faced with some unique dilemmas.

For example, he defines the role of the poet as the voice of the people, yet he cannot lose himself entirely to such a generalized abstraction. After all, the character of Don West is so crucial to his poems that he must retain some individuality in order to seem authentic. Yet by temperament, or perhaps because it might deflect his poetic-political objective, West feels he cannot indulge himself in individualism. Consequently, he offers just a few small glimpses of the private man, so as to convince us of his sincerity, while not crafting a full, detailed portrait of his personal plight. One of his most effective techniques is evidenced in the way he humanizes himself in the 1950s poem "Confession." In lines exuding an excruciating anguish, he expresses his feelings of shame and guilt because, unlike Carl Braden (1914–1975), the redoubtable radical and civil rights activist jailed for his antiracist activities, West held back from speaking out and acting as defiantly as he wished, from fear of going to prison during the McCarthyite witch-hunt:

> I saw him walk through
> The prison gate
> And heard the iron bars clang
> Against his freedom.
> Accused, character assassinated,
> Condemned and forsaken
> By those unfit his shoes to tie,
> He went to serve time in prison,
> And there, but for my cowardice,
> Walked I
> Walked I . . . ![63]

The unnerving directness of the prose masks the text's true function as a palimpsest, with layers of meaning gradually emerging as one meditates on the kinship between the two men, the nature of the unstated "crime," and the ironic connection between the "criminal" and his persecutors.

At first, West might seem dated by his Old Left worldview, but there are strong elements in West's verse that anticipate the themes of post-1960s radical cultural concerns. In particular, there are his emphasis on the hidden history of his region (specifically, his depiction of Appalachia as a colonized area that was actually a cradle of abolitionism), and his Liberation Theology portrayal of Christ as a working man and anticapitalist revolutionary. Yet West evinced some of the weaknesses of the worker-poet tradition. His simple lines frequently voice pieties susceptible to appropriation by all sorts of ideologies, such as his calls for honesty and decency. He also advances what might be construed as anti-intellectual literary values, as in his "Advice to the Would-Be Poets":

> If there is a thing to tell
> Make it brief and write it plain,
> Words were meant to shed a light,
> Not to cover up again![64]

In such sentiments, one can hardly find a more apposite challenge to modernism, and, indeed, to all difficult literature and complicated analysis. West exemplifies a prolific and popular activist-poet for whom both the earlier "proletarian" and later "people's" poetic orientations came naturally. Yet he seems to have operated apart from any Communist Party-led writers groups and was relatively autonomous from Party-sponsored publications, in whose pages he infrequently appeared.[65] Nevertheless, his particular populist version of romanticism was not the only variant extant among the Left literary milieu.

## Revolutionary Romanticism

Several Left poets and poetry critics in the United States held sundry notions and theories about romanticism and modernism as interlinked stages in poetic development, less intricate and studied but not dissimilar from the fashion in which naturalism and modernism are complexly adjoined in Georg Lukács's theoretical work on the novel.[66] One such account, appraising modernism as to a large extent idealized romanticism, and accordingly philosophical idealism, was expressed by transient fellow traveler Edmund Wilson in *Axel's Castle* (1931). Divergent opinions of these terms come to the fore in a three-way exchange about romanticism, Communism, and modernism that preoccupied the *New Masses* in mid- to late 1934. The discussion began with an essay on "Three English Radical Poets," by New York University professor Edwin Berry Burgum (1894-1979), who would later lose his job as a victim of McCarthyism. Burgum attempted to map what is now called "The Auden School" of revolutionary poets in relation to both its counterparts in the United States and earlier poetic traditions.[67]

Burgum claims that the romantic poetic tradition, especially the work of Shelley, is the ultimate inspiration for the pro-Communist but modern-experimentalist "Auden School" in England, although Shelley's philosophy is infused with a "less Platonic" conception of love by W. H. Auden (1907-1973), the fiction writer Christopher Isherwood (1904-86), and Stephen Spender (1909-1995), among others. Burgum additionally argues that the most politically and poetically advanced adherent of the Auden School is C. Day Lewis (1904-1972), for whom "Marxism is . . . the next stage in the development of Rousseauism." Burgum observed that, in his Communist-inspired masterwork, *The Magnetic Mountain* (1933), Day Lewis creates a symbol of "the classless society, the universal soviet that shall be the human race, towards which we are drawn by the irresistible flow of history as to a magnet under the co-operation of our own desire, the urge of our iron-like nature." Day Lewis's outlook is assessed by Burgum as nothing less than a voluntaristic break from positivist versions of Marxism. According to Burgum, Day Lewis is said to bid "his readers cease from their capitalistic delusions and follow frankly by what may seem an almost mad break with the past the course dictated by the virile demand for constructive activity and fraternal joy in action of what is to [Day] Lewis the undegenerated nature of man." Burgum's interpretation, with its romantic rejection of rational, linear progress in favor of a mystical flow leading to a breakthrough, somewhat anticipates aspects of Walter Benjamin's "Theses on the Philosophy of History," written later in the decade, at the time of the Hitler-Stalin Pact.[68]

A few weeks after the appearance of Burgum's essay in mid-1934, Genevieve Taggard, who once wrote that reading Keats in Hawaii sired her own poetic sensibility,[69] contributed to the *New Masses* a provocative response called "Romanticism and Communism."[70] Her question to Burgum and the Auden School was direct: "Should the poetry about to be born belong to the Romantic Family? Should Shelley and Whitman and the 'revolutionary' Swinburne come to the christening?"

In an unusual move, the editors of the *New Masses* (presumably those who were the more literary ones, Stanley Burnshaw, Michael Gold, Granville Hicks, and Joshua Kunitz) appended a seventy-line response to the Taggard article, questioning her definition of romanticism. In their view, Taggard failed to make distinctions among trends within romanticism; in particular, she missed seeing the possibility of a " 'revolutionary romanticism' – a poem, story, or play projecting a vision of a socialist society: an outgrowth of the dialectical forces perceived in the present breakdown of capitalism."

Moreover, while agreeing with Taggard that modernist art (the editors refer specifically to Dadaism, Stream of Consciousness, the Revolution of the Word, Objectivism, and Futurism) is certainly the final literary stage of bourgeois romanticism, and therefore a form of "literary suicide," they see a potential ally in "the individualistic rebel – the bourgeois romantic," who could embrace either revolution or reaction. Then, borrowing (without attribution) Trotsky's argument articulated in his 1922 book *Literature and Revolution*, a source that it would have been impermissible for the editors to openly cite, they conclude: "In Italy the Futurists have gone with the Fascists; in the Soviet Union the Futurists became part of the proletarian revolution. The fate of the bourgeois romantic is fundamentally dependent on his historical milieu."[71]

The argument here advances a number of parallels with topics pivotal to the recent effort of the Brazilian-born Marxist Michael Löwy to retheorize the relationship between Marxism and romanticism. Löwy locates, and identifies with, a sub-trend of "revolutionary romanticism" which means more or less the demand for a renaissance of precapitalist elements of social existence "worth conserving."[72] Löwy is entirely sympathetic to a notion of historical recuperation inspired by Walter Benjamin. In a 1981 essay, "Marxism and Utopian Vision," Löwy's characterization of social transformation also echoes Burgum's description of Day Lewis's appropriation of Shelley's "mad break with the past": "the revolution is not 'progress,' improving the established order. . . . It is a 'messianic' interruption of the course of history . . . the emergency brake that brings to a stop the headlong rush of the train toward the abyss."[73] Revolutionary romanticism, then, is a plausible slant for divining those ingredients within Left cultural practice that are confederated to a universal vision and the total regeneration of the human race. Especially in light of Marxism's repudiation of linear evolution in favor of a dialectical leap produced by social contradictions, it would be overhasty to theorize literary Communists chronologically as a modern extension of attenuated romantic intensities that followed the decline of the French Revolution. If they are to be judged romantics in any sense, the Left poets might be distinguished as returning to the revolutionary amplification of the romantic vision at its height.

Whatever formal ideological adherence to Stalinist-positivist versions of Marxism many Left-wing poets might have had, the tropes of romanticism, especially of a utopianism etched in preindustrial society, can be discerned even in the most modern of the Left writers. Throughout the writing of Horace Gregory in the 1930s, for example, one finds many archetypal features associated with revolutionary romanticism; both a "romantic hindsight" and "melancholic gaze" are brought to bear on an urban culture transformed by industrialization and market capitalism.[74] What is uncommon in Gregory's vision is the frequent invocation of both classical style and symbolism, as when he formulates his socialist utopia in contrast to the bourgeois world:

Wake here
    Atlantis under hard blue skies

35

> Thy Indian summer bride is like the spring
> Roof-tree in light
>> Thy blossoming
> In fire to love returns.[75]

Gregory, a skillful translator of Catullus, was perhaps best known in these years for his elegiac monologues, yet beneath the narrations of personal anguish was a consistent aspiration: to reconnect the Marxist dream of fraternity and equality with a romantic nostalgia often energized by precapitalist longings.

Most commonly, romanticism was visible in the endorsement of Walt Whitman, the poet most adulated by the Left. Whitman's work embodies not only facets of classic romantic ideology but also a robust proletarianism, and perhaps even a proto-modernism indicated by his free verse catalogues and use of common speech.[76] Taggard was exceptional in her questioning of Whitman's rightful presence at the "christening" of a new revolutionary poetry. From the beginning to the denouement of the Communist cultural tradition, most Communist poets would invoke Whitman as a model. When Meridel Le Sueur published *Annunciation* in 1935, she was hailed in the *New Masses* as "something of a female Walt Whitman."[77] Even among African American poets, Langston Hughes was adamant that Whitman was "the greatest of American poets" and explained in a 1946 Communist Party edition of Whitman that his "I" was not "introspective" but "the cosmic 'I' of all peoples who seek freedom, decency, and dignity, friendship and equality between individuals and races all over the world."[78] Only the young and radical Robert Hayden (1913–1980) reproached Whitman for not recognizing the Black slaves who fought in the Civil War.[79] But motifs from Whitman are revealed in the work of such a contradictory mélange of writers, including in the early proletarian poetry of African American Communist Richard Wright, the religious mysticism of Kenneth Patchen (1911–1972), and the Marxist-scientific modernism of Muriel Rukeyser, that it is difficult to generalize about the precise influence of Whitman.[80] Perhaps the most striking manifestation of the Whitman cult can be found in the career of Mike Gold, for Gold's trajectory is but a twentieth-century version of Whitman's.

Both men spent their youths primarily surviving as moderately successful journalists known for their polemically sharp tongues, and both had a penchant for conventional romantic poetry (Whitman's taste being far worse than Gold's). In their salad days, both produced numerous mediocre poems and thin, somewhat affected, stories. In mid-life, both men – Whitman at age thirty-six and Gold at thirty – reinvented themselves before a substantial public audience as men of the people, voices of the democratic masses. For Whitman, who had been something of a dandy, the new persona was embodied in the engraving that appeared in *Leaves of Grass* (1855) in place of his name; here Whitman is pictured with a beard, a large hat, an open shirt collar showing his flannel underwear, and worker's trousers.[81] For Gold, whose individualism had led him from Greenwich Village Bohemia to Harvard Yard to Mexican oilfields, it was the literary portrait of the slum child of *Jews without Money* (1930); here his lower-middle-class businessman father was transformed into a house painter, and his radical younger brothers changed into a sister who was killed in the streets by a blond German wagon driver.

Both of these well-read writers would spend the rest of their lives insisting that they were not "literary" men, not college trained or products of genteel literary culture; when they spoke it was as instruments of the people. Among the clearest signs of this populism was the broad sentimentality both now professed toward home life and especially toward their angelic mothers.

## CHAPTER 2

# Inventing Mike Gold

## "A Kind of Cheeky Krazy Kat"

As a Communist writer for most of his life, Mike Gold was often miscast by his critics and later historians as a Party spokesman or even a cultural bureaucrat. The Communist Party did, in fact, appoint officials such as Alexander Trachtenberg (1894-1966) and V. J. Jerome (1896-1965) to annunciate policy and guide practical activity. Such men had power, however, only in certain contexts or at particular moments; they were merely elements, albeit influential ones, of a vital and fractious cultural movement. Their authority was due primarily to their connections with the Party apparatus, but they were never the movers and shakers of practical literary activity at the movement's base.

Far more vivid in the lives of the tens of thousands of readers of the Communist press was the personality aura – partly a myth created of their own desire – of Mike Gold.[1] First as editor of the *New Masses* from 1928 to 1930, and then as a member of its editorial board until 1934, Gold appeared regularly in its pages. He also became a prolific writer for the *Daily Worker*, beginning in 1933 with his "Change the World" column (originally called "What a World"). Gold was never a member of any leading Party committee, nor was he intimate with or particularly trusted by Party leaders, but he was an enormously popular speaker and debater who frequently toured the country; he authored introductions to books by Langston Hughes and other Left poets and artists; and, despite the resentment of some members of the New York John Reed Club who chafed at his "star" status, he was a nationally known symbol of the fully "committed" writer who had a genuine public following. Simply put, no single individual contributed more to forging the tradition of proletarian literature as a genre in the United States after the 1920s. All who came after Gold would stand on the shoulders of his legacy.

Part of the explanation for Gold's impact was his colorful semi-autonomy from the Party officials such as Jerome on the Party headquarters' "Ninth Floor." The dazzling blend of proletarianism, bohemianism, romanticism, and even a strain of modernism that comprised the early 1930s mix of Left poetry was quite evident in Gold's own personality and career. "A kind of cheeky Krazy Kat bouncing rocks off the crania of his adversaries" was the way the Marxist playwright and novelist Philip Stevenson (1896-1965) remembered Gold. He was "sentimental about the socialist future, always ready to fight for his beliefs, overcorrecting opportunism with doses of leftism."[2] One of his most renowned polemics indicted the poetry of Archibald MacLeish for expressing a "fascist unconscious."[3]

Some of the confusion that exists in scholarship about the policies and practice of the Communist Literary Left flows from a basic tension in the life of Gold, a man riven by strong contradictions that he held together by promoting in his critical statements and imaginative writings the self-image of a fully integrated revolutionary artist whose commitment to the working class was total and dependable.

This toughness convinced the African American writer Shirley Graham Du Bois (1896-1977) that, in her battle against racism, "Mike so perfectly symbolized the fact that I was not struggling alone. . . . [A]s long as there are people to fight for, Mike Gold will burn a light. Mike Gold will be there in the corner for us to gather around and know."[4] A Pennsylvania miner who later lived in the Soviet Union, Ed Falkowski, recalled that Gold's name became a "household word" among radical workers in the 1920s and 1930s because "He seemed to *know* – to be *certain* – of final victory for the working class. There was no wavering in him, no doubts to put to sleep."[5] Such a persona was constructed over many difficult years by a man who regarded himself as "soft" and "almost mad with the overflow of pity and sorrow I feel for this goddamned mess of a world."[6] Gold's lifelong friend Dorothy Day (1897-1980), founder of the *Catholic Worker*, regarded him to the end as a "gentle and loving spirit."[7]

Gold emerged from an anarchist political background that he never completely transcended; his personal instability before the mid-1930s and his lifelong battle with diabetes, exacerbated in his last three decades, curbed his activities in the Party to contributing columns, usually polemical and humorous, and giving speeches. In his declarations on cultural matters, he promoted values of simplicity and directness which reached an apogee in his 1930 nine-point program of "Proletarian Realism" that advocated writing akin to a clean, swift knock-out punch to the collective chin of the bourgeoisie.[8] Gold's own creative writing, when he exercised discipline, as in his much-revised *Jews without Money* (1930), or in some of his experimental drama, possessed a refreshing lyricism portending other major achievements that never came. In a response to Genevieve Taggard's introduction to the poetry anthology *May Days,* Gold explained his view of reconciling craft with commitment:

> [T]here is no doubt that the Russian Revolution has brought a wiser, harder intellect into being; and this intellect cannot accept the muddle of individualism and communism that appeared in the *Masses* pages. . . .
>
> The new revolutionary artist has no compartments in his mind, one for individualistic art and the other for communist revolution. He is so saturated in the Communist world that he is incapable of creating art that is not communist, any more than Michael Angelo or Dante could have created art that was not medieval.[9]

This ideal anticipates the single-minded psyche of male protagonists in several Left-wing novels depicting martyrs to the revolutionary or antifascist causes, especially André Malraux's Kyo and Katov in his *Man's Fate* (1934) and Robert Jordan in Hemingway's *For Whom the Bell Tolls* (1940).[10] The famous Whitmanesque mysticism of Gold's February 1921 manifesto, "Towards Proletarian Art," appears to have been superseded in the late 1920s and early 1930s by a publicly expressed unity of political and artistic objectives.[11]

Such a new attitude was formulated in the years of Gold's greatest creative ferment. In his early thirties, he had just returned from an exhilarating experience in the Soviet Union; he was also seeing his plays produced by the New Playwrights Theatre, which he had helped to found with a $50,000 contribution that he charmed from Otto Kahn, a Jewish businessman.[12] But this energetic avowal of Gold's consummate Communist artist masks a personal story of emotional pain and instability, a nostalgia and guilt for a lost childhood happiness that he sought to reconstitute by transforming himself into the beloved patriarch of Left-wing culture. In the process, Gold would organize his emotional and intellectual life around a predominating military vision of the class struggle that naturally gave rise to a view of "art as a weapon." This was also the well-known Communist slogan of the John Reed Clubs at the time, indicating that Gold was hardly alone in believing that cultural statements might affect life-and-death struggles.

The cost of Gold's vision of cultural warfare is hard to reckon. By the time Gold turned forty, his literary career had been remade from creative writer into popular Left journalist, although his prose was never as academic, and rarely so stultified and colorless, as that of functionaries such as V. J. Jerome. But Gold's lack of time to create a literature to match the Marxist program he devised may not have been his only obstacle. He also made a dramatic turnabout in his personal life through a strong commitment to marriage and raising his children, while additionally suffering from declining health and engaging in a fight for economic survival, his livelihood largely dependent on churning out daily newspaper columns.

## "By Street Life and Thunder"

Walking through Greenwich Village on a hot summer evening in 1955, the former *New Masses* editor Joseph Freeman stepped into a bar on Greenwich Avenue to call home. Approaching the only phone booth in the establishment, the fifty-eight-year-old Freeman almost did a double-take as if confronting an apparition. A short, slim man in his early twenties with a mop of thick, dark, shaggy hair and swarthy features was holding open the booth's door for air while declaiming free verse into the receiver. For a moment Freeman imagined that he had been propelled back in time thirty-five years, and that standing before him was Mike Gold from their *Liberator* days of the early 1920s. Taking notice of the older man's interest, the fledging poet quickly introduced himself as Gregory Corso (1930–2001).

Relishing memories of those long-ago times when he and Gold used to "bat poems around," Freeman listened a bit to Corso's side of the telephone debate about whether a certain line of poetry should be cut. Soon Corso put Freeman on the phone with his interlocutor, another aspiring writer by the name of Allen Ginsberg (1926–1999). Freeman instantly determined that this was the son of Louis Ginsberg (1895–1976), the socialist poet whose verse used to appear in both the *Liberator* and *New Masses*. Ginsberg's mother had been an active Communist, and the preadolescent Allen had attended Party-sponsored meetings where he learned to sing "The Red Flag" and union songs.[13]

Freeman and Corso ended up having drinks together, after which Freeman examined some more poems and told Corso that "in the old days" he and Gold would have surely published them (minus Corso's generous use of four-letter words) in their revolutionary magazine. This led to a series of meetings between Corso and Freeman to discuss literary matters. Corso eventually found work as a seaman and took off on a ship, but Freeman continued to read the poetry of the Beats. After Ginsberg's book *Howl and Other Poems* appeared in 1958, Freeman bumped into both Corso and Ginsberg at a 1959 New Year's Day party at an art gallery. When Ginsberg insisted to Freeman that Corso was the "better poet," Freeman offered his own view that Corso's strength was his "imagination" but that Ginsberg's was "feeling." He then urged both men to look up Mike Gold on their next trip to San Francisco; they would surely find a kindred spirit. Six days later he mailed off a report of these events to Gold, with whom he had recently resumed communication, after nineteen years of silence.[14]

Although no evidence exists that a West Coast rendezvous actually occurred, Freeman's intuition of a resonance between Gold and the early Beats was perceptive. In 1957 Gold had attended a poetry session in San Francisco at The Cellar featuring Kenneth Rexroth (1905–1982), whom he had first met in 1923,[15] and Lawrence Ferlinghetti (b. 1920); both performed their work to the "obligato of a progressive jazz trio." Gold linked the former to the French surrealist (and French resistance fighter) Paul Eluard (1895–1952) for his "simple statement of indignation and love," and admired the latter as "an enemy of all that destroys man's joy of living." Gold was also familiar with Ginsberg's poem "Howl," which he characterized as "the most heartbroken lamentation over the epoch that I ever read." What drew Gold to this new movement was its "life," the sure sign of which was police harassment. He noted that Ginsberg was only following in the steps of Walt Whitman, who also had been subjected to the charge of "obscenity." While Gold had no sympathy for drugs and homosexuality, or what he believed to be Ginsberg's "Trotskyism," he saw the Beats passing through a stage parallel to that of the Russian poet Vladimir Mayakovsky (1893–1930) in 1914. To his *People's World* readers, Gold observed: "Yet he grew, and they will, too."[16]

That the trajectory of Mayakovsky should spring to mind as a point of reference had a basis in Gold's personal history. Both men were born in the same year, passing through a tumultuous youth and early manhood in which they aspired to combine poetry and modern theater. Both, around 1914, developed loyalties to the working-class movement, subsequently moving forward to embrace the Russian Revolution with every fiber of their beings. During the 1920s, as Mayakovsky became the voice of revolutionary art, Gold himself became increasingly drawn to Futurism, capped by a visit to the Soviet Union from late 1924 to early 1925, where he immersed himself in the theater experiments of Mayakovsky and Vsevolod Meyerhold (1874–1940).

In the fall of 1925, Mayakovsky made a tour of the United States, and during his New York sojourn he was hosted at a party by Freeman and Gold. According to Freeman, "Gold recited 'A Strange Funeral at Braddock,' broke into tears and made an eloquent speech about the proletarian revolution." When Freeman expressed concern about the quantity of alcohol being consumed by these aspiring proletarian revolutionaries, Gold dismissed him by observing that "Mayakovsky drinks three times as much as we do." Mayakovsky then confessed: "Yes, I am a bohemian. . . . That is my great problem:

to burn out all of my bohemian past, to rise to the heights of the revolution."[17]

Mayakovsky's 1930 suicide, not long after Gold visited him in Moscow, coincided with the final stages of Gold's own transformation into a celebrated novelist and regular *Daily Worker* columnist. Although never quite disappearing, Gold's erratic bohemianism was progressively displaced as he assumed the responsibilities of marriage, a family, and unyielding Party commitment. Gold rationalized Mayakovsky's sad end as the result of harassment by "little people on the make . . . climbers and careerists."[18] He turned to a substantial consideration of the Russian poet only during the early years of World War II.[19] This was after he accidentally discovered David Burliuk (1882–1967), the painter and poet who was a founder of Russian Futurism and a mentor of Mayakovsky, living in obscurity in a tenement in the Ukrainian section of New York's East Side. In a brochure about Burliuk that Gold prepared for the A.C.A. Art Gallery on East 57th Street, he discussed his affinity with both men.

In Mayakovsky Gold saw a young rebel who, to quote the Soviet poet Nikolai Aseev, had been ruled "by street life and thunder," until Burliuk bullied him into assuming his responsibilities as a poet who understood "the harsh and crude realities of the proletarian struggle." Significantly, Burliuk himself is presented in the brochure by Gold as having made a personal transition of his own. Gold quotes Burliuk as telling him that he eventually forsook aggressive experimentation aimed at only the destruction of "old forms in art," to bring "poetry back to the people by stressing the dramatic and epic, by heroic oration, not morbid introspection." In due time Burliuk's paintings themselves became what he called "primitive."[20] Thus Gold saw in the lives of both men patterns justifying the narrative of his own struggle to gain control of his emotional and personal life, exemplified by a removal from the literary experiments of his younger self.

Although it is likely that some of the breakdowns and depressions that marked Gold's youth were the consequences of his protracted combat with diabetes,[21] his flamboyant behavior recalls that of several generations of rebellious youth gifted with literary precocity. Gold emerged from painful poverty in New York City as something of an autodidact, becoming in his teens a devotee of the American writers such as Whitman, Twain, and Sandburg, and Russians such as Gorky and Dostoyevski. When he showed up in Boston at age eighteen, he lived in an anarchist commune, embraced vegetarianism, and, like Allen Ginsberg twenty years later, was nicknamed "Professor." At one point neighbors complained about Gold's insouciant habit of exercising stark naked before an uncovered window with a big cigar in his mouth.[22]

During the 1920s, Gold was, on the one hand, an eccentric Communist who preferred a good joke to a political speech;[23] but he also privately wrestled with a variety of insecurities as he tried his hand at writing poetry, drama, fiction, and reportage, as well as editing Left magazines and producing plays. Gold was invigorated by his personal contacts with Futurists in mid-decade, and it was the shock of the Great Depression, the inspiration of the Party-led movement of the unemployed, and the triumph of Hitler that enabled him to visualize a new identity as America's foremost committed writer. It was through the stern tutorial of the Communist movement that Gold had found stability and salvation as "the people's writer . . . fearless and incorruptible, pouring forth what seemed like a torrent of words from the heart."[24] Thus he felt he had a debt to the Communist movement which he would honor for the rest of his life. His early undisciplined experiments in art and life brought with them the dangers of self-centered individualism, a bohemianism that needed to be, like Mayakovsky's, "burned out." As he forged this new identity, he shed his own "street life and thunder." He retained this self-selected personality, never losing control over what he was and represented, to his last day. Yet he retained to the end an incandescent warmth, compassion, and empathy for that rebellious stage of youthful angst and hi-jinks in which he now hypothesized the Beats to be.

## Poverty Is a Trap

Gold's biography has been recounted several times but is too often confused with that of the persona of his novel *Jews without Money*, which he claimed was "85% autobiographical."[25] He was born Itzok Granich on 12 April 1893, in New York City's Lower East Side, the first surviving child of Charles Granich, who emigrated to the United States from Jassy, Rumania, in 1885, and Kate Schwartz, who left for the United States from Budapest, Hungary, one year later. Gold anglicized his first name to Irving at the behest of his schoolteachers, and then to Irwin when he started publishing.

Gold's father, in contrast to Herman, the working-class house painter of *Jews without Money*, was self-employed as a suspender maker and salesman who owned his own manufacturing shop with several employees. Although he was incompetent in dealing with commercial matters, Charles Granich was an engaging storyteller with a vast knowledge of the theater, and adored by his first-born son, who sat at his feet for hours, lost in a fantastic tapestry of Old World tales and extemporaneous dramatizations of Yiddish and

European plays. Hence young Michael was devastated when his father fell mysteriously ill, became bed-ridden, and died when his son was only eighteen. A year before his death, Charles Granich made several unsuccessful suicide attempts by slashing himself with a knife. His son, who discovered the bleeding body and heard his pleas for death, was horrified to find himself hating his father and wishing for his demise in order that the family might be free of this burden.[26] Charles's economic incompetence and illness required that his wife find work in a restaurant; Gold himself was forced at age twelve to quit school and to start work at a gas mantle factory, followed a year later by a job at the Adams Express Company. The parents quarreled bitterly over their dilemma, and thus was born in Gold the "consciousness of guilt for duty undone."[27]

The loss of his father as a powerful source of joyous entertainment haunted Gold for the rest of his life, even as he carried on Charles's tradition of singing folksongs (often in Yiddish) and public storytelling. Gold's writing had actually begun at age fifteen while his father lay ill; he wrote tales, entitled "Tenements," "Nails," and "Ghost Story," that were published in a settlement-house newspaper.[28] Several of Gold's early published writings refer to the death of fathers and father figures, events usually associated with political action. In a 1919 poem, "To One Dying," Gold tells of the passing of an old revolutionary who will be replaced by a young disciple.[29] In "A Great Deed was Needed," a striking coal miner's son, Buddy, weeps at the loss of his father, then transforms his rage into desire for class war with the cry, "The world needs a great proletarian deed!"[30] A few years before his own death, Gold insisted that he still meditated daily on his father's fate.[31] Charles Granich's death was also decisive in his son's leftward turn, for Gold formed the belief that the prevailing social system was at fault for never giving his father a chance to reach his full powers: "[H]e had not been given an honest chance to discover his own make-up, and to work toward his own special career. I felt that he had been robbed. It was this sense of injustice to my father that had prepared me so readily for my contact with the revolution."[32] In *Jews without Money*, originally called "Poverty Is a Trap,"[33] Gold created a myth to dramatize this conviction by remaking his father into a working-class house painter who injures himself in a fall from a ladder and then slowly languishes from lead poisoning due to breathing the fumes of his paint.

This brilliantly realized character, who fused Gold's own personal anguish and his political convictions, retains Charles Granich's personality and role as a victim of capitalist society who lacked consciousness of the forces destroying him. But the occupation of painter and the illness that killed him were drawn from the life of Gold's friend, the worker-poet Jim Waters (dates unknown), who lived with Gold at the time he was finishing *Jews without Money*.[34] Gold transferred to the working class the love and idealized childhood adulation he had felt for his father; hence a victory of the working class over capitalism became a legitimate dream for him as a partial compensation for the loss of his father.

The life of Kate Granich is more faithfully portrayed in the novel. Gold intended Katie to be a symbol of socialism, albeit a romanticized one, who is depicted in the chapter "Mushrooms in Bronx Park" as closely linked to nature. Indeed, the social and cultural critic Lewis Mumford (1895–1990), who met Gold just before World War I and remained friends with him through the next decade, recalled years later that Gold was "a passionate, brilliant, vehement youth . . . a romantic and an anarchist, closer to Rousseau and Stirner than to Marx."[35] Throughout the novel the son, searching for an emotional center to his life, fails to recognize that it is his mother who is the ultimate object of his own desire; unlike his dreamy father, she lives socialist values in her altruism, generosity, and explicit hatred of capitalist exploitation. Only on the final page does young Mike's quest for a savior shift from the illusions of religion (his fantasy of a Messiah) and of popular culture (the Messiah begins to look like Buffalo Bill) to working-class revolution. Such a revolution will be the instrument that will "destroy the East side" and "build there a garden for the human spirit."[36] Through this indirect reconciliation with the spirit of his mother, animated by a socialism of natural love, an alternative foundation is created for a new kind of family with Gold himself assuming the role of family avenger and protector.

*Jews without Money* contains a second invention about his family. In the novel a sister, Esther, one year younger than the protagonist, is killed by a delivery wagon. Young Mikey's relations with Esther are surprisingly sadistic, provoked by the nurturing role she plays in relation to his sick father. With mother Katie working in a restaurant, Esther assumes the part of housekeeper and nurse. Thus she earns a higher place than Mikey in their father's affections, expressed so effusively to young Esther as to assume sexual overtones.[37] The more innocent, kind, cooperative, and generous Esther's behavior becomes, the more young Mikey torments, ridicules, humiliates, and even beats her. On the evening when she is killed by a blond, German American wagon driver, young Mikey is lost in a book about Richard the Lion-Hearted.

The Granich family consisted only of Mike and his two younger brothers, George, born in 1895, and Emmanuel ("Manny"), born in 1898. Several years before Mike's birth, a sister had died at the age of four of natural causes.

Esther, the invented sister in the novel, has many characteristics borrowed from an aunt, and the wagon accident is based on an incident when Mike's brother Manny was run over in the street and injured. By practically eliminating his brothers from the narrative and moving the death of his sister from the past to the present, occurring as Mikey approaches adolescence, Gold dramatizes the complex feelings of a surviving child. Possibly he believed that the sister who pre-deceased him had served as the object of an idealization by his father against which he could never measure up, or else the sister is a stand-in for the role Gold wishes he had played in relation to his parents. The invented tale of Esther invokes emotions of self-hate and jealousy on the part of young Mikey that otherwise appear to have no explanation, other than being the manifestations of an exaggerated sibling rivalry. Moreover, the linking of Esther's death to the family's poverty — she is killed when she is forced to seek firewood on a cold stormy night because her father is sick and Katie is working — shows once again Gold's tendency to assuage his personal pain by channeling anger in the direction of an inegalitarian social order.

Readers and scholars have reacted variously to the rapid transmogrification of the protagonist at the climax of *Jews without Money* from a candidate for suicide to a proletarian revolutionary. This is said to have occurred several years after Mikey turned fifteen, and is portrayed as a cure-all to his various problems. Specifically, in the final chapter, the post-adolescent protagonist declares for proletarian revolution after hearing a man on a soapbox speak at a political rally. Later, Gold claimed that this was based on an incident in 1914, when he was twenty-one, and that the speaker was the "Rebel Girl," Elizabeth Gurley Flynn (1890-1964), at the time a fiery leader of the Industrial Workers of the World (IWW) and later a Communist spokeswoman. One of Gold's sons believes that the speaker may not have been Flynn but Emma Goldman (1869-1940), the anarchist who was anathema to the Communist Party by the time *Jews without Money* was published.[38]

Moreover, it is likely that radical politics were well known to the three Granich brothers from their youth, with each brother influencing the other. The youngest brother, George, became a founding member of the Communist Party in 1919, which suggests a time of radical activity going back to an even earlier date. As with Mike, his commitment was life-long. After a period of hoboing, George married, and he and his wife, Gertrude, then ran a children's camp in Woodstock, New York. The Graniches subsequently established an after-school center for children in the basement of their home on MacDougal Street in Greenwich Village. *Jews without Money* is dedicated to George and Gertrude's son, Michael. When George died of cancer in 1946 at the age of forty-five, Gold devoted three of his *Daily Worker* columns to expressing his grief.[39]

The brother between Mike and George, Manny, worked in the shipyards during World War I and then took an interest in engineering. In the early 1920s Manny traveled to California, where he organized agricultural workers for the IWW. Sometime during the 1920s, Manny joined the Communist Party, and in 1932 he traveled to the Soviet Union, where he helped build factories in the Ural Mountains. In 1936, Manny (now sometimes called "Max") and his wife, Grace, were asked by the Comintern to travel to China, where they edited *Voice of China*, working with Madame Sun Yat-sen to rally the Chinese against the Japanese. After returning to the United States, Manny worked as the chauffeur, secretary, and body guard for the Communist Party general secretary Earl Browder while Grace was employed at Party headquarters, on the famed "Ninth Floor." When Browder was expelled from the Party in 1946, Manny turned bitterly against him. Manny's loyalty to the Party lasted until the 1961 Sino-Soviet dispute, after which he became a supporter of Mao and a passionate defender of the Red Guards during the Chinese Cultural Revolution.

Whatever the precise stages of Gold's radicalization were, it seems to be the case that, at the time that he heard Flynn (or Goldman) address the rally in Union Square, he purchased a copy of the *Masses* and later submitted to the magazine a poem in the style of Walt Whitman, about the death of three anarchists, which appeared in the August 1914 issue.[40] He became regularly associated with the *Masses* and its successors, initially as Irwin Granich and later as Mike Gold. Less evident from his novel is that the young Mike Gold was also ambitious in a conventional way, perhaps seeking to achieve the economic security that had slipped from his father's grasp. First, he took extra courses in night school to compensate for his failure to finish high school. Although he never disclosed this information himself, documents found by his literary editor (see endnote 25) after Gold's death reveal that he was hired by the *New York Globe* from 1913 to 1914, and used the credentials he acquired there to attend New York University to study journalism for a year. He also worked on a number of suburban newspapers in the New York area and managed a printing plant. Based on these accomplishments, he received special permission to attend Harvard University as a provisional student in the fall of 1916 – an uncanny parallel to the biography of Gregory Corso, who attained the same status in 1954. While matriculated, Gold penned a chatty column that appeared six days a week in the *Boston Journal* called "A Freshman at Harvard."

His efforts to become "Joe College" ended in catastrophe. Only a semester later, Gold suffered a nervous breakdown so severe that he always considered it the lowest point of his life. Setbacks in his romantic life had triggered a delayed reaction to his father's death, during which repressed feelings powerfully reasserted themselves. Fifty years later he recalled:

> [My father's] memory . . . obsessed me more than did that beautiful girl I was in love with. Every day I thought of him . . . I think the thing that hurt me most was that I had adored him as one of the most brilliant people I had known.[41]

Gold fell into a paralyzing depression and sold all his books. He walked around in dirty rags that deteriorated to the point where his genitals could sometimes be seen through the cloth. He began to scrounge money for food, thought endlessly about his dead father, and continued to pursue the hopeless love affair. Still, during the illness and his recovery in these years just prior to World War I, revolutionary politics were never distant. He joined the IWW and frequently resided in an anarchist commune, run by the Boston Left personality Polly Parrot. There he was active in supporting local strikes, editing an anarchist newspaper called *The Flame* with a millionaire friend,[42] and working in the Boston birth control movement. He frequently contributed to the Socialist *Call* in New York.

Gold's Boston experiences were the nadir in terms of his effort to establish a sense of self and control over his destiny. While the pain of his first loss in love may well have set the stage for the reappearance of powerful, suppressed feelings about his father, he could also blame his personal crisis on his having held naive illusions in achieving stability through a Harvard education that would lead to a normal professional career. Although he cited his Harvard sojourn in an application to the Guggenheim Foundation in 1936, exaggerating his stay to six months, he omitted it in his 1928 application and otherwise denied that he had ever attended.[43] There is evidence that he was neither lying nor joking in this attitude, but trying to express some essential verity that the "facts" of the situation did not communicate.

## Meyerhold in Harlem

Leaving Boston, Gold began to live out his father's legacy by devoting himself to the theater, first demonstrated through his association with the Provincetown Players.[44] In 1917 Gold's *Down the Airshaft* was performed, followed immediately by *Homecoming*. Both short plays are noticeably based on events in Gold's life. The first tells of a Jewish boy longing to leave his mother and take to the road until he hears the artistic muse of his own environment through the sound of a flute coming down the tenement air-shaft. The second depicts a dead Russian father, killed in battle at the front, returning briefly to his family as a ghost until he is exposed by news of the actual events of the war reaching home.[45] That same year Gold, now a member of the Socialist Party, escorted Theodore Dreiser, in search of material for a play about tenement life, to view the Chrystie Street apartment he shared with his mother. Furthermore, his own first sketch of an episode from *Jews without Money* appeared as "Birth: A Prologue to a Tentative East Side Novel" in the November–December 1917 issue of the *Masses* under the name Irwin Granich.

In late 1918, however, Gold crossed the border into Mexico to escape the draft. There he passed more than a year working – sometimes translating for the press, sometimes doing physical labor – as well as carousing. He was also active on the Left, proclaiming an anarchist politics opposed to all states and political organizations but still sympathetic to the Bolshevik Revolution. At one point, collecting money in the streets of Mexico City for a Spanish translation of the Soviet Constitution, he encountered the African American boxer Jack Johnson, with whom he was acquainted, and received a $10 contribution.[46] His time in Mexico resulted in a full-length play, a short story, an unfinished novel, and a life-long love of Mexican songs, the spirit of the Mexican Revolution, and the Spanish language.[47] Back in Provincetown in 1920, he saw the Players perform his work *Money*, a one-act play climaxing in a scene in which Mendel, a factory worker, describes his political transformation when hearing a street corner speaker on the East Side predict a classless society.

In January 1921 he had become a member of the editorial board of the *Liberator* under the name Michael Gold, which he used for protection during the post–World War I wave of antiradical repression. The pseudonym was borrowed from a friend of his father who was a northern veteran of the Civil War, a war in which Gold *did* believe. Around this time he joined the Communist movement, although his membership status may not have been consistent until the early 1930s. By January 1922 Gold and Claude McKay were jointly appointed executive editors of the *Liberator*, but by October Gold, who was temperamentally incompatible with the fastidious and somewhat aristocratic McKay, had gone West.

From 1922 through 1924, Gold lived in Oakland, California, writing for the *San Francisco World* and other papers. He published a series, "The Life of John Brown," in the *Daily Worker* which subsequently appeared as a Halderman-

Julius Publishing Company pamphlet under that name. After a period in Chicago, when a collection of his narratives called *A Damned Agitator and Other Stories* (1924) was published as a pamphlet by the *Daily Worker,* he traveled to London, Paris, Berlin, and the Soviet Union. There he was profoundly affected by the Constructivist theater of Meyerhold that employed pantomimes, acrobatics, formalized scenery, and other techniques to emphasize his plays' nonverbal aspects.[48] Decades later, Gold enthusiastically recalled how he attended the theater every night of his stay, and also spent long hours in the company of Meyerhold (who spoke English) in the green room of his theater. To Gold, the plays were impressive for their ability to express emotions through the movement of the body, and he saw a unity between words and muscular activity. Observing a Meyerhold performance "had the effect of sculpture that came to life under your eyes." He was also fascinated by the extraordinary stage, an old barnlike house containing all kinds of structures and several floors, as well as by the "noble" appearance of the German Jewish Meyerhold.[49]

The impact on Gold, who was also acutely sensitive to the visual and physical, was monumental.[50] Returning to New York, "I felt as if something had left my life and must be replaced by something as close to the original as possible." Gold threw himself back into journalism, helping to launch the *New Masses* as a Left publication friendly to but independent of the Communist Party. He worked on some short plays and dramatic sketches, including an influential "mass recitation" called "Strike!" that appeared in the *New Masses* in July 1926. He also completed chapters of a novel-in-progress based on his own youth that he would soon recast as an autobiography. But he remained committed to recreating some version of Constructivist theater in the United States. In 1927, with John Howard Lawson, John Dos Passos, and others, he organized the New Playwrights Theater, which took its name from "The Playwrights Theater," where the Provincetown Players first performed in New York City. Then a well-to-do supporter of revolutionary arts, Florence Rauh (sister of Max Eastman's former wife, Ida Rauh), offered Gold her apartment while she went on vacation. Gold went into a "trance" and started to write a full-length play, *Hoboken Blues.* When finished, he realized that it was in "Futurist style," something that had not been a conscious choice but happened "automatically." He sent the manuscript off to the *American Caravan,* a new annual of avant-garde literature. The editors – Van Wyck Brooks, Lewis Mumford, and Paul Rosenfeld – accepted it at once with great eagerness, and it appeared in 1927. This was the same year that Gold was arrested during a demonstration to protest the execution of Sacco and Vanzetti.

An experimental drama set in Harlem, New York, and Hoboken, New Jersey, *Hoboken Blues* was intended to have an entirely African American cast with white characters played by Blacks in white masks. The subtitle was *The Black Rip Van Winkle: A Modern Negro Fantasia on an Old American Theme*, and the protagonist is a Black man, Sam Pickens, who travels from Harlem to Hoboken seeking work as a banjo player in a circus.[51] After being attacked by white policemen, Pickens awakens to find himself in a communist utopia. When he decides to return to Harlem to retrieve his wife and daughter, he discovers that he has actually been asleep for twenty-five years.

Gold's plans received a setback when he went to the flat of African American singer and actor Paul Robeson (1898–1976) to ask him to play the role of Pickens. Robeson had read the play, but felt it was inappropriate for him because it seemed politically "hopeless" in spirit.[52] Moreover, Gold was never able to assemble an all-Black cast, and its production by the New Playwrights Theatre in 1928 was a failure, although the *Daily Worker* published a supportive review by James P. Cannon.[53] *Fiesta*, another full-length play but written in a conventional style, received more favorable reviews when it was produced at the Provincetown Playhouse in 1929. But Gold was bitter about changes made in the production; he felt that the directors had debased the Mexican peons whom he wanted to embody the spirit of the revolution. Gold was further distressed by the abandonment of the New Playwrights Theater at that time by the other writers; he believed this to have been engineered by Lawson, who did not share his confidence about winning a working-class following. Then there was a nagging sense of inauthenticity about his own efforts to dramatize African American and Mexican life in the plays; although he felt knowledgeable and respectful of these cultures, the effects were not at all what he had intended. For the most part *Fiesta* ended the playwriting phase of Gold's career. But in 1936 the Federal Theatre Project produced *Battle Hymn*, a drama rewritten with Michael Blankfort (1907–1982) from a biography of John Brown that Gold had originally published in 1924, and in 1948 he released parts of a play based on the life of Communist Party New York City councilman Pete Cacchione (1891–1947).[54]

Gold's clumsy efforts at Black dialect and his depiction of African American stereotypes in *Hoboken Blues* seem somewhat inexplicable in the context of Gold's militant antiracism. In the early 1920s, Gold had criticized Upton Sinclair for his creation of an "old-fashioned stage darkey," so one might have expected Gold to avoid the subject if he were unable to do better.[55] What seems likely is that Gold was attempting to recreate Black urban culture with the same humor and earthiness with which he was depicting Jewish ghetto culture in his East Side novel; but the effort failed due to his lack of intimate familiarity with the materials and his primary focus on producing a Futurist spectacle.[56] Moreover, Gold, who would occasionally make odd-ball statements about Black music in his columns in the 1930s, may have been caught in cross-currents of Left thinking at the time. At first there was a celebration of "Negro primitivism" in the Harlem Renaissance; later many radicals, Black and white, denounced the Renaissance jazz culture as the creation of wealthy and decadent white patrons.

Gold had long felt a strong affinity between the African American and Jewish situations. This was not premised on a disparagement of his own culture, nor was it an expression of Negrophilia. Gold, dissimilar from some other Jewish radicals who seemed to be captivated by a bleached-out ver-sion of "universalism" – in which their ethnic identity became unmention-able – felt at ease in his culture and community. If he showed signs of any Jewish "nationalism," it was unquestionably a "proletarian nationalism" premised on class alliances.[57] Even before the Communist movement theo-rized a Black national liberation struggle as the key to transforming capi-talism, Gold saw common roots, experiences, and a future between the two targets of extreme bigotry in his day, Blacks and Jews.[58] In 1923 he published a powerful story about racism in a hospital, "Death of a Negro," and soon after proclaimed John Brown his hero.[59] Scholar William Maxwell observes aptly that "the notion of the shared fate of Jews and African Americans that led him to Brown also urged him to resist Americanization via black hating." Gold was the scourge of those second-wave immigrants who were "paying the ticket price of citizenship with professions of whiteness"; instead, he devoted himself to "exposing the bond" between Yiddish culture and Negro spirituals.[60]

Reminiscing in the 1960s about his relationship with Claude McKay, Gold characterized racism as the "White Problem" (instead of the "Negro Problem"), recollecting that he had regarded the persecution of the Jew as that of a "White Negro."[61] Letters preserved from the time exhibit Gold's identification and empathy with Blacks, devoid of liberal paternalism. Of course, Gold's views would be refracted through the changing opinions of the Party to which he gave allegiance; for example, during World War II he wrote several columns denouncing the "Harlem Riots" as an expression of a "perverted Negro nationalism" that may have been inspired by "fascist hoodlums organized by a Negro Hitler."[62] Notwithstanding his vision was somewhat skewered by the priorities of the antifascist struggle, he returned in the Cold War years and afterward to clear-sighted and uncompromis-ing exposés of racism. At the time that William Faulkner presented a pub-lic statement against compulsory integrationism, Gold rendered a powerful public riposte in "A Reply to William Faulkner's 'Thinking with the Blood.'"[63]

## The Van Gogh of a Darker Time

During his discussions with David Burliuk in the early 1940s, Gold was particularly struck by the obscurity into which the painter-poet had fallen: "This artist who discovered Mayakovsky, who exhibited with Picasso and Kandinsky, who knew Gorky, Verhaeren, Repin, who organized one of the intellectual currents that burrowed under the feudal throne of the Czardom, is living in an East Side tenement."[64] To give Burliuk some perspective, Gold reminded him of the example of Van Gogh, offering a description that one might bring to bear on the later career of Gold as well:

> The critics completely ignored him, or scorned him. He did not fit into their categories. He was like the sunset. He was full of contradiction, like nature itself at work. He was a man. He suffered deeply for the wrongs done the working class. He adored the violence and tenderness of his Mother Nature. He was a humanist. He was a painter of man and nature.[65]

Gold, too, had been among the cultural luminaries of his generation; a friend and associate not only of Leftists such as Eastman, Dell, Reed, McKay, Dreiser, Dos Passos, and Sinclair, Gold was also championed at different intervals by Eugene O'Neill, Edmund Wilson, H. L. Mencken, and even Ezra Pound. By the time he encountered Burliuk, he, too, was beginning to be scorned and ignored. In Gold's parting toast to Burliuk, the close identification of the two men was clear: "My children and your children will see a humanist world. And you, the Van Gogh of a darker time, will be famous and loved."[66]

When *Jews without Money* appeared ten years earlier, few would have predicted that its author would end his career in poverty and near obscurity. The book, however, was atypical of Gold's oeuvre in terms of the amount of time devoted to its production, the deep wellsprings of personal and group life that it expressed, and, of course, the propitious moment in which it appeared — one year after the stock market crash and on the eve of Hitler's ascendancy to power. As early as 1917, Gold began publishing autobiographically based fiction in the *Masses,* and throughout the 1920s published more of such writings in journals such as *American Mercury, Menorah Journal,* and *New Masses.* These contributions were heavily revised to appear as the book-length *Jews without Money* in 1930. The book was extremely popular, elicited rave reviews, and acquired a reputation as the founding novel of "Proletarian literature," despite certain unorthodox features.[67] That same year, Gold achieved national attention through his assault on the writings of Thornton Wilder that was published in the *New Republic,* and from Sinclair Lewis, who praised Gold in his Nobel Prize acceptance speech.[68]

Yet the background to the construction of *Jews without Money* requires further attention. An examination of Gold's correspondence with Upton Sinclair, and with his future publisher, Horace Liveright, indicates a significant modification in perspective on the book following his return from the Soviet Union. Prior to that time, Gold had maintained that he was writing a novel based on autobiographical experiences. Yet scholars have observed that the earlier published versions of chapters, and related stories, seem to depict Gold's life more accurately than the manuscript that was ultimately marketed – at Gold's insistence – as an autobiography.[69] What changed was the creation of a more positive view of both of his parents, as well as a celebratory attitude toward the ghetto culture that was previously depicted mainly as stifling and oppressive. A noteworthy example is that his early writing represents his mother as a symbol of narrowness, a figure to be escaped rather than embraced.[70] Once his new orientation was established, Gold became adamant that the book was no longer fiction but mostly truth. Gold's mother in his finished work would become a sacred "mother-legend," similar to the mother in Walt Whitman's fictional persona.[71]

Gold's experiences in the Soviet Union appear to have triggered a rebirth, encouraging him to take a fresh approach to the earlier events in his life. In the *Nation* he described the revolution as tantamount to the apocalypse – "The world was upside down; the money-maker was a pariah and outlaw; the revolutionists became the pillars of society. . . . It was . . . the end of everything – the beginning of everything."[72] To Upton Sinclair he affirmed that "One feels so normal and strong in Russia," and that everything now seemed "simple and real"; after all, he had witnessed "The earth in the throes of the birth of a new race of giants."[73] The Soviet sojourn, repeated in 1930, was the final stepping stone toward the creation of a Mike Gold whose faith was firm and unyielding. In the same letter to Sinclair in which Gold had lamented his being "soft," he had added that "I know therefore that I am not the leader and I am willing to follow the Lenins and the like."[74]

Several years later, Gold was able to publish a fuller statement of his political creed in the *New Masses.* "Why I am a Communist" challenges the reader to name a party more successful in organizing the struggle for socialism than the Communist Party; if one cannot, then one should abandon all efforts to build rival parties and help advance the best one extant. Gold lists all the achievements socialism will bring – "It will free the factory slaves, the farm drudges, it will set woman free, and restore the Negro race to its human rights" – and he uses representative romantic imagery to promise a working-class victory in his lifetime: "I know that the world will be beautiful soon in the sunlight of proletarian brotherhood." He concludes that the struggle requires that "I accept its disciplines and necessities; I become as practical and realistic as possible for me; I want victory." Complementing the argument for putting the Party first on tactical grounds, however, is Gold's testament to the centrality of the Communist Party in providing intellectual and emotional stability. He explains how, in the process of making his Communist commitment, "My mind woke up like a suppressed volcano. I can never discharge this personal debt to the revolutionary movement – it gave me a mind."[75]

Gold's credo was thus forged not on orders from Moscow, but developed out of his own life experience. From the emotional turmoil of his youth he gradually assembled a new world outlook that provided an explanation for the fate of his father, his own situation, and the oppression of others with whom he identified. The solution was socialism, and the instrument for realizing the solution was the Communist Party. Art and culture could be weapons to advance that effort, wielded by those who shared a common vision. Such a vision worked pragmatically to improve his own life, as shown by the success of *Jews without Money* and the national attention garnered by his essay on Wilder in the *New Republic*; moreover, in the excitement of the early 1930s, the vision seemed to be working for others as well. Unfortunately, what Gold believed to be the opening of a new epoch, leading forward to socialism, was but an anomalous moment in a sequence of unexpected events, a series of limited victories to be followed by many serious defeats. Gold, however, remained more or less frozen in the instant of his glory days. Nearly fifteen years later, on the eve of the worst antiradical repression in modern U.S. political history, and Gold's departure from his native land for a three-year exile in France, he declared:

> Marxism flourished . . . during the first half of the 1930s. . . . New writers wrote "proletarian novels," plays and poems and became a main stream in our national culture, that formed the finest literary epoch our country has known since the Golden Age of Whitman, Emerson and Melville.
>
> It was a fighting art, a Marxist art and frankly a weapon in the class struggle then raging so openly. . . . We must find our way back to the main highway. . . . We must rebuild the Marxist cultural front, with its literary magazines, theaters, music and art.[76]

Unfortunately, that cultural front would never be rebuilt. Instead, the rudimentary Communist cultural tradition would barely survive for another decade or so, although a number of honorable contributions would be made. Gold, however, would be a very minor participant; it was what he *had* done, what he *had* stood for, not what he *would* do that would count for subsequent generations. From the mid-Depression on, his life became something of a holding action. Moreover, circumstances conspired with his own personal weaknesses to prevent the completion of the major books that one expected to follow his first success.

In 1930, with $6,000 in royalties from *Jews without Money,* Gold purchased land in Bucks County, Pennsylvania, for $3,000, which he later sold to the Leftist humorist S. J. Perelman (1904–1979). Gold seems to have had at least three major prose fiction and nonfiction projects in mind at this time. One, dependent on financial backing, was a volume to be called "Jews of the World," consisting of impressionistic pictures of life in Palestine and the ghettos of Europe. Another was a novel about a Harvard college student, of which three chapters were completed. The narrative concerns the ordeal of Ernest Lowell, a devotee of Thoreau and Whitman who falls under the corrupting influence of an English professor devoted to Proust, Gide, Eliot, and Huxley. The student has a fatal flaw — prejudice against working-class Italians. Oddly, Lowell resembles Gold in having a father who is both economically incompetent and physically ill. The most fully conceptualized of Gold's future projects was a novel about the struggles of the unemployed. The hero is a young Irish American iron worker who loses his job and finds himself caught between a radical friend wanting him to organize, and a wife who pressures him to make whatever compromises are necessary to find work.

This last manuscript had the most promise since, like *Jews without Money,* it grew out of the anger of his childhood poverty and oppression. It also had a conspicuous and compelling theme: that unemployment is not an individual problem, and that its solution requires one to think and act socially. Moreover, Gold's brother George had been a leader in the Unemployed Councils, and Gold himself had participated in demonstrations. Gold even took a leave from his newspaper column to focus on the project. But soon he found the subject "too huge to be confined within the framework of fiction." He later reminisced that "I could find no form for all this bleeding chaos, this welter of millions of individual tragedies. There were too many stories and not the one inevitable one." Within a short time he found himself transforming some of his research materials for the novel back into articles for the Communist press.[77]

By temperament, Gold was simply not suited to sustaining his focus for months or years in isolation on one big project. *Jews without Money*, of course, had been crafted from dozens of short, discrete vignettes, published over a decade and reworked into a loosely unified volume with much agony. Gold's companion of the 1920s, Helen Black, told novelist Albert Maltz that Gold was simply incapable of revision. He would ask her if a story needed further work; if she replied that it did, he sent it out anyway, moving on to the next project.[78] No doubt Gold's growing medical condition, his active life, and his constantly changing living conditions contributed to an inability to concentrate on long-term writing projects. By 1936 Gold was writing Sinclair that he was out of funds and back to the days of sleeping on the floor: "I'm afraid that as usual I will have to forget fictioneering and get some work to do—may go back to the *Daily Worker* column, which pays a small wage but takes every bit of creative feeling out of me."[79] And so he did. Back in 1933, with money in his pocket and still optimistic about future books, he was so incensed by the triumph of Hitler that he had talked to the *Daily Worker* editor Clarence Hathaway; they arranged to launch his "Change the World" column at $15 a week, and Gold was even reluctant to accept that much. Now he returned to the job for more businesslike reasons.

Another change had occurred as well. In June 1935, en route to Paris to attend the Congress for the Defense of Culture, Gold was seated with other single travelers at the ship captain's table facing a young French woman, twelve years his junior, named Elizabeth Boussus. Elizabeth was a French teacher at Rutgers University and was returning home for a visit. She was struck at once by Gold's articulateness, confidence, and athletic build, which was that of a gymnast. Gold squired Elizabeth around Paris during the congress. They were married in April 1936 in a civil ceremony in Brooklyn. Their first son, Nicholas Francois Granich, was born later that year in Los Angeles, where they lived for a while, and a second, Carl André Emmanuel Granich, was born in 1940 in New York.

In the late 1930s, Gold was constantly on the move, frequently shifting residences and doing a great deal of public speaking. In 1938, however, the Gold family began paying installments on a summer cabin in a "Single Tax" colony in Plainfield, New Jersey, called "Free Acres." Between 1938 and 1941 they mostly lived there. Their plan was to rent it out, but a fire eliminated that possibility and the cabin was eventually sold in 1947. The Gold family spent the rest of the year living in a cold-water flat on New York's Lower East Side or in uptown Manhattan. Having an undisciplined writing schedule, Gold sometimes received complaints from neighbors for typing late at night; nonetheless his *Daily Worker* columns arrived on time. Politically he had a special status in the Party due to his national reputation, one that allowed for his rarely attending neighborhood cell meetings.

In 1940, Gold was suddenly hospitalized with severe diabetes. He had long shown episodic signs of the illness, but the stress of the moment probably elevated the disease to a more dangerous state. Not only was Elizabeth in the final stages of her pregnancy, but, stunned by the Hitler-Stalin Pact, Gold had ceased writing his column for a month. He then became convinced of the Pact's justification and embarked on a vigorous speaking campaign in its defense, as well as writing a series of *Daily Worker* articles castigating literary backsliders for departing from the Communist-led cultural movement in the wake of the Pact. These polemics were collected as *The Hollow Men* (1940), one of Gold's weakest tracts; his friend Sender Garlin called it "a hollow book."[80] The night that their son Carl was born, Mike as well as Elizabeth was hospitalized, and their son Nick was left home alone.

After that crisis, Gold's stamina significantly decreased. Eventually his energy began to flag after only two or three hours at the typewriter. For the next two and a half decades, until be became blind and died, Gold had to take sixty units of insulin a day, and to carefully monitor his hours of work and sleep. Still, he continued his public speaking, even though it usually involved long walks and train rides. He did this not only out of a sense of duty and for the pleasure of receiving the warm response he usually was accorded, but also because the *Daily Worker* columns paid little and the small speaking stipends were necessary to pay his rent, which was usually $25 a month. The Gold family lived without luxuries, and friends in or around the Communist Party provided them with free medical care, free rides, and free or discounted clothing.

In 1947, with the Cold War closing in, Gold decided that his children should get to know the French side of the family. Gold's summer house at Free Acres was sold that year for a good price, and additional money was borrowed. In France, Gold related well with Elizabeth's family; her parents had been adamantly pro-Dreyfus, and Emile Zola's *J'Accuse* was prominently displayed in the libraries of both sides of the family. He learned French to the extent that he could read the papers, understand conversation, and speak slowly. During the postwar period in France, everything was rationed and most people used bicycles for transportation. The Golds lived at several different locations, with their sons receiving their education in Paris for two winters before going to a provincial village school. Politically, Gold was somewhat under wraps. He had dropped his Party membership upon leaving the United States, and carried out only a few activities, such as attending a 1949 Peace Congress in Prague with Welsh Left-wing poet Dylan Thomas.

When the Golds returned to New York City in the spring of 1950, the Communist Party was very weak and under constant attack by McCarthyism. For a while Gold resumed his work at the *Daily Worker*, but fell victim to staff cutbacks possibly connected with internal political struggles. He then worked for a Czechoslovakian news agency and, after that, Polish radio, where he made recordings for "Radio Poland." Elizabeth, who was not a Party member but was sympathetic to the Party, was working in a garment sweatshop, and Gold, who was nearly sixty, even tried factory work for a while. During one summer their economic situation reduced them to seeking work at the Left-wing Camp Unity; Elizabeth was employed as a waitress, and Gold's job was to hand out towels to guests. Under such conditions, it is not surprising that Gold became tormented by a serious writer's block.[81]

In 1955 their oldest son moved to California, and the Golds, at Elizabeth's insistence, followed a year later. At the time of the Khrushchev revelations and the subsequent Soviet intervention in Hungary, Gold was settling in San Francisco. There he gave an interview on radio station KPFK defending the invasion, but felt he did poorly. He continued to write columns for the West Coast Communist paper, *People's World*, and the Jewish Communist *Freiheit*. His eyesight deteriorated to the point where he was totally blind in one eye, and everything he wrote was dictated to Elizabeth. On 16 May 1967, he died of a stroke at age seventy-three during a hospitalization at the Kaiser Foundation near San Francisco.

## The Gold Standard

The cacophony of elements that made up Gold's art is evident in his 1924 poem "The Strange Funeral in Braddock." The verse suggests a folktale with medieval elements – dragons and ogres invoke industrialism and are romantically juxtaposed to the spring sunlight and the soft April air. Gold inserts a Greek chorus to recite the refrain, "Listen to the mournful drums of a strange funeral. / Listen to the story of a strange American funeral," while the dead worker, Jan Clepak, is reincarnated as a Christ figure. Macabre and grotesque in imagery, the poem concentrates on the consequences for three survivors of Clepak's horrific death after he falls into a vat of molten steel. In a proletarian reworking of Shakespeare's song by Ariel in *The Tempest* of a "sea-change," Clepak is literally transformed into molten steel, the will of his observing wife becomes steel, and other material transformations take place as well.[82]

The poems of Gold, which might on occasion be called working-class grotesque, are replete with memorable phrases, often crudely satiric, with allusions to such writers as T. S. Eliot and Sinclair Lewis. In "Ode to Walt Whitman," he declares: "Poetry is the cruelest bunk, / A trade union is better than all your dreams – " and "Hear the shriek of the killer babbitts." In "A Wreath for Our Murdered Comrade Kobayashi," he writes of "bombastic pansies." In "Tom Mooney Walks at Midnight," a satiric reference to Vachel Lindsay's "Abraham Lincoln Walks at Midnight," he declaims: "One race – one class – one dream: Communism!"[83]

The fragmented, disrupted, and discontinuous images that marked Gold's career are appropriate to a literary legacy that oscillates between the outrageous and the pedestrian, between brilliant and banal, between warmth and vitriol. It is hard to justify the consistent application of literary terms such as naturalism and romanticism to very many aspects of the improvisational, indeterminate, open, and aleatory features of his writing. Indeed, his nine-point program for proletarian realism, usually read as socialist-realist didacticism, actually has aspects of a satiric incorporation of Ezra Pound's declarations on Imagism. At times, even a proto-"surrealist" Mike Gold can be detected in his Constructivist drama and poetry of the 1920s and very early 1930s, not to mention in his 1930 children's book, *Charlie Chaplin's Parade*, which describes a city with skyscrapers "like giant brooms . . . rocking in the wind, and scraping chunks of cloud from the sky, which fell into the street like dust."[84]

Gold was an especially unlikely paramour of the bisexual Walt Whitman in light of his tendency to bait middle-class writers as "pansies."[85] But he gave a boost to the Left-wing association with the Good Grey Poet through his 1935 "Ode to Walt Whitman," which includes passionately romantic stanzas such as this one:

O Walt Whitman, they buried you in the filth
The clatter speedup of a department store basement
But you rose from the grave to march with us
On the picket line of democracy –
Sing sing O new pioneers with Father Walt
Of a strong and beautiful America
Of the thrushes and oceans we shall win
Of sun, of moon, of Communism and joy in the wind
Of the free mountain boys and girls –
It will come! it will come! The strikes foretell it!
The Lenin dreams of the kelleys and greenbaums
Deep in the gangrened basements

Where Walt Whitman's America
Aches, to be born — [86]

Whitman is likened to a reborn Christ, to the spirit of communism, to nature, and to Bolshevism; that is, he serves as the multipurpose icon of Gold's multiethnic cultural mosaic. According to Walter Lowenfels, "Mike was an early pioneer in claiming Whitman for the working class. He campaigned year in and year out for Whitman observances among workers, for a Whitman monument in Brooklyn, etc."[87]

Stanley Burnshaw, the poet and critic who served with Gold at the *New Masses* in the early 1930s, and who remained in touch with him for many years afterward, believed that Gold "suffered from being a bundle of selves."[88] This seems confirmed by the recollection of others who were his contemporaries. For example, to the young New York Communist writer Nathan Adler, the older and more established Gold "was a self-involved guy, with no openness, no response." Gold stood in sharp contrast to the well-dressed, charming Joseph Freeman, a marvelous dancer in his Russian boots, who spoke to young men passionately of life, love, and revolution "in Proustian sentences with subjunctive clauses."[89]

At the *Daily Worker* office in the mid-1930s, sports columnist Lester Rodney heard Gold referred to as "a sort of prima donna," mainly from Joe North, who still bore a grudge against Gold from conflicts during the John Reed Club days. But Rodney was primarily impressed by the fact that Gold "met his deadlines on the *Worker*, and we all, to my recollection, found him a bluntly honest guy with an unmistakable passionate sincerity about life, art, people and the sins of capitalism."[90] Rodney was also "fascinated" by Gold's face: "Except when he was smiling, it seemed to reflect the pain he felt for all the tragedy, poverty and injustice he had witnessed."[91]

The FBI was also fascinated by Gold's face. In the files released under the Freedom of Information Act, FBI agents refer to one Irwin Granich, "alias Isaac Granich, Isadore Granich, Mike Gold, Michael Gold, 5' 7½ inches, 153 pounds, black hair, brown eyes, dark complexion, scar on right cheek" and "Jewish-appearing features."[92] Yet Gold's son insists that he had no scar on his cheek, and, while Gold did become dark and swarthy when tanned, he was mainly taken for a Native American Indian.[93]

The "real" Mike Gold, however, is hard to disentangle from the contrasting auras he inspired among FBI informants as well as his many admirers among the 1930s and 1940s Left. One informer regarded Gold as especially dangerous because he had "better than average intelligence" and was a "forceful public speaker."[94] The critic, editor, and film producer Bernard

Smith, who worked with Gold on the *New Masses* in the late 1920s, found Gold friendly and open to discussion, but always "remote": "I simply could not get to the core of the man."[95] When John Dos Passos contrived a literary portrait of Gold in the New Playwrights Theater days in his novel *Most Likely to Succeed* (1954), he seems to have created two characters embodying alternative aspects of Gold's life and personality—Eli Soltair, an anarchist who is full of fun, and Lew Golten, the dour fanatic. The general perception of Gold by rank-and-file Leftists is uniquely captured in the 1991 recollections of the poet Aaron Kramer, who was a teenager in the 1930s and whose idolatrous response to Gold's mystique may well have been shared by thousands of others:

> Gold [is] a figure so complex in my psyche that I've held back from saying a word [until now]. . . . Even as a pre-teener I turned to Gold's *Daily [Worker]* column before reading the most sensational page one news item, and mastered it thoroughly. . . . What stays with me is the keenness of his intellect and the vigor of his style—whether slashing or exuberant.
>
> He had my brain in his grip for many years. I used to wonder when writing a poem: How would this piece fare under Mike's penetrating stare? I held back from certain subject matter, such as love or nature, fearing that Mike would deem it slight or soft.[96]

Women felt a special attraction to Gold, most of whom regarded him as handsome. Edward Dahlberg recalled that the "first time [I] set eyes on Mike Gold," he "had a cigar in his mouth and his arms around the bodices of two young women."[97] The Australian-born novelist Christina Stead was quite infatuated when she met Gold shortly before his marriage. She added yet another fictional version of Gold to the small body of literature about him.[98] He became the model for Jean Frere in her novel *House of All Nations* (1938), described as follows:

> He had a dark broad face . . . a dark, rosy skin, shining dark eyes and a rather large, but well-formed mouth, with the lower lip pouting often. . . . He had extremely thick long curly coarse brown hair, growing low and irregularly on the broad forehead. When he smiled his eyes went into slits the shape of snowshoes and his mouth elongated like a longbow over his regular white teeth. He was thickset with a short thick neck, a large widespread nose, with a faintly Negroid air.[99]

Yet Josephine Herbst, reminiscing in a letter to Genevieve Taggard about Gold's affair with life-long Communist Helen Black, describes him as "the good, Newfoundland type. . . . Around every night, just to sit or go to supper.

Very domestic. Affectionate. He would be nice and simple with a woman. Like a child. Only children never make great lovers."[100] Gold's relationship with Black extended through the late 1920s and early 1930s, and it was Black, as much as Gold, who renounced marriage as "bourgeois."[101]

Gold was excoriated as a "lowbrow" by anti-Stalinist critics Irving Howe and Lewis Coser in the 1950s. Yet this self-representation was often contrived for purposes of humor.[102] Norman MacLeod recalled a debate sponsored by the John Reed Club at which Gold, preparing to do battle with journalist Heywood Broun (1888–1939), arose before the crowd with a cigar jammed in his teeth, "spitting out of the tough guy side of his mouth."[103] Gold could sound vicious in his columns – Dahlberg described him as "the barking Cerberus of pleb fiction"[104] – but he also mocked his own ostentatious proletarianism, as when he signed letters to his millionaire patron, Otto Kahn, "your class enemy."[105] Gold mostly held a reverent attitude toward the standard literary classics of Western culture, especially those written by the leaders of the American Renaissance.

True, there were certain writers of the modern period that he detested beyond all reason – Henry James ("an insufferable bore") is a prime example.[106] And he didn't hesitate to call political-literary enemies "rats" in his column, nor to offer crude denunciations of Hollywood culture that his editors sometimes tried to change.[107] But he would give one's due as a craftsman even to a reactionary such as Ezra Pound. A more telling weakness was the paramount importance he assigned a writer's "position" in relation to the Communist Party and the Soviet Union. A writer who was moving toward Gold's own political stance was warmly encouraged; a writer departing the fold was treated brutally. The redirection of their trajectory determined the weight he might give to denunciations of writers for elitism, obscurantism, symbolism, and other nonrealist literary crimes. Gold became self-critical of this tendency on his part in the final years of his life. While never relenting in his hatred of "Trotskyites," he acknowledged a flaw in what he called his "outlaw personality," which he suspected to have developed from the insecurities of his youth. Convinced in the early days of his career that he had no real friends, he attempted to defend himself by ruthless criticism of all whom he believed to support capitalism. Later he recognized that there were fine and sensitive people who were not radical at all, and he wished he could write something to make amends.[108]

While Gold is given credit for championing and developing the concept of "proletarian literature" in the 1920s and the early 1930s, there appears to have been an evolution in the term's meaning.[109] At first, Gold presented proletarian writing more as a unique contribution to literature, rather than an

opposition to the dominant literature. When socialist writers of the time denounced "capitalist" literature, Joseph Freeman recalled, they were referring
to "the tripe of the popular magazines which were full of lies not only about
the system but about life in general."[110] By the early 1930s, Freeman began
to feel that Gold represented a trend in the Communist cultural movement
that attacked select writers, with whom they politically disagreed, on the
grounds that the writers had gone to college. This approach evolved after
the 1930 Kharkov conference. At that time the sectarianism toward leftward-
moving big-name writers was repudiated, but, in Freeman's view, Leopold
Auerbach (the leading critic in the Soviet Union) also sanctioned the advocacy of "proletarian literature" as a political weapon to police the Left:
"Stalin and his mob had not the slightest interest in literature; they were
using an alleged literary criticism as a weapon for destroying intellectuals
suspected of being in favor of Trotsky, against Stalin or simply neutral."[111]
Gold, unconsciously, and in his own erratic manner, adapted this stance,
which fit well with his longstanding "outlaw personality."

   An example of the manner in which Gold's political views tended to over-
ride all else is his literary assessment of the fiction of John Dos Passos, with
whom he had collaborated in founding the New Playwrights Theater. At the
time Dos Passos published *Manhattan Transfer* (1925), Gold issued a review in
the *New Masses* that was as competent as any that appeared in the popular
press, including one by Sinclair Lewis, and superior in critical nuance and
sensibility to those of the novelist D. H. Lawrence and the humanist scholar
Paul Elmer More.[112] During these years, Dos Passos was moving toward the
Left, and in 1933, when Dos Passos was probably closest to the Communist
Party, Gold published a fine study of his fiction in *The English Journal*, which
contained superbly adept characterizations of Dos Passos's literary strategy:

> There are really a dozen novels in these two books [*The 42nd Parallel* and
> *1919*], fitted together in a continuity and context that makes each narra-
> tive a comment on the other. Dos Passos ranges through all the strata of
> the social order. He is the geologist and historian of American society. . . .
>
>   To add historic poignancy to these individual lives, and to relate them
> to their background, there is a Greek chorus of newspaper headlines and
> Americana. This adds to the strangeness of the novels, yet, after careful
> reading one finds them an organic part of the massive effect at which Dos
> Passos was aiming.
>
>   So, too, are the score or more of cameo biographies of significant Ameri-
> cans which Dos Passos has interpolated on his narrative . . . these terse
> bitter passionate portraits add an extraordinary flavor of historic truth to

the novels, and contain, besides, germs of the future revolutionary growth of Dos Passos.

It is chaos again, but Nietzsche said "one must have chaos to give birth to a dancing star." In the complexity and confusion of these novels the drive is felt toward a new communist world; and, if the aesthetes and gin-soaked Harvard futilitarians are present, it is that they may serve as a contrast to the obscure, almost unmarked hero of this epic canvas – the rising Proletaire.[113]

By 1938, however, Dos Passos had openly renounced Soviet policy and the Communist Party. Gold published a column in which he reevaluated Dos Passos's work as a mere reflection of bourgeois decadence, full of *merde*.[114] This last characterization, unfortunately, is the exclusive comment by Gold on Dos Passos quoted by Gold's hostile critics.[115]

Whatever Gold's genre, the visions he transmitted of the Soviet Union were dead wrong. On occasion Gold did speak out against official Communist Party policy – his criticism of the dissolution of the Communist Party into the Communist Political Association during World War II caused Party leader Robert Minor to publicly reply[116] – but Gold never dissented on the more crucial matter of the Party's uncritical support of Stalin's dictatorship. Gold was emotional, and he had a tendency to glibly and confidently make predictions based on wishful thinking long before his "Change the World" days. In 1926 he professed in a letter to Charles Erskine Scott Wood (1852–1944) and Sarah Bard Field that

It is foolish to air the whole Trotsky thing in the capitalist press . . . I was pro-Trotsky, too, but I think Max [Eastman] is making a mistake to get so heated over it. In two years the controversy will be forgotten, Trotsky will be back on some big job, and Russia will still be marching on.[117]

There existed a pattern in which Gold would react honestly and emotionally to new events at first, but within a short time accommodate himself to the Party's new and previously unacceptable position. Joseph Freeman recalled that he had run into Gold soon after receiving the news that the *Communist International* had denounced his 1936 *An American Testament*. Gold was dumbfounded and announced that he would immediately go to Party general secretary Earl Browder and arrange a meeting to straighten out the matter. Shortly after, he returned to Freeman and explained that Browder was too busy to see him, but that everything would work out all right in the end if Freeman continued to act loyally. That was the last contact Freeman had with Gold until they began corresponding in 1958.[118]

Gold's *Daily Worker* and *New Masses* columns also caused genuine mental anguish to fellow revolutionists, whom he frequently challenged if he sensed a deviation from his understanding of the Communist Party's orientation. In a draft of his unfinished autobiography, "A Calendar of Commitment," John Howard Lawson wrote that his first reaction to Mike Gold's attack on him, which appeared as "A Bourgeois Hamlet of Our Time," in *New Masses* on 10 April 1934, just a week after Lawson's play *Gentlewoman* closed, was "blind rage." He had trusted Gold as a friend, and felt betrayed that, when he was down and out, Gold ignored even the good will that had gone into his dramatic effort:

> It was the method of Gold's criticism to link the attack on an author with personal judgments of the author's life and motives. . . . There was one passage written by Mike that made me feel I had lost my reason, struck me like a blow [this sentence was lightly crossed out on one version of the manuscript]. Mike wrote: "The declassed bourgeoisie of America are not feeling futile. . . . They are beginning to organize, in one form or another. . . . The fact that Lawson cannot see this is another of the penalties he pays for his delayed adolescence."
>
> I rubbed my eyes and asked myself, where had I been during the past year? And where had Mike been? I had organized the first trade union of professional people in a big industry controlled by finance capital. I was spokesman for the writers against the film monopolies, and my statements had been carried by all the New York newspapers.[119]

Albert Maltz, on the eve of his blacklisting and imprisonment, felt the same anguish when he read in the *Daily Worker* Gold's claim that Maltz was opposed to the "Art as a Weapon" slogan because he had sold out to the blandishments of Hollywood.[120] Although Gold apologized to Maltz in the late 1950s, he repeated the insult by attacking in his column former Left writers living in Mexico for allegedly complaining about the cost of maid service. Maltz considered this a slander and, while he donated money to assist with Gold's medical expenses, he refused to give the eulogy for Gold at the Los Angeles memorial meeting.[121]

After a "Change the World" column in which Gold trounced as a renegade a man who was a loyal supporter of the Abraham Lincoln Brigades, novelist Nelson Algren commented wryly in a letter to Richard Wright: "It's wonderful the way a mutt like Mike will, out of a clear sky, start slugging a passing stranger who, it turns out, should remain definitely unslugged. I always thought that the proper Marxian approach toward the middle class was to win them first and slug them later. Mike has the cart before the horse."[122]

On occasion Gold would review books and plays, or respond to newspaper reports of opinions by writers, without having read the material first. Sometimes, as with Lillian Smith's controversial *Strange Fruit,* he was obliged in a later column to modify or even retract his opinions.[123] His review of O'Neill's *The Iceman Cometh* begins: "I haven't been to see the Theater Guild's . . . *The Iceman Cometh,* yet from the reviews I can almost tell what the play is like."[124] Still, in 1940, when African American Communist Party leader Benjamin Davis unfairly attacked Richard Wright's novel *Native Son* for political deviations in Wright's depiction of events as well as the character of Bigger Thomas, Gold stood firm in his praise of the novel.[125]

The literary achievement of Mike Gold is comprised of a haunting novel, some provocative plays, stories, and poems, and, as Walter Lowenfels put it in a letter to Joe North, a *"ganze gestalt* [that] was something more than any individual excellence. . . . He had perspective and vision and anger as well as love."[126] But this affection didn't stop Lowenfels from writing a more critical letter to Phillip Bonosky, the Communist novelist who published a highly laudatory 1962 tribute to Gold in *Mainstream:*

> In my book, Mike has been an *ambivalent influence* in left cultural life in the USA the past 25 years. I feel he has done our cultural movement more harm than good by his continual carry over of a past cultural approach that dates back to the 20s and early 30s.

Lowenfels, for one, saw "The Gold Standard" as a problematical foundational component of the tradition that animated the literary Left in the United States in the mid-twentieth century.

Yet Gold's critical pronouncements, weak as some obviously are, constitute a body of work that cannot simply be vulgarized as intellectual hackwork dictated by Stalinism. He was a writer first, then a political activist; over the years, however, an increasing amount of his criticism evolved into journalism that grew out of the process by which he organized his emotional life around the Communist Party and the Soviet Union. Considering the background from which he came, and the time in which he wrote, Gold probably gained more than he lost by placing a faith in institutions of the Left analogous to the manner in which many people place their hopes in a pope, the Republican Party, "Science," or the president of a union. His literary influence and reputation before the Cold War have yet to be fully assessed; especially neglected are transnational dimensions, as in the case of Gold's mentor relationship to Brazilian novelist Jorge Amado (1912–2001). Once he made the very human decision to invest his confidence in the Communist Party, he suffered many crises and episodes of frustration, but stood by his Party to the end; thus his career appropriately mirrored the decline of his Party's fortunes. To his credit, however, his life's literary activities as a whole bear out Joseph Freeman's later judgment that Gold was distinguished from many other writers on the Left because he "really cared about socialism more than he cared about his personal career."[127]

## CHAPTER 3

# The Great Promise

## Living in a "State of Emergency"

No matter how stirring the demand for simple, working-class literature of the kind promoted by Manuel Gomez, editor of *Poems for Workers* in 1926, or by Mike Gold in his "Change the World" columns in the 1930s, there was no proletarian purity in the actual yield of radical poets in the Great Depression and after. From the dawn of the 1930s, their poetry was a mélange, a bubbling cauldron, reverberating with sundry aspirations and levels of talent. Their verse, of course, percolated through the predilections and vantage points of disparate editors, who in turn were swayed by their interpretations of Communist policy as well as by their personal acquaintances with the poets and the customary kinds of mitigating contingencies besetting an editor regardless of political persuasion. As Stanley Burnshaw mused in 1961 about his cohort of *New Masses* editors in the mid-1930s: "To think that the Marxist critics were an undifferentiated right-thinking Left phalanx is to create a monster that simply did not exist. Not only were the wars within the compound frequent and fierce. Even more important: any number of these writers were troubled or torn, each for his own private reasons."[1]

Indeed, the Literary Left can only be fathomed as a social arena within which contests occurred among a diversity of qualifying factors. There were, naturally, the overarching constraints of the national economic situation that created a desperate insecurity about income for all but the elite. Then were felt the various pressures, real or imagined, placed by the dominant culture on writers to adhere to literary styles, themes, and even modes of acceptable personal behavior if they hoped to see publication of works and some degree of financial remuneration. (For example, in November 1939, Horace Gregory steered a young disciple toward publication of a review essay in the *American Scholar*, but alerted him to avoid any mention of Marx.)[2] Finally there were the idiosyncrasies of diverse personalities in respect to their talents, opportunities, animosities, rivalries, and networks of personal friendships.

One of the salient characteristics of these associations for Leftists was an intellectual or culture symbiosis that can be understood as an "elective affinity"; that is, a convergence of individuals of diverse origins – for example, of different genders, ethnicities, and class backgrounds – into a common configuration that became the pro-Communist sphere. Such significant federations occurred through self-selected commitments and reciprocal attractions. These led first to mutual world outlooks, under the tangible state of affairs of the Depression, centered on the vanguard role of the working class under Party and Soviet leadership. In due time the writers so galvanized came to common projects and organizational affiliations.[3] Moreover, the individual cultural products – poems, novels, plays, criticism – of such cultural workers with this shared world vision were potentially marked not only by Marxist themes (customarily the effort to decode commodity culture and dereify social phenomena), but also by common structural patterns. Ultimately, the overarching "force field" in which writers produced also embodied institutions founded and led by the Communist movement in ways that were sometimes paradoxical and discrepant.[4]

The politics of the movement expressed an indigenous revolutionary trend that freely subordinated its autonomy to the leadership of the Soviet Union. Yet the impact of the Soviet Union on cultural work in the United States, although vivid and multifarious, was far from all-encompassing. The pages of the *New Masses, Daily Worker, International Literature,* and other Communist Party organs reproduced articles by Soviet luminaries, very often commenting on U.S. writers and journals,[5] and published overwhelmingly laudatory reviews of Soviet literature, film, and art. Indeed, another *New Masses* editor, Joseph Freeman, heartily endorsed a remark by the literary radical Floyd Dell in a 1952 speech at the Newberry Library that "what happened to American literature was the Russian Revolution."[6] But that was not all that happened. Many cultural workers in the United States assuredly identified with Soviet revolutionary literary exemplars such as Maxim Gorky (1838–1936), but it is more likely that pre-Russian Revolution books by socialist writers such as Upton Sinclair (1878–1968) and Jack London (1876–1916) made a tangibly greater impress on their formative years.[7] For those less centrally involved in Party institutions, the Russian Revolution was a crucial achievement, but received more in idealized form – as a democratic upheaval compelled into a cruel contest for survival – than through a command of complex, and sometimes convoluted, cultural policies and models.

A more cautious generalization about the sweeping authority of the Soviet Union upon Left literati in the United States might be that the Soviet "experiment" as a whole represented a hope or promise that inspired a near-military ethos for the "committed" artist or intellectual in the era of the Depression and the rise of fascism. It was not so much that the assumption of art as a "weapon" – in the class struggle, or against fascism – distinguished the Communist cultural Left from non-Communist cultural workers. Walt Whitman was scarcely alone in declaring "literature as only a weapon, an instrument, in the service of something larger than itself."[8] Moreover, it would be arduous to name a single twentieth-century writer in the United States who did not have his or her own mix of implicit or explicit political concerns, including those who ostensibly held to an "apolitical" stance – the creation of an imaginary "world elsewhere" – as a means of coping with the social reality of the times.

The collective urgency, however, of the Communist cultural movement is more differentiating. The metaphor of class "warfare" is as much the source of the profuse crudities, superficialities, knee-jerk judgments, two-dimensional fictional characters, hastily selected and clichéd language, and the vulgarized use of Marxist categories that have troubled many readers and critics, as is the movement's political Stalinism. As Joseph Freeman recalled,

> There was a genuine faith in the Great Promise as represented by the Communist Party and Moscow; and there was a fear of fascism and war abroad and fear of reaction at home – and a determination to fight it. . . . We were men in war; we were soldiers in the "class war" of the socialist revolution . . . we hurled ourselves into life because life now meant the transformation of life into a higher, better, freer life – more just, more true, more beautiful – and for everybody, for the whole human race.[9]

In recent decades the conception of living "in a state of emergency" was popularized among Left intellectuals by the writing of Walter Benjamin, albeit without much heed to whatever potential ill-effects such an existence might have on artistic and intellectual production.[10] As Burnshaw's professor of English at Cornell, F. C. Prescott, counseled when his student gravitated toward Communism, "One doesn't play the violin when the house is on fire."[11]

An illustration of literary appraisal according to the Party's "state of emergency" mentality is the 1935 *New Masses* review of Party sympathizer Horace Gregory's work by Moshe Nadir (1885–1943), a Communist poet well known for his writing in Yiddish. Not only does Nadir take the standpoint of an alleged "proletarian reader" to expound that the content of Gregory's *Chorus for Survival* is really "the chorus for the survival of the unfittest emotions, cryptic soul searching – rather than the survival of those laboring masses fit to take hold of the world and thus create a new life." He also exhorts that

Gregory return to the John Reed Clubs (of which Gregory was a founder) to become reeducated in Marxism, and take up activity in the Communist movement, so that his poetry will "cry 'hold the fort' to those who fight underground in Hitler's Germany, in Schuschnigg's Austria, in Mussolini's Italy, in Leroux-Roble's Spain or in our own growing plague spots."[12]

Yet if Nadir's admonitions seem to dodge many of the pertinent aspects of the creative process, there were also positive aspects of such an urgency for Freeman's generation: the Communist literary movement's passion, internationalism, anti-elitism, and especially the encouragement of collaborative enterprises that gave rise to a community of cultural workers. The tenacity of that community is what kept the Left literary tradition alive through so many difficult decades. Nonetheless, the community was linked to a specific party, and the party became crucial to the durability of the main organs of collective expression of the community. What sort of creative interaction took place amidst the "state of emergency" mentality fostered by world events in a force field that included Communist Party–led institutions?[13]

While no cultural dictator of the Left in the United States emerged to issue marching orders to an army of "artists in uniform,"[14] there was among Leftists a greater willingness than is usually found among writers to engage in projects such as creating national organizations of writers (the Rebel Poets Society, John Reed Club, League of American Writers, Labor Poets of America, Contemporary Writers, the Committee for the Negro and the Arts, and the Harlem Writers Club) and supporting national publications. No activities of this sort remotely commensurate in size or cohesion – as well as in degree of sacrifice by writers of time, money, and personal risk – occurred among other literary circles such as the Southern Agrarians, New Critics, or the Beats.

It is conceivable that research in archives of the former Soviet Union may someday divulge that financial aid and/or practical political direction for some of these Left literary groups originated in the Soviet Union. On a national level, of course, these organizations were Communist led, and their foremost activists tended to follow the example of Moscow because they held that this was to the benefit of the advance of socialism.[15] But there is such copious corroboration of grassroots Left literary activity and support for at least the John Reed Club and League of American Writers that it seems unlikely that the domestic authenticity of this literary rebellion could be fundamentally compromised. The Cold War–era liberal American Committee for Cultural Freedom, in contrast, founded as a legal organization in 1951, had a membership (mostly paper) that numbered in the hundreds. But the organization's leaders junketed around the world, and it bankrolled its publications with massive subsidies from conservative foundations, with the funds in some cases originating with the Central Intelligence Agency.[16]

In the "hot-house" atmosphere of the Depression, individuals more seasoned in revolutionary activity, and especially those who appeared to have the trust of top Communist Party and international Communist bodies, were treated deferentially. Starting in the early 1930s, the determinations of various full-time Communist functionaries whose numbers increased dramatically, and the opinions they offered in book reviews and debates, came to carry increasing import. There is evidence that certain cultural statements were carefully reviewed by experienced Party intellectuals.[17] A writer who received pointed disapproval in the Party press, or whose works were rejected or ignored, might well feel as if he or she were being discarded or persecuted. Even non-Marxist poet Wallace Stevens (1879–1955) was adequately distressed by the comments on his poetry by *New Masses* critic Stanley Burnshaw to rejoin Burnshaw in verse.

Yet such rebukes, including those reviews that contained political polemics accusing writers of harboring anti-Marxist and reactionary tendencies, did not always have the status of being ex-communicatory.[18] Most literary reviews were by individuals of different temperaments, tastes, and agendas. Literary editors and the managing editors would read over reviews before publication, blue-penciling them for style, and at intervals offer opinions about the contents of the review. Likewise, the Communist Party leadership followed the contents of the *New Masses* and intervened at times, but the surviving papers and reminiscences of the most prolific reviewers and columnists – Granville Hicks, Joseph Freeman, Michael Gold, Stanley Burnshaw – offer no evidence of their literary judgments being suppressed or altered against their will in the 1930s.[19] These cultural helmsmen themselves, especially Mike Gold, were sporadically subject to blunt criticisms of their literary judgments in print.[20] Often there would be interchanges betwixt various writers, and understandably some readers might be dazzled by the Party status of one or another participant. Still, when they had a chance, authors who had been subjected to criticism in the *New Masses* magazine rudely retorted, without necessarily communicating a sense that the opinions to which they objected carried any more institutional weight beyond that of the critic who wrote the review.[21]

There was, of course, at least one notoriously negative side to Party publications: it was rare for any living writer known to be opposed to Party policy (especially its view that Stalin's leadership of the USSR was a force for democracy, peace, and progress) to receive approbatory mention, and often he or she would be liable to scurrilous personal attacks. There was also the proclivity for reviewers and editors closest to the Party apparatus to make judgments elevating short-term political expediency over larger, more complex questions. Statements published by Soviet writers' organizations, especially if they referred to the United States, might be invoked as authoritative guidelines and cited to promote or change some literary practice.[22]

Publications supported and/or led by the Party, such as the *New Masses* after its first few years, sporadically held meetings between its editors and members of the Communist Party's Political Bureau (a subgroup of the Party's Central Committee in charge of day-to-day affairs), and in times of transition or crisis the Political Bureau might assign a particularly trusted Communist to serve on the *New Masses* editorial board.[23] There were also several individuals dispatched by the Party to cultural work on a national level who became exceedingly influential in literary matters.

## "Waiting for Trachty"

The most commanding of those who furnished direction for the "cultural front" was Alexander Trachtenberg (1884-1966), popularly known as "Trachty."[24] He had no particular literary credentials but did have a extraordinary background that included participation in the events leading up to the 1905 revolution in Russia, for which he was imprisoned. After a year of military service in the Russo-Japanese War, he emigrated to the United States. Trachtenberg received a scholarship to Trinity College in Hartford and then a fellowship to Yale University to do graduate work in economics and labor, where he became busy in the Socialist Party. His dissertation at Yale, "The History of Legislation for the Protection of Coal Miners in Pennsylvania," was later published as a book. In 1915 he left Yale to become a teacher at the Socialist Party's Rand School of Social Science in New York. He energetically opposed World War I and became an ardent supporter of the February 1917 revolution in Russia, although he was hesitant at first to identify himself forthrightly with the Bolsheviks.[25]

By 1921 he had become an adherent of the Communist movement and in 1924, with his friend Abraham Heller, founded International Publishers, where he served as president from 1924 until 1962. In this capacity, combined with his personal links to officials in the Soviet government,[26] he became crucial in determining the contents of books and pamphlets issued by this highly professional Party-led operation, as well as in formulating policy for various Party-led cultural organizations, schools, and public events. By 1934, International Publishers had issued an imposing list of skillful translations of many classics by Marx and Engels, as well as works by Lenin and Stalin, and many books by U.S. radicals. That year a tenth-anniversary celebration was held at the New School for Social Research for Trachtenberg and the publishing house. The sponsors included B. W. Huebsch, vice-president of Viking Press; Bennett Cerf, president of Random House; Alfred Knopf, owner of Knopf Publishing Company; and W. W. Norton, owner of W. W. Norton and Sons; as well as leading book critics of the day such as John Chamberlain of the *New York Times* and Lewis Gannett of the *Herald Tribune*.

By the early 1930s, most matters connected with Communist Party cultural and publishing questions were Trachtenberg's bailiwick; the major exception was the *New Masses*, to which Party leader Earl Browder paid especial attention. There was one incident, however, when Trachtenberg was invited to a conference at the *New Masses* office at the time novelist Theodore Dreiser (1871–1945) came there to protest Mike Gold's attack on him for making anti-Semitic remarks in another publication. According to Joseph North, Trachtenberg convinced Dreiser that his anti-Semitism was faulty by showing Dreiser an article written by Lenin clarifying anti-Semitism as a legacy of Tsarism.[27]

Trachtenberg attended the fraction meetings of Party members active in the Party-led John Reed Clubs, and Party members who wanted to apprehend the Party leadership's views dealt with him directly. To the extent that Trachtenberg served as a sort of "godfather" to the clubs, he warrants credit for battling rather successfully with a difficult task. The New York John Reed chapter alone included 125 artists and another 125 writers, who were engaged in considerable internal feuding. The members' skills and degrees of reputation, and even their relationships to explicitly literary or artistic concerns, were at best uneven. In the regions outside the centers of New York City, Chicago, and Los Angeles, various chapters attracted more teachers, lawyers, dentists, and other professionals than practicing artists or writers. Many of the regional chapters published their own magazines, sometimes crude and other times professional. A national committee was based in New York City, but it did not have an adequate financial basis to function properly. Scores of future writers and artists of note got their start in the clubs. The John Reed Clubs, despite direction from the Communist Party, had some semblance of a separate revolutionary political organization but were lacking in stable and coherent leadership.[28]

In 1934, Trachtenberg gave a momentous speech urging the John Reed Clubs to dissolve and support the holding of an American Writers Congress, a move that was obviously the result of a high-level decision of the Party.[29] He soon afterward played a role in selecting the signers of the call to the congress, confining the names to trusted intellectuals. Next he directed the formation of the League of American Writers that was launched on the last day of the event, becoming the Party's adviser during the crucial time that it evolved from a revolutionary to a Popular Front organization. Officially Trachtenberg served on the league's Executive Committee for the first two years, until he was replaced by the up-and-coming Party cultural leader V. J. Jerome in 1937.

Trachtenberg was a short, swarthy, chubby man who stood a couple of inches over five feet, with a large head, jet-black eyes, and a great, stiff black mustache that he stroked thoughtfully. Mike Gold declared that his extraordinary energy and enthusiasm gave him "the zip of a child early on Christmas morning."[30] The Communist journalist and pulp writer Walter Snow (1905-1973) found him likable and "ebullient," with a sense of humor ("I'll only fight you politically" was one quip) and one who "always seemed ready to listen sympathetically."[31] Matthew Josephson recollected that Trachtenberg, "encircled by his apostles," had "the air of an anxious mother hen guiding her chicks around."[32]

Franklin Folsom, executive secretary of the League of American Writers, recalled Trachtenberg as being impressed with big names.[33] Walter Snow thought Trachtenberg was also impressed with large women, especially writer Meridel Le Sueur, who with her dark hair looked powerful and muscular. Then again, it might have been simply large people who impressed him, for Snow also believed that six-foot-tall Philip Rahv, with "his football lineman's build, his pose as a radical Don Juan . . . , and his passion for obscure pedantic words," exercised "a Svengali sway over little Trachtenberg," until Rahv came out for Trotsky.[34] *Daily Worker* journalist Sender Garlin recalled Trachtenberg's excitement when Party member Ruth McKenney's play *My Sister Eileen* (1941) became a big success; he rushed over to the *Daily Worker* crying, "She's getting more publicity than Marx and Engels got together!"[35]

Folsom reminisced that Trachtenberg would attend the Party's Book and Magazine fraction, acting as if he were everyone's father. He was prone to talk abstract theory, endlessly dispensing one cliché after another, but suddenly, after a half hour or so, would come up with a very sensible idea. *New Masses* editor Joseph Freeman conjectured that Trachtenberg had a superior regard for intellectuals if they were not members of the Party or if they were only fellow travelers. Trachtenberg also had "a dread of offending the leadership here and in Moscow." In the 1950s, Freeman described Trachtenberg as "by turns a cunning and a tough official representing the official Line in literature."[36] Another Party writer, A. B. Magil, came to see Trachtenberg as "an interesting character," but bureaucratic and with no feeling for literature, expressing "entirely utilitarian values in all literary activity."[37]

Nevertheless, as director of International Publishers, Trachtenberg discharged outstanding services to literature in the United States by publishing books on aspects of working-class life rarely portrayed in fiction, such as Myra Page's *Gathering Storm: A Story of the Black Belt* (1932), Mike Pell's *S.S. Utah* (1933), James Steele's (pseud. for Robert Cruden) *Conveyer* (1935), Ben Field's (pseud. for Moe Bragin) *The Cock's Funeral* (1937), Albert Maltz's *The Way Things Are and Other Stories* (1938), Richard Wright's *Bright and Morning Star* (1938), Meridel Le Sueur's *Salute to Spring* (1940), Beth McHenry and Frederick Meyers's *Home Is the Sailor* (1948), and Lars Lawrence's (pseud. for Philip Stevenson) *Old Father Antic* (1961). Translations of Soviet novels issued by International Publishers included Dmitri Furmanov's *Chapayev* (1934), Nicholay Ostrovsky's *The Making of a Hero* (1937), and Petr Pavlinko's *Red Planes Fly East* (1938). In the immediate postwar era, Trachtenberg oversaw publication of a poetry series, several books of Marxist literary and cultural criticism, and a surprising range of science, history, and adventure books for young readers.[38]

Since most of the magazines that sprang up in the Left cultural milieu in the 1930s were inaugurated by rank-and-file members, often with grievances about the limitations of the more established official publications, Trachtenberg intervened on several occasions to transmit the thinking of the Party leadership or to recommend "Party supervision," which usually came in the form of adjoining individuals whom he saw as more reliable to editorial boards.[39] Party activist Alan Calmer[40] believed that Trachtenberg had the sole power to determine whether the New York John Reed Club's *Partisan Review* would or would not become an organ of the League of American Writers, and that he also had the authority to assign Calmer to the publication's staff.[41] On the other hand, Walter Snow insisted that it was not Trachtenberg but Genevieve Taggard, a non-Party member but nonetheless a Party loyalist, who led the fight that prevailed in blocking the move in the governing body of the League to affiliate with *Partisan Review*.[42] Whether she did this independent of a consultation with Trachtenberg is not known.

Trachtenberg remained an untouchable, behind-the-scenes power during the 1940s and 1950s. His primary area of work was International Publishers, where his efforts won the esteem of establishment publishers, especially Alfred J. Knopf. He had also been a founder of the Communist-led Labor Research Association (LRA) in 1927, and he endured as an important LRA collaborator. He ran for public office on the Communist Party ticket on several occasions and was active in organizing Party schools, serving for some years as the treasurer of its Jefferson School in New York. In 1952 Trachtenberg was indicted under the Smith Act and suffered through a nine-month trial, after which he was sentenced to three years in prison. He had served only three months, however, when the principal witness against him confessed to perjury.[43] In 1956 he was retried, but the U.S. Court of Appeals in New York set aside his conviction upon appeal. In 1966, four years after retiring from International Publishers, Trachtenberg sustained a stroke at the age of eighty-two, dying three days later without regaining consciousness. He had no children and was survived only by his wife, Rosalind; arrangements were made to bury him near the Haymaket Martyrs Memorial in Waldheim Cemetery in Forest Park, Illinois, a suburb of Chicago.

## The Black Cultural Front

One component of the Communist-led cultural movement had a claim to semi-independence derived from political theory as well as practical exigency. The African American Communist tradition, pioneered by activists and intellectuals around the *Crusader* magazine and African Blood Brotherhood in the post–World War I years, came into its own during the crisis of the Depression through theoretical writing and activities that sought to reconcile the dynamic tension between nationality and class. On the one hand, Communist Party publications and tactics featured a political and cultural orientation rooted in the Black proletarian/peasant national experience of southern folk culture in the United States and the Black church; on the other, the Party promoted a semi-autonomous alliance with workers in the North and in the colonies of European nations (as well as radical workers in Europe), organized around the basis of a common class position. Pioneering Black Communist theorists such as Cyril Briggs advanced contentions as to the momentousness of the singular culture and psychology of African Americans, who for centuries had been the target of a racist onslaught by Europeans.[44]

As a consequence, Black artists drawn to Communism could affirm Black pride and, indeed, develop a semi-autonomous Black aesthetic based on a national culture, while concurrently interacting with a multiracial and international cultural and political movement. Such was the underpinning of the "elective affinity" bringing a range of cultural workers into a relationship with institutions and organizations initiated and led by Party figures such as Trachtenberg, and by African American leaders such as James Ford (1893–1957). Such an orientation placed Black pro-Communist cultural

workers center stage within the modern movement of cosmopolitan in-
telligentsia. That is, these "Afro-Marxists" viewed their particular identity
within an internationalist framework, linking their struggle for liberation
to the liberation of all humankind.[45]

Still, despite the dual components of the Party's perspective, the situation of African Americans facing hostility from whites as a group tended
to be overwhelming in comparison to the relatively few instances of genuine collaboration between Black and white workers. The former, racism
from whites, was a certain knowledge, confirmed by abundant evidence that
might be reworked into art; the latter, interracial unity on a class basis, was
more of a utopian hope, far more difficult to adumbrate with convincing,
well-rounded characters, symbols, and dramatizations. Such an imbalance
is evident in fiction and poetry. Yet in contrast to the imaginative writing
stands the legacy of cultural criticism produced by Afro-Marxists; this can
be found in the pages of *International Literature*, the *New Masses*, *Negro Quarterly*, and, in the post–World War II years, *Harlem Quarterly*, *Freedom*, *Masses &
Mainstream*, and *Freedomways*.[46] These journals, even when reviewing books
and plays, foreground in cultural terms the programmatic argument for the
synthesis of class and nationality.

The first Black writer of national reputation to become associated with
the Communist movement in the United States was the poet and novelist
Claude McKay (born Festus Claudius McKay, 1890–1948). McKay emerged
from a middle-class background in Jamaica, where he initiated a career as
a poet, alternating between conventional British forms and island dialect
verse. He published *Songs of Jamaica* and *Constab Ballads* (reflecting his brief
experience as a policeman) in 1912, before removing to the United States to
study agriculture at Tuskegee Institute and at Kansas State. Within two years
McKay moved to New York, where he held an assortment of working-class
jobs and was drawn to the Left.

In Harlem he associated with Black socialists such as Hubert Harrison,
Cyril Briggs and Richard B. Moore and held membership briefly in the
Industrial Workers of the World and later the revolutionary nationalist African Blood Brotherhood. He also developed personal friendships with Max
Eastman and his sister Crystal, who brought him wide recognition by publishing in the July 1919 *Liberator* his poem "If We Must Die," a militant response to the 1919 race riots. McKay then joined the editorial board of the
*Liberator* and collaborated regularly with the Communist Party throughout the 1920s, probably joining it for a brief time. His proud and indignant
sonnets of the early 1920s are a fundamental contribution to Black Marxist
culture.

McKay, who was bisexual and had a penchant for bohemian living, was committed to the Communist movement but equally devoted to vagabondage. During 1919 and the early 1920s he traveled around Europe and lived in England, where he wrote for *Workers' Dreadnought*, published by the English Socialist Sylvia Pankhurst, and issued a volume of poetry, *Spring in New Hampshire* (1920). Back in the United States, McKay became involved in personal and political quarrels with Mike Gold and Max Eastman about which kinds of poetry and articles were suitable for the *Liberator*. There was unease between McKay and the editorial group in general over the obligatory balance between articles focusing forthwith on race issues and those stressing class issues. A more destabilizing disharmony grew out of the temperamental disparity between the affectionate, patrician McKay, with his taste for sonnets, and the affectedly proletarian, tough-talking Gold, whom McKay considered "filthy" in his personal mien and who sought to publish poems of raw emotion. At one point, after hearing a story about Gold, an amateur boxer of some repute, swaggering in an aggressive manner into a gathering of pacifists, McKay insulted his manhood. The enraged Gold sought him out at an Italian restaurant, challenging McKay to box. Although the encounter ended with the two men laughing together over a bottle of dago red, McKay knew that their collaboration was over. When a vote of confidence was taken by the *Liberator*'s editorial board, Gold triumphed and McKay resigned.[47]

McKay then spent twelve years in Europe. He was present at the Third Congress of the Communist International in November 1922 and passed six months lecturing on art and politics throughout the Soviet Union. He wrote numerous essays for the Soviet press on Marxism and African Americans which appeared in a Russian collection, *Negroes in America*, published in 1923, the same year that his fourth poetry volume, *Harlem Shadows*, was published.[48] During his European residence, he wrote prose works celebrating working-class and vagabond life and values, including *Home to Harlem* (1928), *Banjo* (1929), *Gingertown* (1932), and *Banana Bottom* (1933).

By the time McKay resumed habitation in the United States in 1934, his radicalism had become markedly anti-Stalinist. He was also ill and broke. Yet, perhaps out of curiosity or to gather information, he joined the League of American Writers. In July 1937 he received an invitation to sit on the dais at the opening of its second American Writers' Congress, but he stood up and departed from the stage when hearing the remarks of Party general secretary Earl Browder.[49] That same year he issued his autobiography, *A Long Way from Home*, and he was criticized at length for his "disloyalty" by Alain Locke in the Black pro-Communist journal *New Challenge*.[50] Thereafter he appeared on several occasions in the socialist publication *New Leader*.

In 1940, however, he published *Harlem: Negro Metropolis*, which harshly attacked both the Communist Party and the socialists. Thereafter he became increasingly conservative, converting to Catholicism in 1944 and dying in Chicago in 1948. Although McKay did not play a personal role in nurturing the Black Literary Left, his literary and political trajectory anticipated aspects of the Black revolutionary Marxist tradition that cohered during the first part of the Depression; as McKay had done, Black writers personally and artistically blended literary trends from the Harlem Renaissance and the new proletarian literature orientation promoted by the Communist Party.

In some instances the fraternization of the two trends was cursory, resulting mainly in a few antiracist poems and some political endorsements. This seems to be the case with Countee Cullen (1903–1946), a leader of the Harlem Renaissance with degrees from New York University and Harvard. There are many uncertainties about Cullen's personal background, and his career was marked by a sensational scandal in 1928 when his highly publicized marriage to the daughter of W. E. B. Du Bois, perhaps the most elaborate social affair in Harlem up to 1928, collapsed immediately because of his homosexuality. A Left political orientation was first evidenced in 1932, when Cullen endorsed the Communist Party's presidential ticket, and in 1935 he was elected to the Executive Committee of the League of American Writers.

Cullen's principal literary influence, however, was prior to the Depression; it came in the latter days of the Harlem Renaissance when he published *Color* (1925), *Copper Sun* (1927), *The Ballad of the Brown Girl* (1927), and *The Black Christ* (1929). His preferred verse forms were sonnets, quatrains, and ballads in the English tradition. Thus there is little to connect him to the cultural work of the 1930s and 1940s Black Left other than occasionally through his sympathies, starting with his early expression of a passion about Africa.[51] In the 1930s Cullen taught French at Frederick Douglass Junior High School in New York, published a satirical novel, *One Way to Heaven* (1934), and a collection of poetry, *The Medea and Some Poems* (1935). Before his death in 1946 of uremic poisoning combined with high blood pressure, he published several books of children's verse and began to collaborate with Arna Bontemps on the musical *St. Louis Woman* (1946).

More pivotal for the advance of a Black cultural front was the work of two critics drawn very early to the John Reed Clubs, and who never publicly repudiated their pro-Communism; their writings were crucial in crafting the textual arguments supporting the Harlem Renaissance and proletarian synthesis. These were Eugene Gordon (1891–1974) and Eugene Clay Holmes (1905–1982), who used the Party name Eugene Clay. Although numerous other Black cultural figures drifted toward cultural institutions of the Party, these two intellectuals furnished a stability and continuity within the social arena that also expedited the melding of nationalist and class-based trends into a common tradition.

## African Americans and the John Reed Clubs

Gordon was born in Oveida, Georgia, graduated from Howard University, and became a second lieutenant in the U.S. Army during World War I.[52] In the 1920s he became a feature editor for the *Boston Post* and in 1928 edited a literary publication called *The Saturday Evening Quill* that was sponsored by the Saturday Evening Quill Club of Boston. As an aspiring novelist and painter, he identified with the Harlem Renaissance. Next, at the outset of the 1930s Gordon professed that he was a Communist and was eminently visible in the Party's literary affairs. His transformation was denounced by the ex-radical Black journalist George Schuyler.[53] In 1933, Gordon wrote a short story about a Black Communist organizer in Georgia, "Agenda," that was a prototype for the early fiction that would soon make Richard Wright famous; it won honorable mention in a fiction award from *Opportunity*.[54] In the April 1934 issue of *International Literature* he published a substantial autobiographical essay, "Southern Boyhood Nightmares." The following passage augurs many of the same themes that Wright would later popularize in his treatment of African American psychology in the chapter "Fear" in his novel *Native Son* and in the early sections of his autobiographical *Black Boy*:

> My whole boyhood in the South was darkened by a lowly lying cloud of subconscious fear that at times burst through to open terror. . . . It was . . . an accumulation of ideas suggested by countless agencies – my mother, my teachers, the pastor of our church, the children with whom I played in the gutters of New Orleans, the very atmosphere I breathed, my whole environment – the white man was my natural and eternal enemy, regardless of the guises he might assume or the methods of approach he might take.[55]

Gordon started out principally as a literary critic in John Reed Club publications, the *New Masses*, the *Daily Worker*, and *International Literature*. He co-authored a Party pamphlet, *The Position of Negro Women*, in 1935. He also addressed the First Congress of the League of American Writers, and served a brief time on the editorial board of the *New Masses* in the mid-1930s, after which he traveled to the Soviet Union and wrote for the *Moscow Daily News*. In the 1940s he kept on writing for the *Daily Worker*, often on Black cultural matters, and for a while he assisted on its staff. Married to a Euro-American woman, and with a son, he contributed to the *National Guardian* during the Cold War and then drifted into obscurity.

Holmes was born in Paterson, New Jersey, and received a B.A. from New York University in 1932, where his cardinal preoccupation as a student was literary criticism. His first published article, "Jean Toomer: Apostle of Beauty," appeared in *Opportunity* in 1932.[56] He began teaching at Howard University as an instructor in 1932, partly intrigued by the outlook of the chair of the philosophy department at that time, Alain Locke, who was also concerned with Black cultural criticism. Although Holmes was initially captivated by pragmatism and John Dewey's instrumentalism, at Howard he encountered a core group of Black Marxists in the Division of Social Science, including William Alphaeus Hunton, Doxey Wilkerson, Abram Harris, and Ralph Bunche. Within a short time Holmes was won over to dialectical materialism and would become a virtuoso in teaching it to other Communists in the Washington, D.C., area.

A close relationship was cemented between Holmes and Locke because Holmes was a popular teacher, while Locke was not, and Holmes helped sustain the credibility of the department. Moreover, Holmes was willing to cover for Locke when Locke departed on long weekend trips. Holmes was also a facile writer who would help Locke in completing manuscripts. After a few years of teaching in the precarious situation of an instructor, Holmes wrote to the Communist critic Granville Hicks in 1935 that there was a good chance of his being retained at Howard if he could find funds to pursue graduate study. Although Holmes was now a Communist Party member, he felt that his membership must be kept secret from the Howard University administration; even Locke, who suspected where Holmes's sympathies lay, did not yet know about his Party membership. Furthermore, the Washington, D.C., Party leadership had a high regard for Holmes's work in building a chapter of the National Student Union and a faculty union at Howard, as well as for drawing Black faculty closer to the Party.[57] Holmes subsequently earned an M.A. in philosophy from Columbia University in 1936, and a Ph.D. in philosophy from Columbia in 1942, during which time "his philosophical outlook was forged in the context of the struggle between dialectical materialism and pragmatism."[58] In 1939 he married Margaret Cardozo.

Holmes was an assistant professor at Howard from 1937 to 1946, an associate professor from 1946 to 1961, and a full professor from 1961 until he left the university in 1970. In 1952 he succeeded Locke, who died two years later, as chair of the Philosophy Department, which he held till his retirement. Holmes's Marxist critique of pragmatism is articulated in his doctoral dissertation, *Social Philosophy and the Social Mind: A Study of the Genetic Methods of J. M. Baldwin, G. H. Mead and J. E. Boodin* (1942). There Holmes argues that Darwinism and pragmatism have become wedded as a social philosophy under the banner of science, thus offering a philosophical apology for bourgeois democracy. Another book-length project, "The Life and Times of Alain Locke," was never finished.

Holmes retained his militant commitment to the Black liberation movement long after the 1930s. During the Cold War, when grants for social science research were denied to Howard University faculty, and governmental committees charged that Howard was under Communist influence, he helped organize a conference on "Academic Freedom in the United States" in 1953. In 1958 he arranged for W. E. B. Du Bois to deliver a lecture against U.S. Cold War policy. Du Bois also condemned the execution of Julius and Ethel Rosenberg. Many of Holmes's writings after the death of Alain Locke were devoted to explaining Locke's life and work. In addition to submitting essays to the *Journal of Philosophy, Philosophy and Phenomenological Research,* and *American Journal of Physics,* he was a contributor to the *New Masses* and a sponsor of the Communist-initiated academic journal *Science and Society.* Simultaneously he expounded on the philosophy of science, especially by applying higher mathematics and physics to the study of space and time.[59] In the 1960s Holmes persevered in applying a dialectical materialist analysis to the Black experience in articles he wrote for *Freedomways* about the lives and works of Locke, Du Bois, and Langston Hughes.[60] He died of cancer in Washington, D.C., at age seventy-five.

The John Reed Clubs, to which Gordon and Clay belonged, placed a distinct weight on leading Black writers to the revolutionary movement. The May-June 1934 JRC *Bulletin* carried an article called "Negro Intellectuals and the John Reed Clubs," in which the national office of the John Reed Clubs reprinted excerpts of interviews it had conducted with Black John Reed Club members. Gordon, who was a member of the organization's National Executive Board, observed that the small number of Blacks recruited to the John Reed Club in Boston was due to the "petty-bourgeois national-mindedness" of Black intellectuals from more privileged economic backgrounds, causing them to want to preserve their parasitic relation to the Black poor.

Langston Hughes, in a friendly contribution, implored that the same methods practiced in approaching other writers should be used to come closer to Black authors:

If the JRCs in the larger centers would send speakers and contact the Negro literary clubs and student groups, we might be able to catch the coming artistic generation while they are still on the wing. A lecturer going forth and pointing out to them the part which artists and writers have played in the liberation of the working class in Russia, and the part which they can play here, might do something toward winning the younger Negroes to our side.

Holmes, at the time a member of the Philadelphia John Reed Club, suggested that the writers' group of the clubs had long ago explored this question and drawn certain inferences. In contrast to Hughes, who thought that Black journalists might be approached, Holmes considered most Black newspapermen and pulp fiction writers to be "hopeless":

> Where the wedge should begin ... is with advanced university students. . . . Then . . . all those younger artists and writers, who have been declassed, who do not know what it is about, politically and socially. . . .
>
> Further, every effort should be made ... to stage more and more lectures on Negro art, literature, etc., so as to penetrate the bourgeois intellectual Negro audience. These lectures should be competently given and from a Marxist-Leninist point of view. Notices of these lectures should always be sent to the Negro press.

In inspecting the present situation, the *Bulletin* editors noted that their superior accomplishments so far had been in St. Louis, where "a score of Negro artists from the Urban League joined the JRC," and in Cleveland, where "the Club has attracted a number of Negro intellectuals." In contrast, the New York Club had no active Black members among the club's writers' group.[61]

There were, nonetheless, little-known African American contributors of poetry to publications such as the *Harlem Liberator*, the organ of the Communist-led League of Struggle for Negro Rights,[62] which also printed poetry and fiction by Don West, essays praising the USSR by Langston Hughes, announcements for the Marxist-Modernist "Vanguard" salon (hosted by sculptress Augusta Savage) and regular coverage of film and theater events. There were likewise Black journalists who were very close to the Party, such as Loren Miller of the *California Eagle*.[63] Moreover, other African American members of the Party, such as the attorney William Patterson, occasionally wrote on cultural matters.[64]

The pro-Communist Left, however, received its biggest boost when, toward the end of the 1920s, sympathy for the Communist Party was indicated by Langston Hughes (1902–1967), a leading Black poet, playwright, novelist, translator, and autobiographer. Hughes was born in Missouri but raised in divers places in the Midwest. He was exposed to radical ideas through his grandmother's devotion to the memory of her first husband, a follower of John Brown who was killed at Harper's Ferry, and by Jewish high school students in Cleveland at the time of World War I. Hughes began to publish poetry even prior to entering Columbia University. He soon dropped out to travel in Africa and Europe. Although Hughes was well versed in the work of Claude McKay as well as the earlier African American writer Paul Laurence Dunbar (1872–1906), the writings of Walt Whitman and Carl Sandburg encouraged him toward verse forms that were more modern yet also non-elitist. His first two published collections, *The Weary Blues* (1926) and *Fine Clothes to the Jew* (1927), were conspicuous for fusing jazz and blues with scenes from Black working-class life.

During the interval that he wrote his first, semi-autobiographical novel, *Not without Laughter* (1930), Hughes had the sustenance of an affluent but conservative patron. When that relationship disintegrated in the early Depression, he voyaged to the Soviet Union, then lived in Carmel, California, where he completed his collection of short stories, *The Ways of White Folks* (1934). Hughes's short fiction in this volume and several others is marked by an easy-going style of simulated simplicity that is often whimsical and controlled, yet forceful. There is an ample sweep of locations around the United States and abroad, and Hughes progresses facilely among an invigorating compass of forms that engage stream-of-consciousness, an omniscient narrator, monologues, and letters. The revolutionary goal is rarely proclaimed in his fiction, unlike in his poems, although an occasional tale, such as "Little Old Spy" (1934), renders his sympathies explicit.[65] Customarily, divers aspects of racial justice are investigated through narratives on the ground of the personal, entailing interracial love, the life of the Black artist, and the misapprehensions of Black life and culture by whites.

In the mid-1930s Hughes finished a number of plays, including *Mulatto* (1935), *Little Ham* (1936), *Emperor of Haiti* (1936), and *Don't You Want to Be Free?* (1938). In 1940 Hughes issued the first volume of his autobiography, *The Big Sea*, which would be concluded in 1956 with *I Wonder as I Wander*. *Shakespeare in Harlem* (1942) and *Jim Crow's Last Stand* (1943) promulgated his dual loyalties to the blues and to the antiracist struggle during the World War II years. In the meantime, his column in the Black newspaper the *Chicago Defender*, featuring the folk hero Jesse B. Semple, called "Simple," won a major audience. Hughes originally designed the character Simple to promote a Left-wing view of why the antifascist war must be supported despite the existence of domestic racism, but Simple acquired a vitality of his own which resulted in the publication of five volumes of Hughes's collected columns as well as his musical *Simply Heaven* (1957). Two postwar volumes of his poetry, *Fields of Wonder* (1947) and *One-Way Ticket* (1949), drew little notice, but *Montage of a Dream Deferred* (1951) embodied new moods and cultural themes in Black urban life. More plays, children's books, histories and biographies treating African-American topics, and anthologies, came forth before Hughes's last two poetry collections, *Ask Your Mama* (1962) and *The Panther and the Lash* (1967).

From the advent of the Depression Hughes collaborated closely with the Communist Party, a partnership that was sustained more erratically in the 1940s.⁶⁶ He joined the John Reed Clubs, published frequently in the *New Masses*, issued columns and a pamphlet praising the Soviet Union's treatment of its darker-skinned nationalities, wrote a poem to honor the 1934 convention of the Communist Party, and was elected president of the Communist-led League of Struggle for Negro Rights. His new agenda of producing "rhymed poems dramatizing current racial interests in simple, understandable verse, pleasing to the ear, and suitable for reading aloud, or for recitation in schools, churches, lodges, etc.," was fully in harmony with even the most extravagant wing of the proletarian literary movement.⁶⁷ Hughes also served as a correspondent during the Spanish Civil War, and his 1938 collection of poems, *A New Song*, was published by the Communist-led International Workers Order (IWO), originally created to provide insurance policies and other benefits for workers. The booklet featured an introduction by Mike Gold, who unhesitatingly declared "the best Negro literature" to be a folk literature, "close to the joys and sorrows of the people." Gold designates Hughes's current verse as the product of a two-stage evolution, moving from nationalist expression (as the articulation of the "hopes, the dreams, and the awakening of the Negro People") to a deeper stage of "a voice crying for justice for all humanity." In effect, the poems were an eloquent testimony to an Afro-Marxist cosmopolitanism. Moreover, by issuing 10,000 copies of the first edition, the IWO also resolved the enigma of locating an audience for writers "snubbed" by the upper classes, thus contributing "mightily to the rise of that democratic culture of which Walt Whitman prayed and dreamed."⁶⁸

The collection began with Hughes's keen, double-voiced "Let America Be America Again." Hughes first presents the words of a naive idealist calling for a restoration of the older America of pioneers seeking freedom; then a second speaker (in parentheses) mumbles that "America never was America to me," and progresses to controvert further myths about the recent loss of "opportunity" and "equality." As this oppositional speaking voice appropriates the standpoint not just of African Americans but of poor whites, Native Americans, immigrants, the young, and, finally, "the people," it seizes complete control of the poem while clamoring that "we must take back our land again." In his closing stanza Hughes enunciates a nearly immaculate declaration of a transformative praxis rooted in the recoupment of a revolutionary and messianic romanticism:

> Out of the rack and ruin of our gangster death,
> The rape and rot of graft, and stealth, and lies,
> We, the people, must redeem
> The land, the mines, the plants, the rivers,
> The mountains and the endless plain –
> All, all the stretch of these great green states –
> And make America again![69]

Thus Hughes premises his scrutiny of national mythology on the bedrock of a people's struggle to make a detour to the future through the past.[70]

Although Hughes was less visible in Party affairs during and after World War II, he supported the Progressive Party presidential campaign of Henry Wallace in 1948, condemned the prosecution of Communist leaders under the Smith Act in 1949, and retained his admiration of the Soviet Union. According to Black former Communist Party member Lloyd Brown, Hughes began to use the telephone instead of personal visits as his primary means of keeping in touch with the Party because he felt obligated to look out for himself; throughout the 1950s and early 1960s, Hughes was especially solicitous of Brown's opinion as to how he should approach controversies with other Black writers, such as James Baldwin.[71] Following receipt of a subpoena to appear before the House Committee on Un-American Activities (HUAC) in 1953, Hughes worked out a settlement in which he resolved to publicly praise HUAC so long as he was not compelled to name names.[72]

The Communist Party did not attack Hughes during this period, although W. E. B. Du Bois wrote that Hughes was "beneath contempt" for omitting Paul Robeson from his 1955 juvenile book, *Famous Negro Music Makers,* and Hughes's former literary agent was not assuaged when Hughes mailed him a copy of the testimony marked "No names mentioned."[73] Some Communist Party members were told that Hughes was placed in a compromised situation due to his homosexuality, threatened with public scandal if he didn't make a deal.[74] After Joseph McCarthy died, the Party literary journal contacted Hughes for a contribution of poetry, but Hughes replied that he had no poems on hand.[75] Nevertheless, the Party continued to feature Hughes's earlier work in its publications.

Somewhat under Hughes's influence, Richard Wright (1908–60) began his literary career as a poet in Communist and John Reed Club publications in the early 1930s.[76] He was born in Natchez, Mississippi, the grandson of slaves, and was raised by his mother, a country schoolteacher, and other relatives. In 1927 he moved to Chicago, where he held various jobs. While working in the post office he met Communists and future members of the John Reed Club, such as Abe Aaron (who published fiction as "Tom Butler"), as early as 1930.[77] Soon after becoming busy in the club, he also joined the Communist Party at some point during 1932 or 1933. He was quickly established as a revolutionary poet, but by the mid-1930s, when he joined the Federal Writers Project, he had begun to write fiction, earning Hughes's nickname of "The Negro Gorky." His Black proletarian novel about postal workers, *Lawd Today*, was not published until 1962, but his first collection of four stories was issued in 1938 as *Uncle Tom's Children*, whose theme as well as title recall Mike Gold's preceding essay in *Negro*, "A Word as to Uncle Tom."[78] A fifth story was issued as a Communist Party pamphlet in 1939, *Bright and Morning Star*, and was annexed to the second edition along with "The Ethics of Living Jim Crow," formerly appearing in the WPA book *American Stuff* (1938).

Following discord with local Black Communists during which he was charged with Trotskyism, Wright departed Chicago for New York in 1937, where he anticipated embarking on a more auspicious literary career. At that point there was some vacillation about his future in the Communist Party due to his negative experiences in Chicago, and he engaged in a friendly correspondence with pro-Trotskyist James T. Farrell (1904–1979).[79] However, once in New York, Wright reconciled with the Party and rose to become director of the *Daily Worker* Harlem Bureau. After a brief marriage to a Jewish Communist dancer, he wedded a Jewish New York Party organizer and became a national Party speaker in defense of the Hitler-Stalin Pact. While presenting his views as a spokesman for African American opposition about U.S. intervention, Wright did not fail to advance the Black-Jewish unity that was one of the Communist Left's primary accomplishments: "Who can deny that the Anglo-American hatred of the Negroes is of the same breed of hate which the Nazis mete out to Jews in Germany?"[80]

The unfriendly reaction of a number of Black Party activists to Wright's portrayal of Bigger Thomas in his 1940 *Native Son*, of which he had heard oral reports, disaffected him, even though the novel was lionized by the leading critics in Party literary organs and received the personal endorsement of Earl Browder.[81] Mike Gold declared *Native Son* the equal of *The Grapes of Wrath* as one of the two major novels of the 1930s.[82] *New Masses* writer Samuel Sillen became a particular Wright enthusiast, also commending the 1941 theater version of *Native Son* in the strongest conceivable terms, and declaring Wright's *Twelve Million Black Voices*, a historical narrative published that same year, a "magnificent literary and pictorial study."[83] In letters to Wright, Sillen astutely noted that a penchant of Left criticism was to be too concerned with the potential reaction of "other people" to *Native Son*, rather than honestly discussing one's own reactions.[84] He also accentuated that the *New Masses* was utterly behind the novel, welcoming the debate and the issues it raised, and that William Z. Foster and other Party leaders "downtown" exemplified "a powerful current of opinion . . . in favor of the book."[85]

In the meantime, Wright applied himself to an unfinished novel about women in the United States, for which he enlisted Ralph Ellison as his research assistant. He also wrestled with the technical problem of creating fiction with a range of believable characters beyond the protagonist.[86] Together the two men developed an intellectual rapport, based partly on the younger writer's adulation of Wright's fiction, but also on their conjoint devotion to studying Marx, Hegel, the classics of Western literature, as well as the psychology and folklife of African Americans. When Black poet Melvin Tolson (1898–1966) wrote to Wright from Texas that "the best laboratory of the Marxist is the race problem," he could hardly have found a more amenable audience.[87]

By 1942, however, after the Soviet Union was hammered by the Nazis and the Communist Party was no longer opposed to the war, Wright resolved that the Party had accommodated far too much to its Western allies. He was especially incensed by the Party's toning down of the battle against racism in the United States and temporarily dropping its opposition to the segregated armed forces. Consequently he began to withdraw from any association with the Party until 1944, when he held a public press conference in his publisher's office to announce his resignation. At the same time he published in the *Atlantic Monthly* a compelling but inexact version of his experiences in the Communist Party that had been excised from his 1945 autobiography *Black Boy*.[88] Among other inaccuracies, Wright depicts himself as leaving the Party at the time of the Moscow Trials, about seven years before his actual departure. In the *Daily Worker*, Black Party leader James Ford asserted with incredulity that "It seems strange that Wright in his *Atlantic Monthly* articles did not mention his experiences in New York where he was honored and respected by the Communist Party and he himself seemed proud of the Communist Party's appreciation of him."[89] Notwithstanding, year by year his antagonism toward the Party grew more resolute until he postulated that "the concepts that lay at the bottom of my work now are in direct opposition to those espoused by the Communists."[90]

With his wife and older daughter, Wright moved to Paris in 1947, where he became the dominant member of a circle of Left-wing African American expatriates. He also secured friendly relations with Existentialist radicals such as Jean-Paul Sartre and Simone de Beauvoir and traveled to Africa, Indonesia, and Spain, each of which became topics of his nonfiction books. Wright continued to publish forceful novels with strong psychosexual and antiracist themes, especially *The Outsider* (1953) and *The Long Dream* (1958). *Savage Holiday* (1958), whose characters are all white, was designed to be released under a pseudonym, but Wright's publisher reneged on the agreement for fear of losing sales. Wright remained committed to the need for a revolution against capitalism and colonialism, but he was subjected to pressure by the French government as well as by the FBI and the Central Intelligence Agency.[91] The stress took a toll on his personal life as well as his literary career, and he died in 1960 under somewhat mysterious circumstances at the age of fifty-two.[92]

Wright's evolution contrasted dramatically with that of a fellow African American pro-Communist, playwright, Theodore Ward (1902–1983). An autodidact from Louisiana, the eighth of eleven children, Ward left home at thirteen when his mother died.[93] After roaming around the United States in the 1920s, he started taking poetry classes at the extension division of the University of Utah, and in 1931 was awarded a Zona Gale Scholarship in Creative Writing that brought him to the University of Wisconsin for several years where he gained some experiences in radio. Arriving in Chicago in 1935, he was quickly drawn to the Left and became a founder of the Chicago South Side Writers Group, sometimes referred to as the Chicago Negro Writers Group, as well as the local chapter of the League of American Writers. By this time Ward had turned his efforts to playwriting, and completed a radical drama in 1937 called "Sick and Tiahd." In 1938, his most influential play, *Big White Fog*, a critique of the procapitalist Marcus Garvey and a defense of Communism, opened in Chicago with the endorsement of Federal Theater Project director Hallie Flanagan. In 1940 it was performed at the Lincoln Theater in Manhattan. Ward moved to New York City as well, establishing the Negro Playwrights Company with other Black radicals such as Langston Hughes, Paul Robeson, Richard Wright, Alain Locke, Owen Dodson, and Theodore Browne (1911–1979). The company, however, was not financially viable, and Ward fruitlessly sought support from the Writers' War Board for a play about Frederick Douglass to be performed for Black troops. In the ensuing period he shined shoes and worked in a war plant while writing a play about longshore workers, *Deliver the Goods* (1942).

Subsequent to receiving an award from the Theatre Guild, Ward wrote *Our Lan'* (1941), pertaining to the dispossession of freed slaves of their land in the post–Civil War era. Two productions, including one on Broadway, were engineered in 1947. That year Ward also wrote an unproduced drama about Black and white workers who contract silicosis, entitled "Shout Hallelujah!" With a Guggenheim fellowship for 1948, Ward began research for a major play based on the life of John Brown. A rudimentary version was acted in a converted garage on the Lower East Side, but he was never able to refine it into a successful version.

When his friend Wright acquitted himself of the Party during World War II, Ward was disgusted at what he regarded as a betrayal, reaffirming his own pro-Communist convictions by becoming a stalwart supporter of Party literature projects throughout the Cold War era. Although he denied holding actual membership, he had access to Party meetings and leaders, and was perceived as the equivalent of a member by Ralph Ellison and others. By 1964, however, when he returned to Chicago, such associations had atrophied, albeit he remained independently militant. In 1967, he established the South Side Center for the Performing Arts. Although the production of two new plays, "Candle in the Wind" and "Whole Hog or Nothing," failed to materialize, he revived *Our Lan'*, which played for nearly a year in one of Chicago's poorest communities, and then he toured the South in the late 1970s under the sponsorship of the Free Southern Theater.

The poet Robert Hayden (1913–1981), a member of the Communist-led John Reed Club of Detroit and later a historian and researcher for the Federal Writers Project, was popularly known as the "People's Poet" of Detroit.[94] Hayden was raised by a foster family in a depressed section of Detroit known as "Paradise Alley." He read voraciously as a teenager. He first associated with Communists during his theater activities, and was acknowledged as the contact person who could recruit Black actors and actresses for productions of pro-Communist plays. One of these was the Detroit production of Paul Peters's *Stevedore* in 1936, in which Hayden himself acted.[95] That same year he performed in Langston Hughes's *Drums of Haiti*, and met Hughes in person; Hayden handed over to Hughes an unpublished batch of his poems for an evaluation. Working in both the Detroit chapter of the John Reed Club and the Left-wing New Theater Union, Hayden was respected as a reliable Left-winger; although his bisexuality was known to some of his Communist associates, it was simply accepted. In 1936, Hayden, who had been attending Detroit City College (which later became known as Wayne State University), joined the Federal Writers Project to research Black history and folk culture. The following year, his folk drama about Harriet Tubman, *Go Down Moses*, was performed by the Paul Robeson Players at the Second Baptist Church in Detroit, under Hayden's direction. In 1940, he published a volume of revolutionary poems, *Heart-Shape in the Dust*, which was praised in the *New Masses* in an unsigned review for its "affirmative" character but reproved for its insufficient use of folk culture and "over-conventional use of diction and rhythm."[96] The publisher of the poetry volume was Louis Martin, Left-wing editor of the *Michigan Chronicle*, and the African American Communist Party member and United Auto Workers activist Christopher Alston raised the funds from fellow WPA workers. That same year Hayden married and soon enrolled at the University of Michigan, where he studied under W. H. Auden. Receiving an M.A. in 1942, Hayden taught at Fisk University from 1946 to 1969, then returned to the University of Michigan.

During World War II Hayden underwent a religious conversion to the Baha'i faith, and later dismissed his former writing. In the 1960s he objected to critics who discussed his early poems as meaningful to his career, and he refused to allow their republication, with the one exemption of a Broadside Press edition of his work "Gabriel," about the slave rebel Gabriel Prosser.[97] He relaunched his career as a poet during the Cold War with *The Lion and the Archer* (1948) and *Figure of Time* (1955), followed by *A Ballad of Remembrance* (1962), *Selected Poems* (1966), *Words in the Mourning Time* (1970), *Night-Blooming Cereus* (1972), *Angle of Ascent* (1975), *American Journal* (1978), and *Collected Poems* (1985). These collections combined unique meditations on Black history and culture with poems on metaphysical and aesthetic themes. Hayden's writing honored the Black oral tradition and seemed to motivate political views that were in accord with the new Black Left of the 1960s, but he antagonized members of the younger generation by refusing to call himself a Black Poet or support the notion of Black Art.

## Gender and Party Commitment

The Communist movement of mid-century prioritized class and race, and the Afro-Marxist cosmopolitanism of the Black writers and intellectuals drawn to the movement began to acquire recognition from the outset. In contrast, it has only been since the 1960s that four pro-Communist women novelists have accrued a substantial audience due to their perceived vocalization of protofeminist concerns—Tess Slesinger (1905-1945), Josephine Herbst (1992-1969), Meridel Le Sueur (1900-1996), and Tillie Olsen (b. 1913). Yet even the work of these most "advanced" writers embodies qualifying factors connected with the historical moment of the mid-twentieth-century Left. One is not faced with a categorical "Communist Women's Literary Tradition" but more customarily with constructions of female subjectivity by circumscribed women in particularized situations, perhaps disclosing an elective affinity for a relatively shared ideological world outlook. This state of affairs is equally applicable to Great Depression-era novels by Fielding Burke (pseud. for Olive Tilford Dargan, 1869-1968), Grace Lumpkin (1892-1980), Ruth McKenney (1911-1972), Myra Page (1897-1993), Agnes Smedley (1892-1950), Leane Zugsmith (1903-1969), Mary Heaton Vorse (1897-

1966), and many others.[98] What might be resolved is that this collection of writing is peerless in that it treats female sexuality, desire, and consciousness in the context of class and the exploitation of labor, often accompanied by insights into racial oppression. Moreover, the social actuality and arising panorama of the environment are premised on a roughly estimated assumption about the path to major change. In sum, this is gender-conscious writing but literature that does not necessarily privilege the creation of a unique female voice, especially in terms of textual play.

The fragmented consciousness evidenced in Olsen's *Yonnondio* (written in the 1930s but published as a novel in 1974), for example, certainly yokes the novel to modernist and postmodernist language experiments that contemporary French feminist theorists valorize as crucial to liberation from phallocentric master narratives. Yet this trait is largely the outgrowth of the unfinished character of the text; if the circumstances of her life as a working-class woman had not interfered with Olsen's completion of the novel in the mid-1930s, it might well have cohered in a unified narrative with the female protagonist fulfilling herself through more conventional masculinist political activities. Herbst's accomplishment in the Texler Trilogy (*Pity Is Not Enough* [1933], *The Executioner Waits* [1934], *Rope of Gold* [1939]) is most compellingly defended as the achievement of a woman who strove, albeit with the deficiency of an unsystematic comprehension of the intersections of many-sided oppressions, to synthesize her gender consciousness with her discernment of racism and class exploitation.[99] Tess Slesinger's *The Unpossessed* (1934), while praiseworthy for its luminous presentation of the view that "the personal is political," is troubled by a central ambiguity; conceivably, Slesinger consciously attributes essentialist features to men (logic) and women (emotion), or at least treats maleness and femaleness as equally destructive to psychological health.[100]

The ambivalences of this literary trend can be observed in the literary persona that has become the site for the most contested interpretations, retrospectively inscribed, of the relation of female Marxist cultural workers to the organized Left during the mid-twentieth century; this persona was produced by the writing of Meridel Le Sueur, who died in November 1996 with a copy of Walt Whitman's writings at her bedside. The Communist Party's *People's Weekly World* published an obituary noting that Le Sueur remained a Party member to the end, testimony to an unbroken allegiance of more than seven decades. The avowal was based on a February 1995 interview where, in reply to "the question," the bed-ridden Le Sueur quipped: "Prone, but still in!"[101] In contrast, the *New York Times* obituary for Le Sueur made no mention of her having any Communist or Marxist inclinations, describing her as one "who reported on the plight of the poor during the Depression and celebrated the free spirits of early Americans in her fiction for children."[102] The *Nation* mentioned Le Sueur only as having a negative relationship with the Communist Party, based on the dubious allegation that the Party tried to "censor her output" because of "her writings about women and children and the close inspection of their lives." The *Nation* journalist acknowledged that Le Sueur was hounded by the FBI and blacklisted, especially during the McCarthy era; but that this was not due to her Party membership – rather, it was "because of her radical connections with the Industrial Workers of the World, the Populists and Farmers Alliance."[103] The bulk of appreciations of Le Sueur that followed her death consisted of memoirs by other aspiring writers who were individually touched by her unflagging devotion to the working class, her continuing literary vitality, and her personal accessibility.[104] Such a combination of presentism and political amnesia at the time of her death has worked to memorialize a hodgepodge of Le Sueurs, each with little connection to the others.

Nonetheless, Le Sueur's career is commanding testimony to the particularities involved in the interrelationship of profeminist consciousness, cultural production, and the constraints as well as freedoms provided by Party commitment and ideology expressed through the institutions of the mid-twentieth-century cultural Left. Le Sueur began her life as a writer in the mid-1920s as a radical bohemian with deep roots in the Midwest, although she had already traveled to both coasts. Just after World War I, she studied at the American Academy of Dramatic Art and acted on the New York stage, rooming with the anarchist Emma Goldman in a commune. From 1922 to 1928, she unsuccessfully pursued a career in film (as an extra and stunt woman for *Perils of Pauline* and other movies), stage acting, and on radio (as the voice of Betty Crocker). She joined the Communist Party in 1924 or 1925 (no documentation exists, and her responses to interviewers varied), and in 1926 she married a labor organizer named Harry Rice. Under the influence of two midwestern fiction writers, Zona Gale (1874-1938) and Margery Latimer (1899-1932), and with the aid of Latimer, Le Sueur launched her literary career by publishing an allegorical story, "Persephone," in the May 1927 issue of the *Dial*.[105] That same year, while in jail for participating in a demonstration protesting the execution of the anarchists Sacco and Vanzetti, she decided to have a child. She soon moved to Minneapolis, where two daughters, Rachel and Deborah, were born in 1928 and 1930. More of her stories appeared in *American Mercury, Pagany, Scribner's, Fantasy, The Magazine, Windsor Quarterly,* and similar magazines.

Her early work seems most firmly influenced by D. H. Lawrence with its emphasis on male "rational" and female "emotional" natures, alongside a view of heterosexual intercourse as a transformative experience for the female through the agency of a virile male.[106] Le Sueur came from a Left-wing family. Her parents taught at the People's College in Fort Scott, Kansas, and they acquainted their daughter with a panoply of diverse rebels including Eugene Debs, John Reed, Helen Keller, Theodore Dreiser, Carl Sandburg, and Margaret Sanger. This heterogeneous radical background molded her consciousness in the 1920s, although she also often referred back to troubling memories of her grandmother's fanatical convictions against sex and alcohol.

Prior to the Depression, Le Sueur's contributions to the Communist movement were mainly through articles published in the *Daily Worker* and the *New Masses*. In the early 1930s she reaffirmed her commitment to the Communist Party more resolutely. In her noted essay, "I Was Marching," published in the 18 September 1934 issue of the *New Masses*, she chose to describe her conversion to Communism as if it were recent and that of a middle-class intellectual resolving her isolation through active support of the Minneapolis Teamster Strikes.[107] A year later, in "The Fetish of Being Outside," also published in the *New Masses*, she trounced the politically wavering poet Horace Gregory in the same publication for suggesting that, although he had been pro-Communist since the 1920s, he did not feel that Communist Party membership would advance his art.[108] Her statement is often noted for its emphasis on the Communist Party's providing a "communal sensibility" as an alternative to decadent, bourgeois individualism; this ambience was due more to the Party's organic roots in the working-class struggle than to any specific ideological positions it held.[109]

By the mid-1930s, Le Sueur was making a distinct contribution to Marxist cultural theory as a passionate advocate of midwestern literary realism. Her speech to the 1935 American Writers Congress—she was the only woman to make a major presentation—argues that revolutionary regionalism is an authentic people's culture. She characterizes the Middle West as the target of intense "laissez faire colonization," yet also possessing a regional culture unburdened by an "old tradition" that obscures and muffles the organic connection between the "communal artist" and the new rising class of workers.[110] In 1940, the Party's International Publishers produced *Salute to Spring*, a collection of Le Sueur's short fiction and reportage.

Le Sueur persevered in writing with modest attainment during the 1940s; her regional history *North Star Country* was published in 1945. During the peak of the Cold War, however, she justifiably assumed the mantle of a blacklisted cultural martyr, harassed by the FBI and betrayed by her comrades.

She was tight-lipped about her personal life, but apparently suffered a difficult relationship with the Minneapolis painter Robert Brown. For years she held menial jobs, raising her two daughters virtually on her own. During this nadir of her national reputation, her work appeared mainly in the pages of the Party's redoubtable magazine *Masses & Mainstream*. However, the Blue Heron Press, established by the Marxist historical novelist Howard Fast after he was released from prison only to find himself blacklisted, published her book about her parents, *The Crusaders* (1955). She also instigated a new phase in her career by writing half a dozen volumes of children's literature, most of which are still in print.[111]

Le Sueur's literary career was revitalized as a result of the radicalization of the 1960s. Small press editions of her stories and poems began to appear, including *Corn Village* (1970) and *Rites of Ancient Ripening* (1975). Then, through the extraordinary efforts of the independent West End Press, whose editor was friendly to the Communist cultural movement, *The Girl*, a curious novel of the 1930s, was assembled from various of Le Sueur's manuscripts and published in 1978. Employing the forms, themes, and techniques of popular crime stories to advocate proletarian feminist solidarity, *The Girl* became one of the most recurrently discussed texts of radical women's literature in the next decade and went through several editions. During the same period, the West End Press published *Harvest* (1977), *Song for My Time* (1977), and *Women on the Breadlines* (1977). After the Feminist Press published her *Ripening* (1982), which was ubiquitously reviewed, Le Sueur was hailed as an icon of feminism, celebrated for her devotion to working-class women and her ardent feelings for nature and Native American culture. For many veterans of the 1960s, Le Sueur's career was living proof that a modern Left-wing women's culture had existed much earlier and in more intricate ways than had been formerly acknowledged.

The specificity of Le Sueur's legacy is given its most detailed treatment in an essay on the impact of the Communist Party and gender written by Linda Ray Pratt, "Woman Writer in the CP: The Case of Meridel Le Sueur."[112] Pratt illustrates that these two facets informing Le Sueur's creative output are joined in more exact ways than generalizations about the oppositions of gender and class (or sometimes gender and Party) have allowed. Pratt's thesis is that "CP involvement may have been a crucial support to Le Sueur's survival as a woman writer even as it has had a dampening influence on her lyrical portrayals of women."[113] She commences her case by observing that, although contemporary feminists and others repeatedly point to Le Sueur's brief association with people like Emma Goldman, her more formative political influences were Communists including William Z. Foster,

Robert Minor, and Clarence Hathaway. Le Sueur also served at times in Communist Party leadership capacities; for example, as an alternate member of the National Executive Committee of the Communist Political Association (the organization launched when the Party temporarily dissolved during World War II) and as chair of the Minnesota-Dakotas District of the Communist Party.

Pratt then addresses Le Sueur's oft-quoted recollection that some Party members criticized her work for being too lyrical. Here Pratt provides documentation that Le Sueur herself esteemed that particular criticism and thought it justified. Although Pratt prefers her more lyrical texts, Le Sueur in her last decades repudiated her early use of "beautiful language" and the "mysticism and vagueness" which she felt obscured her writing as late as 1939.[114] Moreover, Pratt observes that claims about Le Sueur's "feminism" need to be tempered by a recognition that her anti-male literary portraits were always of non-Party members; when Party males appear in her work, they "help female characters recognize their true identity as members of the communal group."[115] Such a literary strategy enabled a reconciliation, on a broad plane, of her feminist outlook with her Communist views, although it dodges a more exacting analysis. In sum, Pratt believes that the influence of the Communist Party encouraged Le Sueur's non-lyrical and, for Pratt, stylistically weakest writing. Yet she concludes that it was also the Communist Party that fostered the most prophetic and enduring feature of Le Sueur's artistic achievement, her sense of women's collective power, and her vision of solidarity among women, which Le Sueur derived from the Communists' view of solidarity among workers.

Pratt's treatment of Le Sueur offers a refreshing respite from propensities to uncritically venerate Communist women cultural workers' resistance to patriarchy, or to focus solely on the more retrograde masculinist features of the Communist cultural movement. For evidence of the latter, one has only to thumb through the pages of the *New Masses* to see that one of the most frequent motifs for ridiculing fascists, racists, labor fakers, bosses, liberals who were opposed to Party policy, and Trotskyists is to feminize them — especially by dressing them in women's clothing, often in poses suggesting a female sexuality rendered grotesque by obesity and residual male features (mustaches, five o'clock shadows, hairy legs).[116]

In addition to using feminine features to ridicule conservatives and political rivals on the Left, some Left-wing literary polemics associate feminine qualities with the middle or upper classes, or else with effete intellectuals frequently depicted as not being "man enough" for class combat. This meshes with the trend in Left-wing literary criticism that portrayed "bad writing" as having feminine features – lacking punch, robustness, and machine-like precision.[117] The tradition of identifying revolutionary efficacy with male political potency is clearly evident in a poem by H. H. Lewis, "The Man from Moscow" (1932), in which all political rivals are sexual failures compared to the Bolshevik:

> The Knight of Labor was a nervous kid and passed off
>     before coming into his own.
> The Anarchist never did learn how.
> The Wobbly was game, he plunged in for direct action
>     but soon petered out and went haywire.
> The A.F. of L.-ite has been *fixed* so that he cannot
>     create abomination against respectability.
> The Proletarian,[118] strumming the Marxian uke and croon-
>     ing one manifesto after another, gets no further.
> And the queer Socialist, – tsk, tsk, shame forbid![119]

Lewis was an eccentric voice, known for excessive effusions in which satirical and earnest beliefs were hard to disentangle. Yet his verse resonates with the broader sensibility of the Left-wing edifice of revolutionary proletarian identity, one that often counterposed a masculine image of class war to a feminized middle-class culture. In yet another suggestive variant, Mike Gold theorized his class and ethnic identity in terms of gender: "Working class America is my father, working class Jewry is my mother."[120]

Much Communist literature, by men as well as women, however, did stray from the dominant construction of gender ideology that featured a male obligation to "protect" women. More often, poetry by Leftist women depicted instances of females affirming their revolutionary credentials by attempting to "act like a man." This effort is apparent even in a report on a public meeting that appeared in the Boston John Reed Club journal written by Rivka Ganz (dates unknown). Ganz offered the following description of the Young Communist League Organizer Sylvia Shreves: "There is something shy about her soft, fluffy hair, but her slim body thrusts itself bold and strong, forward to right and left, emphasizing every one of her short forceful phrases. She wears a worker's white shirt, sleeves rolled to the elbow."[121] In this illustration, the proletarian prototype retains male features to which a Communist woman might conform. The results were somewhat different in more sustained efforts of pro-Communist women novelists to actively structure the meaning of sexual difference in capitalist society. In writings of Olsen, Herbst, Slesinger, and others, the female characters that are depicted may start out by trying to assume masculine roles – as rebels, organizers, professional writers, sexually autonomous beings – but their full-blown portraitures often defy and profoundly transgress the gender categories previously constructed through the prevailing literary tradition.

Much of the scholarship of the last decades leans toward the interpretation that the Communist movement empowered women by imparting confidence and offering forums for expression, while at the same time it constricted women in ways that reflected the gender hierarchy of the dominant culture. To be sure, Left women writers did not exist in a vacuum as mere creatures of the Communist movement; like other writers they were formed by the events of the time, ranging from the personal matrix of their home and families to the national and international events that escalated to a high pitch of horror in the 1930s and 1940s. But the Communist cultural movement did provide an institutional framework with some precision. The Soviet Union was upheld as a model, and the Communist Party projected itself as the vanguard of the American working class. This meant that a woman's individualism was always qualified by certain loyalties to a political organization, social class, and even a foreign utopia, that were instrumental steps to self-liberation through group emancipation. One obvious manifestation of this Soviet dependency that fettered the expression of feminism was a growing parallel emphasis on the traditional family in the United States as the political orientation of the Soviet Union evolved toward a similar emphasis during the Popular Front.[122]

Still, one cannot look to a single determinant to explicate the creative efforts of the women writers, or African Americans, who comported themselves within the force field of the principal cultural institutions spawned by the Left in mid-century. Within this field, the *New Masses* was supreme. Yet this oft-cited but little understood publication was riven by multifarious pressures. On the one hand, there was a sweep of male personalities, each with irregular talents and disparate literary tastes. Then, pressing upon this hardworking and often shifting circle of editors was the increasing drive of the Communist movement for homogeneity and loyalty to an egregiously idealized Soviet leadership. The outcome was a magazine of many faces as it negotiated the traumas and blows of national economic collapse and the belligerency of international fascism.

## CHAPTER 4

# The New Masses and the Social Muse

## "Bloody Anarchists"

When the New Masses was founded in 1926, there was virtually no Trachten-
berg-type "Party supervision" – and scarcely any curiosity exhibited – by the
national or international Communist leadership. This loose state of affairs
persisted through the first years of the Depression when Walt Carmon (1894–
1968) moved to New York City from Chicago. In Chicago, Carmon had once
worked for the Labor Defender (the publication of the Party-led International
Labor Defense) and also assisted as circulation manager of the Daily Worker.
In New York, he served as managing editor of the New Masses from 1929 to
1932.[1] By the time he arrived, the $27,000 originally donated by the radical
Garland Fund to launch the publication had been depleted, and Carmon
was frantic to locate new funding sources. Within a short time he devised
a program of fund-raising masquerade balls during the fall and spring at
Webster Hall in Manhattan.

Carmon was a Party member but didn't pay dues or attend Party meetings; his wife Rose recalled that he was a disciplined Communist only when
it served his purposes. Carmon saw the New Masses as a literary-art magazine with a Left slant rather than as a political organ. In his view, politics
was the province of the Daily Worker, which was why staff salaries there were
far more regular than at the New Masses, where contributors received no
payments and staff members were lucky if they got $5 a week. Carmon was
an anomalous Communist literary functionary for New York City; he was
not Jewish (although he loved Yiddish expressions), nor even an Easterner.
Midwestern novelist Jack Conroy and other writers from outside New York
felt particularly comfortable in dealing with him.[2] Moreover, Carmon was
priceless in directing non–New York writers toward publishers potentially
interested in their work.

The free-wheeling atmosphere of the New Masses office was reflected, per-
haps in extravagant fashion, in the recollections of the radical poet Norman
MacLeod (1906–1985), who worked with Carmon and became his friend.[3]
MacLeod's father was an alcoholic businessman from Scotland who met and

married MacLeod's mother in Utah, then divorced her and disappeared. His mother took graduate studies in London and taught at universities in Montana, Iowa, and southern California, finally becoming head of the speech department of Mount Holyoke College in the 1930s. MacLeod attended high school in Montana and Iowa but was disoriented and unhappy due to the uprootedness of his youth, the ups and downs of his family's financial situation, and unpleasant memories of both his father and his mother's second husband. He held a number of jobs and hoboed extensively before attending the University of Iowa for three years and finishing at the University of New Mexico, where he received a B.A. in 1930. His interests included literature and anthropology, and he pursued graduate work at other schools for several more years on and off during the Depression. MacLeod episodically edited poetry magazines and held teaching jobs, but drinking and marital problems pursued him like furies to the end of his life.

MacLeod started writing poetry at the age of thirteen, and his work appeared in the 1920s in several little magazines, including *Jackass* and *Troubador*; later on he personally edited certain others, such as *Morada* and *Front*.[4] His first two books of poetry, *Horizons of Death* (1934) and *Thanksgiving before November* (1936), are noteworthy for their blend of imagism and regionalism. He subsequently wrote a novel about the Federal Writers' Project, *You Get What You Ask For* (1939), and a semi-autobiographical work covering the years 1917–20, *The Bitter Roots* (1941). MacLeod envisioned himself as a revolutionary after 1928, and in January 1931 joined the staff of the *New Masses* on which he served for eight months, solely editing the March 1931 issue that featured Whittaker Chambers's widely discussed story, "You Can Make Out Their Voices."[5] In late 1931 MacLeod was in southern California, where he briefly held membership in the Party and helped to set up the Hollywood chapter of the John Reed Club. After that he sojourned in Europe, the Soviet Union, and sundry parts of the United States. Although he was distressed by the Moscow Trials, he was determined to keep antifascist work his top priority; this enabled him to uphold the stance of an independent Communist until the 1939 Hitler-Stalin Pact.

MacLeod's recollection of the semi-bohemian ambience of the *New Masses* in the early 1930s suggests one of the reasons why Carmon's managing editorship came under fire. He recalled that Carmon kept a drawer full of poems and selected ones for publication based on the number of lines he had available.[6] This drawer was adjacent to another one that housed the scented love letters that poured in for Mike Gold. Gold only came to the office at odd intervals, but he did appear shortly after the novelist Charles Yale Harrison (1898-1954), a pro-Communist writer who authored the successful *Generals*

*Die in Bed* (1930), had fallen into disfavor for alleged Trotskyist sympathies. Gold noticed a copy of Harrison's novel on the desk, took one look at the inscription ("For MG, Yours for the Revolution, Charley"), grunted, and tossed it out the office window.[7]

MacLeod later insisted that "I knew Mike and Wally were members of the CP-USA, but while I was on the *New Masses* nobody ever suggested that I join the Party and I didn't." He recalled three decades after his disaffection from the Party that he "never saw any indication that [Wally] was not his own man, no evidence that he was controlled and dictated to by the CP-USA."[8] MacLeod claimed as well that the formation of the John Reed Clubs was not initiated by the Party leadership; it had been organized after Carmon kicked a bunch of young writers out of the *New Masses* office. They had been hanging around too much, and to get them out of his hair he told them to "go out and form a club."[9] Rose Carmon confirmed the story and recalled that Carmon added, "I've even got a name for you – call it the John Reed Club."[10]

The advent of the John Reed Clubs, nonetheless, created a new complication, because among the hundreds of young radicals drawn to it were many Young Turks with ultrarevolutionary opinions. This was especially conspicuous among members of the New York Club, the most consequential one, who soon began aiming their fire at the older generation, pontificating their super-Left, sectarian views. The young members held that the *New Masses*, even while under the Carmon regime, was too immersed in a project of courting well-known, middle-class writers. From their perspective as outsiders to the literary establishment, even Mike Gold, the major proponent of "proletarian literature" in the United States, was objectionable. They griped that he was not very engaged with the John Reed Clubs and rarely came to a meeting. They thought that he was a prima donna, mainly preoccupied with Mike Gold, and more engrossed in winning big-name writers to Communism than in developing unknown revolutionary writers. Not only did they declare Gold an undisciplined Communist; they also concluded that his writing was ideologically weak. *Jews without Money* was knocked as petit-bourgeois, not proletarian, literature, and they reasoned that at times Gold seemed to be writing from the standpoint of the lumpen proletariat.[11]

Only a year after the clubs were formed, a capital donnybrook erupted when the Soviet-led International Union of Revolutionary Writers announced a meeting to be held in Kharkov in 1930. Gold received a personal invitation to attend and arranged for his friends, the novelists Josephine Herbst and John Herrmann, to receive payment for all their expenses so that they could accompany him as observers. The John Reed Clubs did not receive an invitation until later, as if it were an afterthought, and New York members were outraged at the favoritist way that Gold acquired accreditation for Herbst and Herrmann, since the two were at that point supposed to be merely fellow travelers. The previous antagonism the John Reed Club members felt toward Gold was thus exacerbated.

The Party's point man in the clubs, Alexander Trachtenberg, agreed that the John Reed Clubs should be represented at such a momentous conference. When the clubs decided to send Harry Alan Potamkin (1900-1933) and William Gropper (1897-1977), neither of whom were then Party members, the Party fraction voted to add A. B. Magil to the delegation. The clubs were agreeable to this, and all three traveled together on a ship.[12] As it turned out, Gold adhered to the literary views closest to those promoted by the conference. Like Gold, the International Union of Revolutionary Writers saw its project as winning established writers to a proletarian Communist perspective, not driving away middle-class writers and replacing them with self-proclaimed proletarian writers. In his "Notes from Kharkov" published in the *New Masses*, Gold stressed that the endeavor to activate the writing of proletarians was in no way to be counterpoised to the effort "to enlist all friendly intellectuals into the ranks of the revolution."[13]

Further evidence of the erratic nature of the Party's influence on the early *New Masses* is revealed in a letter from Carmon to Walter Snow, reacting to Snow's political dissatisfactions with a *New Masses* review:

> You are absolutely correct. . . . I didn't read the book of course. The review arrived before I had seen it. It was a mistake. . . . and I can assure you that it is not going to happen again. That we have not been slaughtered by the movement for doing it is simply due to the fact that as yet the Party has not yet created the means by which such a necessary check up is made of its publications. So bloody anarchists like ourselves get away with murder.[14]

Consequently, in the first years of the Depression, Carmon's free-wheeling, pragmatic managing of the *New Masses*, and Trachtenberg's mechanical, politically motivated approach to decisions on cultural matters, represented both the past and the future of the Communist literary institutions that were pledged to realize "the Great Promise." The Trachtenberg approach would grow steadfastly more commanding, at least until the political crisis brought on by the Khrushchev revelations in 1956, when for several years afterward there was a rethinking and something closer to an actual laissez-faire policy predominated. Between the contrary approaches of Carmon and Trachtenberg, however, the mediating process was complex and uneven. An investigation of the interplay among *New Masses* editorial board members—all of whom were pro-Communist, but who often dissented on how to run the magazine – permits some appreciation of the complicated elements that must be factored into any appreciation of the resulting public record.

In 1961 Stanley Burnshaw went to extraordinary lengths in a *Sewanee Review* essay to provide the historical context in which he had produced his 1935 *New Masses* commentary about Wallace Stevens, called "Turmoil in the Middle-Ground."[15] The review had elicited Stevens's famous and much discussed "Mr. Burnshaw and the Statue," which later became Part II of Stevens's "Owl's Clover," reckoned by some critics to be his finest long poem. Yet Burnshaw noted in a letter to the editor of *Sewanee Review* that in twenty-five years not a single scholar of Wallace Stevens, or of poetry for that matter, had ever contacted him to request information about the episode, even though Burnshaw had become a highly visible poet, novelist, critic, and publisher after the 1940s.[16] Interpretations of Burnshaw's original argument, necessary to judge Stevens's perception of it, were in Burnshaw's estimation deduced from the general premises about Left criticism that emerged in later decades. Even though the participants in the affair were living, the famous exchange was not recreated and reconstituted in the terms appropriate to the writers in their own time. To clarify for the contemporary reader his aims and goals in the review, Burnshaw felt it indispensable to discuss his personal definition of Communism in the 1930s and thereafter, and the specific features of his divided state of mind as a poet and activist. He also provided six paragraph-long glosses on matters of terminology and tone, to allow the reader in the 1960s "to interpret the originating circumstances from within its period context."[17]

Burnshaw's point was that one cannot decipher the critical writings that appeared in the *New Masses* externally, from outside the elements at work in the system of relationships that produced the writings. At various times, the elements that inspired the Communist cultural movement included general policy turns emanating from Moscow; personal frictions among sensitive, egocentric, and ambitious editors; conflicts and resentments between editors closer to or further from the Party's Political Bureau; and resentment between those who saw themselves as self-sacrificing and highly disciplined, and others they perceived as self-indulgent and bohemian. Sixty years later one can have little hope of recreating that fractious system of relationships with any completeness or guarantee of utter accuracy; but a look inside the editorial process, using memoirs, correspondence, and interviews as well as published material, may at least detach one from "the absurdity of the unhistorical view" about which Burnshaw was so aggrieved.[18]

## Becoming a Weekly

In the 1950s, former *New Masses* editor Joseph Freeman asked former Communist Party chairman Earl Browder if he could put his finger on the date when pressure from the Party leadership and Moscow began to circumscribe Communist literary policy more directly. Browder "thought a moment and said, 'After the assassination of Kirov,'" which had occurred in 1934.[19] At first Freeman agreed with Browder, but later he found a 1931 memo documenting a major controversy between the *New Masses* and the John Reed Club of New York City. The strife, however, was not about the Party's top-down control of the *New Masses*, but, rather, pertained to a state of affairs in which a group of Party members and their close allies in the club were endeavoring to secure their own hold on the publication. Still, the discord precipitated an intervention by the Party leadership, and Freeman saw this as a forerunner of later developments.

Conflicts at the *New Masses*, and interventions in the affairs of the magazine by the Party's Political Bureau, seem to have eventuated about every two years after 1931, although one could retrospectively also include the predicament of the magazine in 1928, occasioned by an increasing irregularity of production and an impending financial collapse that Walt Carmon was asked to stem. Each emergency was linked to earlier ones, and usually several factors joined to create each new upset. The key dates of disruptive controversies prior to the McCarthy era are 1931–32, 1934, 1936, 1938, 1939–40, 1945–46, and 1948. Through an investigation of the sequence of conflicts involving the *New Masses* during the 1930s and early 1940s from the point of view of members of the editorial staff, one may gain insight into the practical constraints of publishing a magazine that mediated between a Party organically linked to a Soviet-led global Communist movement, and an indigenous cultural rebellion that spawned its own personalities and concerns.

The first issue of the *New Masses* appeared in May 1926. Until September of 1933 it was published as a monthly. The issue of 2 January 1934 marked its debut as a weekly. Early sales figures are not accessible, but the magazine's circulation enlarged from 6,000 as a monthly in late 1933 to 25,000 during its second year as a weekly in January 1935; at that juncture it was outselling the *New Republic* and had newsstand sales greater than both the *New Republic* and the *Nation* combined.[20] It endured as a news and cultural weekly until March 1948, when it merged with the Communist Party's literary publication *Mainstream* to reappear as *Masses & Mainstream* under the editorship of Samuel Sillen and Milton Howard.[21]

In the late 1920s and early 1930s, the *New Masses* did not really have an authoritative editor. While Mike Gold's name was recorded in this capacity for several years, he was under siege by his critics in the John Reed Clubs and appeared at the editorial offices with less frequency after the 1920s. An editorial board did exist which appointed whoever was at hand and had time to work in the office to carry out editorial tasks in consultation with the board. The appointment of Whittaker Chambers in an editorial capacity in 1932, which has drawn attention due to his eventual role as a Soviet spy, was no doubt a more purposeful assignment but was still largely based on an assessment that Chambers had some open time as well as editorial ability. If Chambers chose to act like a "commissar" in trying to enforce a more orthodox, less literary, and more political orientation for the *New Masses*, this was due as much to Chambers's temperament as Walt Carmon's "anarchist" reign reflected his more haphazard predisposition.[22]

At the time of the 1931–32 conflict with John Reed Club members, Joseph Freeman believed that Joseph Pass (1893–1978), whom he saw as an ambitious but frustrated writer, wanted to replace Gold as editor of the *New Masses* and that illustrator William Gropper wanted to supplant artist Hugo Gellert (1892–1985).[23] He also believed that Joseph North (born Joseph Soifer, 1904–1976, a foremost Communist journalist and editor, and brother of composer Alex North), who would supersede Joseph Freeman as *New Masses* editor in the late 1930s, was pulling the strings.[24] While the backers of the attempted coup were all members of the Party, or were at least pro-Party, the Party leadership, represented by Trachtenberg, had more confidence in Gold and Gellert. The result was a compromise establishing a "Relations Committee" after the fall 1931 blowout, which expanded the editorial board to include one representative each of the dissident writers and artists and held out the possibility that, in the future, the magazine might become the organ of the John Reed Clubs.[25]

Such was the state of the conflict between members of the John Reed Clubs and the *New Masses* at the time when Joseph Freeman returned from California in late 1931. Party leaders Earl Browder, Clarence Hathaway, and Alexander Trachtenberg then asked him to join the magazine's editorial board. Assessing the situation, Freeman prepared a written report to the editorial board and the Party's Political Bureau, urging a total reorganization of the publication and its staff, in order to "make it a magazine which a trained mind would listen to with respect and intellectual profit."[26]

According to Freeman's notes from the time, he was convinced that under Carmon the *New Masses* "was rotten with the worst characteristics of dilettantism. It tried to be 'light,' 'humorous' – succeeded in being infantile and dull. While *New Republic, Nation,* etc., *Modern Quarterly* were publishing serious articles pretending to be Marxian, the *New Masses* insisted on running 'proletarian' but really bohemian stuff (lousy, crappy, were 'Marxian' terms)."[27] Freeman's harsh assessment, although it had some basis, was characteristic of his critique of the *New Masses* at every point when he had not been one of the leading editors. Throughout the 1930s he considered himself superior to his peer group (that is, those of his colleagues who were younger or less important than Trachtenberg, Jerome, or Browder); he saw himself as the most qualified to give the magazine direction and frequently insisted that most of its problems stemmed from a failure to heed his guidance.

No action was taken on his proposal, and the two-pronged crisis continued over the next year. Several new organizations, separate from the *New Masses,* emerged to meet the needs of Left-leaning professionals and writers; in particular, the League of Professionals for Foster and Ford, comprised of intellectuals supporting the Communist Party 1932 presidential campaign, and Pen and Hammer, an organization of Marxist academics that had its own publication.[28] Meanwhile, the internal situation in the John Reed Club worsened. Thus a second conference between the Political Bureau and *New Masses* editors was held on 4 November 1932.

This conference set the stage for the removal of Carmon as de facto editor. His official departure in the early spring of 1932 was recalled by his widow as the result of a Party decision, although it was not due to any political disagreements. The Party leadership thought that Carmon "shouldn't be editing the *New Masses* because he didn't have a big enough name." There were also myriad complaints about the quality of his editing from a professional point of view, and Carmon, whose personal life was additionally complicated by an affair with the magazine's business manager, Frances Strauss, was close to a breakdown when he took a vacation in Florida in the winter of 1932. Mike Gold apparently opposed the decision to replace Carmon but lacked the will to fight it.[29]

The situation had still not reached the point where the Party leadership placed a markedly high priority on directing the *New Masses* editorial policy. The most professional journalist who joined the *New Masses* editorial board, serving from 1934 to 1938, and making possible its transformation into a weekly, was not a political appointee who enjoyed the designated trust of the Political Bureau. Herman Michelson was asked to join the board because he had a long history of working on newspapers, including the *Socialist Call,* the *New York World,* and the *Herald Tribune.* His skill was not in writing, of which he did little, but in his ability to focus on editing the work of others.

Michelson was considered loyal to the Party, and he was the husband of a well-to-do Party stalwart, Clarina Michelson, but he was not regarded by the Party's Political Bureau as politically shrewd.[30]

Joseph Freeman, who joined the board before Michelson, following the 1931 crisis, was also more respected for his professional skills than political leadership. His background in journalism included working in Europe in 1920 for the *Chicago Tribune* and *New York Daily News,* serving as associate editor of the *Liberator* during 1922–23, and handling the cables, mailers, analyses, and feature articles for TASS, the Soviet news agency in the United States, on and off from 1925 to 1931. Freeman had spent 1927 in the Soviet Union, where he sometimes worked as a translator for the Comintern. For a period in 1929 he was in Mexico as the TASS correspondent. Just before his assignment to the *New Masses* editorial board, he had briefly worked on a script in Hollywood. Freeman knew French, German, Spanish, and Russian and had published *Dollar Diplomacy: A Study of American Foreign Affairs* (1925), co-authored with radical economist Scott Nearing, and *Voices of October: Art and Literature in Soviet Russia* (1930). His book *The Soviet Worker: An Account of the Economic, Social and Cultural Status of Labor in the USSR* would appear in 1932.[31]

After 1932, the various appointments and assigned responsibilities were made with greater attention paid to an individual's personal and political reliability. The Party's leaders desired not so much individuals who would submit every word they wrote or every decision they made for inspection; to the contrary, they sought editors who could be trusted to make appropriate decisions on their own. For example, when the magazine became a weekly in 1934, Joseph North, who increasingly had the faith of the Party leadership, was assigned to the board. Stanley Burnshaw, who served on the *New Masses* editorial board from 1934 to 1936, thought of North, whom he respected for his knowledge of poetry and his piano playing, as "the political watchdog." But Burnshaw, who refused to join the Party, and who believed that he held heterodox views on both Communism and literature, always felt that he had North's full confidence.

In 1967, fifteen years after his total disillusionment with the Soviet Union and the Communist movement, Burnshaw recalled in a letter to New Left Marxist critic Lee Baxandall:

> I was never bothered by so-called political pressure when I wrote for the *New Masses:* none that I can recall, and I have a good memory. Nor do I recall any inward pressures which my political self might have made me feel. I was about as free an agent in the *New Masses* as I have ever been. I said what I believed and that was that, and I can't recall anything of mine having been corrected or revised or otherwise altered to suit *anyone else.*[32]

*The* New Masses

While it is always perilous to propose a "representative" figure, Burnshaw's history in relation to the Communist-led cultural movement is particularly instructive because he never held Party membership, clandestine or otherwise. Yet Burnshaw was unequivocally part of the institutionalized leadership of a "movement" bound together by a common worldview cohering around a set of propositions that were the equivalent of a Communist outlook. To regard Burnshaw, and thousands like him, as not "Communist" because of their failure to pay fifty cent dues, is to miss apprehending the rudimentary glue of this remarkable movement. The bond can be fathomed less fittingly as top-down Party discipline than as elective affinity stemming from common longings, dreads, and experiences. Moreover, Burnshaw's poetry, during and after his Communist period, resonates with the utopian urge emblematic of the revolutionary romantic inheritance that branded the early 1930s origins of the Left tradition.

## Portrait of a *New Masses* Literary Editor

Burnshaw was the son of Jewish immigrants from Russia who came to the United States in the late nineteenth century; he would picture their escape from Czarist oppression in his novel *The Refusers* (1981) and in his poetry published in *Caged in an Animal's Mind* (1963).[33] His father, who had earned a Ph.D. in philology at Columbia University, inaugurated his career as a teacher of Greek and Latin. His father's dream, however, was to administer a home for Jewish orphans with a year-round curriculum combining academic and manual labor intended to produce a contemporary "Renaissance Man." The elder Burnshaw launched his experimental school in New York City, then relocated to the rural setting of Pleasantville, twenty miles north of the city, when his son was six.

Throughout his youth, Burnshaw, who attended the experimental school, idealized his father's learning and humanitarianism, and reveled in the surrounding pastoral countryside. Starting college at Columbia University, Burnshaw transferred to the University of Pittsburgh when his family moved to the city, graduating in 1925. He then wrote poetry while working for a steel corporation as an apprentice advertising copywriter in a nearby town. In the late 1920s he established a minor literary reputation with verse that appeared in the *American Caravan, Midland Voices, Echo, Palms,* his own magazine *Poetry Folio,* and in privately published editions. Simultaneously, he was profoundly aroused by the horrors of industrial life, both human and environmental, that he witnessed in the steel company town of Blawnox, Pennsylvania.

Burnshaw afterward ascertained that he had been transformed into both a communist and conservationist (in the sense of wishing to protect nature from the ravages of industrialism) by his dream that "the whole world would belong to the people." He grasped this as an emotional rather than an intellectual development, one that became a kind of faith: "I had never had any political ideas in my life. This was an overwhelming apocalyptic conversion, and once I had it there was no question about it."[34]

During a year spent in Europe with his first wife, where he studied at the University of Poitiers and the Sorbonne, he fell under the influence of the Jewish socialist French poet André Spire. Burnshaw returned to New York and began working as an advertising manager for the Hecht Company. In his auxiliary time, he pursued graduate work at New York University and later received an M.A. in English from Cornell. He joined V. F. Calverton's journal *Modern Quarterly* as a contributing editor, married a second time, and worked on a book, eventually published as *André Spire and His Poetry: Two Essays and Forty Translations* (1933).[35]

The very week that Burnshaw returned from Europe he picked up a magazine at a New York newsstand that he had never seen before. It was the *New Masses,* and in its pages he read with rapture the spellbindingly original prose of a section of Mike Gold's *Jews without Money* (1930). Burnshaw began submitting poetry and reviews to the *New Masses,* and eventually went to the magazine's office to meet Gold in person.[36] Soon he was following the Communist press, and, although he knew that the Party program did not address his fears about industry and technology, "the question disappeared under deepening waves of people victimized by the ever enlarging Depression."[37]

In late 1933, Burnshaw first began working part-time and then full-time for the *New Masses.* As part of this association, he published an open letter breaking off relations with V. F. Calverton as "an enemy of the American working class" because *Modern Monthly* had published Max Eastman's charges of repression of the arts in the Soviet Union. Burnshaw, in contrast, held that "all of the facts at my disposal clearly show that there is actually more freedom for artists in the Soviet Union than in any other country."[38]

The Australian novelist Christina Stead remembered meeting the short and trim Burnshaw in the *New Masses* office at 31 East Twenty-Seventh Street in 1935: "a neat, limber young man with clear large appraising eyes. He might have been an Anatolian or other fresh-skinned country visitor from a distant place, considering the city ferment."[39] For Burnshaw, the *New Masses* years were more productive for his prose than for the kind of meditative poetry he aspired to write. In addition to his industrious editing, he completed a stream of reviews and essays for a number of publications; occasionally, when writing on political topics for the *New Masses*, he used the pen name "Jeremiah Kelley."

Burnshaw's essays and reviews of poetry were consistent in their content with the views of the Kharkov Conference. In " 'Middle-Ground' Writers," which appeared a few months prior to the advent of the Popular Front, Burnshaw declared that the task of the Marxist critic was to reach out to "every ally who can be enlisted." While Burnshaw's critical work promoted orthodox Communist politics (despite his private misgivings about the Party's adulation of industrialization), he devoted greater attention to more strictly literary issues, and evidenced a commitment to convincing, not merely denouncing, writers who held "confused" or "wavering" positions that he characterized as "middle-ground."[40] During the later part of his tenure on the editorial board, he engaged in discussions with Joseph North about visiting Robert Frost (1874-1963) to discuss the idea of altering one of Frost's poems that he had seen in manuscript, possibly for publication in the *New Masses*. Burnshaw felt some sort of rapprochement was conceivable after Frost praised Burnshaw for vanquishing *Poetry* editor Harriet Monroe (1860-1936) in his 1934 debate with her about "Art and Propaganda."[41] Sometime later North or perhaps Alfred Kreymborg did approach Frost, but a negative *New Masses* review of Frost's *A Further Range* (1936) by Rolfe Humphries apparently drove Frost away.[42]

Burnshaw was primarily responsible for selecting the poetry that appeared in the journal. His background was strong in modernism and his book on André Spire emphasized the virtues of free verse experimentalism. Nonetheless Burnshaw was in full agreement with the *New Masses'* prioritization of publishing poetry that addressed social conditions, and his book reviews bluntly accused writers of producing escapist content; moreover, he saw no virtue in formal features as such. In a letter rejecting a poem submitted by the young Communist poet Willard Maas,[43] Burnshaw criticized the poem for being "too chockful of startling imagery." By this he meant that "instead of its being realized as a poem, it concentrates on arresting the attention, by its technical feats."[44] Burnshaw later denied that the selection of poems was politically determined by the *New Masses* editors. His denial, though, was slippery, in that he suggested that political "watch-dogging" simply wasn't necessary. As the *New Masses* became increasingly perceived as the cultural arm of the Communist movement, writers who expressed views that differed from the movement, or who employed styles of which the movement seemed not to approve, were less likely to submit their work to the magazine.[45]

By 1936, Burnshaw was finding it difficult to write his own poised and contemplative poetry while carrying out his editorial responsibilities. He departed at the end of the year, primarily because of his unhappiness with the return of Joseph Freeman to the board, his financial problems, and uncertainty about his own creativity. The skillful anticapitalist poems he had been writing since the late 1920s appeared in the 1936 collection, *The Iron Land: A Narrative*; they were marked by a structural strategy of rhetorical questions and innovations. One that was selected for inclusion in the 1935 anthology *Proletarian Literature in the United States* suggests that, while it may be difficult to "play the violin when the house is on fire," as his professor had warned him, one might perform quite well with alternative, louder instruments, such as trumpet and drum. In "I, Jim Rogers," Burnshaw declaims his views in the kind of public voice that many on the Left thought necessary to answer the challenge of the "American Jeremiad"; that is, how and in what manner should a poet speak in the face of mass suffering.

Described as a "Mass Recitation for Speaker and Chorus," the poem enables the diminutive Jewish intellectual Burnshaw to become "Jim Rogers," the powerful voice of a de-ethnicized, "universal" working class, a personal witness to the devastation of unemployment in the Depression. Rogers, standing in line in a city relief office, watches a woman carrying a dead child – "the thing" – returning each day after being told the building is too crowded, refusing to recognize that her child lives no more. The strategy of the verse invokes the power of individual testimony to span the bridge of differential class experience and affect those who learn of suffering only from a safe distance:

> I, Jim Rogers, saw her
> and I can believe my eyes
> And you had better believe me
> Instead of the sugary lies
> You read in the papers. I saw her
> Slip into our waiting room
> Among us thin blank men
> And women waiting our turn.
> But none of us looked like her
> With her starved-in face, dazed eyes,
> And the way she clung to the thing
> Her arms pressed against her bosom.

When the woman is finally interviewed by the bureaucrats, she refuses to accept the loss of her child and flees into the city streets.

Jim Rogers then roams the passageways and alleys, picking up the fragments of her story. Her husband had lost his mill job in New Jersey after she became pregnant, and he committed suicide by jumping off a ferry. The woman then gave birth and found temporary work in a store basement, only to be fired because she was too weak to keep up the pace. While Rogers relates her tale in verse, he offers a pledge of solidarity as he elevates her as an example to humanity:

> And if I
> knew where to point my voice to
> I'd yell out: Where are you? Answer!
> Don't run away! – Wait, answer!
> Whom are you hiding from?
> The miserly dog who fired you?
> Listen: you're not alone!
> You're never alone any more:
> All of your brother-millions
> (Now marking time) will stand by you
> Once they have learned your tale!

The public voice by which Burnshaw breaks from the past to challenge the ruling order has completely overwhelmed the intimate inscriptions of his earlier work. In Burnshaw's conclusion, Rogers, the proletarian surrogate through which the middle-class poet speaks, passionately attempts to galvanize passive observers into active agents; he turns to directly face the reader:

> – If any of you who've listened,
> See some evening walking
> A frail caved-in white figure
> That looks as if one time
> It flowed with warm woman-blood.
> See her ghosting the street
> With a film of pain on her eyes,
> Tell her that I, Jim Rogers,
> Hold out whatever I own
> A scrap of food, four walls –
> Not much to give but enough
> For rest and for arming the bones –
>
> And a hard swift fist for defence
> Against the dogs of the world
> Ready to tear her down. . . .
> Tell her I offer this

> In these days of marking time,
> Tell our numberless scattered millions
> In mill and farm and sweatshop
> Straining with arms for rebellion,
> Tie up our forces together
> To salvage this earth from despair
> And make it fit for the living.[46]

Rarely has the moral and political case for Communist solidarity been expressed so cleanly and eloquently.

Shortly after leaving the *New Masses*, Burnshaw entered the college textbook field. In May 1939, he founded the Dryden Press, where from time to time he hired friends from the Party to work in various capacities, such as translating and editing. Although he was troubled by Marxism's ability to reveal social truth so well while failing to address crucial issues of human consciousness, emotion, and perception, Burnshaw still was friendly to the Party and to the Soviet Union, even at the time of the Hitler-Stalin Pact.[47]

In April 1940 Burnshaw's year-old daughter died, leaving him in a state of deep depression. For five years he published almost nothing until his verse play, *The Bridge*, appeared in 1945. This was a political allegory reconsidering the role of technology in social progress, suggesting that art might possibly counter technology's perversion by greed. Burnshaw was pleased when he learned that Mike Gold, whom he had always admired as the personification of socialist idealism, praised the play in the *Daily Worker*.[48] Burnshaw also published a long poem that year, *The Revolt of the Cats in Paradise* (1945), and three years later a novel, *The Sunless Sea* (1948), both of which were satires suggesting a further devolution from his explicitly revolutionary position the 1930s.

Burnshaw's disaffection from the Left was completed when he read about the anti-Semitic charges of a "Doctor's Plot" against Stalin in the Soviet Union in 1951. When Granville Hicks gave anti-Communist testimony shortly thereafter, naming names before a government committee, Burnshaw sent him a supportive letter.[49] He then announced a new, more philosophic poetic direction in *Early and Late Testament* (1952), which included revisions of his early poems in a way that tended to heighten their obscurity. Burnshaw added further to his reputation with his edition of *The Poem Itself: Forty-Five Modern Poets in a New Presentation* (1964) and his scholarly *The Seamless Web: Language-Thinking, Creature-Knowledge, Art-Experience* (1970). More of his novels and poems, increasingly on Jewish themes, appeared regularly through the 1980s.

Yet Burnshaw never repudiated his revolutionary past, which he defended with feistiness when queried in the 1960s and later by scholars who were seeking information about his old literary friends and associates. Moreover, from Burnshaw's many reworkings of his earlier texts, there emerged a striking instance of utopian socialist verse, crystallizing in allegorical form the view of those who retained their communist dreams while losing hope as to the revolutionary means of realizing them. His poem "The Bridge," echoing Hart Crane (as did Burnshaw's 1945 play by that name), had appeared in a less developed form as Section Two of "Fifth Testament: Dialogue of the Heartbeat" in his 1952 collection *Early and Late Testament.* In the version published twenty years later, Burnshaw depicts in direct and clean free verse stanzas the efforts of an idealistic collective ("We") to construct "a bridge-head from here and now to tomorrow," reaching across the water, spanning a veritable sea, leaning "toward the far horizon," with arms that "Reach out to greet the future." The builders of Today work industriously in anticipation that from the other direction, Tomorrow, where they discern a "far light flooding," will come a second bridgehead "with outstretched arms." Then "the two bridgeheads may meet, the old and the new / Join hands to close the ocean."

In the last stanza the builders are confronted with a doubter who sees no distant light and who questions that the "outstretched arms" will ever emerge from the other side. To this, the builders of Today reply:

> We see it
> Whether or not they range the air: half of whatever we see
> Glows in cells not signaled by our eyes.
> If men only lived by the things they knew
> The skin of their hands could not touch, they would soon die
> Of starved need. The shapes of sensate truth
> Bristle with harshness. Eyeballs would cut the edges
> Of naked fact and bleed. The thoughtful vision
> Projected by our driving hope creates
> A world where truth is possible: without it
> The mind would break or die.[50]

Once he had made the case for Communist action in practical terms; now it is the dream alone that motivates a purposeful life.

As a non-Party member of the *New Masses* editorial board, Burnshaw was free to do as he pleased — no words of his were ever changed for political reasons — because, as he later recalled, "he *would* do no wrong." Through his conversation and behavior, he convinced the other board members that, "like the others around him, he deeply believed in the necessity for promoting the Ultimate Good, whatever the circumstances," which at that moment in history translated into defending the program of the Party.[51]

His relations with Party member Joseph North disclose additional aspects of Burnshaw's political status. North gave books to Burnshaw to read, but he would never issue him orders. Still, it was clear that the Communist Party leadership put its trust in North more than Burnshaw. Not only did North seem to be someone who might serve as a "political watchdog" in case of trouble, but, unlike Burnshaw, he also made himself available to be moved to other assignments when needed. In fact, North soon left the magazine to begin editing the Weekly Section of the *Daily Worker* when Clarence Hathaway became the editor. After that North went to Spain, returning in 1938, to once again join the *New Masses* editorial board.

## Poetry and the Popular Front

Burnshaw's tenure at the *New Masses* essentially coincided with the moment when the old combination of anarchy and sectarianism that dominated the magazine was overthrown, and the views promoted by Mike Gold and the Kharkov Conference prevailed. And yet, not every editor was gratified by the new direction. Just prior to his own departure from the board in 1934, Joseph Freeman wrote in the *New Masses* that a "sectarian" attitude had dominated the Communist press until 1933. "As recently as last year it was easier for a camel to pass through the eye of a needle than for a 'fence-sitter' to appear in the pages of the Communist press. The 'line' was jealousy guarded." Suddenly, however, "fence-sitters" were happily embraced: "our press is his and he can say anything he likes, however remote it may be from revolutionary thought."[52] The first characterization seems exaggerated in light of the haphazardness of the Walt Carmon era; and the second seems to have been stuck in to give the impression of fairness and balance. Freeman is chiefly out to combat the Left of the movement but makes a preemptive strike to insulate himself from the insinuation that he conciliates fence-sitters.

As was the case with his 1931 report on the *New Masses*, Freeman's 1934 statement may have been calculated to bolster his own position as a reliable guardian of orthodoxy, yet one who was open to reason – the perfect shepherd for the entrance of leftward-moving intellectuals into a Communist-led literary movement. In the next few paragraphs Freeman proceeded to denounce a "laissez-faire" attitude in the Party press, demanding that writers with a liberal past must now prove themselves Communists. Yet within this framework, he went on, writers who, during the last decade, were perfecting their craft but were now joining the revolutionary camp (John Howard Lawson and Isidor Schneider are mentioned) can come together with writers who had a decade of Communist loyalty (this seems to be a personal reference) and whose only need is to further perfect their craft.

Freeman, however, was probably not referring to a political laxity in the form or content of poetry or fiction so much as in articles and reviews that offered Marxist judgments; the magazine's selection of imaginative literature does not appear to have been addressed in the early 1930s on a policy level, nor even subjected to much collective decision making. The testimony of Burnshaw suggests that the decisive factors influencing the publication of poetry and stories principally related to the kind of material submitted (which was already self-selected due to the frankly revolutionary and "proletarian culture" orientation of the "Third Period") and the tastes of the particular editor who appears to have had free reign and was on occasion called the "poetry Czar."[53] Although a Party cultural leader like Trachtenberg or Jerome might promote the work of a certain writer, the areas in which the Party's Political Bureau intervened mainly concerned matters such as professionalization of the publication and its distribution, personality conflicts, and the editors' ability to carry out policy in a broad sense.

Such policy issues were especially acute at the beginning of the Popular Front, starting in mid-1935, and again after the crisis precipitated by the Hitler-Stalin Pact, in September 1939. In the first instance the Party leadership felt it could take another chance on Freeman; in the second, the more trusted Joseph North and A. B. Magil were put in charge. Freeman was already a bit of a political risk in 1936 because of the circumstances under which he had departed from the New Masses in 1934. He claimed in all of his letters to friends and in his public statements that he wanted to spend the next eighteen months working on his autobiographical *An American Testament: A Narrative of Rebels and Romantics* (1936). Yet in 1937 letter to Earl Browder he states that in 1934, after helping to transform *New Masses* into a weekly, he was kicked out "in a most uncomradely manner," and that he was then subjected to gossip that he had abandoned the magazine at a crucial moment. What can be documented for certain is that Freeman had been involved in a major conflict with Herman Michelson, although Freeman claimed that he did not understand the basis of it.[54]

Before leaving the *New Masses*, however, Freeman asked Granville Hicks (1901–1982) to join the editorial board starting in January 1934. Hicks was a literature professor at Rensselaer Polytechnic Institute who had a year earlier published a Marxist history of literature in the United States, *The Great Tradition* (1933), and who would join the Communist Party a year later. Among others serving on the editorial board at the time of the Popular Front were Mike Gold, Joshua Kunitz, Herman Michelson, Joseph North, and the African American lawyer and journalist Loren Miller (1903-1967).[55]

Freeman rejoined the editorial board in March 1936 at the personal request of Browder, who asked him to step in for at least a year to pull the magazine out of crisis. He remained until mid-1937 when he was officially disciplined by the Party for the first time, on the grounds of irresponsible personal and political behavior (see discussion in Chapter 5). During his tenure on the board throughout 1936 and 1937, numerous conferences about the direction of the New Masses were held between the editors and members of the Party's Political Bureau.

The immediate problem that had to be addressed was a serious lack of financial resources. Many Left writers were now finding jobs in paid outlets in the publishing houses and magazines that had been closed down in 1932; new houses and magazines were being founded while older ones expanded. This reduced the number of active contributors. At the same time, the Party's People's Front orientation attracted many writers and professionals who were looking for a fresh venue to correspond to the changed times, not the same old predictable formulae. Moreover, the latest techniques of "bourgeois journalism" – manifest in Time and Esquire, and marked by innovative formats, layouts, condensed and witty presentations of material, and photographs – made the New Masses seem antiquated. Finally, the New Masses was trying to do too many things at once by publishing news, Marxist editorials, exposés, eye-witness accounts, theory, art, satire, and literature.

The magazine's editors and the Party's Political Bureau settled on the idea of publishing a new kind of Popular Front weekly with a Literary Supplement. On 29 December 1936, a staff conference was held at the New Masses office; invited guests included Alex Lehv of Soviet Russia Today and Herbert Kline of New Theater. The conference group concluded that the magazine should be a 64-72-page weekly with a colored cover and numbers of photographs aimed at achieving a circulation of at least 100,000.[56]

Committed to his own vision of what the magazine should be, Freeman had rejoined the New Masses that spring in a combative mood. In his characteristically hypercritical manner, he later recalled that "I returned to find that certain New Masses staffers were trying to cripple our literature by theories and practices which were sectarian and narrow-minded in middle-class rather than in proletarian cant."[57] Who exactly was to blame for this state of affairs is not specified, although the names of Burnshaw and North were soon missing from the editorial board. Hicks had moved on to an advisory capacity while working on his biography, John Reed (1936), and Isidor

Schneider (1896-1977), a poet, novelist and prolific reviewer, joined the board. But since Schneider was to depart for the Soviet Union with a Guggenheim fellowship at the end of the year, he recommended a new young writer and Party member, F. W. Dupee (1904-1979), to temporarily take his place.[58]

Freeman wrote Granville Hicks that he hoped that, once finished with his book, Hicks might take a permanent position as the magazine's literary editor. But Dupee's work pleased Freeman, and Hicks, in the meantime, indicated that he preferred to serve the magazine in an advisory capacity from his home in upstate New York, contributing a "journal of the month."[59] Freeman was fearful that, if *New Masses* did not undergo a change that reflected the Popular Front orientation, it would be lost to the Communist movement as was *Partisan Review* (at that time in limbo, before its reappearance four months later with a semi-Trotskyist political inflection) and the recently defunct *New Theater*. Thus he plunged ahead with his concept of turning the magazine into a weekly like *Time* that would periodically feature a Literary Supplement. In late 1936, he traveled about the United States raising thousands of dollars to realize this goal.

A few months afterward, in the spring of 1937, Freeman planned, wrote the prospectus, and laid the foundation for the *New Masses* Literary Supplement which was to be published sometime later that year as an inserted magazine section coming with a *New Masses* subscription; the Supplement, he believed, would be the authentic heir of the original *Masses, Liberator,* and the early *New Masses*. Yet by the summer, with the Supplement still not available, he was in trouble with the Party leadership for other reasons and was asked by the Party's Central Committee to leave the magazine. The reasons were that Freeman had not returned from a *New Masses* assignment in Mexico until many weeks after he was due home, and his 1936 autobiography had been criticized by high Soviet officials for gossipy indiscretions and for favorable references to exiled Bolshevik Leon Trotsky.

After the autumn of 1937, Freeman never returned to the *New Masses* office. The *New Masses* published a statement in its issue of 7 September 1937, claiming that, due to the dangerous international circumstances, Freeman "will leave shortly for a trip abroad in behalf of this magazine and a publisher who has commissioned him to do a book on the European situation." The announcement promised that Freeman would continue to appear regularly in its pages through "a series of interviews from key points and with key personalities in Europe."[60] No such interviews ever appeared, although Freeman did publish some book reviews over the following months, one of which was a sectarian attack on critic Edmund Wilson. "Edmund Wilson's Globe of Glass" explicitly defends the Stalin regime and attributes Wilson's alleged faults to an attraction to Trotsky; thus the polemic appears to have some features of an effort on Freeman's part to reestablish his own credentials as a Party loyalist.[61] The masthead replaced his name as editor with that of his old antagonist, Herman Michelson, just returned from a long stay in the Soviet Union.

The Literary Supplement itself never lived up to Freeman's expectations. In the months prior to its advent in December 1937, an altercation broke out between two of the supplement's editors, Granville Hicks, the publication's principal literary critic, and Horace Gregory, who was the core of an aggregation of Left-wing modern poets. Gregory had begun his teaching duties at Sarah Lawrence College in the fall of 1934, continuing his arm's-length literary collaboration with the Party. With a background as a teacher and lecturer for the New York John Reed Club, Gregory had maintained his association with the Party throughout the transition to the Popular Front era; he joined the National Council as well as the Executive Committee of the League of American Writers in 1935, and signed the call for the Second Congress in 1937. Nevertheless, Gregory and his wife, poet Marya Zaturenska (1902–1982), had powerful convictions about their own superior abilities to judge verse, and an obsession bordering on paranoia about literary log-rolling in the establishment as well as in Left publications.

In the fall of 1937, Gregory launched his own book series, *New Letters*, to be issued twice a year by W. W. Norton and Company. The purpose of the first selection, presenting nearly forty poets and fiction writers from the United States and Western Europe, was primarily to feature "young writers . . . whose work has been deeply affected by a new conception of human consciousness which arose after the World War and began to be assimilated after 1930."[62] In private correspondence Gregory more directly referred to the younger writers in the collection as emerging out of the Communist cultural movement.[63] Thus Gregory was taken aback when Granville Hicks launched a full-blown assault on the publication, under the title "Those Who Quibble, Bicker, Nag, and Deny," in the 28 September 1937 issue of the *New Masses.*

Was this a personal attack motivated by malice and envy; or did it reflect genuine political differences, perhaps even an orthodoxy sponsored by the Party's cultural leaders (Jerome and Trachtenberg)? Retrospectively, it seems that Popular Front culture, a product of both changing social conditions and of policies championed by influential Communist critics such as Hicks, operated on the terrain of a fairly precise contradiction. On the one hand, in the search for political and cultural allies against fascism, the yard-stick of revolutionary purity no longer applied; the borders between Communism and New Deal liberalism became blurred, and popular writers who might earlier have been regarded as suspect due to their market orientation were embraced if the author and the cultural product seemed compatible with the antifascist crusade. On the other hand, there seemed to be much less tolerance for the atmosphere of despair characteristic of early Depression poetry and fiction, or of techniques and vocabularies that smacked of introspection, uncertainty, and ambivalence.

Granville Hicks, an English professor emerging from a devout Unitarian and Universalist church background, is aptly depicted by his biographers as possessing an "evangelical strain in [his] personality"; he also became a near-pristine example of the fellow traveler who exemplifies Enlightenment faith in rationality and progress.[64] After several years of contributing to Communist publications primarily about fiction and criticism, he joined the Party in 1935, becoming a nationally recognized voice in letters for the politics and culture of the Popular Front. In Hicks's address to the Second American Writers' Congress, collected in a volume where poetry noticeably took a back seat, he exuded optimism and certainty while extolling the need for a literary leadership to create books that will "march in step with the marching feet of millions."[65] The orientation was accordant with Party general secretary Earl Browder's call at the same congress for a literature "permeated with faith in the creative powers of the masses" with "one of its greatest themes [as] the dramatic world changes effected by mass creative power when it is organized, disciplined and directed."[66]

In spite of the fact that Hicks had given the impression that he wanted to pull back from literary infighting when he refused the magazine's post of literary editor under Freeman, there was no sign of magnanimity in his assault on fellow *New Masses* contributing editor Gregory's volume. Obviously much of the writing anthologized by Gregory was an affront to the Popular Front sensibility championed by Hicks, but he may also have seen Gregory as a potential threat or rival, especially since the collection contained a piece of literary criticism by William Phillips and Philip Rahv that designated Hicks's work as "more in the sectarian tradition of Upton Sinclair than in the great tradition of Karl Marx."[67] Two-thirds of the seventeen-paragraph-long essay was devoted to expanding on the theme that "Communism is good news," and the condemnation of numerous writers, mostly already out of political favor (such as James T. Farrell and John Dos Passos), for delineating despair more than hopefulness. When he at last addressed the contents of *New Letters*, the contributors (many of whom had previously appeared in the *New Masses*) were arraigned for a Spenglerian bleakness and creating a mood more appropriate to the 1920s than the 1930s. "All this," he closes, "confirms the impression that it is difficult to render in literature the substance of the Communist hope."[68]

The rebuttal by Gregory and two other writers was introduced in a neutral tone by the New Masses editors in the issue of 12 October. Gregory, whose contribution was longest and appeared first, commenced by reminding Hicks that he had heard the call that "Communism is good news" first, as early as 1924. He then turned the tables and insisted that it was Hicks who was lost in the 1920s – the 1920s of H. L. Mencken. The evidence was that Hicks had displayed wild enthusiasm over Sinclair Lewis's novel It Can't Happen Here (1935) – which turned out to be a terrible misjudgment because Lewis "is now reported to be writing an anti-Communist play" and heading "straight in the direction of Leon Trotsky's friends." The problem was that "the actual center of Mr. Hicks' review is a defense of a kind of realism that was ably practiced during the 1920s," but which became "his only scale of measurement." Searching for a poet "who would be a combination of Walt Whitman and Emily Dickinson," he failed to appreciate that "poetry is reviving under the stimulus of more than one literary tradition." The issue dividing the two men was not that of enforcing a Communist Party political line – for both he and Hicks "believe that the U.S.S.R. is building an enduring civilization, and that Trotskyism is a disease" – but that Hicks was unable to read poetry.[69]

Muriel Rukeyser, closely allied with Gregory, more directly accentuated the topic of whether the "application of a rigid standard of the (moral) happy ending" was superior to a "sensitive straight facing of present scenes and values." The real choice was between what is "inert" and what is "living." Rukeyser did, in fact, find "hope" in the poems anthologized, but "a steadier, less blatant hope than Mr. Hicks demands – a hope to be worked for continually, not shouted before its time."[70] A third, brief intervention simply observed that the terms and categories of political action are improper for assessing lyric poetry.[71]

Hicks's rejoinder acknowledged agreement with Gregory that "Communism is good news," but exhorted that "most of our writers don't make me feel that they know that in the very depths of their imagination." Gregory had evaded the task of explaining whether or not he agrees with such a judgment, while Rukeyser had provided only a few unconvincing examples of a dubious "hope." The other topics raised in passing – the decline of melody in poetry, alternatives to realism, the unique qualities of the lyric – were treated less dogmatically, and the reply ended with a call to continue the discussion.[72]

The next stage in the debate came in the form of an exchange between a young disciple of Gregory's, T. C. Wilson (Theodore Carl Wilson, 1912–1950), a poet and critic equally facile in modernist and proletarian genres, and Samuel Sillen (1911–1973), a young New York University English instructor who had recently joined the *New Masses* board. Wilson proposed that the central issue in dispute was the "form" in which Communist hope was to be expressed, not the question of whether a particular group of writers was expressing it. Not only was "clear-headedness about the present" a superior criterion for literary judgment than "optimism about the future," but the division itself was "critically meaningless," since many outstanding works of art contain both. Hicks's fixation on his formula led him to a basic error in equating the emotions expressed by writers in *New Letters* with the despair and bitterness of those of the 1920s: "What he significantly neglects to point out is that whereas the young writers of the twenties were generally content to express those emotions and stop at that, the young writers in Mr. Gregory's collection, though they may convey a feeling of despair, also attempt to reveal its underlying causes." Rather than succumb to the state of affairs producing despair, they demand that such conditions be changed.

The most literary-specific aspect of the interchange centered on realism and naturalism. Wilson reasoned that Marxism enabled the artist to command a more complex social vision than other worldviews, thereby requiring an extension of realism "to include perceptions and awareness impossible to convey within the confines of naturalist fiction." Less consequential than the amassing of data (which Gregory had chastised as a feature of "pragmatic naturalism") would be the "selection of *significant* fact"; documentation would remain vital but would be accomplished through "interpretation." Moreover, in the new push to "render an object, a scene, an event, or character so that it will possess both a factual and symbolic meaning," techniques such as the fable (already employed by Kafka, Henry James, Thomas Mann, and several Soviet writers) would be employed. The merit of such a technique should be judged by determining whether "the objective fact is made to stand as a symbol of some emotion, ideal, or belief that is larger than itself."[73]

Wilson was rejoined by his contemporary, Sillen. Negotiating between what he posed as two extremes, Sillen affirmed that Hicks had neglected the necessity of multiformity, but noted that Wilson had made a more serious misjudgment in his claim that the "battle has now been won" in terms of rallying young writers to a "well-developed political consciousness" and "an intense hatred of fascism." Wilson was mistaking the status of a minority, and one "on the offensive," for the larger milieu of cultural workers who had not yet heard the "good news." This suggested that Wilson was in some cases mistaking claims of Marxist commitment for their actuality – a sloppy procedure that was particularly dangerous in light of the attraction for some intellectuals of Trotskyist pretenses to being pro-socialist or anti-fascist. The task of the literary critic was not to extol political consciousness in a general sense but to separate "the genuine from the spurious."

Wilson also erred in his promotion of fables, especially those of Kafka, as far surpassing the realist tradition. Realism must be flexible, and certainly not bound to naturalism; but Sillen saw the American tradition of realism in the category of "great historical sources," while the fables of Kafka and James were at best "enriching streams" to be subsumed into the larger project. To Wilson's endorsement of Kenneth Burke's critical work *Attitudes Toward History* (1937), Sillen counterposed the volume by the British Spanish Civil War writer Ralph Fox, *The Novel and the People* (1937).[74]

## The Last Refuge

On 7 November 1937, the first Literary Supplement appeared. The four editors were Gold, Gregory, Hicks, and Joshua Kunitz (1897-1980). The hindmost was a serious scholar who had traveled around the Soviet Union and had written a Ph.D. dissertation at Columbia University, published as *Russian Literature and the Jew.*[75] Kunitz was among the most highly educated Communist intellectuals and the Party's undisputed authority on Russian literature. Sometimes Kunitz was called upon to defend controversial Soviet policy, as in the case of the Moscow Trials. Yet he was not thoroughly trusted by the Party leadership.

In the early 1930s Kunitz wrote for the *New Masses* as "J. Q. Neets," and was considered a Party member even though for years he never attended a meeting. He was a more active presence in the John Reed Clubs, where he was outspoken in defense of the importance of literary style, and happy to debate comrades such as Mike Gold and Henry George Weiss, who, in his view, failed to appreciate the culture of the past.[76] Then Kunitz was spotted talking to the novelist Edward Dahlberg (1900-1977) after Dahlberg had broken with the Party. When reprimanded, Kunitz testily replied, "I'll talk to whom I please." He subsequently agreed to leave the Party of his own accord, and, although he habitually contributed to the Party press, he was regarded behind his back by some Party leaders as a "Menshevik."[77] Nevertheless, he continued to write for publications associated with the Communist movement until the late 1970s. In the intervening years he published many books, including *Dawn over Samarkand* (1930), *Russia: The Giant That Came Last* (1947), and *Russian Literature since the Revolution* (1948). He also taught at academic institutions such as the City College of New York, Cornell University, and Middlebury College until he was blacklisted at the beginning of the Cold War.

In line with the special prerogative of each critic, Hicks contributed an essay to the supplement exposing the "Trotskyism" of the *Nation* magazine's book-review section, while Gregory extolled the virtues of diverse literary techniques in his review, "Poetry in 1937." Verse by Rukeyser, British Communist Hugh MacDiarmid (1892–1978), and several others was published, ranging from the moderate difficulty of the former to the more conventional forms and explicit content of the latter.

Within a few weeks, the *New Masses* editors published an editorial, "Is Poetry Dead?," referring to a debate held in Toledo, Ohio, between an English professor and a CIO organizer. The former insisted that the public no longer cared for verse; the latter maintained that, while the American people had lost interest in poets "who were obsessed with images of death and decay," the rebirth of the labor movement had produced a vital interest in poetry "in the tradition of Whitman" that "talks the language of the people." The editorial called for readers, including poets, to take sides – to explain which writers are "reaching large audiences," and the reasons.[78]

The terms in which the issue was posed could hardly do less than elicit the most anti-intellectual sentiments; who, after all, would wish to join the bourgeois professor against the idealistic worker, or stand on the side of "death and decay" against "the language of the people"? In the second Literary Supplement (now retitled "Literary Section" due to a post office requirement), two letters were published in response, both castigating the verse of Rukeyser for its amorphousness and lack of verbs. One of the authors, folksinger Lee Hays (1914–1981), further indicted James Agee, Richard Eberhart, and other *New Masses* contributors for "regurgitation of their own lives." His recommendation was to "let Horace Gregory sell the *Daily Worker* on the subway for a year if he doesn't know what I mean." Hays then concluded, "I sometimes wish Uncle Mike Gold would rise and slay these demons for us, for he is a sensible voice crying in what appears to be a wilderness of ivory towers."[79] Indeed, Gold himself had recently been embroiled in a parallel debate in the *New Masses* around the legacy of Isadora Duncan (1878–1927) in relation to modern dance in the 1930s. In his depreciation of the latter, Gold used every opportunity to take swipes at the influence of T. S. Eliot and "deliberately unintelligible and overtechnicalized" modern poetry. He concluded with the statement that "in our revolutionary poetry and dance I would like to see more beauty and romanticism – the sort one finds in all folk ballads, for instance. I just don't like cerebral art, and don't believe I ever will."[80]

The second edition of the Literary Section, itself, noteworthy for the initial appearance of novelist Thomas Wolfe (1900-1938) in a Communist venue, contained little poetry – only a short piece by Party member David Wolfe (a pseudonym for future screenwriter Ben Maddow [1909-1992]), and translations of Federico Garcia Lorca by Langston Hughes. The sole essay addressing poetry was an academic piece by future English scholar Dorothy Van Ghent (1907-1967), then a Ph.D. candidate at Berkeley and the lover of poet Kenneth Rexroth. She surveyed trends in modern poetry and called for a "dialectical materialist" attitude among Marxist poets.[81]

A few weeks later, Martha Millet (b. 1919), a teenage Communist who identified herself as secretary of the "Poetry Group," joined the discussion on the side of the CIO activist and against the recent verse publications of the New Masses. Her organization advocated poetry that was not "confusedly ornate, pretentiously intellectual, and 'cerebrally' dull." The essence of poetry was rhythm, "an aspect of power, including political power," demonstrated by the efficacy of the slogan "workers of the world, unite." Therefore, "The Popular Front needs rhythms . . . in order to combat the profit system." Although high standards were necessary, "the popular front has to become popular," mandating that "poetry has to become popular." Moreover, the key to popularity is when verse "attains a rich and accurate simplicity and directness."[82]

In the following week the New Masses printed a purported survey of the 389 poems published in the poetry journal Westward, which were simplistically classified as "Descriptive Poetry," "Poetry of Frustration," and so forth. The surveyor concluded that 85 percent of the poems were "worthless," from the viewpoint of subject matter.[83] The following page offered yet another letter on the poetry debate, this time endorsing Lee Hays's call for Mike Gold to take action against cerebral poets, to which he should also add critics such as Dorothy Van Ghent.[84] A week later, Robert Forsythe (a pseudonym for Kyle Crichton [1896-1960], a well-known writer for Collier's magazine) used his column, "Forsythe's Page," to enter the fray. Under the rubric "Wanted: Great Songs," he urged novelists to produce novels that were "simple, eminently readable," such as those of John O'Hara and James M. Cain. As for poets, the priority should be ballads in the vein of Robert Burns's "A Man's a Man for A' That." Forsythe urged that Lee Hayes and others should be heeded as nothing less than the voices of "workers [who were] protesting that the poems which appear in the New Masses mean nothing to them." In his own way, Forsythe was frankly acknowledging that art must be subordinated to the requirements of "living in a state of emergency." He explained that publishing the work of a "second-rate poet" was of no consequence because "I want the struggling people of this world to have all the help they can get. . . . Perhaps this is a period in history when survival is more important than art." What was imperative, then, was "a poem that will set me cheering . . . a new revolutionary song that will set my heart afire."[85]

After this, the now one-sided debate subsided. Moreover, with the appearance of the third Literary Section on 8 February 1938 devoted entirely to the translation of a Japanese novelette, the *New Masses* announced a major financial crisis; the editors appealed for $20,000 partly due to the added expense of the supplement. Urgent appeals continued throughout March. When the fourth supplement appeared on 12 April, the only poetry in it was a forty-stanza long anti-Trotskyist satirical ballad by Granville Hicks called "Revolution in Bohemia."[86] Gregory's name remained listed as an editor of the Literary Section and contributing editor of the journal, but the voices of himself and those with his perspective had nearly vanished.

A fuller understanding of the public debate can be obtained by examining private correspondence of the same months. In November 1937, Gregory confided to T. C. Wilson in Columbus, Ohio, that he had joined the board of the *New Masses* Literary Supplement with the idea that, when Wilson returned to Manhattan, the younger man might simply take over Gregory's position. But now that Wilson was delayed, Gregory felt beleaguered by Hicks, Gold, and Joshua Kunitz; moreover, the future of *New Letters* was in crisis due to the conversion to Trotskyism of his assistant, fiction writer Eleanor Clark.[87] In an earlier letter, Gregory had explained that those opposed to him also included "the bourgeois Left," by which he meant the *New Republic* and its literary editor Malcolm Cowley (1898–1989), whom he believed to be a master at planting reviews to reflect his prejudices. Nevertheless, Gregory was convinced that the controversy over *New Letters* would lead to a whole "new phase" of the cultural movement.[88]

Over the next few months Gregory's aspirations were scaled down. He began to write to Wilson that his success had been mainly in keeping Hicks from "taking over full charge of the literary section."[89] Next he announced that he had decided to give up on *New Letters*, convinced that Clark was sabotaging its promotion in order to force Gregory to turn for help to the newly reorganized, and semi-Trotskyist, *Partisan Review*. By now he wanted out of *New Masses* as well: "The whole weary fight . . . is a fight for power." Gregory saw himself under attack by the New York literary establishment, the Communists, the Trotskyists, and the conservatives. Some of the resentment, he believed, was simply against "new writing, not a personal resentment but the general feeling of POWER slipping. The old babies on all fronts grow frightened at the large number of new names I have published within the last two years." Instead of his efforts fomenting a new movement in poetry, Gregory had come to realize that only Wilson and Rukeyser would openly back his position.[90]

Another angle on the dispute can be seen in the correspondence between Samuel Sillen and Wilson. While Wilson was thoroughly under Gregory's influence, to the point where he often sent advance copies of his reviews and letters to the older man for coaching before submission, Sillen nonetheless opened the *New Masses* door wide to Wilson's participation. To Ohio, Sillen sent letters praising Wilson's essays in the *New Masses* and *Yale Review*, inviting him to New York for discussions of their differences, appealing to Wilson to submit poetry, book reviews, and literary essays.[91] As tensions increased and Gregory continued to mail Wilson venomous reports about the allegedly poor quality of the new Literary Section, Sillen continued to answer Wilson's queries and protests with patience.

Sillen pointed to the concerted effort made by the *New Masses* editors to give book reviews to individuals thought to be sympathetic to the particular school of literature (such as the assignment of works by the Auden Group in England to Wilson himself). He also emphasized that the opinions of various columnists were theirs alone. He claimed (less convincingly) that the "Is Poetry Dead?" editorial was not an attack on Gregory, but that the contents of the letters that arrived did show an unsympathetic attitude to certain kinds of writing among the readership that could not be neglected. Moreover, he insisted that of the hundreds of poems that arrived every week at the *New Masses* office, most were of truly poor quality; the few that made it into print were simply the best of what they received, not selected because they were of the "oompah" (cheerleading and optimistic) type. His last communication ended with an unrequited plea:

> We want the best that we can get. When gifted writers like yourself refrain from giving it to us, our battle is tougher, no doubt, but we keep on going. You have again and again been invited to write for the magazine. You have been published in it. At no time was your stuff blue-pencilled into vulgarity. If you want a better magazine you've got to chip in and help. Nothing else will do.[92]

Wilson, however, was finished; Gregory remained in name only; Rukeyser, who had other connections to the movement beyond the *New Masses*, donated an occasional review.

The disaffection of a writer as eminent as Gregory from the *New Masses* no doubt influenced the attitude of other potential contributors and supporters. Yet the consequences were as short-lived as those of earlier departures – of Dos Passos, Burnshaw, Freeman – inasmuch as the Communist-led cultural movement was still on the ascendancy. The reservoir of talent for the review section, in particular, seemed endless. If James Agee and Mark Shorer stopped writing, there were Joseph Frank, Sidney Alexander, S. J. Perelman, Louis Zukofsky, Barrie Stavis, Eleanor Flexner, Langston Hughes, Dorothy Parker, Richard Wright, Ralph Ellison, Meyer Levin, Richard Rovere, Milton Meltzer, Bernard Grebanier, and many others ready to take their places in the pages of the Communist publication. Moreover, in the post-Gregory period, women – such as Marguerite Young, Barbara Giles, and Ruth McKenney – became more visible in editorial and staff roles.

Although the Literary Section would get smaller and appear with less frequency until it was dropped, the 10 May 1938 "Federal Writers' Number" issue was a landmark, featuring Richard Wright's "Bright and Morning Star." The issue also included several young fiction writers who would become known in the 1940s and 1950s, such as Sam Ross, Arnold Manhoff, and Saul Levitt; and a range of poets in various stages of their careers, such as Kenneth Rexroth, William Pillin, Kenneth Fearing, Alfred Hayes, Weldon Kees, Maxwell Bodenheim, Willard Maas, and Eli Siegel. The special guest editors were two poets to whom Gregory and his wife were antagonistic, Sol Funaroff and Willard Maas.

Funaroff provided a concluding retrospective for the issue by tracing the "literary class of '29" from its creation of a new genre of proletarian "little magazines," supported by labor groups or collective efforts of young writers. Ultimately feeling dissatisfied with their limited means of reaching the public, the writers more aggressively affiliated with social movements and also turned to film and theater, if not to union organizing or fighting fascism in Spain. Then came the Federal Arts Projects offering temporary relief from the problems of economic insecurity, although the "proper function of the creative writer under government sponsorship" remained to be solved. Funaroff closed with an optimistic prediction for this new generation, now that it had decisively left behind "the eclectic art of coteries" and "the egocentric figure of the bohemian outcast" for "an art serving the public need": "The relationship between the American public and its writers whom it subsidizes through governmental agencies will find expression in a people's literature."[93]

A few weeks later, the *New Masses* announced a proposal from Mike Gold

for a People's Culture Day to coincide with the anniversary of Walt Whitman's birth. The editors extolled Whitman as a writer who "participated
heartily in the life of his countrymen"; who "derived his theme and his
speech from the masses whom he celebrated in everything that he wrote";
and who employed "sweeping rhythms" to express his "passionate affir-
mations" that had been recalled in 1936 by Carl Sandburg's *The People, Yes.*
Whitman's "faith in the common man," they concluded, "is embodied in
the work of the proletarian writers."[94] This Whitmania continued in the
lead article in the Literary Section of the 14 June *New Masses* by playwright
and novelist Philip Stevenson; he acknowledged that Whitman was "never
a thorough-going Socialist" but nevertheless "*the most important example of,
and spokesman for, the transition in American literary tradition between the idealism of our revolutionary middle-class democracy and the materialism of our coming
revolutionary-working-class democracy.*"[95]

Thus Whitman was configured as the consummate icon for the Popular Front, a bridge between Left liberalism and proletarianism, embodying
the common ideals of both groups. The point was consolidated by a theoretical essay by Joshua Kunitz, explaining the compatibility of both terms,
"people's literature" and "proletarian literature"; the former expressed the
Popular Front Alliance, the latter the outlook of the working class.[96]

Only one small note of dissent, a harbinger that some of the disputed
issues were going rise again in the 1940s and 1950s, came in a late May
1938 letter from Clarence Weinstock (better known under the pseudonym
Charles Humboldt [1910-1964]), editor of the Party-led *Art Front.* Called "Ivory
Tower or Hole in the Ground," Weinstock's letter questioned whether those
who had complained of the difficulty of *New Masses* poetry and urged songs
of uplift, had genuine credentials as the voice of "the common people."
While Weinstock acknowledged that the sentiments expressed "have considerable backing among your readers," it was not clear to him that such a
perspective really reflected a higher level of political consciousness of "the
people," or simply a failure to rise above the superficial education in the arts
purveyed by public schools:

> I am beginning to think that just as patriotism is the last refuge of a
> scoundrel, so the people are the last refuge of a philistine. What does a
> philistine want of art? Something that will give him the most exalted
> feelings with the least effort, something profound, but easy. His idea of
> poetry is the recitation, of painting the virtuously accurate description of
> nature. He wants nothing to do with that radical transformation of the
> world of nature and society ... which is the essence of great art.

Weinstock ended by noting passages from Lorca and Mayakovsky that, out of context and without effort, would also appear meaningless, and Marx's preference for Balzac's "The Unknown Masterpiece," a story that prefigures the development of abstract art and the artist's effort "to create a new language which even his fellow artists do not understand." If Weinstock's view stemmed from life in an "ivory tower," the counterview, expressive of an "unrevolutionary laziness," was a consequence of existing in "a hole in a ground."[97]

The dispute between advocates of a tolerance for literary forms that might be interpreted as difficult, communicating despair, and elevating fable over realism, and those calling for optimism and the use of the "people's language," occurred with relative autonomy from the Party leadership. In their autobiographies, neither of the central antagonists, Hicks or Gregory, nor secondary participants, such as Forsythe (Crichton), refer to external promptings.[98] All acted from their own convictions, and all felt that they were more truly representing the Party's interests. Clearly the problem of determining criteria for priorities in the publication of poetry in a time of social crisis, with a constituency of readers such as that associated with the New Masses, could only be resolved – if resolution on a policy level was even possible – through debate and practice.

Moreover, the issue in dispute was hardly a sectarian or a nonliterary one; the crux was a frank confrontation of the dilemma of selection criteria, a matter of concern to all journals but usually masked behind a powerful editor's claim to "taste." The New Masses' construction of an editorial board for the Literary Supplement embodying a range of perspectives on criteria, and the aggressive encouraging of readers to voice opinion on policy, constituted an experiment in democracy rare for any journal in the United States with the caliber of writers available to the New Masses. The sectarian and bizarre elements of the discussion were generated by the obligation of professing allegiance to the Soviet Union and the belief that Communism was "good news." This led to the contributions being somewhat deformed by the need of the authors to ritualistically disassociate themselves from any taint of suspected "Trotskyism," and to coordinate their arguments around a premise of proving optimism in poetry that was very often arranged around other aesthetic and emotional priorities.

To what extent did either side hold the superior theory in terms of conjoining culture with revolutionary practice? Ironically, both Gregory and Hicks were less than two years away from breaking with the Party at the time of their debate; the announcement of the Hitler-Stalin Pact in August

1939 became the vehicle for them as well as Crichton and Cowley to sever connections. This indicates that no formal "position" in the literary debate was objectively more conducive to Party loyalty. Such an abrogation of ideological predestination runs counter to the retrospective illusion that final events in a sequence are always the logical results of earlier behavior. The evolution of Hicks and Gregory was the outcome of numerous components of the force field of the cultural Left.

Moreover, neither man's cultural orientation was particularly decisive for the quality of literature that was promoted in their respective forums. The New Masses continued to publish significant poets, along with lesser figures, although some of the poetry selected (for example, by Zukofsky and Rexroth) would not be regarded by future scholars as their consequential work. While a number of the figures associated with Gregory's New Letters evolved to become productive and influential, their success was linked to a very different period in cultural life. His collection is less known today than Hicks and Gold's 1935 Proletarian Literature in the United States, and Gregory's own poetic reputation remains firmly rooted in his Communist works.

What may be more significant for understanding the force field of Left writing is that the blows in the Communist Press – struck by Gold, Forsythe, and readers who claimed to speak for the working class – intimidated and paralyzed the opposition within the Communist-led cultural institutions. Even though the quantity of these assaults was not great, it is surprising how quickly Gregory's side gave in through failing to fight back in their own letters to the editor after the initial exchanges, and then by withdrawing their own poetic contributions. Clearly these writers did not wish to subject themselves to charges of being elitist and anti-working class, despite the efforts of certain editors, like Sillen, to maintain a pluralistic balance.

Weinstock furnished an astute criticism – one that remained unanswered – when he asked why the insistence of a few individuals that their own demand for anti-intellectual poetry also represented the voice of "the common people," should be taken either as genuine or as necessarily a class-conscious attitude. In part, the answer to Weinstock's query lies in the Left's oversimplified correlations of its own Communist Party with the objective interests of the working class, the Soviet Union with world socialism, and of literature with a "weapon." A surfeit of oversimplified propositions became the groundwork of the movement's shared outlook, creating a subculture in which demagoguery about "the people" was seductive as well as terrorizing. That is, among the Left-wing audience one might claim to represent the point of view of the working people, or some especially oppressed group, and simply attack a complex or difficult artistic statement on the grounds that it was not immediately accessible to oneself. If the author of the statement was not himself or herself a bona fide proletarian, or member of an oppressed group, it would be difficult to reply. Consequently, in a peculiar way, the "cultural capital" and "symbolic capital" of the Left could too often be anti-intellectual posturing.

Guy Endore. An eccentric Communist for several decades, Endore produced singular novels in diverse genres such as mystery, horror, and popularized biography, while also pursuing a career as a Hollywood screenwriter, until he was blacklisted in the McCarthy era. (Courtesy of Marcia Endore Goodman)

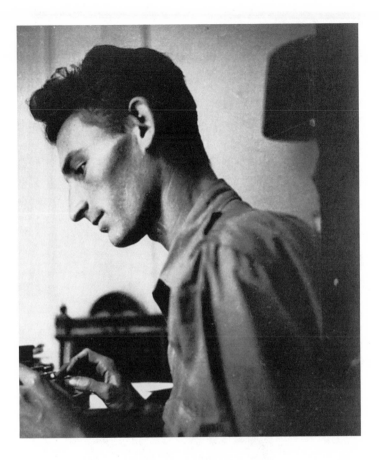

Top left: Don West. A Communist organizer in the Deep South, West was a prolific poet in the plain style of the worker-writer tradition, infusing his ballad-like forms with regional themes. (Courtesy of George Weissman)

Bottom left: Joseph Kalar was a promising proletarian poet in the late 1920s and early 1930s. (Courtesy of Richard Kalar)

Above: Edwin Rolfe, described by a friend as "a Jewish replica of Keats," was a poet who volunteered for service in Spain with the Abraham Lincoln Brigades. (University of Illinois Library)

Above: John Dos Passos and Michael Gold, collaborators in the New Playwrights Theater in the mid-1920s. (University of Michigan)

Top right: Two portraits of Michael Gold, a colorful personality and avant-garde playwright of the 1920s who transformed himself into a symbol of Communist proletarian rectitude in the 1930s. (Courtesy of Gold family)

Bottom right: Michael Gold and his brothers, George and Manny, also members of the Communist Party. (University of Michigan)

Top left: Alexander Trachtenberg, founder of International Publishers and an authoritative adviser in Communist Party cultural matters. (Courtesy of International Publishers)

Bottom left: Claude McKay, the first pro-Communist African American poet of major stature. (Courtesy of Carl Van Vechten Collection, Yale University)

Above: Langston Hughes, a leading poet, fiction writer, and playwright of his generation, was sympathetic to Communism and the Soviet Union from the late 1920s into the Cold War years. (Courtesy of Carl Van Vechten Collection, Yale University)

Left: Richard Wright launched his literary career as an ardent Communist poet in the early 1930s. After turning to fiction, he moved to New York City, where he served on the *Daily Worker* staff and then became disaffected from Communist Party policy during World War II. (Yale University Library)

Above: Eugene Clay Holmes, a Communist Party member who taught at Howard University, sometimes publishing under the name "Eugene Clay." (Moorland-Spingarn Research Center of Howard University)

Above: Meridel Le Sueur, an active Communist Party member throughout her life, whose work was responsive to gender and class oppression. (Courtesy of Tilson family)

Top right: Horace Gregory, a leading poet of the 1930s and literary editor for the pro-Communist *New Masses*. (Courtesy of Patrick Gregory)

Bottom right: Granville Hicks, an English professor and Communist Party member frequently embattled for his approach to Marxist literary criticism. (Syracuse University Library)

Left: Two portraits of V. J. Jerome. An aspiring
poet and playwright, Jerome rose to become head
of the Communist Party's Cultural Commission
and served a prison sentence under the Smith Act
in the McCarthy era. (Courtesy of the Marxist
Center for Reference Studies)

Above: Francis Winwar. A popular novelist and
biographer, Winwar was an independent radical
first married to longtime Communist cultural
leader V. J. Jerome and then to Bernard
Grebanier, a Communist English professor-
turned-informer. (Courtesy of Jerry Winwar)

Above: Joseph Freeman, poet, Don Juan, and *New Masses* editor in the 1930s. (University of Michigan)

Top right: A. B. Magil, the son of a Hebrew scholar in Philadelphia, became a full-time Communist Party journalist and functionary. (Courtesy of A. B. Magil)

Middle right: A self-portrait by Herman Spector, an avant-garde Left poet in the late 1920s and early 1930s who reworked forms and themes of the High Modernists. (Courtesy of Synergistic Press)

Bottom right: Sol Funaroff, the guiding spirit of *Dynamo*, a pro-Communist journal of modern poetry, whose haunting verse invoked themes from Apollinaire. (Courtesy of Nathan Adler)

151

Above and right: Three portraits of Alfred Hayes, around 1930, 1940, and 1950. With Byronic aura and a penchant for hanging around pool halls, Hayes evolved from a Communist poet to a popular novelist, playwright, and writer for film and television. (Courtesy of Josephine Hayes Dean)

153

Top left: Genevieve Taggard, a prominent Left poet for three decades and professor at Sarah Lawrence College. (New York Public Library)

Bottom left: Ruth Lechlitner, a leading Left poet of the 1930s, was responsive to feminist and environmental concerns. (Courtesy of Anne M. Corey)

Above: Joy Davidman, poet, novelist, and film critic, was a Communist party member first married to pulp writer William Lindsay Gresham and later to Christian apologist C. S. Lewis. (Marion Wade Center, Wheaton College)

Above: Alain Locke, the eminent Howard University professor who was sympathetic to the Communist movement during the 1930s and 1940s. (Moorland-Spingarn Research Center of Howard University)

Top right: Arna Bontemps, author of revolutionary fiction during the 1930s. (Syracuse University Library)

Bottom right: Sterling Brown, a major U.S. poet who was sympathetic to the Communist Party during the 1930s. (Moorland-Spingarn Research Center of Howard University)

Above: Margaret Walker, a Communist Party member in Chicago during the late 1930s who became a leading writer of her generation. (Courtesy of Carl Van Vechten Collection, Yale University)

Right: William Attaway was a Communist Party member and author of brilliant radical novels who turned to writing music arrangements, screenplays, and television scripts. (Courtesy of Carl Van Vechten Collection, Yale University)

Above: Ralph Ellison, author of Marxist fiction and criticism during the late 1930s and early 1940s. (Library of Congress)

Right: John Malcolm Brinnin, a young Communist poet in Detroit who became an influential critic and anthologist. (University of Delaware Library)

Muriel Rukeyser in Hollywood about 1937.
Rukeyser was a pro-Communist poet in the 1930s
who never abandoned her early commitment to
social justice. (Courtesy of William Rukeyser)

# Yogis and Commissars

## Love and Revolution

In the title essay of the 1945 collection *The Yogi and the Commissar*, Arthur Koestler (1905–1983), a former Communist Party member turned novelist, posits two extremes betwixt which the conscious intellectual must negotiate a course. At one end the Yogi represents self-absorption to the point of passivity; at the other the Commissar stands for ruthless immersion in the world of action to the stage of losing moral autonomy. Koestler by no means promotes the latter over the former, nor suggests that intellectuals can or should be free of either impulse. Rather, his aim is to render the reader cognizant of one's own drift. If the cultural historian could simply divide mid-century U.S. Left cultural workers into the pristine polarities of uncontaminated artists seduced by power-hungry political automatons, matters would indubitably be simplified. Yet the record, for those who seem to have been victimized by the Communist Party as well as those alleged to have done the victimizing, rarely lends itself to such unalloyed archetypes.

The Communist Party official most visibly guiding cultural policy from the mid-1930s to the early 1950s appears in many memoirs and studies to be a stone's throw from the "Commissar" end of the spectrum, a rigid, bureaucratic personality maladroitly superimposed on the temperament of a man ultrasensitive to art and poetry.[1] V. J. Jerome (Jerome Isaac Romain [1896–1965]), was born in a Russian-Polish shtetl in Lodz, and at the age of nine joined his parents in England, where he went to high school.[2] In 1915 he disembarked in New York City at nineteen and worked his way through several years at the City College of New York doing odd jobs. Already radicalized, he was equally enthralled by modern art and drawn to the Imagist poets of England and the United States, with H.D. and Richard Aldington as his favorites.[3] He dropped out of college when he married Frances Winwar in 1919. She, too, was Left-wing, having contributed poetry to the *Masses*. Their son was named "Germinal," after Zola's novel.[4] At the time of his marriage, Jerome used the last name "Roman"; he later changed it to Romain, and other relatives used the name Roram (including his younger brother,

Nathan) or Rourman. In the early 1920s Jerome worked as a bookkeeper for the International Ladies Garment Workers Union. In 1924 he joined the Communist Party. That year he was divorced from Winwar; she left him for an aspiring concert pianist, Bernard Grebanier (1903-1977), who would also join the Communist Party in the next decade. Winwar herself was a distinguished figure on the Left in the 1920s and 1930s.

Born in Sicily in 1900, she had come to the United States in 1907. Her father was a singer, Domenico Vinciguerra, brought to New York by the family of the wealthy State Department luminary, Christian Herter. Vinciguerra thought he had been transported to the United States to pursue his singing career, but soon learned that he was to serve as a handyman on Herter's Long Island estate.[5] His daughter, Frances, who had raven hair and dark eyes, and delicately classical features, weighed one hundred and ten pounds and was precisely five feet tall. In the 1920s, she published articles on culture under the name Frances Vinci Roman.[6] Adoring music and painting, she became co-founder of the Leonardo da Vinci Art School in New York. While pulling close to the Communist movement at times, she stayed an independent Marxist throughout the 1930s. After marrying Grebanier, she initiated an exceptional career writing in many genres, beginning with historical romances. *The Ardent Flame* (1927) and *The Golden Round* (1928) are novels set in the thirteenth century; others are set in Massachusetts, Sicily, and France. She was even better known for her popular biographies, usually sentimentalized, of famous artists. Many of these featured collective protagonists: Dante Gabriel Rossetti and Algernon Swinburne in *Poor Splendid Wings* (1933); Byron, Shelley, and Keats in *The Romantic Rebels* (1935); and William Wordsworth, Dorothy Wordsworth, and Samuel Taylor Coleridge in *Farewell the Banner* (1938). Other of her fictionalized biographies were of Oscar Wilde, Walt Whitman, George Sand, Joan of Arc, Elizabeth Barrett Browning and Robert Browning, Gabriele D'Annunzio, Edgar Allan Poe, and Jean-Jacques Rousseau.

During the Depression, Winwar was engrossed in the League of American Writers from 1936 to 1939, serving on its Executive Committee, National Council, and other bodies. In 1936 Winwar published a commentary on the life of suffragist Susan B. Anthony in the Popular Front publication *Woman Today*.[7] She resigned from the league in 1939, along with Grebanier, who had served as the chair of the New York chapter and taught at the New York Writers School. After divorcing Grebanier in the 1940s, she married twice more. Continuing to publish through the 1960s without evidencing any more radical political sympathies, Winwar developed senile dementia in the

1970s and vanished from the public eye until news of her death was reported in July 1985.

Grebanier, whose only marriage was to Winwar, was born in New York City and in 1926 began teaching as an instructor at Brooklyn College; he lasted there until his retirement in 1964. Grebanier persevered in playing the piano and also became a collector of paintings, sculptures, tanagras, intaglios, and vases, which he acquired during many trips to Europe, especially to Italy. Renowned for his wit, as well as his obesity, both of which recalled Samuel Johnson, he wrote numberless scholarly books on English literature and theater, directing several off-Broadway plays as well. Grebanier's scholarly reputation rested primarily in the field of Shakespeare, where he produced decidedly anti-Freudian studies.

During the Depression, Grebanier became an activist in the Teachers Union and joined the Communist Party in 1935, leaving in 1939. The gay poet Harold Norse (b. 1916 as Harold Albaum), a literature student and Communist activist at the time, recalled Grebanier as "a leviathan of a man whose resonant bass voice and flamboyant manner kept the students enthralled" even as he "heaped scorn on those who rejected the Communist faith." Yet,

> a less unlikely Stalinist . . . would be hard to find. In mustard corduroy suits with silk foulards beneath many chins, and three or four massive rings on each pudgy hand, which he flourished in sweeping gestures as he bellowed his epigrams. . . . He minced about in quick little steps that gave his gargantuan frame the aspect of a gaudy hippopotamus.[8]

In 1940 Grebanier reluctantly became an informer during the Rapp-Coudert investigation of Communists at Brooklyn College. While he later contended that the hostile reaction on the campus to his "naming names" destroyed "seventeen years of happy marriage," there is evidence that it was already unraveling due to personal conflicts.[9]

In December 1925, the twenty-nine-year-old V. J. Jerome was single again and began a relationship with the forty-six-year-old Rose Pastor Stokes (1879–1933), at one time a leading socialist and now an important Communist recently divorced from the millionaire reformer Graham Stokes.[10] Rose Pastor Stokes found Jerome "so rare and fine a spirit that it would take more than human will to resist his appeal."[11] They were secretly married in February 1927. Stokes obtained nothing from her divorce settlement, and for three years she and Jerome had custody of his son while both took temporary jobs at minimal wages. Jerome usually worked in sales, variously selling insurance, advertising space, and printing. After 1930, Stokes became stricken with cancer and Jerome's son was returned to his mother. When Stokes's fatal illness was diagnosed, Jerome immersed himself in raising funds for her treatment, which included the removal of a breast and a trip alone to Germany in 1932. This was hazardous for a Jewish Communist at the time, but indispensable to receive radiation treatment. Just before her departure she begged Jerome to help her commit suicide because of her unbearable pain, and on board the ship she wrote a letter reproaching Jerome for his refusal to cooperate.[12]

Stokes's death in Germany elicited an outpouring of anguish that Jerome communicated to his and Rose's intimate friend, the poet and novelist Olive Tilford Dargan (1869–1968, who after 1932 used the pen name Fielding Burke). He graphically described Rose's transformation from a beauty filled with vitality and nobility into "a broken, cancerous body with a shaven head anguishing upon a hospital cot – and then gray ashes in an urn."[13] In June 1933 these ashes were returned to the United States and displayed on the platform of a massive Party-sponsored memorial meeting. They were then placed in the safe of the Communist attorney Joseph Brodsky until a decision could be made as to how the Party might make use of them; but at some point during the 1930s Jerome privately retrieved her ashes and their fate remained a mystery to Stokes's biographers.[14] From Stokes's death until his own, Jerome unsuccessfully tried to find a writer who might complete and publish Stokes's autobiography-in-progress. It was finally brought out in unfinished form in 1992.[15]

Jerome had earned a B.A. at New York University in 1930, but he had yet to find a focus for his writing. In her terminal days, Rose Stokes successfully tried to temper his style. She urged him to write always as if he were addressing workers, simply and directly: "After you've written long and involved sentences, cut them up mercilessly. Try to see a concrete image of what you have set down in writing. Revise, revise until it is simple and clear."[16] Jerome had been thrilled by Stokes's poem "Paterson,"[17] which he described in a letter as "a symphony of sullenness, of fist-clenchings, of crouching for the pounce. It is the victor of tomorrow speaking to the victor of today."[18] His initial objective was to write poetry, fiction, and drama carrying forward the spirit he detected in Stokes's verse.

## A Pen Dripped in Vitriol

Jerome's chance to rise to national visibility, however, came not through writing imaginative literature but through his onslaught against the work of the fellow-traveling New York University philosophy professor Sidney Hook (1902–89). Communist journalist Sender Garlin, who knew both Hook

and Jerome personally, was confident that it was Jerome alone who instigated the attack, and that Party leader Earl Browder was in the early stages
anxious to find a means to allow Hook a way out. In an undated letter, Jerome
told Stokes of his plan to write a reply to an article by Hook, "Towards the
Understanding of Karl Marx," that had originally appeared in the *Symposium*, an academic journal sponsored by New York University.[19] Hook had
told Jerome, who was auditing Hook's class on Marxism, that the appearance
of the essay was an example of "boring from within," but Jerome wasn't
convinced: "it's to decide this question that I'm dipping my pen in vitriol."
His use of "vitriol" suggests *a priori* antagonism toward Hook, but Jerome
assured Stokes that his object was to clarify theory, not to attack personalities, and that he was writing without any particular publication in mind,
although he assumed that his essay would be submitted to a Communist
journal in the United States, Germany, or the Soviet Union. He also saw
the essay charging Hook with "revisionism" as part of a larger project that
would go beyond Hook to include V. F. Calverton and Edmund Wilson. "At
last I feel that I'm finding myself in the movement in writing, even more
than teaching. For I have always wanted to plunge into Marxian philosophy,
but the impetus for polemics was lacking."[20] To Dargan he in like fashion
wrote of his Hook essay:

> Please remember that there is nothing "ad hominem" about the attack.
> The matter is purely a question of ideological struggle. It is only because
> this struggle is so vital to us – for it represents zealous guardianship on
> our part of the basic principles of the revolutionary movement against
> adulteration and weakening – that the ideological disputes are for us no
> mere abstract, scholastic disputations, but a life and death conflict.[21]

There would endure a brutality in Jerome's prose polemics; they rank among
the strongest pieces of evidence in the cultural Left in the United States for
the existence of a kind of thinking parallel to that of Stalinist cultural thugs
such as Andrei Zhdanov.[22]

Following publication of Jerome's censure of Hook in the January 1933
issue of the *Communist*, which played a crucial role in fostering Hook's disaffection from the Party, Jerome was asked to collaborate with Sam Don,
editor of the *Communist*, with the consequence that he would be associated
with the *Communist* for the next two decades.[23] This assignment prompted
a comprehensive switch in his focus away from the creative writing that he
had already inaugurated toward polemical scholarship.

Jerome, like Rose Pastor Stokes, who had been the spokesperson for the
Negro Commission of the U.S. Communist movement in 1922 at the Fourth

Congress of the Communist International in Moscow, was much inspired by historical and contemporary instances of African American resistance to racism. He had published several poems on the subject in the early Depression and he was working on a play about the rebel slave Nat Turner (1800–1831). One poem, "Newsboy," features an African American worker speaking in Jerome's rendition of "Black dialect"; the African American urges a newspaper boy, who is yelling sensational and misleading headlines, to voice the truth about the urgency for Black and white workers to fight fascism. The piece evolved into a popular play performed by the Communist-led American League Against War and Fascism.[24]

An example also showing Jerome's use of "Black dialect" is the sentimental, idealized "A Negro Mother to Her Child," which appeared on the cover of the August 1931 issue of *The Rebel Poet* along with a powerful lithograph of a lynching under the stars and stripes:

Quit yo' wailin' honey bo'
'Taint no use to cry
Rubber nipple, mammy's breast
Both am gone bone dry.

Daddy is a bolshevik
Locked up in de pen
Didn't rob nor didn't steal
Led de workin' men.

What's de use mah tellin' you
Silly li'l lamb
Gon'ter git it straight some day
When you is a man.

Wisht ah had a sea o' milk
Mek you strong an' soun'
Daddy's waitin' til you come
Brek dat prison down.[25]

Two years later, however, Jerome wrote to Dargan that the months of labor he had spent on the anti-Hook piece had meant shelving the drama about Turner. Twenty years afterward, in prison, Jerome would still be haunted by a desire to finish the play.[26] Moreover, Jerome's view of workers in struggle, especially African Americans and women, never evolved from the highly idealized and romanticized imagery of his early work. When Party member Howard Fast's *Spartacus* came out in 1951, Jerome waxed enthusiastic in a letter to the author:

How glad I am to see women presented not alone as comforters to their men, but ready and able to fight actively side by side with them, expecting no special consideration. Wasn't it always so among the enslaved men and working classes, and haven't we today the Rosalie McGees, the Amy Mallards, and the Elizabeth Gurley Flynns?[27]

Franklin Folsom recalled Jerome as a small, short, round-shouldered man with a circular face, thick glasses, and a troubled but kindly face. He seemed to be always thinking of higher things, "a wonderful, sweet guy who could be an awful pill" because he could be so "overly zealous about the fine points." At times he performed like a martinet on behalf of the Party's Central Committee, and he could act pompous. Yet he could also be generous, and humorous anecdotes abounded about his forgetfulness. A popular story, told with a few variations, is about the time Jerome noticed his suitcase sitting in Party headquarters. Consequently he picked it up and went to Grand Central Station. Only after he got there did he realize that he had no idea where he was going, so he called the Party headquarters to get the information.

Jerome was apparently not cognizant that some Party members laughed at him behind his back. In response, others felt they had to be protective of him; they didn't want to wound his feelings. Among his traits that were mocked was the formal manner in which he frequently started a conversation: "May I intrude with an anecdote?" Jerome had acquired a British accent while he lived in London's East End, and used language that sounded archaic. Another of his characteristic expressions sometimes imitated was, "paradoxical as it may seem." He regarded himself as a scholar of English literature, and references to Dryden, Milton, and other English writers appeared throughout his rather tedious polemics such as *Culture in a Changing World: A Marxist Approach* (1947) and *Grasp the Weapon of Culture!* (1951).[28] Although it may well have cloaked a more complex individual residing within, Jerome's prose, public and personal, gave voice to the narrowest and simplest versions of Marxism, and his scholarship, even if genuine, seemed leaden. More troubling, Jerome seemed to become more mechanical rather than subtler over time.

His 1933 essay "Toward a Proletarian Novel" offered intriguing perspectives, even if Jerome ultimately sought to force literary practice into categories designating how near or far an author allegedly was from the working class.[29] Characteristic of his literary criticism by the end of the decade was "Edmund Wilson: To the Munich Station," which indicts Wilson for providing "literary service to fascism." Wilson's crime, in addition to writing positively of Trotsky in the *New Republic*, is that he quotes Marx "to deny the truth that Marxism is the scientifically formulated theory and practice of the working class, *made operative through the leadership of the Communist Party*" (emphasis in original).[30] In *The Negro in Hollywood Films* (1950), Jerome addressed a crucial and neglected issue at length with a righteous anger appropriate to the issue of racism. Yet he is relentlessly negative in his bashing of recent films that might at least be the incipient stages of a new direction. Further, in a like manner he attacks Party writers who were more sanguine than himself about the capacity of Hollywood film to use artistry to play an increased positive role. In a 1953 letter to Howard Fast, Jerome angrily reprimanded Fast's draft novel about Sacco and Vanzetti for its complimentary literary portrait of then Professor of Criminal Law Felix Frankfurter in the 1920s: "Is this the same being who today, as Justice of the Supreme Court, has condemned to death the Sacco and Vanzetti of 1953 – Ethel and Julius Rosenberg?" Jerome compared Fast to Joseph Freeman, who, in *An American Testament*, had tried to write of Max Eastman in the 1920s without retrospectively judging the earlier Eastman by his relation to the Communist Party in the late 1930s.[31]

Franklin Folsom wrote that Jerome often acted "rather like a Jesuit or Talmudist" in regard to Marxist icons. He reminisced that Jerome "could always point to a classical text that supported his point of view – a method of citing authority that was not always helpful to writers finding their way in a complex world different from the world in which classical authors had lived."[32] In 1981, puzzling over a reference to Jerome's *Grasp the Weapon of Culture!* as the U.S. government's only example of an "overt act" cited at Jerome's Smith Act trial, *Nation* editor Victor Navasky quipped: "today it seems less calculated to inspire action than somnolence."[33] Jerome's short autobiographical novel of his childhood, however, *A Lantern for Jeremy* (1952), displayed an unexpected capacity for simple, lyrical writing.[34]

Sender Garlin felt that Jerome was an inappropriate choice to be a cultural leader. He was simply "not supple enough for that kind of post." Jerome seemed to think that dealing with the problems of artists was similar to intervening in a longshoremen's strike. Jerome would talk of the "purity and integrity of Marxism" so that one could "almost see the Virgin Mary." He was unquestionably esteemed and needed by many in the Party, but not personally liked, except by a few writers such as John Howard Lawson. Garlin recalls that when Jerome first emerged on the scene as a Party writer he called himself "V. I. Jerome," but underwent so much ribbing for the obviously vain reference to V. I. Lenin that he switched the V. I. to V. J.[35]

Among the reasons that Jerome rose so quickly in the Communist literary movement, as in his ascendancy to editorship of the *Communist* and assignment as head of the cultural commission, were his association with Rose Pastor Stokes and also the Party leadership's assessment that other writers, such as Gold and Freeman, could not be deemed organizationally reliable. Thus an intellectual such as Jerome, although he lacked the formal academic credentials of several members with Ph.D.'s and the national popularity of a Mike Gold, could compensate by providing stability and invoking self-discipline. In 1936 Jerome further proved his mettle as an organizer when he was sent to Hollywood to consolidate a Party branch there. In the Left film community he acquired additional respect as a fund-raiser.

From 1935 until 1955 Jerome edited the Party's theoretical journal, first called the *Communist* and later *Political Affairs*. His personal life improved as his political fortunes grew. For a while he lived with the Party activist Ann Rivington, and in Hollywood he had an affair with the Communist writer Viola Brothers Shore (1891–1970).[36] In 1937 he married Alice Hamburger, a much younger woman, who as "Alice Evans" was executive secretary of the Left-wing New Theater League. They had two sons, their first names Carl and Frederick in honor of Marx and Engels. Eventually Alice became director of the Park Nursery School, having a special interest in autistic children. During the McCarthy era she was fired and blacklisted after taking the Fifth Amendment before an investigating committee. In the same year as his marriage to Alice, Jerome was appointed head of the Communist Party's cultural commission.

## The St. Augustine of Communism

For a small number of intellectuals, Jerome inspired great admiration. Historian Herbert Aptheker regarded Jerome as his "teacher," and was thrilled by praise from Jerome.[37] James Aronson, the talented journalist and editor of the *National Guardian*, gave a personal tribute to Jerome after he died:

> The man with the eternal briefcase and the thoughtful face ... when he approached you, with his furrowed brow and purposeful look – if you did not know him you would be sure he was inviting you to join a conspiracy of gargantuan proportions. In actual fact, he wanted to tell you of a most touching poem he had just read in an obscure quarterly which sang truth to the people. He was a most gentle revolutionary. He had such a deep respect for learning.... He had the strength born of conviction that steeled his soul and mind for six decades. And he carried his lantern with the never-ending curiosity of the youth he ever was.[38]

The painter Rockwell Kent (1882–1971) and the poet Alfred Kreymborg (1883–1966) were enthusiastic about Jerome's polemic against intellectuals who balked at the Hitler-Stalin pact, even though it now reads as a crude and self-righteous piece of writing that defamed many former Party allies, who were still Left liberals, as lackeys of Western imperialism and war-mongers.[39] Another admirer was the poet Archibald MacLeish (1892–1982), who at the time of the Moscow Trials wrote to Jerome, "I wish you were here to answer with your clarifying skill the questions about the new Moscow trial that plague me."[40] Although Mike Gold had engaged in bitter polemics with MacLeish in 1933, Jerome published a sympathetic apprecia-tion of MacLeish's play *Panic* in 1935.[41] As late as the spring of 1939, MacLeish was still praising Jerome's broadsides against his old enemy Edmund Wil-son and others in the *New Masses*, insisting that "my admiration for his [Jerome's] scholarship increases from day to day."[42] Then MacLeish pulled back from his fellow-traveling stance at the word of the Hitler-Stalin Pact, and Jerome singled him out for extended attacks by name in *Intellectuals and the War* (1940).

Samuel Putnam (1892–1950) was an outstanding translator and former ex-patriate who authored the memoir *Paris was Our Mistress* (1947). Joining the Communist Party in the mid-1930s, he contributed to the *New Masses* and then became a regular reviewer for the *Daily Worker* with his own column in the 1940s. Putnam also adored the "intellectual companionship" of Jerome, and remarked that he, like others, "loved to watch your mind at work." He reported to Jerome in early 1944 that his young son, Hilary, later a leading philosopher at Harvard University, "fairly lives on the sustenance that he gets from his talks with you." However, only a year later Putnam underwent a disillusionment and came to the conclusion that "out of misguided hu-mility [he] had forced himself to live in the stifling atmosphere of the party line with all its ruthless intolerance for the process of the mind."[43]

The Left-wing journalist I. F. Stone (1903–1989), however, made no secret of his opinion that he found Jerome's cultural leadership "offensive." In an early 1950s letter declining to sponsor a rally on behalf of Jerome during his Smith Act trial, Stone confessed, "I'd feel like a stultified ass to speak at a meeting for Jerome without making clear my own sharp differences with the dogmatic, Talmudic, and dictatorial mentality he represents. I intend to go on defending him as a Smith Act victim but I can't pretend he's a libertarian."[44]

A characteristic piece by Jerome was his 1937 essay in *The Communist*, "Marxism-Leninism for Society and Science," reviewing the first year of the journal *Science & Society*.[45] It constitutes a tedious checklist of pros and cons of the different articles held up against Jerome's model of orthodoxy. This type of work steadily encroached on his literary scholarship. After a few book reviews published in the 1930s, there was a hiatus in his writing on literature until he projected a full-scale survey of the novel in the United States in the mid-1940s, but this never got beyond the outline stage.[46]

Some evidence of political disquiet on Jerome's part surfaced during the late 1940s and early 1950s. In 1949 Jerome expressed some criticisms of William Z. Foster's article, "The Fascist Phase of Imperialism," scheduled to be published in *Political Affairs,* and he requested permission from Foster to publish some comments along with it. Foster replied that such a move would only confuse the Party: "Either the article, with necessary amendments, is correct and should be published; or it is wrong and should not be published." Jerome then made an unsuccessful proposal to the National Committee of the Party to halt publication of the article.[47] Between November 1953 and January 1954, Jerome complained to the Administrative Committee of the Party that decisions involving *Political Affairs* were being made without him, and he finally resigned as editor, requesting that his name be removed from the masthead.[48]

In 1951, shortly after taking the Fifth Amendment in testimony before the House Un-American Activities Committee, Jerome was arrested together with twelve other Communist Party leaders and charged with violating the Smith Act (allegedly advocating the overthrow of the government). In the summer of 1951, Jerome and the pro-Communist novelist Dashiell Hammett (1894–1961), who had refused to name names in an earlier investigation, were imprisoned together at the Federal House of Detention in New York.[49] Soon Jerome was put on trial as one of the twenty-one so-called secondary Communist Party leaders indicted under the Smith Act. After a nine-month litigation, he was convicted of conspiracy to teach and advocate the overthrow of the U.S. government, and in 1955 he began his jail sentence. He was released in 1957.

Jerome and Frances Winwar had remained cordial after their 1924 divorce and followed each other's literary work, exchanging inscribed copies of books and pamphlets. When a Department of Justice representative approached Winwar for a five-hour interview about Jerome, she acknowledged that he was a Communist but insisted that he was a fine person with whom she had shared an "interest in victims of police brutality." In a subsequent interview with the FBI, she declared that Jerome was essentially a scholar and "the St. Augustine of Communism."[50] While Jerome was in prison, Winwar sent money to Alice Jerome.

Jerome had written poetry while he was in court, and in prison he became more preoccupied with ideas for creative literature, criticism, and historical analysis than with immediate political issues.[51] His first son recalled that "my father always regarded himself as a creative writer," but his biggest problem "was relinquishing a manuscript that had room in the margin for further revision. I have never known such a painstaking lapidarian of prose, far closer in spirit to Flaubert and Lafcadio Hearn than to the insatiable agitprop machine." Over the years Jerome had abandoned many works in progress and often dreamed of new ones but never acted on his dreams. In prison he recalled an artist friend in London

> who worked simultaneously, that is, intermittently on half a dozen can-
> vases with pencil and brush, turning from one to the other as the mood
> gripped him. That is how I have been feeling in the recent period with
> the tugs of the mind alternating from the essay on historiography, to the
> project on humanism, and thence to the Nat Turner play (still a dream),
> and beyond to the theme of the origin of Christianity.

He began to dread the thought of dying without completing his projects.[52]

Part of his inspiration for this new creative upsurge came from pouring over old classics from the prison library such as *Pride and Prejudice, The Scar-let Letter, Jude the Obscure, Jane Eyre,* and *Tom Brown's School Days,* and from conversing with other inmates while working in the prison plumbing shop and mopping: "What deep, buried mines of humanity are here."[53] His wife reported to Albert Maltz that even though Jerome enjoyed such work, as well as helping to prepare prison Passover services and playing on the prison chess team, his health seemed to be deteriorating.[54]

Throughout the 1930s and 1940s Jerome was tediously unstoppable in finding political deviations in the writing and literary views of others; how-ever, he was an equally severe critic of his own writing. For him, the central question was the possible political implications of a cultural argument or artistic image, which can clearly put a brake on creativity and risk taking. Oddly enough, Jerome's private tastes ran toward modern art, a collection of which he maintained in his home, but his public posture on cultural matters was hardly distinguishable from the advocacy of two-dimensional Soviet Socialist Realism. This led Annette Rubinstein to conclude that he was an elitist; simply put, he felt that ordinary Party members and workers were not capable of appreciating advanced art in the manner that he was.[55]

Such a public stance hardly worked to his own advantage as a frustrated writer. In the early 1950s he drafted a poem, "Caliban," and circulated it to friends and associates for comment. His poem presents the view, not uncom-mon today, that *The Tempest,* particularly in its portrayal of the enslaved Caliban, is in part Shakespeare's apology for colonial expansion. Jerome's poem, however, is complicated by its reference to the African American Canada Lee's stage performance as Caliban, and the implications of producing the play during the Cold War atmosphere in which, for the first time, a Black actor portrayed this character. It was additionally significant for Jerome that the performer was Lee, because he brought to the role a Left-wing political consciousness.

In the literary discussion that ensued, Jerome received a taste of his own medicine. The African American Communist writer Lloyd Brown (b. 1913) declared the poem "politically wrong" for a combination of reasons. Brown held that efforts to make seventeenth-century plays responsible for contemporary racism, or in the case of *The Merchant of Venice*, anti-Semitism, were a misdirection of energy. He also reasoned that both the Soviet Union, which claimed to be the foremost "Shakespeare country" in terms of the number of readings and performances held there, and the international peace movement, based their moral claims on the humanist heritage of Shakespeare, Victor Hugo, and other "cultural giants," which validated the progressive fruits of the Shakespeare legacy.[56]

The Jewish Communist critic Sidney Finkelstein (1909-1974), who had an M.A. from Columbia University but spent the Depression working in the Brooklyn Post Office, was more generous to Jerome. He tried to make specific textual changes in Jerome's poem that would show Shakespeare in a more positive light, yet also reveal "that there were limits to his wisdom, things that even Caliban could teach him, that Caliban knew and Shakespeare didn't."[57] This was succeeded by an even more elaborate literary discussion of *The Tempest* and Jerome's poem, in which James Allen (Sol Auerbach, 1906-1990), a Communist Party specialist on African American history, launched a full-scale offensive against the draft poem, and Finkelstein intervened on Jerome's behalf.[58]

Clearly then, Jerome did not have a double standard when using a political yardstick to validate art; the cultural commissar applied standards to himself at least as rigorously as he did to others when scrutinizing the political implications of poetry, and it is hardly surprising that his productivity was so meager. Nevertheless, Jerome's Party post brought him perks; even while he defended Jerome's poem against what he saw as exaggerated and unfair criticisms, Finkelstein felt compelled to complain to Jerome that his own recent book, *How Music Expresses Ideas* (1952), had not yet been reviewed in *Political Affairs* (successor to *The Communist*), whereas "every time you write a pamphlet, you make sure it gets the most immediate and widespread attention."[59] In a letter to the Communist playwright and Hollywood screenwriter John Howard Lawson (1894-1977), to whom he also had sent his draft poem for comment, Jerome acknowledged that the discussion had caused him great "pain," in part because the criticisms made of the poem reflected "extrinsic" tensions; but he nevertheless felt that he had benefited from the criticism and finally published the poem in a special "Negro History Week" issue of *Masses & Mainstream*.

The final version is a marvelous meditation on the ambiguities of cultural production on multiple levels. The long poem is structured as a three-way colloquy among an observer of Lee's stage performance; words quoted from *The Tempest* and other plays by Shakespeare; and an italicized representation of thoughts attributed to Lee. The first stanzas show a harmony between the viewer's perception of Lee as a representative of colonially oppressed people, emerging from his "rock-bound ghetto," and Shakespeare's perhaps inadvertent representation of Prospero as "the white conqueror" demanding service. Then, while the viewer begins to identify Caliban as the "towering fore-shadow / of Red Cloud, / Toussaint, / Jaurez, / Nat Turner," Shakespeare begins to stack the deck by allowing Prospero to depict Caliban as a lying would-be rapist, and giving Caliban replies that appear to confirm the accusations. By the middle of the poem the stream-of-consciousness thoughts of the actor, Lee, dominate the page, the observer's perspective having dissolved completely into those of the Black protagonist. With quotes from Shakespeare now put at the service of the actor, to demonstrate hypocrisy and contradiction, a heroic effort is made to instruct the playwright of the implications of his creation:

> Undo your assent to Prospero,
> lest it be a comfort to the private civilizers
> who come with conquering tread on freemen's coasts –
> who come with trinkets, rum, and Bibles – and guns:
> for the Glory of God
> and the power of Spain
> and the vaults of the Virginia Company.
> Theirs are the roads to the silver mines of Potosí
> covered with Indian dead.
> Theirs the pledges broken, the treaties torn –
> by land-grabber, claim shark, empire builder,
> to the civilizers' war cry, "The savage must go!"
> Theirs the infamy:
> Africa raped –
> torn from birthland, herded in slave-ship, sold
> forced into the canefield and rice swamp,

branded, cropped, castrated,
hunted in the forests and the marsh.[60]

Jerome's poem emerged from the familiar tradition of Left-wing (often Jewish) writers using Black protagonists to fight liberation battles with universal implications. Yet the poem actually leaps forward several decades in cultural debate through Jerome's particular approach to the pivotal location, and intricacies, of subaltern representation.

Not only does Jerome address the ur-text of Shakespeare; he also conveys the context of theatrical depiction in an advanced capitalist society from the perspective of a politically conscious reader responding to the real or imagined signals emanating from an actor with an individualized identity beyond the stage. In the explicit merging of the poet-observer's vista with the one attributed to the Black actor, Jerome implicitly concedes the possibility of projection, and therefore opens the door to himself being interrogated and challenged in the manner that he cross-examines Shakespeare. At the same time, the riddle to be addressed is less focused on Jerome, Shakespeare, and Lee than on the production itself — on the power of art in new contexts to generate diverse meanings to which diverse audiences can relate even as they transcend the author's intent. Whatever his defects in orchestrating Communist policy, the Party's cultural commissar crafted a work of art in which the felicitous relation of form and content smoothly reveals a consciousness of its own production and its function as both a mediated and mediating cultural creation.

From the time Jerome assumed cultural leadership in the Communist Party and all the way through his prison experience, he asserted the view, which he averred to be "Leninist," that the Party must provide leadership in cultural policy, and that its special contribution should be political evaluations of the implications of a work and the views of its author. Naturally, it was hoped that Party cadre members who were artists might be able to make such judgments on their own or in consultation with other experienced members, rather than wait to be reprimanded in the Party press. For instance, in 1936 Jerome had written a poem "To Carl Sandburg," chastising what he saw as a lapse in the old radical poet's social consciousness; but when *The People, Yes* appeared that year, he withdrew his verse.[61] John Howard Lawson, like Jerome, dreamed of producing a "play on Negro life" called "Thunder Morning," the work he saw "closest to my heart." Yet in the face of critical comments he received from Jerome and others, Lawson felt that he had to continuously withdraw and rewrite it. At the time Lawson died, it was still unfinished.[62]

When Jerome emerged from prison in 1957, however, there was a change in his outlook. The dispute in the Party over the Khrushchev revelations was under way, and many Party members assumed that Jerome would ally with the more orthodox Foster faction. Instead, A. B. Magil was astounded to discover that Jerome identified at that point with the Eugene Dennis faction, which appeared at that moment to be headed toward a major democratization and "Americanization" of the Party without dissolving it altogether. On the street, Jerome told Magil that he no longer believed in a Party "line" for literature.[63] In a letter to Albert Maltz that same year, Jerome repudiated the Communist cultural policy of the past as employing the method of "fiat," which of course contradicted the Party's alleged goal of clarification by discussion.[64]

Jerome, however, departed for Poland in 1958 and did not participate in the internal Party fight that was reaching a climax, nor did his later public writing acknowledge any change of view.[65] From 1959 to 1961 he lived in Moscow and worked as an editor of Lenin's *Collected Works*. In 1962, back in New York, he began a novel based on the life of Spinoza. In 1963 creative work continued to obsess him, and he confessed to Walter Lowenfels that he had been too long "occupied with political and theoretical writing" which "drove the muse, like Hagar, into the wilderness."[66] He wrote to exiled American literary agent Maxim Lieber in Poland in 1963 that he was desperately looking for some part-time work that would allow him to write, and that his newest project was a historical novel.[67]

In 1965 Jerome underwent surgery for the removal of a brain tumor. The cancer had caused disorientation and the loss of sensation, vision, and motor power in his limbs. He also suffered depression, impairment in judgment, difficulty in concentrating, and a poor attention span, to the extent that he could no longer care for himself.[68] His domestic situation was complicated because three years earlier, his wife, Alice, and their two sons had broken from the Communist Party and joined the Maoist Progressive Labor Party, although the marriage itself was not disrupted. Jerome died later that year at the age of sixty-eight. His widow moved to Chicago, complaining to John Howard Lawson that the Communist Party was ignoring her proposals to circulate Jerome's sequel to *A Lantern for Jeremy*, entitled *The Paper Bridge* (1966).[69]

## The Red Valentino

If Jerome gravitated toward the role of Koestler's "Commissar" for most of his life, Joseph Freeman was something of an unhappy "Yogi" who, in his years of Party activism, and especially afterward, frequently pined for an increasingly idealized youth of untrammeled poetic expression and sensuality. His purge from the Communist movement in the late 1930s also gives him something of the glow of martyrdom, although none of his poetry and fiction addressing the emotional terrain of the committed writer have survived their time. Freeman is more commonly remembered as the person most associated with the *New Masses*, as editor and critic, during its rise as a potent cultural force in the United States. His own recollections, in letters and conversation, deeply shaped Daniel Aaron's discussion of the *New Masses* in *Writers on the Left*, as well as the work of other scholars after Aaron who independently examined Freeman's papers.

Yet, despite Freeman's obvious literary sophistication, his popularity among the circle of young *Dynamo* poets, and his assertion that he always stood for a more professional publication, he was mistrusted by many of his contemporaries in or around the Party and the broader Communist cultural movement. Freeman's narrative of events is the fullest and most compelling available, in part because no pivotal editor ever sat down to tell the entire history of the *New Masses*, providing supporting documentation. Freeman's version, however, like any other story, must be reexamined in the context of the storyteller's personality and perceptions.

Some who loved Freeman at the outset came reluctantly to regard him more critically as they witnessed him in action. Such was the case with one of Freeman's early protégés on the Left, A. B. Magil (b. 1905). Magil came from a lower-middle-class family in Philadelphia, where his father, Joseph Magil, was a self-employed Hebrew scholar. The senior Magil was the translator of the Pentateuch (five books of Moses) in English and Yiddish, and the editor of a prayer book that was used all over the world. His children became political activists; one of Magil's three older sisters, Rose, was among the few influential women in the Zionist movement in the United States. Magil also had a socialist brother-in-law who worked for a while as city editor of the *Call*.

Magil initially planned to become a writer, hoping to support himself as a high school teacher. While he was a student at the University of Pennsylvania, he took some education courses that disabused him of the latter notion. Meanwhile, he became increasingly drawn to the work of the Irish authors W. B. Yeats and J. M. Synge. He also met Harry Alan Potamkin (1900–1933), the future Marxist film critic, who was five years his senior and was involved in modernist cultural circles.[70] On one occasion, Potamkin invited the nineteen-year-old Magil to a reception for radical Jewish mystic and novelist Waldo Frank (1889–1967), where they sat on the floor with other admirers listening to him.

In 1924, while working as a camp counselor, Magil met Sender Garlin (1902–1999), a radical journalist from Glen Falls, New York, and the brother of one of the camp's owners. Both he and Magil adored the satiric wit of H. L. Mencken. Garlin, politically unaffiliated but already friends with Joseph Freeman, urged Magil to move to New York. After graduating from the University of Pennsylvania with a degree in English at the age of twenty, Magil did just that. He found a job as a copyeditor at *Women's Wear* magazine, and was soon following the disputes between socialists and Communists in the garment industry. Attracted to the Communists, he read the Yiddish Communist newspaper *Freiheit* (Magil was fluent as a writer and speaker of Yiddish). When the *Daily Worker* moved from Chicago to New York in 1927, Magil and Garlin began visiting its office, located in a dingy warehouse. Magil's only literary publications to date were a poem, "Johnny Madeiros Is Dead," about the six-year-old son of a textile striker drowned in a river after the boy was chased by a mounted policeman,[71] and a Yiddish translation in *Menorah Journal*. He soon metamorphosed into a revolutionary activist.

For several years he and Garlin considered themselves to be disciples of Freeman. But the more serious Magil became politically, the more troubled he became about Freeman's tenuous relation to the Communist Party. Freeman's notorious "Don Juanism" was only part of the dilemma. Freeman basically liked to do whatever he wanted to do and resisted political discipline. By the mid-1930s he also had a reputation for defending Party policies in discussions with Party supporters, while equivocating with people hostile to the Party, including those around the right-wing socialist *New Leader* such as Eugene Lyons, a militant anti-Communist whom Freeman had known when they had both worked for the Soviet news agency TASS in the late 1920s.

Magil's negative assessment of Freeman must be qualified because of the hyperorthodox loyalty to the Party leadership that he maintained until 1956. Even Magil's friends, including Garlin, a notorious mimic, joked about Magil as "the Rabbi" and "Straight-line Magil," nicknames prompted by his earnest appearance – he wore very heavy glasses, unusual at that time. Magil was always on call to undertake Party political assignments when needed – in Detroit in the 1930s, in the Middle East in the late 1940s, and in Mexico where he organized a Communist underground apparatus in the early 1950s. Whenever he visited the *New Masses* office, he had the aura of being "the Party Whip"; frequently he would hint that the opinions he held had evolved from discussions with Alexander Trachtenberg and V. J. Jerome.

Many others, from a variety of perspectives, also expressed reservations about Freeman's character and motives; such long-term doubts about Freeman's personal qualities assisted in making his outrageous purge in 1939 all the more palatable. In his voluminous correspondence of later years, Freeman depicted himself as utterly self-sacrificing to the "cause," not only in terms of his time but financially as well, and exploited and ultimately victimized because of his integrity. Various recollections and some documents suggest that Freeman was perpetually in difficulty because of his reckless and undependable behavior. Mike Gold recalled in an obituary for Freeman that, as an editor of the *New Masses*, "Joe had a wonderful way of sliding out of a situation and going to another city to write you a ten-page wonderful letter" in which he provided "all the theoretical ways of solving the particular hell-hole in which you and the magazine had suddenly been thrown by the dropping of some particular floor."[72] A note Freeman received from Bill Browder, the shrewd business manager of *New Masses* and younger brother of Earl Browder, sums up a common attitude toward him, held not just by Party functionaries: "You have a charming personality and that has probably saved your life many times."[73]

While Freeman would always maintain that he quit TASS in 1931 to go to Hollywood and then to join the *New Masses*, there is evidence that he did not leave TASS voluntarily. Freeman's first wife, the artist Ione Robinson, wrote her mother at the time conveying her great distress that Freeman had been "fired" by TASS director Kenneth Durant, whom Freeman had hitherto idolized.[74] The reasons were kept secret from Robinson, but it seems unlikely that they involved any doctrinal political disagreements with Soviet policy, since three Party leaders soon thereafter asked Freeman to join the *New Masses* editorial board. Freeman's own papers suggest that the unpleasantness at TASS may have been due to conflicts with his brother Harry.

Freeman also had antagonists in the John Reed Clubs, such as Conrad Komorowski (sometimes called "Comrade Conrad"), who accused Freeman of not doing as much as he could for the *New Masses* because he was too concerned with writing books and hanging out with big shots outside the Communist movement.[75] Walter Snow was another John Reed Club activist who had a lifelong dislike of Freeman.

Snow, whose Party name was "Robert Clark," was six feet tall and stick thin, with a round face and horn-rimmed glasses. In the 1920s he was a hobo and later a stage hand, but he drifted into journalism and then wrote pulp fiction, specializing in contributing to magazines like *Gang World*. He joined the Communist Party in the late 1920s, but dropped out in the early 1930s while remaining a Party loyalist in the John Reed Clubs. He rejoined the

Party in the years leading up to World War II. Decades later, after reading Aaron's *Writers on the Left*, Snow complained caustically to his step-son, the future historian Maurice Isserman, that Freeman "was a careerist and opportunist, a snobbish revolutionary bureaucrat." Much of Snow's rancor is aimed at Freeman's alleged privileged living conditions: "Freeman...always lived in swanky apartments – a huge skylighted studio in the Village and later Park Avenue swank.... Some argued that it was necessary to maintain Joe... in swank to entertain Corliss Lamont ([Lamont's] father then head of [the] House of Morgan) and other wealthy angels [a term for financial donors]. The Freemans offered a 'proper' New York home for Soviet foreign minister Maxim Litvinoff."[76]

If Snow's account is accurate, it goes directly against Freeman's own self-portrait in which he presents himself as a self-sacrificing movement activist. In reflecting on the *New Masses* crisis that had occurred in 1931, a few years after he and Snow had first met, Freeman avowed that he worked almost alone at the *New Masses* from 1931 to 1933. During those years, "I lived on nothing, worked day and night, broke my health and finally by the end of 1933 was ordered by the doctor to lay off."[77] It seems probable that there is exaggeration here on both sides.

Tiba Willner (1906-1999), the younger sister of Sender Garlin, who worked as promotion manager for the *New Masses* throughout much of the 1930s, adored Freeman as a person. She did not regard him as handsome in a conventional sense, as he had an unusual "Mongolian cast" to his eyes which some people liked and others didn't. Edward Dahlberg recalled that Freeman was "a good-looking youth, quite swarthy and soundly built, but later had a flaccid oleaginous face."[78] When novelist Albert Halper met Freeman in the early 1930s, he thought he had "an oily baboon face."[79] But Willner thought that when Freeman opened his mouth, "he was the most attractive man in the world."

He loved to gather young poets and writers around himself, and was a genius at talking to youthful audiences, displaying a wealth of information and making each person think that Freeman was addressing him or her personally.[80] In private, Freeman was a tremendous charmer; sweet, warm, kind, and able to talk about anything. He was also a woman chaser of the first order. He insisted to Sender Garlin, though, that he was not promiscuous, only "a variationist."[81] To Tiba he bragged that he had seduced a thousand women, and, although she was happily married, he pursued her from the time she was eighteen until she was fifty, after both had left the Party.

Freeman's first wife, Ione Robinson, wrote her mother, when she first met Freeman in Mexico in 1929, that "you would think he was a brother of

Rudolph Valentino by the shape of his head, and his eyes."[82] Almost from the outset of their brief marriage, however, Freeman's former and new girl-friends were omnipresent, sometimes living in the apartment, or else Free-man was away, communicating with his wife by telegram. There were also stories that Freeman had slept with a mistress of Joseph Stalin and that Ivy Litvinov (1890?–1977), the British-born writer married to the Soviet ambas-sador to the United States, was his inamorata as well. A number of literary figures in or around the Communist movement, including Genevieve Tag-gard and Ella Winter, had been his lovers. Winter reportedly broke off with him when she walked in on Freeman with another woman.[83]

Freeman married Charmion Von Wiegand (1898–1983) in 1934. She was the daughter of the conservative Hearst journalist Karl Von Wiegand, and a stu-dent of the artist Piet Mondrian. In the 1930s she became a painter, an art critic, and a representative of artists. The marriage lasted until Freeman's death, but neither partner adhered to conventional fidelity and they con-tinually fought.[84] Garlin remembered that Charmion tended to "belittle" Freeman in public, and her letters to her husband complain of being "emo-tionally starved." She protested Freeman's surrounding the couple with other women – some of whom were old girlfriends – with whom he was emotionally, and not infrequently sexually, involved; about his "explosions"; and about his pressuring her to obtain money from her father under false pretenses.[85] Such a tumultuous personal life unquestionably had political ramifications. Freeman himself attributed his bad relations with Max East-man to sexual competition between the two,[86] and Sender Garlin believed that some of the ill will directed toward Freeman in high Kremlin circles that produced the attack on *An American Testament* had similar origins.[87]

Despite her affection for Freeman, Tiba Willner was well aware of Free-man's unreliability. He was a man incapable of being on time for an appoint-ment with anyone. She believed that he even came late to his own father's funeral, an act that further incensed his brother Harry, a Communist Party patriot already antagonistic to Joseph, whom he called "mushmouth."[88] Franklin Folsom, executive secretary of the League of American Writers, considered Freeman a hard drinker, although not a drunk, who easily con-sumed a quart of whiskey a day. Sender Garlin, himself decried as a "kib-bitzer" by Alexander Trachtenberg, came to realize that Freeman couldn't be trusted by the Party hierarchy. Freeman would never be a foot soldier rising at 5:00 A.M., and "he certainly wasn't tough enough to cut a friend's throat." Although Garlin thought that Freeman was too intelligent to be a bohemian himself, he unabashedly enjoyed the company of bohemians.[89]

For those outside the Party, Freeman could, on occasion, appear to be something of an apparatchik. Halper recalled that during the visit of Soviet novelist Boris Pilnyak to the United States, "Freeman was the interpreter, agent, and Party watchdog for the unwary, doomed Soviet writer, staying at the talented Pilnyak's hotels, accompanying him to Hollywood, guiding and subtly directing his every move."[90] In May 1939, Freeman asked fellow traveler Maurice Hindus (1891–1969) on behalf of *Soviet Russia Today* to drop a paragraph from an article that sounded "needlessly pessimistic." Hindus went into a rage over this effort to tamper with his political analysis, telling Freeman, "It is entirely beneath your intelligence." Freeman, however, replied defensively that Hindus was needlessly expressing "so much indignation over so small a matter." Freeman would have been correct if his suggestion was minor and stylistic; but it was, in fact, a request for Hindus to conform politically.[91]

Freeman's popularity was indeed selective. Matthew Josephson, the historian and a fellow traveler of the Party until 1939, had been a Columbia University classmate of Freeman's, and confided privately to Sender Garlin that he had a longstanding dislike of Freeman.[92] Even the relatively mild mannered Granville Hicks had a stormy relationship with Freeman. In the fall of 1936, when the two were assigned to work together on the *New Masses*, Hicks reminded Freeman of a personal insult that Freeman had avowed in June of that year: Freeman, in defending his public criticisms of Hicks's *John Reed: The Making of a Revolutionary* (1936), had kept Hicks's rebuttals out of the *New Masses* and accused Hicks of lacking "the revolutionary's subordination of personal vanity in the face of truth." As a result, while Hicks would work together with Freeman to carry out common projects, he told Freeman that "the less I have to do with you personally, the better I shall like it."[93]

James T. Farrell's *A Note on Literary Criticism*, appearing in 1936, was an especially problematic book for the *New Masses* editors to review. It was clearly based on Marxist principles with which the editors agreed, yet relentless in its satirical attack on their practice. When Granville Hicks was fair minded enough to take precisely such a position acknowledging agreement on many fundamentals in his review of the book, Freeman sent a letter to Isidor Schneider complaining that Hicks should have argued that Farrell's "viewpoint is not that of a Marxist, though every specific idea he advances may be accepted by Marxists." The reason for this accusation was that Farrell had emphasized the "social" basis of literature more than its "class" basis. To Freeman, it was acceptable to use such a debater's trick to claim that Farrell's Marxist position was merely a liberal one, thereby evading the challenge of Farrell's book.[94]

What is telling about Freeman's response, in addition to his inaccurate characterization of Farrell's perspective, is that Freeman himself was frequently under political suspicion for being a "liberal." Just before he hurled the epithet at Farrell, Freeman had received an angry letter from a leading Communist, Israel Amter, accusing him of "the rottenest kind of liberalism with which our Party is struggling against."[95] Freeman had a tendency to shield himself from Left criticism by throwing the same kinds of charges at others, a practice that would come back to haunt him in 1939.

Stanley Burnshaw had a deep skepticism about Freeman that he retained for decades. When Burnshaw left the *New Masses,* he protested to business manager Bill Browder that "by bringing in four acolytes he was changing the staff of the *New Masses* to a kind of claque."[96] To Granville Hicks, Burnshaw further complained that Freeman had unnecessarily initiated a "personal feud" with him.[97] To novelist Christina Stead, he expressed the view that Freeman had his own faction and sought personal power.[98] Stead had been friends with Freeman, but had concluded that "he is an insatiable sensualist and such a man is absolutely disloyal, and neither men nor women really trust him in their hearts, although they may see with complaisance the agreeable parts of his personality."[99]

## A Divided Life

By the late 1930s, Freeman was certainly feeling uncomfortable, and he was perceived by friends and associates as trying to live a divided life. He had broad literary sensibilities, aspired to write philosophical poetry, desired a wide circle of friends and lovers, yet at the same time craved to be respected as the Communist Party's preeminent cultural spokesman. Later Freeman would conclude that he could never have achieved this goal because a transformation had occurred in the 1930s of which he had not been fully aware. The traditional Marxist view, which he attributed to Lenin, was that "the artist, the writer, the scientist must be won to communism in his own way, through the portals of his art or science." But by 1934, he believed, the view had been supplanted in leading Party circles by a much more manipulative approach. Freeman was haunted by an all-night meeting of the Party's cultural fraction, where Alexander Trachtenberg, once his strong advocate, allegedly rebuffed him by declaring, "Don't tell *us* how to handle the intellectuals. You're a rotten liberal." Although the remarks seem consistent with Trachtenberg's role as the specialist in exploiting cultural opportunities, Freeman was so devastated by the personal assault that he fell ill with a mysterious throat ailment and lost the use of his voice – his most potent feature – for several months.[100]

Still, Freeman never acceded to any interpretation that the Communist Party or the Soviet leadership dictated the *New Masses* literary policy, and to the end he insisted that he had never been forced to lie on behalf of the Party. He held to the formulation that the Communist Party played the role of "guiding" the *New Masses* in the 1930s.[101] He was also adamant against "the narrow notion that Left literature in the Thirties was solely the product of the Kharkov Conference or the John Reed Clubs or the *New Masses*. . . . We ought to see the picture in larger historic perspective."[102] What he meant was that world events pushed writers leftward in complex ways, all of which "led to the dominance on the 'cultural front' of radical writers, artists, directors, teachers, etc."[103] While the Communist Party certainly intervened in the affairs of and presented the prevailing strategy for the *New Masses*, Freeman nonetheless maintained that "the Left did not have to do very much to attract the intellectuals in the Thirties; reeling from the overwhelming shock of the Depression, most of them stormed the offices of the Left magazines and literary groups and begged, pleaded, wheedled and even *demanded* to be taken in!"[104]

Given Freeman's later conclusions about the deleterious effect of Stalinism on the Cultural Left in the United States, one might wonder if he retrospectively came to accept the argument of Max Eastman's *Artists in Uniform* (1934), which he and Joshua Kunitz had bitterly attacked when it was published.[105] However, in correspondence late in life Freeman defended his assault on Eastman's book because Eastman had claimed that the Soviet Union had clamped down on free cultural expression in the 1920s, whereas Freeman believed this had not happened until the early 1930s. Moreover, Freeman made the unconvincing claim that he had to attack Eastman's book because "it gave aid and comfort to the sectarians on the literary Left." That is, by exposing the vulgar trends in Soviet literary practice, Eastman's book allegedly showed the sectarians how they should act if they wanted to be "good Communists."[106]

While Freeman was able in his epistolary reminiscences to conjure up a convincing portrait of his idealism and authentic love of literature and the socialist dream, other materials surviving from the 1930s episodically document ugly personal references to individuals, especially if they were Leftists politically critical of the Communist Party. This dramatically contradicts Freeman's later boast that he, almost alone among the Communist writers, kept his debates and disagreements "impersonal": "I have a temperamental dislike of the ad hominem argument."[107]

Throughout the 1930s, V. F. Calverton (born George Goetz, 1900–1940), Freeman's major contender and rival spokesperson for Marxist culture, was called a "charlatan" and "our greatest danger" on the cultural front.[108] To Malcolm Cowley, he characterized Edmund Wilson (1895–1972) as one of "Trotsky's stooges in America."[109] This came immediately after his return from Mexico when Freeman himself had been subjected to what he believed was personal slander imputing to him pro-Trotskyist sympathies. In the 1950s when novelist Howard Fast engaged in public breast-beating over his mistake of trusting the Communist Party, Freeman declared Fast an opportunist who stayed on the fringes of the Party until the Moscow Trials were long over, and then remained in the Party just long enough to win the Stalin Peace prize.[110]

In 1937 Edwin Rolfe complained that he had heard that Freeman had blocked the publication of an essay by Alan Calmer as a "Critics Group" pamphlet because it was allegedly critical of the recent American Writers' Congress. Freeman was outraged by what he characterized as a slander. What really happened, he explained, was that he had told Angel Flores (1900–1992), the Puerto Rican–born English professor who led the pro-Communist Critics Group, to publish the piece, "despite my opinion that it was not a real criticism but a distortion of history."[111]

In his letter to Rolfe, Freeman further divulged that even before he had taken this action, he had heard rumors about Calmer's ideas and had informed on Calmer to Communist Party leader Earl Browder. When Calmer later ran into Freeman and expressed bitterness about Freeman inducing Browder to "suppress" the essay, Freeman accused Calmer of suffering from an "illusion."[112] The accusation seems more appropriate to Freeman; how could he have imagined that his actions could have had an effect other than discouraging publication of Calmer's essay? Freeman clearly desired to prevent Calmer's pamphlet from getting a hearing but did not want to take the blame for blocking its publication.

Freeman later contended that his decision not to make a public statement denouncing Stalinism, as he had been requested to do by various liberal editors, was consistent with his refusals to make public declarations at the behest of others while he was still in the Communist movement. "I have written many things in my life and many that were wrong. But I wrote them of my own free will and the errors I made were made in good faith. I have never written anything under compulsion."[113] Thus Freeman's version of his final days in the Communist movement emphasizes his independent strength of character. He claimed that when he was under pressure to issue strong public statements supporting the second of the Moscow Trials, he was reluctant to do so and consequently stayed away from New York as long as he could.[114]

Tiba Willner's recollection of Freeman's final days in the Communist movement, when she and her husband were working for the *New Masses,* combines a censure of Freeman for personal irresponsibility along with one for political indiscretion. She agrees that the precipitating episode came when Freeman, who had been sent to Mexico for the *New Masses,* failed to return to New York on schedule. Yet Willner, who resumed her friendship with Freeman after the Khrushchev revelations in 1956, is certain that he was "shacked up" with a woman, and didn't plan to return until he was good and ready. It is impossible to determine, at this late date, which rendition of the reason for his delay is accurate, but the known features of Freeman's career suggest that both could be true. Since Freeman had recently been criticized at a special meeting held at the Kremlin for his insufficiently harsh portrait of Trotsky in his autobiographical *An American Testament* (1937), the issues of political irresponsibility in Mexico and personal indiscretion upon his return to New York City were combined. Freeman was called before a special meeting of the Party's Central Committee and brutally condemned. George Willner, Tiba's husband, was present in his capacity as the recently appointed *New Masses* business manager and was shaken by Freeman's desperate and emotional efforts to defend himself. Some of the arguments that he used to bolster his credibility appear in a letter that he sent to Browder at the time.[115]

In this correspondence, Freeman surprisingly makes no reference at all to the content of *An American Testament,* or to the fact that Party members had read and approved it before publication. Instead, he invokes his record of service to the *New Masses* as proof of his unquestionable devotion to the Party. He reminds Browder that he readily took up the task of working on the magazine in the crisis of 1931–33, and once again in 1936–37, when he believed that a similar crisis was in progress. However, in the second instance, Freeman said he had been suspicious that his assignment of holding down the fort might be a set-up for him to take the blame for the decline of the magazine that had set in earlier. Still, "as a disciplined Communist, I considered it my duty to accept the assignment and to do the best I could to keep the magazine going."[116]

Now, in 1937, due to his disgrace following the Mexican episode, Freeman found that he was about to be "disconnected" from the magazine, and he was in great distress about the situation. He begged Browder to work out an arrangement so that he could continue to submit articles and to help edit the magazine when he was available. He suggested that he simply be described as taking a "leave of absence," and that the rest of the editorial staff be informed by the Party leadership "that I have neither been canned nor have I quit my post." Appealing to Browder to remember that, as a writer, his work was deeply affected by his relations with his comrades, he quoted approvingly a remark that Floyd Dell once made to him: "the Party is my father and my mother, and misunderstanding there is very painful; it paralyzes work."[117] The letter gained Freeman a bit more time before a public denunciation, but his Party career was now over.

Two years later, the *Communist International*, a monthly organ of the Executive Committee of the Communist International (the Comintern), published a statement by a Soviet leader, P. Dengal, damning the British and American Communist parties for having printed favorable reviews of Freeman's autobiography, *An American Testament*. Dengal's attack on Freeman argued that Freeman's was not a case of a confused writer but of one who cleverly uses the mask of objectivity to get across to workers "an anti-working class outlook and arouse sympathy for the enemies of the labor movement."[118] Freeman was charged with not breaking fully with his middle-class bohemianism; and *An American Testament* was scored as having "slight literary value" and being "hackwork," due to Freeman's arrested development. In Dengal's criticisms there is an echo of Freeman's own earlier attacks on writers who failed to break with their bourgeois past, not to mention his criticism of V. F. Calverton's "charlatanism." Although Freeman was never so crude as Dengal, their styles of debate could occasionally be similar.

Freeman, however, never reconsidered nor repented his attacks on rivals, most of which he appeared to forget. Even his later recollections of his "literary line" in the 1930s were organized around the avowal that he had never supported "proletarian literature," and that his disbelief in the genre was always emphasized in what he wrote. Yet his essays in the early 1930s are only a softer and more sophisticated version of the Kharkov Conference orientation. His introduction to the 1935 volume *Proletarian Literature in the United States* appears to be consistent with the predominant *New Masses* position that any writer can produce proletarian literature so long as he or she adheres to a working-class (Marxist) perspective, identifies with the proletarian struggle and cause, treats experience from a proletarian perspective, and reshapes his or her life within the working-class movement.[119] Retrospectively Freeman was able to selectively emphasize certain aspects of his writings, including poems, to make them more compatible with his post-Communist Party anti-proletarian literature stance.

## The Dream with the Changing Name

Freeman's final communications with the Communist Party make pathetic reading. In July 1939 he wrote V. J. Jerome about his difficulty in completing an article due to illness, debts, poverty, and a desperate search for employment. He concludes: "What enables me to bear this suffering and degradation at all is the hope that in the end I shall emerge a better Bolshevik, more useful to the Party."[120] After his excommunication, Freeman went into a deep depression; his body seemed to double in size and he later told Tiba Willner that he had attempted suicide.[121] He had for years received psychoanalytic treatment, but now his therapy became crucial to his survival. The theme of his psychoanalysis was his alleged neglect and exploitation by others, who were motivated by a lust for greed and power. He, on the other hand, subordinated his own career to helping other individuals.

Even though there is no evidence that Freeman became an informer during the two occasions that he was called before governmental investigating bodies,[122] unpleasant gossip circulated about him in Party milieux. A characteristic story was that as a well-paid employee of the E. L. Bernays public relations firm in the 1940s, he wrote the speeches for the National Association of Newspaper Publishers.[123] Franklin Folsom worked for TASS under Freeman's brother Harry in the 1940s, and was surprised that Harry had no contact with Joseph.[124] Yet Freeman's emotional crisis was not permanently crippling. He wrote two novels, *Never Call Retreat* (1943) and *The Long Pursuit* (1947), which allegorically addressed his revolutionary experiences, as well as short fiction and a constant stream of unpublished poetry for the same purpose. He also meditated on the whole course of his life in unpublished writings and dreamed of picking up where he had left off – as a poet, "pure and undefiled"[125] – before his experiences in the Communist Party.

In letters to Floyd Dell and Josephine Herbst in the 1950s and 1960s, Freeman worked his way through to a very simple analysis of the role of poetry and socialism in his intellectual development. As a child he had received intense religious training in Judaism, and until he was twenty he prayed every day. Thereafter the poetry he had been writing became transformed into a substitute for his religion, and "In this way poetry became a preoccupation with the eternal problem of good and evil, the mystery of human nature and conduct in a universe whose riddle remains to be solved."[126] From his boyhood until his old age, with the exception of the 1930s, poetry poured from Freeman independent of the prospects of it ever being published, although as many as a hundred poems found their way into print in the 1920s and early 1930s. Similarly he had drawn every day until he was over thirty, and both his wives were painters. Like his friend Floyd Dell, the poets who nurtured him were the classic romantics, Byron, Keats, Shelley and Wordsworth. These seem logical choices in light of his early childhood, for, until he was seven, he lived in a small Ukrainian village full of woods, hills, and streams, without sidewalks and lights. Fifty years later he vividly remembered "the horses, the cows, the servant girl who took care of me, the church across the road whose bells have haunted me around the world."[127]

Freeman further linked his move from poetry as religion to socialism as religion, acknowledging that his verse was often grim as well as "chiliastic." He offered one of the clearest personal confessions on record of the Jewish-American messianic appropriation of Communism:

> The belief of Chiliasm that Christ will return in the flesh to rule a just world for a thousand years derives from Jewish apocalyptic literature older than the Book of Revelations. It is the Christian, revolutionary version of a persistent Jewish dream – the coming of the Messianic Kingdom. As a child I lived in a landscape rendered grim by pogroms, beautiful by the vision of the Messiah, whom I saw in daydreams riding his traditional white horse as he came to redeem us from exile and suffering. Eventually the Messiah did come for me; he came with hammer and sickle in hand to redeem the whole of mankind. But this savior, like all his predecessors, failed to leave behind him the promised land of universal justice and love. Nevertheless my verse continues to be chiliastic. . . . I cannot surrender my belief . . . that in the end man will free himself of evil and develop his godlike potentials to the full.[128]

As the 1950s evolved into the 1960s, Freeman detached his religio-artistic-socialist vision from the specifics of his Communist Party experience, transforming it into a transhistoric faith in the power of human redemption. His mentor relationship to Daniel Aaron at the time of the latter's study of the cultural Left was a high point of his late middle age; this was dramatized by a moving visit to Smith College in 1958, where he delivered in a public forum a spirited defense of his passionate belief in poetry and the future that he called "The Vision of the Thirties." One year younger than his antagonist, the cultural commissar V. J. Jerome, the Yogi *manqué* Freeman likewise succumbed to cancer in 1965.

## CHAPTER 6

# Three Moderns in Search of an Answer

## The Modernist Temptation

For all the injury perpetrated by Mike Gold in his off-the-cuff *New Masses* and *Daily Worker* columns, he also had the acumen and largesse in the late 1920s and early 1930s to promote such a disconcerting near-modernist figure as Herman Spector (1895–1959), whom Gold declared in 1933 to be "the raw material of New York Communism."[1] Spector was, indeed, a bona fide Communist, but he in innumerable ways also exemplified a broader layer of hundreds of politically unaffiliated writers impelled toward literary and poetic activity in the late 1920s and early Depression years. These were the writers whose work appears in the "little magazines" of the time, magazines that had overlapping avant-garde modernist and proletarian-revolutionary orientations. By the second half of the 1930s, the alienated resentment and gloom marking much of their writing would be less appreciated in the atmosphere of optimism demanded by the anti-fascist crusade.

The modernist challenge to radical poetry was posed most directly by the verse and literary criticism of T. S. Eliot (1888–1965), to judge by the number of direct responses to Eliot's poetry and the centrality of his name in literary debates on the Left.[2] Despite the elitism and arcane quality of many of Eliot's literary allusions, young poets found it unfeasible to ignore the profoundly novel approach to poetic form and sensibility that his verse represented. No Leftist could admit sympathy for Eliot's politics, either those implicit in the despairing poems of his early period, or the more explicitly reactionary ones that he later wrote. But there was contention about the extent to which his technical innovations, as well as those of Ezra Pound (1885–1972), who in the late 1920s personally befriended radicals and for an interval contributed to Left publications, could be assimilated if bereft of ideology.

A sweep of views was investigated in a three-way exchange among writers in the *Daily Worker* in mid-1934. On 5 June, Mike Gold remarked in his column on the baleful influence of Eliot on radical poets of the 1930s: "It is a matter of real wonder to me to see how many try to adapt his sterile, hopeless literary mood to the uses of proletarian literature. I don't believe it can or should be done. . . . They are intellectuals in the worst sense of the word, writing not for the masses, but for the narrow circles of the over-educated."[3] A week later Gold published two contrasting responses.

One, by Leonard Spier (dates unknown), a New York Communist poet devoted to Jack Conroy's *Rebel Poet* magazine,[4] presents the kind of parochial, anti-intellectual judgment that always remained present in the Communist Left and was occasionally promoted by Gold himself: "Eliot's poetry, essentially trivial, pedantic and snobbish, reeking of the library and parlor, is certainly the worst example for radical poets to follow. The proof is: ask any ten workers what they think of the poems in *Partisan Review* [at that time under control of the New York John Reed Club] and elsewhere in which Eliot's influence is conspicuous, and the majority will tell you they don't know what he is talking about."[5] The other opinion was that of Alfred Hayes (1911–85), who sometimes substituted for Gold in writing the *Daily Worker* cultural column. Urging the reverse, Hayes pleaded for revolutionary poets to study Eliot in order to learn from "his ability to make life vivid and concrete, his dramatic power, his diction stripped to the concentration of prose." Hayes also observed that "Our own poetry has lacked this – it is pictureless, unhuman, [un]dramatic. It is poster poetry, holiday poetry, epic poetry with the heroes left out and only the chorus."[6] Hayes evidently believed that one could detach certain features of what has come to be called "High Modernist" verse to render proletarian writing more "modern," in the sense of Hemingway's unpretentious, colloquial style. None of the participants in the discussion showed any appreciation of Eliot's wit as a rare feature of his early poetry, or any empathy for Eliot's view that some social problems might be an irremediable part of the human condition. Yet there was an aspect of his modernism that clearly tempted young poets of the Left; was it merely, as Hayes explained, a question of style, or was the style actually expressive of a more difficult, brainy, and less proletarian content, as others suspected?

In summing up, Gold made his antimodernist views (sometimes controverted by his own practice) explicit and even volunteered some anti-intellectual jibes, chiefly aimed at Martha Graham's latest modern dance performances on revolutionary topics, and "cerebral" music that he heard at "some recent concerts of the Workers' Music League." But Gold didn't advocate Spier's "ask the worker" test of literary quality. Nor did he treat the young and little-known Hayes with disrespect. On the contrary, he toned down the row a bit by observing that very few poets, including such lucid ones as Carl Sandburg, have had many sales of books among workers in the United States because "American workers don't read and love poetry as do

German, or Jewish, or Russian, or Latin American workers." Notwithstanding, since those writers who had reached a working-class audience "came out of working-class life," Gold concludes that, "just as a machine is a different social force in America than in the U.S.S.R., just so the proletarian poet must find a different conception of the function of poetry from that entertained by T. S. Eliot. He cannot be an individualist and ignore his audience. . . . One must become rooted in the revolutionary world."[7] In his antagonism to the "cerebral," his obstinacy that poetry be quickly understood "by the masses," and his stricture against "individualism," Gold appears to be pressing toward a degree of realism and functionalism antithetical to what is normally called modernism.

Such concern about the politics of form in the United States, although set down in terms of comprehensibility, audience, and individualism, roughly parallels on a simpler plane the celebrated debate between Georg Lukács and Bertolt Brecht. Is modernism, the two European Marxists asked, a detachable experiment in form, usable for various ends, or does modernism produce in its very formal features an ideology that replicates rather than transcends the reifications of bourgeois society?[8] The ambiguities in the definitions of terms in the debate, and in the complex relation between literary form and ideological content, as well as the relatively neglected matter of the dynamics of diverse audience reception, account for much of the bafflement that exists about the Marxist-modernist problematic.

According to German playwright Bertolt Brecht, modernism is a set of experimental artistic techniques relatively free of any particular political content, an effective use of which allows the writer to attain a "higher" mode of realism than conventional techniques. According to the Hungarian critic Georg Lukács, modernism is an ideology promoting subjectivism and personalism, mirroring the reifications of bourgeois society and indissolubly interrelated with modernism's characteristic literary forms. While occasional deviations and discrepancies occur, the U.S. Communist editors and critics with the most prestige in the years prior to 1956 – Gold, V. J. Jerome, Joseph Freeman, Samuel Sillen, A. B. Magil, and Joseph North – tended to favor simpler styles and to code "difficulty" as elitist and defeatist, thereby placing themselves on the more extreme edge of Lukács's antimodernism. In practice, however, a significant number of Communist poets, especially in New York, were familiar with Eliot, Crane, and other modernists, and aspired to appropriate for the Left some modernist features. Moreover, Dos Passos's experiments in fiction (moderately "difficult" in comparison to Eliot) were commended so long as he remained a Party ally; eminent Communist writers in other countries who are today often discussed in relation to modernism (Neruda, Brecht, Aragon), were never criticized for being too personal, difficult, or obscure; and there were occasionally double-edged salutes to high modernists such as Joyce for their genius in exposing bourgeois decadence.[9] The meeting ground for most Left poetry of the 1930s was in modern literature, in the sense of support for fresher language, more various forms, and somewhat more difficult ideational content than the worker-poetry promoted in the 1920s, or produced outside New York in the writing of Don West, Henry George Weiss, and divers others. Yet there were certainly moments in the work of many writers, and, in a few cases, entire careers, that can legitimately be called "Red" modernism.

The features of the stylistic legacy of Eliot that challenged Left writers are evident in the first lines of "Gerontion" (1920):

> Here I am, an old man in a dry month,
> Being read to by a boy, waiting for rain.
> I was neither at the hot gates
> Nor fought in the warm rain
> Nor knee deep in the salt marsh, heaving a cutlass,
> Bitten by flies, fought.
> My house is a decayed house,
> And the Jew squats on the window sill, the owner,
> Spawned in some estaminet of Antwerp,
> Blistered in Brussels, patched and peeled in London.
> The goat coughs at night in the field overhead;
> Rocks, moss, stonecrop, iron, merds.
> The woman keeps the kitchen, makes tea,
> Sneezes at evening, poking the peevish gutter.
>     I an old man,
> A dull head among windy spaces.[10]

To what extent are form and content interdependent? Exemplary "Eliotic" traits of these lines are scholarly allusions to history and myth, neologisms (including the title), the unidentified voice of a disillusioned speaker, a longing for symbolic moments of achievement linked to the precapitalist world, possibly paranoid references to a conspiracy theory of Jews as the creators and the economic beneficiaries of World War I, the landscape of a barren field and house intimating the emptiness of twentieth-century civilization, and the negative depiction of the old man's relation to the woman. All of these are memorably wrought in the highly condensed technique of imagism.

An illustrative radical response may be seen in the very first published poem of Herman Spector, which appeared in the January 1928 issue of *Boz-*

*art.* Initially titled "Today and Now" in manuscript, it became "Nightowl"
in the magazine. Ultimately, it was titled "Night Owl in a Decayed House"
when it appeared in the 1933 collection of verse by Communist poets, *We
Gather Strength:*

> there are snow and somewhat frost however
> outside with the white streets and wind.
> the clock tinnily interrupts tolling 2 or 3 times.
> and the old man's snoring is a recurrent bur-zz.
> here between ceiling and floor at the foot of the stairs
> I pause,
> reconsider suicide.
> attenuated loneliness reaches for finality of death,
> the patterns of life grow inept on the carpet.
> today and now the clock ticks
> the telephone is silent and hopeful
> doors are slightly ajar.
> tomorrow will certainly annoy me.
> tomorrow will be somebody's wakeful cough in
>     the still house;
> spying on me, suspicious.
> I will kill myself before I am eaten up
> by the invidious stares of lepers.
> a door opens on its hinge with a burglar's creak.
> this house is rotten with evil
> sweating with suspicions,
> fear
> and the wind drones, winds, blows outside.
> the old man's snore is a violent complaint.
> time for death.[11]

This poem, which would have been unlikely to find its way into the pages
of the *New Masses* during the Popular Front era, is masterful in its use of
inexact but intense realism, fusing images both squalid and vaporous, to
produce an atmosphere of agonizing isolation and forlornness.

Spector's decayed house, like Eliot's, is a negative emblem of the capitalist world, but in Spector's poem it is owned not by "the jew" but by the "old
man." The "night owl" appears to be the poet, Spector, whose self-portraits
from his own drawings invariably show him owlish-looking in spectacles,
roaming about in a night of confusion. In a brilliantly ambiguous touch,
Spector combines the personal with the political to fuse the symbolic notion
of a house as social structure, and the "old man" as the ruler of this system,

with an apparent personal reference to his own father as the "old man," who is also the perpetrator of oppression within his family.

In the same year, Spector's "Night in New York," which appeared in *New Masses* in 1928, responded to Eliot from a different angle, beginning with a reference to the fourth section of "The Burial of the Dead" section of Eliot's *The Waste Land* (1922). Instead of Eliot's "Unreal" City of London where, when the clock strikes 9:00 A.M. to unleash the financial district's commercial crowds who walk in circles as if in Dante's purgatory, Spector offers

> New York, city of chaos;
> confusion of stone and steel,
> the spawn of anarchic capitalism.

In contrast to the clock of Eliot's poem, which points to the ninth hour (the hour at which Christ died) to remind the reader of the death of Christ and thus Christian values as a significant consequence of the commercial world, Spector's clock points to 9:00 A.M. to produce

> pornographic offerings,
> eruptions on the skin of streets
> from the tainted blood of commerce . . .
> electricly alight and lewd.[12]

Following this feverishly sordid imagery is an extraordinary vivification of the New York City landscape, where the elevated train rumbles "a menacing undertone of hate," the city laughs "rattlingly," and "slick, suave limousines sneer." Suddenly, before returning to the opening refrain, the voice of a lone worker is heard:

> all day in the shop and my back hurts,
> my feet are like lead.
> my stomach grumbles . . .
> i belch.[13]

The words are pronounced in the unidealized poetry of the exploited.

## Bastard in the Ragged Suit

While intermittent poems and prose writings by Spector describe the work experience, he does not properly belong among the worker-poets. The point of view dispensed in Spector's writing is that of someone acutely conscious of and angry about class oppression, yet adrift in a world where class relations and social solutions await clarification. Spector did not originate in the

working class; his father owned a small belt-making factory. By breaking
with the family, Spector "descended" into the proletariat. While he wrote a
few poems that idealistically and optimistically call for revolution, in ways
that now seem synthetic and forced, he wrote many more in which he (like
Eliot) confronts his readers with grotesque and repulsive images of people
at the bottom of society, often depicting decadence through the imagery of
female prostitution and sexuality. His strongest poems do not treat work as
such, or speak from the perspective of a worker, but instead depict unemployment, vagrancy, and what in the 1930s was called "bottom dog" life.

Most noteworthy, Spector, recalling Rimbaud's exertions to make himself monstrous by leaping into the unknown, sporadically takes pleasure in
becoming the "other" that the "respectable" middle-class reader often fears
and essays to shun:

> I am the bastard in the ragged suit
> who spits, with bitterness and malice to all.
>
> needing the stimulus of crowds,
> hatred engendered of coney-island faces,
> pimps in a pressed-well parade.

In "Outcast" (1929), the long poem from which this passage comes, Spector
dons the repulsive mask of one who expounds the antithesis of proletarian
class-consciousness; he approximates a lumpen perspective, susceptible at
worst to fascist intrigue. In this gambit, however, Spector reveals by allusion
that the alter ego of "the bastard" is Eliot's J. Alfred Prufrock. The following
lines of Spector's "bastard" rework phrases from "The Love Song of J. Alfred
Prufrock":

> at times the timid christ,
> longing to speak . . .
> women pass hurriedly, disdainfully by.

Spector's closing stanzas in "The Outcast" strongly intimate that the reactionary version of modernism championed by Eliot is designed at best
to channel the outcast's anger away from class consciousness and into passivity:

> recalling the verses of sensitive men
> who have felt these things . . .
> who have reacted, to all things on earth,
> I am dissolved in unemotion.

won by a quiet content,
the philosophy of social man . . .
The high hat gods go down the aisles.
I am at one with life.[14]

Spector's writing in this and additional instances might be described as lodged between modernism and Marxism, rather than comprising a successful arrogation of modernist sensibility for revolutionary ends. His literary record seems to disclose a classic case of what Harold Bloom identified as "the anxiety of influence" in his 1973 book by that title. Spector, in passages such as the above, attempts to slay his predecessor poet (Eliot) to clear his personal space; but his own verse discloses him as a "weak poet" in Bloom's phrase, unable to establish and sustain his own vision and form, despite an enviable modern capacity for objectifying the subconscious.

Such an impasse surely mirrors Spector's painful life. He was born in New York City in 1905, and bragged in the *New Masses* that he had never traveled farther West than 10th Avenue.[15] Five feet ten inches tall, lean with piercing eyes, Spector had sharp features, dark hair, and a medium complexion, and he customarily wore glasses. He surfaced in the Left literary milieu in the late 1920s affecting a "tough-guy persona," with a sharp tongue and precise speech, and full of nervous energy. Through his sardonic remarks, he gave the impression of being a keen judge of character well acquainted with a variety of literary types.

Spector quit high school after three years and began working variously as a lumber handler, shipping clerk, truck driver, streetcar conductor, laborer, baker's helper, Western Union delivery boy, factory hand, butcher boy, envelope addresser, canvasser, and soda jerk. By the time he was twenty-two in 1927, he had published eighteen pieces in little magazines such as *Exile*, *American Caravan*, *Free Verse*, *Transition*, and *Unrest* and in Marcus Graham's *An Anthology of Revolutionary Poetry*. Harry Roskolenko (1907–1980), an aspiring poet who was first a Communist and later a Trotskyist, saw Spector, whom he initially regarded as a distant protégé of Ezra Pound, as "savage, brutal and brilliant." At the same time, Roskolenko remembered Spector as always impeccably dressed in white shirts that he changed several times a day, and a person who "bathed too often," disliked physical contact with workers, and was "frightened of women."[16] In November 1928 Spector became a contributing editor of the *New Masses,* and he joined the John Reed Club when it was founded a year later. Other than his marching in May Day parades, Spector's book reviews and poetry are his only known public means of expressing his revolutionary Communist convictions.

As in the case of Mike Gold, Spector's evolvement to literary and then Marxist rebellion is not reducible to a political explanation. Underlying Spector's sardonic poetry is a two-part tragedy raised to a myth that cryptically motivated his writing behind the scenes, and was visible only in disparate images and obsessive themes. The result is a poetry of retaliation fired by a staccato blues speech and rhythm resounding with anger and literary allusions indicating a self-taught erudition.

The first act of his tragedy involves the bitter particulars of his rejection of his middle-class background. His fury derived from his family's treatment of his older brother, Benjamin, an artist who suffered acute psychological problems. A quarrel between Benjamin and a younger sister resulted in her destroying Benjamin's paintings, after which Benjamin became depressed, withdrawn, and noncommunicative. In Spector's view, his family tried to evade responsibility for its decision to place Benjamin in a mental institution, where he lingered for two decades before dying in the 1940s. An unpublished manuscript found after Spector's death, "Artist into Stone," forcefully reflects the strong feelings of identification between Spector and his brother, Benjamin, coupling the deceased painter-brother to many previous images in his poetry, including the outcast character:

> Am not my brother's keeper
> Not my brother's corpse
> He is in a plain box sleeping
> But I thought I heard him cough;
> The face is pinched and blue,
> The eyes are slits of white,
> The curious stubble of his beard
> Shall flourish through this night . . .
>
> Though he, the mime, is gone,
> The waif who died too soon,
> Whose laughter and whose brush recalled
> The slum, the stone, the afternoon.
> For him, these words of ice;
> For him, a flambeau thrown
> Far into evening space . . .
> Where millioned streets lie stark and still,
> All humming underneath.[17]

Putting into service language as direct and unornamented as the corpse and plain box described, Spector displays an uncanny ability to apply imagist methods to bring his poetry closer to the physical existence of place while simultaneously insinuating a dream-like ambience. The details of the death resound with larger themes of responsibility to humanity, and perhaps even a mourning for the passing of the social art of those, the WPA artists, who painted to impart a semblance of humanity to the slums.

Spector censured not only his family for what had happened to his brother, but also himself for not preventing it. He resolutely felt that Benjamin's institutionalization was not necessary and only contributed to a worsening of his condition. The sister's destruction of Benjamin's art prior to his descent into depression may well have motivated Herman to sustain his own art, despite decades of neglect, as a tribute to his brother and as a hedge against his own despair.

The second act of his tragedy derived from his early marriage to Clara Weissman, born 28 October 1906 on the Lower East Side. They met when she was working at the belt factory owned by Herman's father. Clara was a woman of extraordinary sexual power, beautiful with deep, haunting eyes; she was pictured by her daughter as "a flame, a blazing beauty, a mass of contradictions and the most intense human being I've ever known."[18] In his unpublished autobiographical fiction, Spector painted her in clichés of working-class Jewish female sexuality: "The first time I saw her, it was as if a flame leaped into life, illumining [sic] her eyes and hair, and I saw nothing else.... I felt desire throbbing in me like a tiger.... The very thought of her sent flames soaring, dreams throbbing in my being."[19]

An unplanned pregnancy, however, forced Clara and Herman to marry young, initiating a family without adequate means of support. This placed the already gloomy Spector in the situation of feeling an unrelenting pressure to find a way to earn a living, which came into direct conflict with the time, concentration, and relative peace of mind needed to craft his art. Such conflicted feelings about the role of his wife in his life partly accounts for the disturbing sexual imagery of decay in Spector's work. Here is his description of the Harlem River that lures despondent, unemployed, and heartbroken men to suicide:

> night's breasts were soft, cajoling sleep . . .
> her lewd eyes beckoned their weariness.[20]

In a romantic trope that is also a perverse reworking of the erotics of daily life, the night, seat of unconscious desire, becomes the fatal seducer of the waning authority of consciousness.

Spector's association with the Communist movement gave him some minor prominence in the late 1920s and early 1930s, and it was linked to Mike Gold's patronage. His distinction, however, lasted only until 1934 when the *New Masses*, now "professionalized," moved from being a monthly to a weekly under the guidance of trained journalists such as Freeman, Michelson, and North. Subsequently Spector's contributions only rarely appeared in the magazine. Soon after, the decision of the Communist Party's cultural leadership to cease encouraging the development of small revolutionary proletarian clubs and myriad little publications, in favor of promoting the broader United Front (1934-35) and then of the first Popular Front (1935-39), contributed to Spector's loss of self-confidence. His last great hope had been *Dynamo*, which only lasted four issues in 1934-35. The magazine had a personal significance in terms of his effort at self-recreation, for he envisioned it as "presenting revolutionary literature as an integration of proletarian personality instead of the lopsided abstraction some have tried to make it out."[21]

Small magazines such as *Left*, *Front*, and *Dynamo* had been his mainstay, and he rarely was able to write for others.[22] He announced a book of his own writing, *Sweet like Salvation*, but it failed to appear. Spector made a few sporadic efforts to publish in paying magazines, such as the *Saturday Evening Post* and various pulps. Then he essentially ceased submitting his writing for publication, although he methodically continued to work on revisions. In 1938 Spector joined the "Living Lore" component of the New York Federal Writers' Project. When that endeavor ended a few years later, he wrote exclusively for himself, and then began sketching and drawing in private to express his artistic creativity.

After the 1930s, Spector earned his living successively as a welder in the Brooklyn Navy Yard, a sales canvaser for a photo studio, a pots and pans salesman, and a photo coupon salesman. Around 1950, he became a cabdriver and drove a taxi until his death in 1959. During these years he worked on a promising manuscript, "Call Me Porkchop" (the slang term for cab driver), which he conceived as an urban proletarian version of *Moby Dick*. At times his writing simulated that of the Beats, especially Jack Kerouac, who were achieving prominence in those years. One of his three alternate introductory "proems" begins:

> I am a nightworker who sometimes has daymares. A nightowl Hackie, that stereotype of columnists and nite-clubbers referred to in jest. A pariah of a pave, a modern-day rickshaw coolie with rearview callouses and cannibalistic concepts. This is the image of myself that recurs in the terrifying dream. When I awake, I know the dream to be a reality.[23]

The Rimbaudian impulse to violently thrust himself into the unknown – in this case, the work world of the Hackie – perseveres in yielding a derangement of senses composting conventional perceptions in the unachieved hope of casting up new-sprung forms of cognition.

Politically, Spector persisted in sympathizing with the Left and Communism until his death. At the time of the Moscow Purge Trials, Spector declared to his literary associates that the world was simply divided into two great class camps and one must choose one or the other.[24] Yet after the 1930s his political views were expressed only in conversation with his closest confidants. Publicly, he affected indifference to both politics and poetry, and, furthermore, deceived his old comrades by saying that he had given up his writing.

## Apollinaire of the Proletariat

Examples of hard lives and frustrated ambitions are easy to find among Depression-era poets, but not all specimens of early 1930s Red near-modernism are as grim as the writings of Herman Spector. Sol Funaroff, for instance, crafted an optimistic and explicitly revolutionary response to Eliot's "What the Thunder Said" section of *The Waste Land*, in a 1933 poem of the same name. In it, he strives to reproduce the speech of a revolutionary Russian worker to a crowd of fellow workers while a thunderstorm threatens. Funaroff later avowed that his objective was to "transcribe the speech into poetic form and to transform the metropolitan scene with its vista of skyscrapers, bridges, airplanes, buildings in construction, etc., into a cinematic language which, as in montage, correlates and fuses the objects and symbols that visualize the changing themes of the speaker." He also elaborated that his method of using cross-reference, swift development, and transition of images allowed him "to form a dialectic image pattern which would enable me to present simultaneously sensuous, historical, and philosophical relationships within the poem."[25] Particularly striking is that, unlike Spector, Funaroff sees answering Eliot as only part of his project; his visionary poems are equally marked by prophecy.

A second instance of a revolutionary response to T. S. Eliot by Funaroff can be found in his posthumously published meditation on "The Love Song of J. Alfred Prufrock," which he called "Possessed by Death, 1931." Here Funaroff identifies the speaker of the monologue with Macbeth, instead of Eliot's choice, Hamlet. Funaroff then reexamines and discards the conclusions of Eliot's classic poem in light of Eliot's subsequent religious conversion:

And meanwhile –
what shall he do now? What shall he do?

Retrieve the butt-ends of ancient days
and smoke stale incense of his days and ways
while slowly the censer swings.[26]

Whereas Eliot believed that the church saved him from the despondency evident in his early work, Funaroff proposes that faith in the church transformed Eliot into one of the "hollow men" that Eliot had criticized.

The author of these Left rejoinders to modernist poems, Solomon Funaroff, was born in Beirut, Syria, in 1911. He died at the age of thirty-one in New York City in 1942.[27] The Funaroffs, originally from Russia, were a penniless refugee family, harried and chased from several countries in Europe, the Middle East, and Africa. His father, Levi Funaroff, wrote on social issues in Russian and Hebrew. The elder Funaroff died while the family was living in Palestine, and his wife, Rachel, a Russian revolutionary and Left Zionist, came to New York with her sons to work full-time in a Lower East Side sweatshop.

Two events contributed to the ill health that afflicted Solomon Funaroff from a young age. One was the 1918 influenza epidemic, during which he contracted rheumatic fever that may have impaired his heart. The second occurred while his mother was at work; the tenement in which they lived caught fire, and young Sol was carried out gulping for air and near expiration. Neighbors forced the smoke and fumes from his lungs and wrapped him in a cover while the structure burned down. Doctors diagnosed his case as "Rheumatic Heart" (alternately called "Poverty Heart") and foretold an early death for the boy. Despite such poor health, Sol and his brother, Urie, spent their youth ascending factory stairs in the garment district vending ice cream, candy, and fruit to workers.

Funaroff graduated from Franklin Lane High School in Brooklyn, where he edited the school's literary magazine. At a later date he attended some evening classes at City College, simultaneously assuming the editorship of the Left-wing *College Students' Review*. Most of his classes were during evening sessions so he could work all day as an upholsterer's apprentice, in a baking factory, and as a relief investigator. Lacking books of his own, he frequented the public library where, possibly because he was reading through the poetry section by starting at the letter "A," he stumbled on the modern verse of Guillaume Apollinaire (1880–1918). He was apparently struck by a passage that he would later rework into the opening of "Bellbuoy," which I have quoted as the epigram for this book. Apollinaire's stanzas read:

> Men of future time remember me
> I lived at the time when kings were perishing
> They died in quiet sadness one by one. . . .
>
> One night walking along dark deserted quays
> On the way back to Auteuil I heard a voice
> Which gravely sang with measured silences
> So that the clear lament of other distant voices
> Might reach the banks of the Seine. . . .[28]

The lines apparently resonated with Funaroff's sense that he, a poet-seer, was living in an era of epochal transformations, yet his own fragile grip on life was unlikely to permit him to witness the outcome. Moreover, Apollinaire's haunting strophes correlated with Funaroff's personal temperament, not unfamiliar among the avant-garde, of having a blind faith in a future about which he was rarely specific.

Funaroff was later employed in a matzoh factory, then he obtained occasional reporting jobs for *New York World*, the City News Service, and the Left-wing Federated Press. In his last years he located some editorial work at the *New Republic* and at Scribner's publishing house; then he found temporary employment with Home Relief and the Federal Writers' Project.

It was characteristic that Funaroff was consistently drawn to editorial tasks and literary projects involving other writers. Every year or so he took on some collaborative activity. In 1929, he was editor of Franklin K. Lane High School magazine; in 1932, editor of the National Student League's *College Student Review*; in 1933, poetry editor of *New Masses* and of the collection *We Gather Strength*; in 1934, an editor of *Partisan Review*; in 1934-35, an editor of *Dynamo, A Journal of Revolutionary Poetry*; and in 1936, an associate editor of the pro-Communist *New Theatre Magazine*. Funaroff selected poetry for special supplements of the *New Republic* and *New Masses* in 1934, 1937, and 1938; he was the editor and publisher of the Dynamo series of poetry books; and, just before his death, he was coeditor of a small anthology, *American Writing* (1940), consisting of mostly pro-Communist authors (Ralph Ellison, Ben Field, Joy Davidman) taking their distance from the European war, not yet transformed into an antifascist crusade. In an uncharacteristically generous passage in his memoirs, Edward Dahlberg remarked that "Penniless Funaroff was ready to print any Marxist's verse but his own."[29] In these and other activities, Funaroff aimed to bring socially conscious poets together for a labor readership and audience, especially seeking opportunities to present poetry in innovative forums such as radio, voice recordings, sound film, dance, drama, and music.

His own poetry and criticism showed up under the pseudonyms Charles Henry Newman, Steve Foster, and Sil Vnarov, as well as under his own name. In addition to the *New Masses*, *Daily Worker*, and *Dynamo*, his poems appeared in *Poetry*, *Scribner's*, *Pagany*, *Nativity*, and *Left*, and a few were even anthologized in textbooks of the day. A selection of his work was included in *We Gather Strength* (1933), and two books came out under his own name, *The Spider and the Clock* (1938) and *Exile from a Future Time: Posthumous Poems of Sol Funaroff* (1943).

Throughout his short life Funaroff was tenement-thin and hungry looking. He spent most of his adult years searching for employment, reaching his economic zenith in 1938 when he made $28 a week and had his first private apartment. For many years he was involved with a woman, Natalie, addressed in his poems as his lover. When prospects for improving his health seemed hopeless, he broke up with her and she married someone else.

Like his friend Edwin Rolfe, Funaroff was a pale and slight man who managed to produce writing charged with controlled vitality. Communist filmmaker Leo Hurwitz believed Funaroff to be the driving force of the revolutionary magazine *Dynamo*, remembering him as "quiet little big Sol" – a man who had a "quality of littleness but was fairly tall with sweet shyness."[30] Gertrude Hayes, married in the late 1930s to Alfred Hayes, thought that in appearance Funaroff fit her image of an English poet: He was tall and blond, meticulously dressed with courtly manners, and somehow handsome despite his sickliness.[31]

Due to his modesty and willingness to promote other writers, Funaroff played a central role in a circle of unknown young Jewish writers from the working class who had radical politics and literary aspirations. One of these was Nathan Adler (1913-1994), who had drifted toward the Communist movement a few years earlier. Adler had a reputation as a person of "genuine" proletarian background; his father sold ice in the streets in New York, and Adler had done some writing about his own work in a laundry and the period of unemployment experienced by his father.[32] Whittaker Chambers (1901-1961), a former Columbia University student who published in the *New Masses* and who would join the magazine's staff for a while, asked Adler to read manuscripts for the *New Masses* in the belief that Adler would be able to recognize "the real thing." While performing this task, in 1931 Adler met Funaroff.[33]

Adler had attended elementary school with a Jewish immigrant from England, Alfred Hayes. They had recently reestablished contact, and Hayes introduced Adler to another immigrant who worked as a melamed (Hebrew teacher), Ivan Greenberg (1908-1973). Greenberg had published poetry in *The*

*Rebel Poet* under the name Philip Rahv. Hayes, Rahv, and Adler were of insufficient importance as writers to be admitted to the Communist Party's John Reed Club. Consequently they joined a more free-wheeling Party-led organization, the Revolutionary Writers Federation, which was open to anyone, although much of its base was comprised of Communists who carried on their literary activities in foreign-language organizations. The three men took over the federation's Sunday night forum series as their base. Soon they were joined by Edwin Rolfe, who was employed at the *Daily Worker*. Herman Spector, always a loner, was also present but in the background.

Finding like-minded spirits in this milieu, Funaroff proposed launching a magazine to be called *Dynamo*, which was one of the names originally proposed for the *New Masses*. He grew so devoted to the project that he decided that some of his own contributions should be published under the pen names Newman and Foster, as he didn't want to appear to be writing the entire magazine. *Dynamo*'s sympathetic posture toward modern literature is implicit in its statement of purpose, although high modernism was kept at arm's length:

> There has been a dead calm in American poetry since the "renaissance" of the tens and earlier twenties of this century. We believe that the new generation of American poets is now ready to initiate a new "renaissance" which in compact images and rhythms of poetry can utter the deeper, social and class meanings of the turbulent days around us.[34]

A series of critical essays featured in issue number two of *Dynamo* advanced the theme that the magazine intended to be a vehicle for young revolutionary poets who had followed the development of modernism.

One contributor was William Phillips (b. 1907), then a pro-Communist and married to a Party member. Using the pen name "Wallace Phelps," he declared in "Sensibility and Modern Poetry" that "The linguistic rhythms of the *transitionists*, though based on a theory of language and poetry-audience far from that of revolutionary poetry, have taken some hold on a few of the younger American revolutionary poets." Phillips then offered a fairly precise delineation of the relation of various Red poets to the new phenomenon.

In Phillips's narrative, William Pillin (1910–1985)[35] and Muriel Rukeyser (1913–1980) are cited as the writers most immersed in the *transition* experiment, while Spector and Joseph Kalar (1906–1972) are noted for having made "machine sensibility" compatible with a revolutionary outlook. Horace Gregory is said to represent a group of writers in "transition from traditional to proletarian poetry." Unfortunately, from Phillips's view, poets such as these failed to identify themselves "with the daily life, the idiom, the collective surge of the proletariat. Consequently, their sensibility is largely humanist, and frequently sentimental. They maintain an objectivity poised above the fleshy proletarian struggles. And their imagery is for the most part conceptual." The *transition* poets also echoed a "sensibility of choice" – "the poetic correlative of the intellectual's sense of conflict and the necessity of taking a position." Isidor Schneider (1896-1977) is characterized by Phillips as one who made such a leap: "his early poetry is traditional and his recent poetry is an attempt at direct proletarian poetry." Finally, Phillips argued, other poets have ignored both the influence of the transition poets and the new urban idiom; in particular, H. H. Lewis (1901-85) and Don West have produced "shallow personal effusions," although with wide audience appeal, but "their poetry does not cut into the wealth of perceptions which the best of modern literature has verbalized."[36]

In the same issue, Funaroff, writing under the name Charles Henry Newman, presented "How Objective is Objectivism?," which reflected on a school of poetry that would yield a number of pro-Communists such as George Oppen, Carl Rakosi (b.1903), and Louis Zukofsky (1904-78). (These writers, however, all published little during the 1930s or in some cases the 1940s, so that their poetry evolved external to Party-led literary institutions.)[37] In his critique of their work, Funaroff praised their clear, precise images and firm poetic lines. Significantly, he rebelled against their efforts to minimize the interpretive function of the poet by frequent use of objective nouns for descriptive purposes rather than "as poetically legitimate verbal means for analogy, for symbolical or metaphorical concept." The Objectivists, in Funaroff's view, correctly avoid sentimentality but mistakenly identify it with the expression of emotion. Hence the Objectivists' method fails to organize and coordinate experience most clearly in a social context.

In particular, Funaroff notes that William Carlos Williams (1883-1963)[38] applies his technique of observation to a social object, but falls short because his tools are unable to cope with such a breadth and width of material: "He sees details of poverty but he does not recognize or relate to its cause." Reciting a familiar theme, Funaroff concludes: "Today, the poet . . . must transform himself from the detached recorder of isolated events into the man who participates in the creation of new values and of a new world, into the poet who is proud to give voice to this new experience."[39] Characteristically, Funaroff affirms the modern yet draws back from the brink of modernism in his partisanship on behalf of a realist vision.

In "The Love Campaign," Funaroff surfaces in the pages of *Dynamo* in the same issue writing under the name "Stephen Foster" to offer a fable adapted from a Soviet satirical journal, *The Crocodile*.[40] Funaroff produced the fable in response to perceived demands by the *New Masses* editorial board that poetry be written for special campaigns. In the tale, the "Responsible Editor" of *Left Pass* decides he needs a poem about love to launch a campaign. Hence he summons the writer Kenneth Edwin Haze (a name obviously derived from Kenneth Fearing, Edwin Rolfe, and Alfred Hayes) to produce such a poem to order. At the climax of Funaroff's thinly veiled plea against sectarianism, political criteria are invoked to gut the commissioned poem of its content.[41]

Funaroff was only twenty-one when the landmark volume *We Gather Strength* was published, and most of his contributions to the anthology featuring the work of four poets were written in his nineteenth year. Yet, from the outset of his literary career until his death, he was a beacon among the literary Left—a touchstone for critical observation about the problematics of form and political content. In his introduction to *We Gather Strength*, Mike Gold proclaimed admiration for Funaroff's ability to "combine abstract manifesto and personal lyricism in another curious fantasy. He is eclectic, derivative, and rhetorical, jazz and revolution mix."[42] A few years later Kenneth Fearing wrote in a review of Funaroff's collection *The Spider and the Clock* that his poetry was persuasive but not always poignant; he observed that Funaroff's "bulletins outlining the disasters of the twentieth century, condensed and stark," sometimes tended to cover too much territory, and could be too statistical, lacking a personal slant. Fearing especially admired Funaroff's title poem, "The Spider and the Clock," a work more "wistful" than optimistic, fully charged with the tragic implications of the times. Fearing contended that "a tendency to grandiloquence is his chief fault," but in more personal moments "he is capable of lean and memorable imagery."[43] William Carlos Williams thought that Funaroff's best work was "characterized by technical smoothness, a loveliness of jointure in the words . . . a verbal facility, an ear for the music of the line which is outstanding, a good outline to the image . . . and a clearly indicated relationship of the image to the poem."[44]

Funaroff's capacity to extract the raw materials of his art from the experiences of oppression and to fuse them with romantic images linked to the utopian future is strikingly demonstrated in "Unemployed: 2 A.M." A lone street lamp reveals the destitute of the city collapsed on the benches and grass of a park. As they sleep, the cool grass soothes their bare feet and "The waterfront nearby smells like a black restless wind" with a horn moaning far off that agitates their dreams.[45] "Uprooted" deploys several of the same symbols—an unemployed worker, a street light, a "bare toe." The final stanza implies that the worker's dream can only be realized when passivity is replaced by recognition that directly in front of him stands the "machinery" of society, waiting to be seized:

> The shadows of silent machines
> spread on the walls of the city.
> Amid uptorn pavement of the broken street
> a blanketed steamroller,
> stranded, waits.
> Hands in pockets, he stands at the corner, waiting,
> or walks, a brooding figure, through the streets.[46]

Funaroff's poem thus promotes a complex vision in which nature becomes the stepping stone to a revitalization connected with a mastery of modern city life.

In "To the Dead of the International Brigade," Funaroff praises his fallen comrades by divesting his human self and seeing it transmuted into a force of nature, thus uniting the poet and the environment:

> Let me break down foundations of the earth
> and speak to you in the dust
> as the wind speaks in the dust
> as the dust is carried in the wind
> and the wind makes a speech of it.
>
> Listen to me who hold you in memory
> as a sky holds a cloud tenderly,
> as the earth holds you eternally,
> bearing each Spring green remembrances.[47]

In "The Last Superstition," Manhattan is a graveyard with Egyptian trappings, its subway cars coffins on wheels:

> The city pyramids above the tomb —
> embalmed in oil,
> wound in ticker-tape,
> encased in subway steel.
> As he travels in his coffin,
> his life disintegrates towards his destination
> among the molecules.[48]

In contrast to this near-hallucinatory vision of acute urban isolation, "When the Earth Is Cold" reveals that direct contact with nature revives the soul and instills a will to struggle:

211

> the voices of trees,
> voices that leaf by leaf gather volume;
> now the thunderclap of histories;
> and then the swirling of wind and the dust,
> rain and the seasons.
> And the brown leaves, like letters, vanish in the snow.
>
> We shook our fists at the sun.
> We dug our heels into the mountains.[49]

Such rapid, fierce and immediate lyricism fuses seamlessly with the public moment of the poem's expression of intransigence.

A resuscitation of the modern city through the tropes of romantic love and immersion in nature forms the turning point of Funaroff's nine-part "Dusk of the Gods":

> As a lover's hands evoke desires
> from the body of his love,
> I, too, with fruitful fingers,
> touch with tenderness,
> as twilight a city,
> til electric blooms flower from steel and stone . . .
>
> My hands like hammers,
> my mouth like iron,
> I crushed mountains,
>
> I consumed fear,
> ate darkness.[50]

Funaroff's poet-seer is also a lover whose sequence of neoteric imagery leads to the sensual exploration of new-sprung worlds. Rarely has the desire for erotic-like transcendence been so elegantly fused with the passion for near-violent transformative revolutionary praxis.

Like many of the lesser-known Left poets among the Communist movement, Funaroff felt unappreciated and even somewhat abused by a number of key leaders of the Communist Party's cultural work during the Popular Front era after 1935, when more prominent and established poets were courted by Party-influenced publications and organizations. *Dynamo* and other small magazines were abandoned by the Party, and the *New Masses* became less accessible to minor and novice writers. Funaroff nonetheless accommodated to the pull of the literary Popular Front as it guided writers further away from modernism. The majority of his later poems, after publication of *The Spider and the Clock* (which is largely a retrospective of his young manhood), are noticeably deintellectualized by comparison. His last project was intended to be an anthology of children's street songs.

In a 1938 interview in the *Daily Worker*, Funaroff placed the *Dynamo* and John Reed Club period in historical perspective, characterizing the early 1930s as a time of "literary stimulation" instrumental in "making the literary world realize the significance of a social viewpoint." However, the League of American Writers had become the logical next step in poetic development, with its broader and more encompassing nature. Echoing the *New Masses* call for "a poetry of hope and affirmation," Funaroff spoke about the possibility of "the mass production of poetry in pamphlets that will sell for about ten cents a copy." The *Daily Worker* interviewer praised Funaroff's image as a "regular guy": "S. Funaroff is no long-haired poet with nervous white hands and a strange expression in his eyes. Like most of his contemporaries, Funaroff's appearance is similar to that of any neat young worker." The accompanying photograph showed Funaroff with evenly cropped hair, wearing a checkered tie, white shirt, and double-breasted suit jacket.[51]

Funaroff's grievances about the Party exploded at the time of the Hitler-Stalin Pact, although not so much in objection to the pact itself as to the Soviet Union's subsequent invasion of Finland, and the Communist Party leadership's inept handling of the complex situation. Early in 1940 he wrote a close friend that "there's an urgent need for an independent radical party with a basis and organization in labor."[52]

Funaroff's last published volume of poetry was *Exile from a Future Time: Posthumous Poems by S. Funaroff* (1943). It was graced with cover blurbs by Kenneth Fearing, Alfred Kreymborg, Isidor Schneider, Malcolm Cowley, and Genevieve Taggard. The collection was edited by John Varney (1888–1967), a pro-Communist poet who taught at New York University,[53] and included poems by Funaroff that had been set to music by the African American jazz musician Willie "The Lion" Smith, Paul Bowles, and Waldemar Hill. Before he died, Funaroff also wrote a "Negro Musical," "Tough Scufflin'," and was working on another musical, "King Porter," on his deathbed.

Unlike other Jewish Communist writers and intellectuals who became intimately engaged in African American history and culture from the perspective of championing a Black proletarian vanguard, Funaroff was drawn to the lyricism of African American song from his sense of Blacks as fellow outsiders, like poets and revolutionaries. Concomitantly, Funaroff's visionary writing increasingly took a distinct turn toward Jewish themes. The arc of his ever more demodernized career might be seen in the range of such writings from the troubled allegories of his unfinished "Iron Calf" and "Medieval Jew," to the uplifting and optimistic cantata in five sections, "The

Exiles." In this last work, Funaroff employs in unduly simplified fashion a motif from the Popular Front icon Walt Whitman that Funaroff adapted to the Jewish national resistance struggle: The "people of the grass" bring their wanderings to a climax by gathering themselves "in troops" to destroy "the brown beast."[54]

## Byron of the Poolhalls

Alfred Hayes was born Alfred Haas of Jewish parents in the Whitechapel section of London on 17 April 1911. His mother was the daughter of a butcher who had immigrated to England from Austro-Hungary. She soon met Alfred's father, a veteran of the Russo-Japanese war who had formerly played a wind instrument but was learning the trade of barber. Four months before World War I began, the Haas family moved to New York City where Alfred's father practiced his trade in several hotels. The family name was pronounced "Hayes" in the East End of London, so they decided to adopt the new spelling in the United States.

In the public elementary school in the Jewish section of Harlem where the family resided, young Alfred was frequently asked to read in front of his class. Too young in England to acquire an English accent, he had a voice like a bell; one day he caused a sensation when he was called upon to recite Edgar Allan Poe's "The Bells" before his fifth-grade class. He repeated the performance on many subsequent occasions, thus beginning his early fascination with poetry, as well as drama.

The Hayes family lived on 117th Street in Harlem. After a while Alfred's father acquired his own barber shop; he was also a bookie and played the horses. Alfred started gambling at an early age; as soon as he was able he was shooting craps on the street and betting on the races. Although Hayes's literary and political interests were rapidly growing, his parents insisted that he attend Commerce High School to learn something practical, such as the skills necessary to become a public accountant. The pressure on Alfred inaugurated warfare within the family and he would remain angry at his parents ever after, rendering him unable to have a civil conversation with his father even on the elder man's death-bed. Despite his unhappiness at Commerce High School, Hayes began submitting to the school paper romantic poetry modeled on Swinburne. In private he experimented with realistic fiction inspired by Ben Hecht, and at the age of seventeen he joined the Young Communist League.

After graduating from high school, he attended the City College of New York for six months in 1930. Through his father's connections, he simultaneously obtained a night job as a copy boy at the *New York American*, which was part of the Hearst newspaper chain. One of his first assignments took him to the city morgue where he was overwhelmed by a sense of horror. At the time, he was also reading the Old Testament from which he seemed to absorb the lesson that evil always wins. These two experiences intensified a morose cast from childhood that friends say persisted throughout his life; sometimes it seemed that his demeanor was close to manic-depressive. In the early 1930s, Hayes was mostly unemployed and trying to write; he lived at home and did odd jobs, working as a reporter at the *Daily Mirror*, dishwashing in a summer camp, and holding positions as a delivery boy, waiter, and process server, and even engaged in some minor bootlegging. The cultural sterility of his home, which contained no books, produced in him a terrible hunger for literature; lacking money, he began stealing hundreds of volumes, some from the public library, and educating himself remarkably well. After a visit to Pittsburgh in search of work, and time spent on a farm in Connecticut, he returned to New York to participate in the Communist movement and start publishing in the *New Masses*.[55]

Hayes had a young face, black hair, and was five feet nine inches tall. He was handsome in a Byronic way, and one could sense his intensity; as the years passed, his poetry and fiction would be increasingly marked by the guilt and nostalgia, sometimes recalling Byron's verse, too. At the YMCA he read poetry aloud, and he produced plays at the Left-wing Camp Unity, where he also acted. In his fiction and poetry he prided himself on making the utmost effort to tell what he saw as the truth. At the same time he remained addicted to pinball machines and pool halls. Although he read Hart Crane as he walked the streets of New York, he preferred to hang out with nonintellectuals, spending time with cabdrivers in pinball palaces. He didn't like pretensions and could be quite modest on occasion; for example, he never boasted about his literary achievements in front of those having problems getting published.

Hayes's first ambition was to become a newspaperman, and he worked as a reporter at both the *New York American* and the *Daily Mirror* between 1932 and 1935, before being laid off. After a while he worked in Harrisburg, Pennsylvania, writing a radio drama script for the International Ladies Garment Workers Union. He then worked for the Federal Writers' Project and sold a few poems, but could not get a volume of his poetry published. With Communist composer Earl Robinson, Hayes wrote a May Day verse, "Into the Streets May First!," which appeared on the cover of the *New Masses* and was set to music by the Left-wing composer Aaron Copland.[56] His 1936 poem about Joe Hill was reworked into a famous ballad by Earl Robinson.[57] Occasionally Hayes wrote Mike Gold's *Daily Worker* column for him. Hayes was extremely versatile, moving easily among poetry, short stories, criticism, essays, plays, and, later, film, television, and novels.

After marrying Gertrude, his first wife, Hayes lived on St. Mark's Place in Greenwich Village in the 1930s. Kenneth Fearing lived close by on Bleecker Street, and the Hayeses spent much time at the Fearings'. Hayes became a prominent figure in the John Reed Club and was a noted participant at the Second National Conference, where he was described by the *New Masses* as "dark, Dantean, witty, conscious to imperiousness that he personifies a new sort of 'young generation,' the lyric poet of the New York working class, of the strike front."[58] Although he continued to be publicly identified as a Communist, Hayes's only known political activity in the mid-Depression was with a group who placed people's furniture back in their homes after they had been evicted; he attended the group's meetings as well as participated in its actions. In the late 1930s Hayes began to evidence dissatisfaction with the Communist Party's claims regarding Spain and the Moscow Trials, and what he perceived as its functionalist orientation toward Left writers. He complained to his wife, Gertrude, that he couldn't even write a poem against the church if the Communists were in an alliance with it.[59] While not exactly disillusioned, he found himself at odds with his circle of friends. Sol Funaroff began to complain about Hayes's "bitterness," which he interpreted as "a form of petty, personal dissatisfaction." Funaroff, who no doubt was threatened by anti-Party criticisms, reported to Nathan Adler in mid-1937 that he had seen both Hayes and Kenneth Fearing on the eve of the latter's departure for England on a Guggenheim fellowship:

> Hayes was there and in an awful gripe, carping about the Party stand on Spain, the Moscow Trials, Novelist X, Comrade Y, and Poet Z. He was in a blue funk about his literary self and making the customary wisecracks about the people whom he knew. Fearing replied with his own brand of witticism. It struck me that the difference between the humor of Kenneth Fearing and of A. Hayes is the difference between dead-pan humor and bedpan humor. . . . The latter is dirty and sickly, inspired by maliciousness and envy, and the former is the mask of irony, the defense of a man hurt and embittered by life, and of a mind accustomed to and amused and scornful of the tragedies of ordinary existence.[60]

Funaroff's observations may have been influenced by political differences, which may also be true of Adler's recollection of Hayes's misanthropic interpretation of a strange incident that occurred at the funeral of Funaroff. Sol's brother, Urie, stepped forward and appeared to throw a copy of Sol's *The*

*Spider and the Clock* into his coffin. Later Sol's friends wondered if this was perhaps a ritual of burying a treasured object with a loved one. Hayes, however, insisted to others present that Urie had thrown the book as an assault motivated by envy.[61]

Hayes's growing skepticism allowed him to openly question the Moscow Trials in ways that others in his circle found unthinkable. Once Fearing arrived in England, Hayes begged him to travel on to see the situation in the Soviet Union at first hand. He had doubts about the defenses of the early Moscow Trials that he heard from Joseph Freeman and Joshua Kunitz:

> I know I'd like to take a look sometimes at what I'm supposed to be fighting for and see if it looks anything at all what it's supposed to look like and if it's worthwhile. I might have contracted for something I don't want at all, you can't tell. I made a political blind date and maybe the dame ain't nothing like she sounded over the phone.

In contrast, Herman Spector grimly accepted the necessity of the trials and Edwin Rolfe was among those who would "stiffen up like cats" when Hayes expressed any dissatisfaction with the Party analysis.[62]

Hayes admired Jewish writers such as Moishe Nadir (1885–1943) and I. L. Peretz (1851–1915); while he didn't know Yiddish, he was nonetheless fascinated by the European culture of such writers. Baudelaire, Heine, and Hopkins were also meaningful to him, and he read much of the poetry of William Carlos Williams. In the *Partisan Review,* Hayes wrote that, while influences on his generation can be traced to Crane, Eliot, and Pound, "it was not so much individual poets and poetic methods as general objectives and ambitions in the poetic atmosphere, charge[d], true, by the bourgeois poets of the preceding generation." He was influenced not just by the masters, but by fugitive pieces that appeared in the little magazines.

In the late 1930s, Hayes worked as a "radio hack" and began to regard himself a playwright. Two of his more successful efforts were the Broadway play *Journeyman* (1938) and the musical *'Tis of Thee* (1948). In the early 1940s Hayes served as film critic for the Left-wing publication *Friday.* From 1943 to 1945 he served in the U.S. Army, and while launching a career as a novelist, from 1945 to 1950 he was a writer for Warner Brothers, RKO, and Twentieth Century Fox in Hollywood.

No full-length collection of poetry by Hayes appeared until after the Depression. These volumes reprinted few of the poems from his revolutionary period, and none that expressed his socialist outlook. One of those not included was the poem Hayes considered his most distinguished of the early Depression years, "In a Coffee Pot." In 1934, Hayes had successfully lobbied

Granville Hicks to feature it in the 1935 volume *Proletarian Literature in the United States*, rather than his "Into the Streets May First!" "If you think for a moment of the poems not in terms of their immediate necessities, but from the point of view of the place in the development of our poetry," he pleaded, "Coffee Pot" was far superior. While modestly granting that the poem had "derivative" features and "echoes," he insisted, "It is the first poem I know of in the movement which attempted to create a realistic, representative experience of my generation – a generation which is a decisive factor in the growth of revolutionary consciousness."[63]

The poem beholds the world through a disenfranchised central consciousness, a young man who articulates the collective thoughts of a group of unemployed youth; their brooding is clearly intended to be a prelude to social action:

> And I have seen how men lift up their hands
> And turn them so and pause –
> And so the slow brain moves and understands –
> And so with a million hands.[64]

Hayes's method is to commence with a catalogue of petty grievances and myopic attachments, until a quantity of such perceptions transforms into a qualitative leap in consciousness. A similar theme of isolation is explored even more pointedly in the dramatic monologue of a character called "Singleman," who turns out to be an "everyman." The call for action, though subtle, is again unequivocal: "Yet change dreamed of brings no change."[65]

Communist politics takes center stage in "To Otto Bauer," a bitter denunciation of the reformism of the Austrian social democrat, who delayed calling for armed struggle against the right-wing government until it was too late. The workers who died in battle against the fascists are redeemed by their actions and join the company of the French Communards of 1871 and the German revolutionaries of 1919:

> All honor to them, Bauer! For you
> History prepares a shameful grave. . . .
> But they – they sleep with Communards,
> Their brother Spartacists lie at their side,
> They marched forth Social Democrats but Bolsheviks they died![66]

Another poem, "The Port of New York," satirizes the myth of "the Promised land," and "In a Home Relief Bureau" presents a Prufrockian sensibility coping with a representative Depression reality:

And the minutes. And the hours.
But you have time to wait
Now there is nothing left you have but time.
What you were when you were not this
What you were before time brought you down to this
(Before the last policy was cashed
Before the last ring was pawned)
Now you have time enough to recall.
Think now of the profit and the pride
The ambition fed in furnished rooms
The nails kept clean against the imagined day.
The pressed suit, the manner honest and assured,
The undeceitful face,
Survives for this that once was not to be endured,
This charity, this disgrace.[67]

Once again we have a relentless cataloguing of the objectified consciousness of frustrated desire. His breathless style, persistently urgent in a straight-forward manner, creates an effect both purposeful yet sufficiently subtle to yield an unfeigned political art in concert with his view of historically progressive forces.

*The Big Time* (1944), Hayes's first full-length volume of poems, published with drawings by Beatrice Tobias, vividly paints the realistic, drab inner torments of New York City with its movie houses, dance halls, and bars. But the poems in the collection are devoid of even the rudimentary markers of a transcendent social vision. Moreover, Hayes's project of honing a more realistic and truthful poetry through the respectful study of modernist technical advances has matured in an unexpected manner. Indeed, what Hayes retained from his early mentors is reduced to what Mike Gold called "the sterile, hopeless literary mood" of high modernism.[68] Other than his occasional use of free verse, the language, structure, and allusions in his poems are as lucid and conventional as those embraced by the British Victorians and romantics, and American poets such as Whitman, Robinson, and Frost.

*The Big Time* was well received as a collection marked by emotion that was pure and forceful, and writing that was vigorous and dramatic. But by this time Hayes was too involved with his own private hell of cynicism to qualify any longer as a Left poet. His World War II experiences were exhilarating but left him with indelible pain, and his depression intensified. Class distinctions are omnipresent throughout the poetry collection, but the bitterness of the "have-nots," as depicted in "I Always Come Home" and "My Cousin Herman," is limited to a desire to personally replace or have revenge upon the "haves." Interaction between the sexes is more pronounced than in earlier work, but consistently debased by deception and exploitation, climaxing in the horrifying narrative of a lover's castration by a cuckolded husband in "In the Village."

The poems collected in *Welcome to the Castle* (1950) introduce a somewhat improved mood in that their inner world reflects increasing complexity and subjectivity, ensconced in the grim comic castle of middle age. The first half of the collection is based on Hayes's war-time experiences. A reader could feel that the verse conveys a sense of a sensitive individual with traces of social conscience and vivid historical sense, but also of one who has chosen poetry for reflections because of its succinctness and opportunities for dramatic contrast and suggestive paradox. A closer reading, though, shows that Hayes's World War II poems culminate in an momentous avowal of utter transformation in a dramatic monologue called " – As a Young Man." Reflecting on a photograph of himself at the age of twenty-five, in 1934, "before the present war," the speaker finds his young self and the worldview of the 1930s unrecognizable:

> But who remembers now
> The volunteers to Spain?
> Or how the miners stood
> Sullen and angry men
> In Lawrenceville in the rain?
>
> The boy in the portrait smiles
> But Time has had the ultimate laugh.[69]

The second part of the collection commences with "The People of the Pit," a description of an exile's return to a profit-driven society in which individual survival is the only objective: "You are home again among the familiar cannibals. / Put on the terrible mask, and dress."[70]

Hayes's final volume, *Just Before the Divorce* (1968), is unexpected in several respects. The collection reveals a Hayes who passed through the tumultuous 1960s rebellion of youth against the Vietnam war and racial oppression without registering the slightest empathy or reradicalization. Instead, the political atmosphere of the 1960s inspired in Hayes a return to the haunting moments of a time prior to his Communist youth. The collection published in the landmark year 1968 demarcates the contours of the monumental sadness that colored his writing, though it is troubling that Hayes never seems able to go beyond the vivid dramatization of his own narcissism. The collection opens with "The Tennis Players," showing a thirteen-year-old Alfred lurking by the tennis courts of a summer vacation resort, clandestinely eyeing the wealthy young women with their rackets and split skirts. In this bar mitzvah into the world of envy and lust, the boy, a son of a barber who has been given a room above the garage to house his family in return for his services, seethes with resentment as he reflects on the scene to which he is an outsider by age and class:

> The hotel orchestra agitated the dreams of the barber's son.
>     The women on the lawns
> in the evenings with jewels in their hair and on their arms,
> were more naked than any women he had ever seen. . . .

In the closing lines, the boy reflects as the tennis game ends:

> the tennis players departed.
> He sat, hearing the vast blue fall
>     of night; hearing,
> on some estate, a dog's faint yap.
> Wetly his hands lay in his corduroy lap.
>     His mother, hearing him return,
> Looked up from the stove.
> She saw on her son's face something queer: a flush,
>     blooded, as though he'd sat
> too close to some great fire
> and had come back to her marked by a singular burn.[71]

The burn, unlike the birth deformity of Oedipus's club foot, or the "Mark of Cain" that God inflicted upon Adam's son guilty of fratricide, appears to be the perversion of an image of nature's potential bounty. That is, the boy's face is damaged by the sun rather than beautified, due to the lust of his consciousness.

References to a "father" pervade many of Hayes's other poems in the collection, especially "The Father of Us All," "My Father Was Shaving a Dead Man When," and "To Be a King in Athens." By the middle of the collection, Hayes moves forward in time so that disillusionment with romantic love has become the fulcrum. In the title poem, "Just before the Divorce," the rage of jealousy that earlier fueled bitter meditations on class privilege now becomes transferred to the untrammeled and misogynous violence of a betrayed husband who mentally burns his wife's clothing, rapes her, shoots down "her winged and middle class desires," and then with

> A Zulu spear
> pierces her pierced ear.
> . . . smashes her laughter.

    Machineguns
her smile.
Hangs her perfect breasts from the attic rafter.
    A final shot—
dead, he grins at a twitching twat.[72]

Following this catharsis, the remainder of the poems in the collection range in tone from melancholy to misery as Hayes treats the aftermath of his new life as a tourist in Paris and Japan, an inhabitant of a middle-class house in Studio City, California, and reflects once more on his war-time experiences. Technically, his verse remains an extension of his 1930s blend of motifs from Eliot and Fearing applied to personal and more contemporary experience. Yet such a repetitive, compulsive display of hopelessness becomes increasingly banal in its mechanical cuteness:

Someday, I suppose, the sea, harsh, cleansing,
    will inundate this town.
I hear a homosexual laughter as we drown.[73]

Hayes's novels also reflect a mounting increase in his singly cynical tone. Yet their comparative length tends to promise more, heightening one's sense of a lack of fulfillment. In both genres, it seems as if Hayes's pledge of truthful self-disclosure, in which his art served therapeutic functions, only scarcely pierces the exterior, not probing beyond a certain painful point; Hayes simply could not search deeper into himself. This corresponded to ambivalence that he was unable to master. Initially, he announced that his work on screenplays was just temporary; he planned to go to Hollywood for a maximum of twenty weeks to make some good money, which would enable him to write novels the rest of the year. But his tarriances in California grew longer and longer until he moved there permanently.

Hayes's career as a novelist matured during the war. In the 1930s he had produced little fiction, although he wrote radio plays and was a great admirer of Ben Hecht's slick novelistic facility. However, when he submitted his first collection of poetry to the New York publishers Howell and Soskin, they recognized that Hayes's poems were strongly marked by a drive toward a narrative. They convinced him to try writing fiction. After the war, when Hayes moved on from them in favor of another publisher for his third, best-selling novel, they felt betrayed.

When Hayes was drafted into the army, he allocated part of his salary to his mother and part to his wife. Throughout his maturity he was a chief breadwinner for his family and supported many relatives. Gertrude was astonished that he had the discipline to survive basic training. Soon he was assigned to work in entertainment, serving, among other assignments, as a museum guide under the U.S. occupation of Italy. There he became acquainted with the director Roberto Rosellini and collaborated with him on the script of the successful postwar movie *Paisan* (1946). When Hayes returned to New York City he was invited to work on a Hollywood film, thereby establishing his first links with the motion picture industry.

*All Thy Conquests* (1946) was an stirring first novel about the contrarieties between American troops and Roman citizens. The narrative is based on an factual case of the rise and fall of a fascist hoodlum who became a lackey for the Nazis, and who was eventually lynched by a mob. The Americans depicted by Hayes are homesick, childishly irresponsible but historically alert to possible rebirth of fascism; the Italians are cynical and despairing. The novel was ubiquitously praised for its expert construction, evocation of mood, and sensitive rendering of Italian characters.

*Shadow of Heaven* (1947) is Hayes's most revealing political novel, depicting an aging labor organizer, Harry Oberon. Oberon, whose name recalls the influential romantic poem by C. M. Wieland as well as the King of the Fairies in Shakespeare's *A Midsummer Night's Dream*, has begun to doubt the validity of his calling, life in general, and love. His inner drama is presented in prose that carries shadings and nuances of a Jamesian novel; the dialogue and characterization are vivid. But Oberon, a burned-out crusader, is already so demoralized that he exudes an atmosphere of fatigue.

*The Girl on the Via Flaminia* (1949), Hayes's most successful novel, is about an affair between an American G.I. and an Italian woman during the last year of the war. The novel became the vehicle by which Hayes would finally secure a niche in the world of wealth and privilege to which he so long aspired. In 1954 he transformed it into a play (the genre in which it was originally conceived) which was first performed at the Circle in the Square theater in New York. It then had a successful Broadway run before Hayes adapted it as a movie, *Act of Love*, with its setting transferred to Paris and its central woman character French rather than Italian.

Hayes's subsequent novels attracted much less notice and dwelled almost exclusively on failed marriages and love affairs. *In Love* (1953), a triangular love story, is once more in the Jamesian idiom, told from the point of view of a middle-aged artist. Hayes displays a strong feeling for words and an ability to make them count. *My Face for the World to See* (1958) depicts an affair between a successful New York screenwriter and a young girl trying to break into the movies. Once again, Hayes's strength is in his merciless insight into human behavior. *The End of Me* (1968) is about the termination of the protagonist's second marriage in California, after which he comes to

New York to meet his sullen 26-year-old poet-nephew. *The Temptation of Don Volpi* (1960) consists of three novellas and drew little comment. Hayes's last collection of fiction, *The Stockbroker, the Bitter Young Man, and the Beautiful Girl* (1973), was published in England and attracted no notice in the United States.

After his radicalism waned, Hayes's longtime tendencies toward cynicism and romanticism came to the fore. Yet the modifications in his poetry and fiction were hardly due to opportunism; they faithfully reflected his post-war outlook. The major mutation in his life can be pinpointed to his service in the Army in Italy during the war; the U.S. Army Special Services turned out to be a wonderful opportunity for him when he engaged in entertaining, writing, guiding, and translating (he quickly picked up Italian). The experience was transforming and he blossomed, beginning to feel for the first time his real creative power. Hayes had a new look at the world and it seemed a much larger place than the somewhat parochial one he had known in New York City among the pro-Communist cultural milieu. Italy was the venue of his two most successful novels; he was struck by the suffering of war and also by a feeling that ideological politics had caused these horrors to happen. As in the case of his contemporary Irwin Shaw (1913–1984), who followed an analogous trajectory but with greater success, he started seeing the world less in terms of classes and more in terms of "people," as individuals. He may have remained sensitive to exploitation and oppression, but he did not have the necessary conviction to fight for a cause. Friends remember a great sadness about him.

As Hayes negotiated between his desire to write truthful poetry and fiction, and his attraction to the easy money available in film and television, his road was somewhat rocky. He more or less went his own unswerving way, his independence making things difficult for him in Hollywood. Hayes could not stand stupidity when he encountered it, so that he continually alienated agents, producers, and even friends. Yet he had an intelligence that was highly respected. Moreover, he was sufficiently cautious to refrain from moving to Hollywood permanently until the McCarthy witch-hunt was mainly over. He maintained a New York City apartment during his early visits, and, while still friendly with many Leftists in Hollywood, stayed aloof from their defense campaigns against blacklisting. Film became increasingly attractive to him; it meant high pay, exciting trips, a good life, and meeting interesting Hollywood characters. By the end of the 1960s, Hayes had primarily shifted to writing television shows such as "The Alfred Hitchcock Hour." But frequently his name did not appear in the credits because his task was to doctor and rewrite scripts.

Hayes's reputation faded much too rapidly, apparently because of a con-tradiction between his authentic writing skills and the talent for which he was esteemed. Hayes's poetry was impressive for the way in which he chose his words, but reviews suggest that his popularity was rooted instead in his poems' narrative quality. His novels at first were favored for their blend of historical consciousness and political awareness, without the imposition of a "line," combined with a poet's sensitivity to word use. But after his third novel the historical dimension faded, and all that was left to admire were his language and Jamesian nuances. Still, in the most disturbing of his last short stories, the 1960 "Gondola," Hayes's talents coalesce to provide a powerful retrospective commentary on the illusions of his radical youth.[74]

The story reworks key elements from the Scottsboro trial, a burning cause of the 1930s because, at the time, the political and moral issues seemed clear-cut. In the famous case, attorneys for the accused established that the two white prostitutes in the trial had lied about being raped by the Black youths in a gondola car on a train in Alabama; one of the women, in fact, recanted and toured the country on behalf of the convicted men. In "Gondola," how-ever, everything is blurred, beginning with the dates of the events in Hayes's narrative.

His fictionalized and transformed version of the events portrays a lawyer, limned in a hard-boiled detective style, sent to a small town in the northern United States by a committee in Birmingham, Alabama, seeking justice. The lawyer is investigating a legal case where a young white woman has claimed that two Blacks had raped her in the gondola car of a train while holding a gun on her boyfriend, and that they then killed a brakeman who inter-vened, by throwing the brakeman off the train. The lawyer is convinced that the white woman is lying, and he wants her to return to Birmingham to tell the truth. Strangely, he carries his convictions in something of a restrained fashion. He insinuates the idea that his sole motivation is to establish the "truth"; there is no evidence that he is especially concerned about the racial dimensions of the case or that he holds Left-wing views. He attempts to use a combination of money and moralistic arguments to urge the woman and her companion, Grady, to go back to Birmingham to testify.

When Grady departs the apartment to walk his dog, the lawyer is left uncomfortably alone with the woman. After resisting her attempts at seduc-tion, he listens to her dramatic rendition of the story of her life. When Grady returns, a combination of too much alcohol and the tension of the situation induces her to disclose that she had actually been raped by the white brake-man, and that Grady had been too cowardly to intervene. The brakeman had been killed when he attacked a black youth who had spied on the episode.

In the pandemonium that follows this revelation, the lawyer is attacked by the dog and the couple flee with his money, symbolically tearing up, but not taking, his identification cards.

The most forceful property of the story is its atmosphere. The reader leaves the tale with a resolute impression that "evil" is not so easily classifiable as the Scottsboro case would have one believe. Moreover, one senses that "evil" is linked to a trait rudimentary to humanity, one's "animal" nature; the dog serves as an objective correlative for the growing violence of the narrative and it attacks when threatened. At the same time, one's behavior is very much connected to controlling factors in life beyond one's choice; the down-and-out woman, and Grady, act according to their brutal environmental conditioning. Nothing really can be done; but the half-hearted lawyer, a stand-in for Hayes, must continue to combat evil without any illusion that he is fighting for a righteous "cause."

Hayes's political disillusionment is understandable and even compelling in light of his individual experiences; but it is not particularly representative of his generation of Left poets, most of whom chose to redefine their socialist commitments during the postwar years without abandoning them completely. Of course, the one-time "have-not" Hayes modified aspects of his personality accordingly as he became transformed into one of the "haves." His old friend Nathan Adler recalls meeting Hayes for dinner on San Francisco's Fisherman's Wharf in the mid-1950s, after Hayes had married the beautiful daughter of an eminent Hollywood director. Adler, whose perception may have been influenced by his continuing Left commitment, recalled that he was stunned by the imperious manner in which Hayes pronounced his food improperly prepared and ordered it returned to the kitchen.[75]

More considerably, Hayes's literary evolution typifies the failure of high modernism to really take root among the majority of Communist poets most drawn to Eliot, Pound, and Crane in their formative years. To be sure, the Depression-era poetry and aesthetic orientations of Herman Spector, Sol Funaroff, Alfred Hayes, and the better-known Kenneth Fearing all provide persuasive indications that a strong current within the Communist cultural movement embraced many features of modernism and the avant-garde. All were capable of exceptional phrasing and innovative approaches, and in their prime they deployed experiments in form to dramatize and depict working-class experiences, dereify perceptions, and promote revolutionary perspectives. Yet all suffered from the consequences of their economic insecurity – the premature death of Funaroff, deflection of the potential of artistic fulfillment for Spector, an enforced new career as the author of thrillers and mysteries for Fearing, and an evolution toward an alternative artistic vision that may not have done justice to the talents of Hayes. The self-generated institutions of the Left, of course, were too fragile and embroiled in too many inherent contradictions due to the growing demand for uplifting verse, to provide adequate sustenance or long-term cultural nourishment. In a way, briefly summarized, the revolutionary pilgrimage of Spector, Funaroff, Fearing, and Hayes is the story of rank-and-file, organizationally committed 1930s Left poets for whom the temptations of modernist culture provided palpable stimuli but few enduring answers.

## CHAPTER 7

# Sappho in Red

## Loyalties

One of the most acclaimed Communist poets lived her intimate life and forged her career as a modern feminist, but in her cultural theory and practice she professed to eschew loyalties based on gender difference. The avowed meager investment of Genevieve Taggard in gender identity is perplexing but not anomalous among the Literary Left. Her poetic credo is concordant with the antiromantic stance of her critical statements:

> The reader will misunderstand my poems if he thinks I have been trying to write about myself (as if I were in any way unique) as a biographer might – or as a Romantic poet would, to map his own individuality. Since the earliest attempts at verse I have tried to use the "I" in a poem only as a means of transferring feeling to identification with anyone who takes the poem, momentarily, for his own. "I" is then adjusted to the voice of the reader.[1]

Yet Taggard did write several poems strictly about female life experiences, such as "To My Mother," recalling her mother's domestic labor, and "Proud Day," about the Black singer Marian Anderson, which begins: "Our sister sang on the Lincoln steps."[2] She also proclaimed forthrightly in the book-jacket blurb of her Collected Poems that "Many poems in this collection are about the experiences of women. I hope these express all types of candid and sturdy women."[3] Taggard's intricate and perhaps contradictory approach to gender can only be fathomed in the context of the particularities of her personal and political evolution.

Born in Washington State in 1894, Taggard was the eldest of three children whose parents were schoolteachers of Scotch-Irish and French Huguenot lineage. They were pietistic members of the Disciples of Christ Church, and occupied her childhood with the Bible and hymns.[4] Until the age of two she lived on an apple farm in Washington, after which her parents moved to Hawaii to work in the public schools and start a missionary program. There, Taggard grew up among children of Hawaiian, Chinese, Portuguese, and

Japanese descent, an experience that created a sense of racial equality and community amidst a refined indigence. Her remembrance of this childhood would differ vividly from her experiences on the mainland when the family twice returned for visits to their erstwhile domicile in Washington due to her father's lung ailment and for economic reasons. The racism and class exploitation she beheld in Washington shaped her impression that she had been momentarily cast out of Eden.[5] At the age of thirteen, back in Hawaii, Taggard became engrossed in Keats, writing imitations of his poems. For eighteen years she lived in a setting she would later idealize for its guilelessness and for the rectitude of her family's courtly pauperism. Thus her artistic discernment became molded around contrasts branded by repulsive realities (Washington State) and the intimation of a finer life (Hawaii), with her poetry constituting the transit between the two.

In 1914 Taggard was granted a scholarship to attend the University of California at Berkeley. Her father was by now too afflicted to work, so her family moved to the San Francisco Bay Area where her mother ran a boardinghouse for students, with her assistance. Genevieve took assorted jobs to raise money for family expenses, which lengthened her undergraduate career to six years. Superior in literature, Taggard became editor of the college literary magazine, *Occident*. Inflamed by writers who had been associated with *Occident*, such as Frank Norris (1870–1902) and Jack London (1876–1916), she began thinking of herself as a socialist. Her writing teachers included Leonard Bacon (1887–1954) and Witter Bynner (1881–1968). In these years, Taggard was lofty and slender, with delicately sculpted features and brown hair. She spoke and read poetry with a rich, warm voice, and decades later Bacon remembered her as sweet-natured, radiantly pretty, and full of vital energy.[6]

With her verse published in a few national publications, Taggard came to New York in 1920 to work in the publishing house of B. W. Huebsch. Soon Van Wyck Brooks (1865–1963) was asking her to review for the *Freeman*. Taggard then initiated her own little poetry magazine, the *Measure: A Magazine of Verse*, with Maxwell Anderson (1888–1959), Elinor Wylie (1885–1928), Louise Bogan (1879–1970), and others, which lasted for six years. In 1921 she married a Jewish radical from Cleveland, Robert Wolf, and their daughter, Marcia, was born soon after.

Five books of her poetry appeared in the 1920s, amalgamating love lyrics, exotic recollections of Hawaii, and a Marxist sensibility: *For Eager Lovers* (1922), *Hawaiian Hilltop* (1923), *Words for the Last Chisel* (1926), and *Traveling Standing Still* (1928). In 1930 she published an acclaimed scholarly volume, *The Life and Mind of Emily Dickinson*, concentrating on the Dickinsons' father-daughter kinship. The volume had taken Taggard eight years to research and write, and was grounded in abundant primary materials and interviews. This substantial achievement was succeeded by more poetry: *Remembering Vaughan in New England* (1933), *Not Mine to Finish* (1934), *Calling Western Union* (1936), *Collected Poems: 1918–1938* (1938), *Long View* (1942), *Falcon* (1942), *A Part of Vermont* (1945), and *Slow Music* (1946). In the late 1920s Taggard was temporarily an instructor at Mount Holyoke College. In 1931 she was honored with a Guggenheim Fellowship to pursue her poetry writing, which permitted her to take her daughter to Capri and Mallorca. She booked passage back to the United States to become one of the first faculty members at Bennington College. After 1934 she taught permanently at Sarah Lawrence College. That same year she divorced Robert Wolf and a year later married Kenneth Durant, the U.S. director of the Soviet news agency TASS. All through the 1930s Taggard's books received complimentary reviews, and she enlarged her creative work to encompass collaboration with composers who put her poetry to music.

By the late 1940s Taggard began to show multiplying marks of illness due to hypertension; she retired from teaching in order to concentrate on her writing while living in the Vermont home she shared with Durant. In May of 1948 she was given an award from the American Academy of Arts and Letters but failed to appear at the presentation ceremony. Taggard died in a New York hospital that November, shortly before her fifty-fourth birthday.

Taggard was able to intermix a career as a remarkably flourishing writer and teacher with a split personal life: initially, as a free-spirited bohemian radical; later, as a resolute and constant Communist fellow-traveler. Following her landing in New York, "Jed," as Taggard was nicknamed by her friends, was introduced to the *Masses* and *Liberator* circle by Max Eastman, who would afterward be among her lovers, as would Joseph Freeman and playwright Maxwell Anderson (1888–1959). Her relation to Robert Leopold Wolf was tempestuous and convoluted. Wolf, born in 1895 to a wealthy Cleveland family, graduated from Harvard and made national news in 1916 with his first marriage, to a Bryn Mawr student, which was ratified by a signed contract in which both parties "promise to faithfully perform to the community all the duties and obligations of marriage necessary to the community's welfare."[7] From the time Wolf divorced his first wife and married Taggard, monogamy was not a priority for Wolf, and for some time he doubted that he was the father of their daughter.[8] After the child was born, Taggard conjectured that Wolf was angry because the new responsibility encroached on his dream of becoming a novelist. She also hypothesized that Wolf suffered a severe inferiority complex due to his self-hatred of his Jewish background.[9] Later Wolf participated in a *menage à trois* with Josephine Herbst, who was Anderson's lover as well.

A tall, nervously alert, wiry slim man with dark eyes, Wolf began his literary career as a disciple of D. H. Lawrence and Floyd Dell. In the 1920s, he issued a book of poems and some erotic stories about group sex and wife swapping. He then evolved into an early proponent of proletarian literature and traveled to the Soviet Union.[10] Dell was initially announced as the godfather of Wolf's daughter, but this status was afterward rescinded when their intimacy cooled. By the end of the decade Wolf was showing signs of psychological illness; institutionalized, he attacked a guard and was committed for life.

Taggard, devastated by Wolf's retraction from her, was drawn to Kenneth Durant (1899-1972) during the late 1920s, when Durant was still married to Ernestine Evans, an editor at J. Lippincott. Joseph Freeman, employed by TASS at that time, mediated among the various parties as Durant's marriage unraveled. Durant was born to a wealthy Philadelphia family in 1889; his grandfather had made money by investing in railroads in Russia. Durant graduated from Harvard in 1912, where he was friends with radical journalist John Reed, and then held jobs with the *Philadelphia Bulletin* and the Federal War Information Agency. Through a friendship with the American diplomat William C. Bullit, Durant assumed the post of aide to Col. Edward M. House, the adviser to President Woodrow Wilson, and was asked to attend the Versailles Peace Conference.

Roused by the Russian Revolution, Durant returned to the United States to become press secretary to the then unrecognized Soviet envoy. After publishing an official Soviet English language magazine for several years, he opened a bureau for the Soviet news agency TASS in 1923. Durant managed the TASS bureau for two decades until the onset of Taggard's illness in 1944. Brokenhearted by her death, he retired to Vermont to write articles on outdoor subjects and a book about the Adirondacks. Durant became the director of the Blue Mountain Museum and married Helen Van Dongen, previously the wife of the Communist filmmaker Jorge Ivens. In 1972, Durant was stricken by a fatal heart attack.

While never a member of the Communist Party, Durant was dogmatically pro-Soviet and never demonstrated an autonomous or critical outlook. Taggard, although a free spirit in the 1920s, appears to have adapted to Durant's political stance in the 1930s. Her correspondence at the time of the Moscow Trials with two close friends and literary mentors, Charles Erskine Scott Wood (1852-1944) and Sara Bard Field, reveals a zealous obstinacy in her devout credence in the guilt of the framed-up victims of the Moscow Trials.

She accredited every allegation about Trotsky and his followers colluding with the Nazis.[11] Her poetry collection *Falcon* was devoted utterly to pro-Soviet effusions, hinting at the manner in which her utopian fantasy about Hawaii had become reworked to cohere around a set of sites and symbols in the Soviet Union, including geographical ones such as Stalin's birthplace (Tiflis) and a rest home on the Black Sea. At the peak of the Moscow purge trials she venerated the Soviet Union as "A country come forever past the shade / The dark, the stormy death that on this planet lies." Its resolute action in defeating its enemies is "good news":

> The worker and the idle worker hear
> The simple facts that crooks cannot confuse.
>
> See, on this planet one large patch is changed.
> The other areas work like chemical dyes
> To blot the color out . . . maps daily ranged
> In new alliance with new elaborate lies.[12]

While the utopian longings for a world they would never see were corroded by pessimism in the poetry of Herman Spector, cut short by the premature death of Sol Funaroff, and transmuted into nostalgia and guilt by Alfred Hayes, the example of Taggard suggests a trajectory in which vestiges of intellectual and moral doubt are increasingly absolved by a political piety of the emotions. Within this framework, the poems that Taggard came to cherish most were those optimistic about the hopeful possibilities of Communism.

In 1937, when Granville Hicks disapprovingly reviewed the poetry and prose selections in Horace Gregory's volume *New Letters in America*, he assailed many selections for negativism. Nonetheless, he initiated his comments with a statement recalling his early training for the ministry: "Communism is good news." From her desk at Sarah Lawrence, Taggard dashed off a letter to Hicks fully endorsing this uplifting sentiment, and urging him to look at her recent *Collected Poems*: "Some time ago I said what you only partly said in your *New Masses* piece. I said it well; I put it into portable form, I wished it to be used." She then identified five key poems – "Image," "Remembering Vaughan," "Funeral in May," "Definition of Song," and "Lark" – as her legacy to the Left.[13]

The reigning themes of the first four poems are that joy comes in response to death and suffering, "reality" is what one discerns in the beauty and clarity of moonlight, and the duty of poetry is to infuse speech and movement with hope. Yet it was with the fifth poem, "Lark," that she chose to close her collected works:

233

*Sappho in Red*

> O lark, from great dark, arise!
> O, lark of light,
> O, Lightness like a spark,
> Shock ears and stun our eyes
> Singing the day-rise, the day-rise, the great day-rise.[14]

The proposition, that poetic optimism is the antidote to mental despair, seems to have evolved initially in the early 1930s when Taggard may have suffered a breakdown. During those years she also made her pledge to Communism and consolidated her relationship with Kenneth Durant. By the time of her death, it was her anthem.

## The Rational Ecologist

Ruth Lechlitner was one of the most intellectually exacting of the poets who were pro-Communist. In her contribution to the 1935 *Partisan Review* discussion of revolutionary poetry conducted prior to the First American Writers' Congress, she assented to many of the shortcomings of Left poets that had been cited in the introductory statement by Edwin Rolfe. Lechlitner, however, offers an alternative explication for the problems Rolfe noted of "static, fragmentary, repetitional and superficial" work. In her view, these deficiencies were the result of a lack of seriousness in the poets' political absorption of the theory of the revolutionary movement. Lechlitner provides a minilecture on Hegel and dialectics, beseeching a greater understanding of the laws and processes governing the universe. Returning to the mid-nineteenth century for analogies, she reasons that the typical Left poet of the early Depression resembled John Greenleaf Whittier, who focused on the abolition of slavery and sought practical solutions to immediate problems. A superior model could be found in Whitman, she argues, who "saw also above and beyond [the immediate problems], finding a symbolical significance in the force actuating a group movement that is as true and applicable to our time as is his." Lechlitner demurs from citing an exemplar of her own time, but affirms a series of watchwords as her closing advice to "the young revolutionary poet":

> think first; use the findings of philosophy, history, science as body and background for your own perceptions; learn that separate persons, objects, or places as subjects have no significance except as related to the force that has brought them into being; finally, don't exploit your subject for all it is worth: bring something of rational and vital worth to it.[15]

Lechlitner had been born on 27 March 1901 in Elkhart, Indiana, the daughter of a builder named Martin Lechlitner, of Pennsylvania Dutch-German background, and Jessie Wier James Lechlitner, of Irish ancestry. She initially wrote poetry in high school and began publishing while achieving her B.A. in English at the University of Michigan. She secured the degree in 1923, by which time she was already persuaded by radical ideas. After teaching high school in Michigan, Lechlitner was hired in New Mexico but then fired for teaching Flaubert. She was afterward employed as *Midland* magazine's editorial assistant and she also enrolled at the nearby University of Iowa.

While working to complete her M.A. degree in 1926, Lechlitner met a literary-minded undergraduate, Paul Corey. Concurrently they moved to New York's Greenwich Village to embark on their writing careers and were married there in 1928. For their honeymoon they voyaged to Europe and then spent time living and writing in France, Spain, and England. After a second sojourn in New York, where they held office jobs, they moved in the spring of 1931 to reside on a few acres of land on the Hudson River near Cold Spring, New York. There they began a life of erecting their own houses, raising their own vegetables and chickens, and living independently on $1,000 a year. Lechlitner and Corey saw themselves as revolutionaries who believed in ecology and a back-to-the-land ethos as key elements of the Communist project. Lechlitner did some editorial work in New York City and was a routine reviewer for the *New York Herald-Tribune*.

Although Lechlitner later claimed that she was "never a Communist" and only barely a fellow-traveler, this is deceptive.[16] The politics of both Lechlitner and Corey were on the whole pro-Communist in both the ultra-revolutionary and the Popular Front days of the 1930s, although their main activities were literary. Lechlitner contributed to the *New Masses* and the early *Partisan Review*, where she appraised poetry from a revolutionary Communist perspective, and she afterward became an active member of the League of American Writers, chairing the Book Distribution Committee and teaching at league schools. At the time of the rupture of *Partisan Review* from the Communist Party, Lechlitner and Corey named two of their chickens, destined for the axe, Rahv and Phillips, after the *Partisan Review*'s main pro-Trotsky editors. Later, however, they felt that the Communist Party had gone overboard in its anti-Trotskyist polemics, and the couple moved toward independent radicalism, and, finally, toward liberalism.[17]

Ruth detested jewelry, perfume, furs, cosmetics, and hairdos. She kept her hair quite short and wore no-frill dresses. Meticulous about her poetic craft, she published a book of poems during each of four decades – *Tomorrow's*

*Phoenix* (1937), *Only the Years: Selected Poems, 1938–44* (1944), *Shadow of the Hour* (1957), and *A Changing Season* (1973). Her husband, meanwhile, wrote an auto-biographical trilogy of radical farm novels about Iowa — *Three Miles Square* (1939), *The Road Returns* (1940), and *County Seat* (1941). In 1946 he published *Acres of Antaeus*, a political novel about the strife of small farmers in the 1930s, with one of the characters, Smiley, modeled on the novelist-turned-organizer, John Herrmann (1900–1959). Later Corey became a prolific author of juvenile and young-adult fiction, often with conservationist themes.

In 1947 the two writers, accompanied by their only child, Anne, migrated to the Sonoma Valley in California, where they once more built a domicile, grew produce, raised chickens, and kept a house full of cats. Lechlitner occasionally worked as a substitute teacher in the Sonoma Valley Unified School District. She organized local literary groups and even contributed poetry to the New Left Marxist journal *Praxis* in the 1970s. After a long illness in a convalescent hospital, she died in 1989 at the age of eighty-eight. Corey passed away two years later.

Lechlitner's poetry is consecrated to the deliverance of humanity from superstition, fear, and cheap escapist sedatives in which it has been indoctrinated by the state, religious leaders, and industrialists. A lament that closed her first collection, "To a Future Generation," concerns the failure of her own contemporaries, "who walked in the shadow/ Of a world ending." She fixes the discrepancy between objective need and the blindness inculcated in people by the social order:

> The mind found
> In desperate confusion
> Waste, poverty, greed;
> But our habits
> Were gardened, familiar; the new road
> Unposted (we thought) unpaved.
> And we answer:
> The mind knew our need,
> But the hands, long bound
> To an accustomed task, a charted yesterday,
> Were not young hands to hold
> Firm to the changing course:
> Another way.
> Not the mind, but the hand failed us:
> And the heart — bond-slave to childhood —
> Looking back, betrayed us.[18]

Even in her occasional literary criticism that addresses fiction, Lechlitner dwelled on the need for an author to devise symbols aimed at disclosing causal connections to the reader, as in her observation about John Herrmann's *The Salesman* (1939):

> This is not just a book about a salesman – though the publishers seem to think so. It is (or rather should be) a book about a house [in the novel, that belonging to the mother-in-law of the salesman Crawford]. The one weakness of the novel lies in the fact that this theme is almost buried: the house as a symbol is only vaguely hinted at, not logically, cleanly used to knit together and give depth and meaning to the book as a whole. By so doing, Herrmann could have shown us more surely the forces behind Crawford's failure as a salesman; and why the young couple, bound to the values of the past, emerge with no new set of values on which to build their future.[19]

In Lechlitner's philosophy, "wholeness" is to be regained by contact with nature, the forging of community, and the development of creative reason. In a familiar Left-wing gesture, she eschews individuality to the extent that, even in a poem called "Notes for a Biography," she becomes the voice of the entire nation, urging the United States to pass into a maturity of brotherhood. In a further poem, "This Body Politic," she designates "the great I" as the servant of fascism.[20] Lechlitner, however, in several poems dealt with women's oppression more explicitly, and with greater rage, than had Genevieve Taggard. "Lines for an Abortionist's Office" is written in the form of a prayer addressed to the state:

> Close here thine eyes, O state:
> These are thy guests who bring
> To gods with appetites grown great
> A votive offering.
>
> Know that they dare defy
> The words of law and priest –
> (Better to let the unborn die
> Than starve while others feast.)
>
> The stricken flesh may be
> Outraged, and heal; but mind
> Pain-sharpened, may yet learn to see
> Thee plain, O state. Be blind:
>
> Accept love's fruit: be sleek
> Fat and lip-sealed. (Forget

That Life, avenging pain, will speak!)
Thrust deep the long curette![21]

The bitter sarcasm of the verse is intensified by the tightly controlled stanzas with a perfect ABAB rhyme scheme. The female speaker, depicted as the voice of an individual but actually responding on behalf of a community of women who are "guests" in the abortionist office, sardonically urges the rulers of society to persist in their pretense of ignorance about the suffering they enforce. Religious references – the votive offering, the stricken flesh, the achievement of wisdom through suffering, the ironic use of "love's fruit" to refer to the aborted fetus – powerfully accumulate to explode in the disconcerting image of the abortionist's curette as the male phallus about to "thrust deep."

Lechlitner's "Case Recruit" magnifies the critique of patriarchy as the male ego is placed on full display. Desperately apprehensive of relying on its own resources, the ego finds gratification only in an audience that is nothing less than a maternal surrogate: "O – / The womb-encircling mother." Lechlitner's attacks on an ego so steadfastly male-identified indicates that her project may indeed have been a complex revision of Eliot's modernist call in "Tradition and the Individual Talent." In that essay, Eliot called upon the poet to eschew individual feeling in favor of a certain kind of historical consciousness, to achieve a perspective from "the mind of Europe."[22] Lechlitner, in contrast, repeatedly assumes the voice of an omniscient consciousness, but one that is frankly partisan and collectivist, as if her antipatriarchal attitude led logically to a rethinking of the material and natural world in revolutionary terms. Thus she concludes "Garland for Spring, 1937" with a ringing declaration that fuses female fecundity and proletarian utopia: "Spring is an international season."[23]

## Waltzing Mouse

Joy Davidman was far more engrossed in Communist literary institutions than either Taggard or Lechlitner. Born Helen Joy Davidman in 1915, she was descended from Jews who had emigrated to the United States from Eastern Europe in the latter part of the nineteenth and the beginning of the twentieth century.[24] Her father, Joseph, came to the United States with his family at the age of six from Poland. He was the son of a street merchant and religious zealot who died of pneumonia contracted while making the somewhat unusual effort to convert Christians to Judaism in the street during the winter. Joseph, in direct response, became an atheist, a biology teacher, and ultimately a junior high school principal. In 1909 he married Jeannette Spivack, who was college educated and came from a liberal intellectual family. After a change of residence to a middle-class neighborhood in the Bronx, their two children, Helen Joy and Howard, were born immediately before World War I.

The parents, known as "Joe and Jen," afforded a comfortable household, even during the Depression. But Joe was infamous for his parsimony and exactitude; he even liked to convene his children by sounding a metal whistle, expecting them to run to him instantaneously as if they were trained dogs. Moreover, he was unmerciful in his requirement for intellectual achievement; when Joy broke the scale on an I.Q. test he was content, but when Howard only scored 147 he was acutely displeased.[25] To satisfy her father, Joy read H. G. Wells's *Outline of History* at the age of eight, and then avowed that she was an atheist. At the age of twelve she professed her design to become a writer. There was also ample stress in the household due to encounters with anti-Semitism, the most painful occurring while on their seasonal vacations, where they encountered the ubiquitous threat that they might be refused lodgings once their ethnicity was known.

Joy was beset furthermore by health uncertainties from an early age. These drove her into a preoccupation with fantasy, not only the study of ghost and science fiction stories but actual clandestine visitations to the zoo at night where she supposed that she was communing with the giant felines. Frequent traumas influenced her to imaginatively picture a sheltered hideaway. Her first trauma may have been caused by her mother's sudden separation for several weeks immediately after Joy's strenuous birth; a physician had counseled her to go to a dude ranch alone to recuperate from the tribulation. Then, while still quite small, Joy began to feel discomfort when she went to bed. This turned out to be the consequence of a crooked spine, which troubled her for years before it was correctly diagnosed. Next, her parents became anxious about her protruding eyes. The reason was ascertained to be hyperthyroidism, which, after many misdiagnoses, was treated with a radium belt arranged around Joy's throat for twenty-four hours once a week over the passage of a year. The procedure seemed to work at the time, but it was presumably the cause of the cancer that would riddle her body following her fortieth birthday. A more instantaneous side-effect of the radium-belt strategy was that Joy began to sicken from exorbitant insulin secretion inducing a low sugar level in her blood that generated tremors, cold sweats, fainting, and a major appetite increase.

After attending Public School 45, where one of her classmates was Julius Garfinkle, subsequently the actor known as John Garfield, she enrolled in

Evander Childs High School. There two more infirmities, scarlet fever and anemia, obliged her to forego classes for drawn-out periods. In these years she began to have a persistent dream that continued into her early thirties, when she finally reproduced it in a poem called "Fairytale":

> At night, when we dreamed,
> we went down a street
> and turned a corner,
> and there, it seemed,
> there was the castle.
>
> Always, if you knew,
> if you knew how to go,
> you could walk down a street
> (the daylight street)
> that twisted about
> and ended in grass;
> there it was
> always, the castle.
>
> Remote, unshadowed,
> childish, immortal,
> with two calm giants
> guarding the portal,
> strong to defend,
> stood castle safety
> at the world's end.
>
> O castle safety,
> love without crying,
> honey without cloying,
> death without dying!
> Hate and heart break
> all were forgot there;
> we always woke,
> we never got there.[26]

This yearning for personal security, with the idealized likeness of parents before the family home ("two calm giants/ guarding the portal" of the "castle safety"), eerily invokes Franz Kafka's *The Castle* (1926); it is also easily comprehensible in light of Davidman's incessant illnesses. Yet her judgment to publish the verse as a contribution to a collection of antifascist poetry in the early days of World War II insinuates that the imagery resonated with political concerns for her as well.

A feeling of fragility merged with her need to satisfy her imperious father, not to mention her anxiety as a small woman (five feet two inches tall) and a Jew. Her uneasiness about her Jewish identity should not be deprecated; her earliest mental connections with the name "Christ" tended to be dread. Moreover, she felt "cold chills" at the mention of "Jews," who had become in the hands of Christians the object of "floggings and burnings, 'gentleman's agreements,' and closed universities."[27] This terror accounts for the inordinate total of allusions to Christ, crosses, and the New Testament found in her poetry, beginning with her very first contribution, "Resurrection." Her poem "Waltzing Mouse" exhibits the fear of death that stemmed from her sundry insecurities as well as from the brittle health of her youth:

Impulse as I was when I was born,
caught upon time's nether horn,
murdered through and through with birth,
cankered with corrupted earth. . . .
Every hour of sunlight I
watch my body partly die. . . .
. . . I see my painful track
blotted out behind my back
till I die as I was born,
slain upon time's other horn.[28]

In this specimen the conventional form and formal diction once more manifest the need for a brawny and stable structure, a kind of backbone, to bear the tormented body and mind of the poet.

With a high school diploma at the age of fourteen, Joy was admitted to Hunter College in the Bronx in the fall of 1930. At the time she had penetrating brown eyes, short dark hair, and an exquisite complexion. But she was also slightly chubby and infamous for her inferior refinement in clothes. She briskly became an English major and peerless friends with Bel Kaufman, the granddaughter of Sholem Aleichem, afterwards known for her novels *Up the Down Staircase* (1964) and *Love, Etc.* (1979). Concurrently they plunged themselves into literary activity. Joy became associate editor of the Hunter College *Echo*, where she published short fiction, poems, and translations. She also embarked on a love affair with a professor, a Phi Beta Kappa with a Ph.D. from Columbia who was mature enough to be her father.

Davidman's recurrent dream of a quest for sturdy security that always stays out of reach foreshadows her drift toward older men. It furthermore augurs the manner in which she eventually related to Communism, as well as her ultimate religious conversion. Moreover, a prize-winning story she wrote at Hunter College, "Apostate," portends additional aspects of her life and work. Appearing in the November 1934 issue of the *Echo*, the narrative concerns the Jewish daughter of a miserly father in a Russian village. Up in arms against her parents' scheme to marry her to a weak-willed Jewish man, the young woman contracts a furtive arrangement of her own to marry a strong-appearing Christian, with the contingency that she must be baptized and forswear Judaism. At the instant her conversion is to take place, her father and brothers emerge and start thrashing and kicking her, while her Christian fiancé stays inert and the Christian spectators chortle. The unrefined substance of "Apostate" came from accounts that her mother told her about her mother's native village in the Ukraine, but her story also reveals an apprehension that her obsession with finding a person of strength might lead to her perpetrating some species of elementary disloyalty.[29]

Davidman radicalized in the same mode as did many other students during the Depression, dazed by the inequalities and hardship that surrounded them. In the spring of 1934, near graduation, she was profoundly shaken when she eyewitnessed a young woman, driven by the desperation of destitution, leap to her doom from a rooftop. That autumn, Davidman started teaching high school English while also matriculating at Columbia in an M.A. program in literature. When her thyroid problem returned, she continued the familiar treatment, abandoned teaching, wrote poetry, and completed her degree with honors in December 1935. In the fall of 1936 she discovered herself in the classification of "permanent substitutes" when she endeavored to continue her public school vocation, which meant low salaries and supplementary distasteful tasks, such as floor scrubbing.

In the summer of 1937 Davidman resigned as a substitute and, encouraged by the presentation of an assortment of her poems in the January 1936 and March 1937 issues of *Poetry*, determined to take advantage of her parents' munificence to write full-time. Later that year, with the aid of *Poetry* editor Harriet Monroe's devising for her to meet the poet Stephen Vincent Benét (1899–1943), Davidman proffered a collection of her poems, mostly unpublished, to the Younger Poets Series that Benét edited for Yale University Press. *Letter to a Comrade*, eighty pages of verse, appeared in 1938 with an introduction by Benét. The reviews, mostly by women, were approbatory. Her association with Benét led Davidman to a lifetime alliance with the Brandt and Brandy literary agency, and also with the MacDowell Colony in New Hampshire, where Davidman passed the summers of 1938, 1940, 1941, and 1942. In July 1940, Davidman published her novel *Anya*, also grounded, like "Apostate," in her mother's yarns about her youth in Eastern Europe. The main figure in *Anya* is a sexually emancipated woman who has affairs before and after marriage, asserting that "no man shall have power over me."[30] The dust-jacket blurb likened Davidman's work to the fiction of D. H. Lawrence. What is unusual is that Anya's sensuality stems mainly from the zest of her senses, which brook no limitations or constraint, rather than from promiscuity or lust. The response of reviewers was again approving; they applauded the deftness of the writing as well as the depiction of the main character.[31]

Although Davidman took pleasure from her literary successes during the late 1930s and her fraternization with the artists with whom she was now in touch, she continued to be obsessed by the experiences of the Depression and, step by step, apprehended that her opinions were like those of a Communist. The most attendant issue provoking her to join the Communist Party was the Spanish Civil War, which became the topic of various of her poems. Yet she also felt obliged to take some kind of personal activity on behalf of her beliefs. Years afterward she recollected that, when a Communist acquaintance asked her if she was joining the Party to aid others (hinting at a sort of paternalism), or out of her own self-interest, she "lied" and explained that it was the latter.[32]

After several efforts to join the Communist Party at large gatherings, she achieved membership in a Manhattan Party unit and briefly used the party name "Nell Tulchin"; Tulchin was the name of the village in the Ukraine from which her mother had emigrated, which she also used in *Anya*. Her parents were aghast at the news, but slightly palliated shortly thereafter when *Letter to a Comrade* won $1,000 in a prize from the National Institute of Arts and Letters.[33] Davidman was then solicited to work (with no salary) at the *New Masses* as the poetry critic. Among her first determinations, she bragged, was to reject submissions by Oscar Williams (1900–1964), a popular anthologist who had extended one adverse observation in his otherwise positive review of *Letter to a Comrade*.[34]

Hardly had she made her mark at the *New Masses* before the Hollywood studio, Metro-Goldwyn-Mayer, which had requested names of possible screenwriters from one of Davidman's Hunter College professors around the same time that *Anya* had been accepted for publication, proffered her an invitation to come to Hollywood to try writing screenplays at fifty dollars a week for six months. She concurred, but the Hollywood experience brought only rebuff of her work by the studio as well as a miserable love affair. She spent much of her time in Hollywood at Communist Party social and political events. Back in New York by the fall of 1939, she rejoined the *New Masses* in time to bolster morale at the magazine with her fervid support of the Hitler-Stalin Pact. She also became active in the League of American Writers. Her major contribution to the League, *War Poems of the United Nations* (1943), was a collection of 300 poems by 150 poets from different countries, for which she did many translations on a haphazard basis and allegedly devised two poets from England for the selections to reinforce that country's representation.[35] She edited, as well, the posthumous poems of Alexander F. Bergman (1912–1941, born Alexander Frankel), a staunch young Communist whose writings were collected in *They Look like Men* (1944). In 1941 and 1942, Davidman taught a class on poetry at the league's New York Writers' School. Due to her Hollywood experience, Davidman was habitually assigned films to review, and she proved to be a harsh judge of popular Hollywood entertainment while virtually uncritical of Soviet productions. Soon her *New Masses* job became salaried.

## And God Came In

At a 1941 meeting of the League of American Writers, Davidman first saw a radical folksinger, William Lindsay Gresham (1909–1962). Less than two years later in August 1941 they were married. Almost instantaneously she found herself less interested in attending Communist Party functions, which afterward led her to reflect that a good part of her motivation and that of other young people to join the Party was to find a mate. Moreover, Gresham was already personally demoralized about prospects for the Left, and, once Davidman gave birth to her first son, she recognized that children came before everything else. By 1943 she was no longer reviewing films, and her contributions to the *New Masses* diminished to poems and book reviews, ceasing altogether in the summer of 1945. In 1944, she contributed seven poems, most of which were militantly antifascist, to the landmark volume edited by Thomas Yoseloff, *Seven Poets in Search of an Answer*. In April 1946 her name was dropped from the *New Masses* masthead, and she no longer showed up at any Communist Party meetings.

Davidman had always subordinated herself to older men and strong authority figures, rebelling mainly by swapping loyalties from one to another. But in Gresham, approaching his mid-30s, a veteran of the Spanish Civil War and already divorced, the twenty-seven-year-old Davidman had found someone far more complicated than she had anticipated.[36] At the time they met he was six feet tall, lean, with dark eyes, a deep baritone voice, and demonstrative body language that proclaimed sensuality.

Born in Baltimore in 1909, of a southern family, he had lived in Fall River, Massachusetts, and then graduated from Erasmus Hall High School in Brooklyn. Gresham was thus able to baffle people by affecting a Southern accent and impersonating a backwoods preacher even as he fit comfortably into Manhattan's East Side. He began to support himself in the early 1930s by taking odd jobs and singing folksongs in night clubs. After two years in the Civilian Conservation Corps, he met and married Jean Karsavina (1908–1989), an unrestrained bohemian from a well-to-do Jewish family who was embarking on a career as a pulp writer and life-long Communist.[37] Gresham was a reviewer for the *New York Evening Post* for a while, and also worked writing advertising copy while he made an initial foray into pulp writing. About 1936 he joined the Communist Party, but he was feeling disconsolate in his marriage. When he learned that a friend of his was killed fighting the fascists in Spain, he felt moved to volunteer for the International Brigades in which he served as a medic for a year and a half. When he returned to New York he was alcohol dependent, on the threshold of a nervous breakdown, and still embroiled with Karsavina in a marriage that was basically over, although not officially so until the beginning of 1942. After a blundered suicide attempt – he had hung himself with a leather belt in his closet, but the hook broke – a Communist Party friend devised for him to undergo a psychoanalysis that continued for several years.

In the course of his therapy Gresham was compelled to face his painful youth. In particular, he focused on the summer of his sixteenth year when he seemed to experience an intellectual and artistic awakening, finding himself astonished by his responsiveness not only to poetry but to the "loveliness of each blade of grass and dandelion."[38] The moment was broken by his parents' divorce, resulting in a disaffection from his father whom he did not see for the next seven years. He postulated that the trauma produced a case of acne so hideous that people on the subways seemed to be edging away from him. As a consequence, Gresham stood in front of the mirror performing for hours how to be winning, studying to sing and play the guitar, and immersed himself into the world of magic tricks and carnival lore.[39]

His marriage to Davidman did not terminate Gresham's love of the fellowship of carnival people, who used to congregate at the Dixie Hotel in Manhattan. Nor did it end his heavy drinking and his ardor to continue therapy, paid for by Davidman's twenty-five-dollars-a-week salary from the *New Masses*. After moving to Sunnyside in Queens, where many other Leftists lived, Davidman gave birth to two sons, David in 1944 and Douglas in 1945. Then Davidman detected that Gresham was having an affair – she alluded to the incident in a poem published in the *New Masses*[40] – and she requested firmly that they move out of the city, to Ossining, New York, on the Hudson River. After the move, the friction between them only grew worse. One day Gresham phoned from New York and declared that he was in the midst of a nervous breakdown; he professed that he was in a state where he couldn't

stay where he was and he couldn't return home, and then hung up. Davidman spent the rest of the day making phone calls in a frenzied attempt to
locate friends to help find him, then put her sons to sleep. Alone in the dark,
she experienced what she later claimed was a thirty-second visitation from
God, which caused her to drop to her knees in prayer.

When Gresham returned after several days, he acknowledged her claim
that she had a spiritual experience and together they began reevaluating
their philosophy. Davidman, in particular, felt that she had to settle accounts with Marxism and for the first time read Lenin's *Materialism and
Empirio-Criticism*. Ungratified, she felt she should give Judaism a chance, but
found that what she read about Judaism did not harmonize with what she
had felt in her instant of elation – "the conviction of sin followed by the
assistance of God's grace."[41]

In the meantime, their resolve to set out on a new course seemed to acquire a helping hand when Gresham published his first novel, *Nightmare
Alley* (1946), a grisly tale of carnival life which would become a pivotal text
of *roman noir*. The central character, Stan, has many traits of Gresham as a
youth, and the work was conceived with the conscious inspiration of Marx
and Freud. The novel might conceivably be regarded as Gresham's forecast
of where he could end up without the ballast of a guiding philosophy – it
climaxes with a now-alcoholic Stan earning money for booze as a geek bit-
ing heads off live chickens in a carnival show. The book was a commercial
success beyond all expectations, and even brought an unanticipated $60,000
movie contract.[42]

Before Gresham could drink up the money, Davidman induced him to invest it in a southern-style mansion on twenty-two acres of land in Pleasant
Plains, New York. It was there that she and Gresham became enchanted by
the writings of the English Christian apologist C. S. Lewis, and then drawn to
his most illustrious disciple in the United States at the time, the poet, priest,
and Beloit College professor Chad Walsh. In the summer of 1948 Davidman
and her sons, with Gresham's blessing, were baptized at the nearby Pres-
byterian church that they had all been attending. Soon after, however, the
family switched from this Calvinist denomination to an Episcopalian con-
gregation. Davidman then initiated a correspondence with Chad Walsh that
would last to the end of her life; she also began writing a novel that would reveal her new faith. Concurrently, Davidman collaborated with Oliver Pilat,
a journalist for the *New York Post*, in a long series that appeared from October to November 1949 called "Girl Communist," covering her Communist
Party experiences. Davidman was adamant that most Party members were
merely well-meaning people who were self-deluded, but her account was

spiced with hilarious as well as outrageously unfair anecdotes and observations about her former comrades. Meanwhile, Gresham published his
second novel, *Limbo Tower* (1949), dedicated to the poet Alexander Bergman,
depicting life in a hospital with the main character a zealous revolutionary
dying of tuberculosis.

## The Apostate

At Walsh's recommendation, Davidman inaugurated a correspondence with
C. S. Lewis, writing to him as "Mrs. W. L. Gresham," in which she advanced
inquiries about his notions. The two rapidly became ardent pen-pals. In the
meantime, although Gresham and Davidman had publicly announced their
conversions from Marxism to Christianity in the 1951 book *These Found the
Way*, Gresham had further evolved to become an enthusiast of L. Ron Hub-
bard's Dianetics. This new obsession coexisted with his Christianity for a
brief time, but his next infatuation – Zen Buddhism – was clearly incon-
gruous. That was followed by an enthrallment with the I Ching, Tarot cards,
and yoga.

In the 1940s, Gresham joined Alcoholics Anonymous and seemed to have
his drinking under control, but there next emerged a profound strain with
Davidman over their rivalry as writers. Gresham also habitually pontifi-
cated male chauvinist ideas about how to handle women, including crack-
pot theories about the menstruation cycle and the uprightness of the double
standard in sexual life. When Gresham lost his temper, he would go down
to his basement and shoot a rifle.[43] Davidman, in the meantime, plugged
away on the work of fiction that would reflect her new philosophy. In 1952
she published *Weeping Bay*, a revamped proletarian novel with a religious
worker-hero. Set in Canada, the novel depicts a Catholic union organizer
who defies an alliance of the religious hierarchy and businessmen. Although
there were strongly positive reviews, Davidman believed that distribution
of the novel was undermined by a Catholic sales manager at Macmillan's
publishing house who was affronted by her handling of the church establishment.[44]

In 1952 Joy's younger first cousin, Renée Pierce, came to live in the Gresham home with her two children. She was in concealment from a drunken
and brutal husband in the South. With this new domestic situation, Davidman announced that she needed to make an expedition to England to confer
with C. S. Lewis in person, leaving Renée in charge of the household. The
story of Davidman's meetings with Lewis in England, her gradual enchant-
ing of Lewis and his brother, and the circumstances leading to the stun-

ning marriage of Davidman to the life-long bachelor Lewis in 1956, received widespread notoriety in the 1992 motion picture *Shadowlands*. The film also depicts Davidman's up-and-down battle with cancer before she died at the age of forty-five in the summer of 1960.

A less-idealized consideration of the circumstances of the break-up of her marriage with Gresham suggests that Davidman probably arranged the domestic situation so as to precipitate a turn of events allowing her to absolve her obligation, as an Episcopalian, to resist divorce. She may well have conspired to leave her attractive younger cousin – who was herself in the midst of a break-up of a marriage – alone for months in the same house as the charming and womanizing Gresham. Based on past experience, Davidman must have known that this would lead Gresham to temptation. Moreover, Renée, in contrast to Davidman, was of a predilection to dedicate herself exclusively to her husband and offer no intellectual rivalry; this rendered her especially tantalizing as a long-term surrogate for Davidman. Not surprisingly, while in England Davidman received a letter from Gresham proclaiming his resolution to divorce her and marry Renée. Davidman showed the letter to Lewis, who gave her on-the-spot guidance to go ahead and concur in the divorce offer, then he told her to bring her children to England.

After Davidman's death, Lewis was shattered; he followed her to the grave within three years. Gresham's descent was even more pathetic. Surviving by writing articles on carnivals and magic in men's magazines, he also lectured on side-show acts where he would demonstrate fire-eating. One of his most popular performances over the years, sometimes done at local libraries, was "The Human Volcano." For this act, Gresham took a sip of lighter fluid and sprayed it at the lighted torch "with a satisfying woosh! that scared the pants off some of the old folks."[45] A chemical in the lighter fluid apparently induced cancer of the tongue, and by the early 1960s Gresham was in constant pain and able to consume food only through a straw. On 14 September 1962, Gresham checked into the Dixie Hotel, a carnival workers' hangout in Manhattan, under a false name. He downed a bottle of sleeping pills and this time successfully killed himself.

Gender issues are manifested complexly in Davidman's poetry. In public statements made after she left the Communist Party, she described Party women as "feminists." Her grounds were that the women mainly wanted equality with men. Davidman also derided Party efforts to root out male chauvinism as petty and ridiculous.[46] This, however, was written retrospectively, during her Christian phase, and the attitude Davidman satirized may well have been more her own than that of others. Despite her fascination with strong faiths and strong men, it should be recognized that the faiths she chose were enveloped by a considerable intellectual apparatus, and her erotic attractions were evident in all phases of her evolution – from her early affairs and the celebration of infidelity in *Anya* to her obsession with the womanizing Gresham, and to her romantic infatuation with her religious mentor C. S. Lewis.[47]

A plea for women's independence is clearly intended by the tough, clean, pure image of her poem "This Woman" in its call for women to forsake ribbons and ornaments in order to "go bare, go bare." Moreover, since the phrase "This Woman" comes from the marriage ceremony, the poem must be taken as a declaration of emancipation from conventional marital expectations. Nevertheless, Davidman as a poet has to be apprehended as one who negotiates cross currents; that is, she moves against some patriarchal conceptions of gender construction but reconstitutes others. As she shifts her loyalty among various authority figures, she is simultaneously disobedient and obedient. This is evidenced in her poem "Letter to a Comrade." The piece is dedicated to a woman (Ellen Weinberg), and its invocation of the "wanderer" seems to conjure up an empowering female quest-figure. Yet the world is seen through ostensibly "genderless" eyes, and conventional images of masculinity and femininity abound.

Prevailing gender representations are also characteristic of the extraordinary number of warlike poems that appear in *Letter to a Comrade* and her contributions to *Seven Poets in Search of an Answer* (1944), often featuring martyrs who are either historical males (the slave rebel Spartacus, the German Communist Ernst Thaelmann) or figured as males. In "The Princess in the Ivory Tower" she describes a male seeking to escape the horrors of the "real world" by climbing to utopia by way of the golden hair of the fairy-tale character Rapunzel. "Twentieth Century Americanism," which memorably asserts "America" as urban and ethnic, speaks in a powerful voice in a huge arena. The poetic act may be that of a woman who has emerged from the private and protected world of conventional gender construction, but the voice aspires to be gender neutral. "Prayer against Indifference," in a style recalling that of Edna St. Vincent Millay (1892–1950), moves away from Davidman's more customary stance; the "I" is evidently the poet, swearing fidelity to a life of political commitment, and the opening references are in language associated with female experience:

> When wars and ruined men shall cease
> To vex my body's house of peace.
> And bloody children lying dead
> Let me lie softly in my bed

> To nurse a whole and sacred skin
> Break roof and let the bomb come in[48]

Some of Davidman's curious inversions in other of her poems upset customary gender depictions. In "Skeleton," beauty, usually associated with a female, becomes a wolf who "has eaten out my soul / and left me empty."[49]

In further poems there are several points at which a complex dialectic of gender in binary relations comes into action. "Obsession," a compelling invocation of one's erotic need for a recipient of hatred, presents the object of obsession as a male and the speaker implicitly a female. The object has power over the female – yet the female takes pleasure from the relationship while understanding the mutual dependency for what it is:

> This hate is honey to my tongue
> And rubies spread before my eye,
> Sweet in the ear as any song;
> What should I do, if he should die?[50]

In "Jewess to Aryan" the former is depicted in positive terms that are female, while the latter, in negative terms that are male:

> I have resented you; a parasite worm
> drinking the female. . . .

Nevertheless there is the same eerie kind of indispensability of the "Jewess" for the Aryan as in "Obsession," a disturbing form of love that will evaporate if the former is sapped in power. Hence the mysterious ending: "When I have no more strength / you might be afraid of me." The contention here recalls that of Jean-Paul Sartre's Hegelian essay *Anti-Semite and Jew* (1947) in which each element of the equation is defined only by its relation to the other.

Yet Davidman is hardly consistent in her reliance on such dialectical lines. Like Funaroff, and so many others on the Left, she could readily fall back on romantic pieties. "End of a Revolution," for example, returns her to the tradition of familiar Whitmanian imagery:

> When I am born again
> I shall come like the grass-blade;
> I shall be fertile and small
> As the seed of grasses.
> Rain shall breed me;
> Earth shall bear me;
> I shall smell of the sun over the green fields.[51]

Here the poet-seer breaks down in the face of imagining a post-revolution-ary society, retreating to pastoral utopian clichés.

In a comparable manner Davidman's love poems often cast males and females in customary roles:

> Now under a rainstorm corn is come again
> and it shall ripen into the body of my love.

> Now birdseed scattered falling makes again the summer
> burning with leaves, bringing the pollen grain,
> the rain falling like seed the firseed fallen
> the honey thick in trees and the smell of rain
> and the bird crying alone. I for my lover
> cook magic over woodfires to call him home

Such incantatory rhythms and erotic imagery have an aura of recorded dream sequences, hinting at mythologies and rituals of a collective uncon-scious. Yet there are also moments in her love poetry that her lines are full of sensuous, materialistic desire that come close to constituting acts of de-fiance against Communist poetic decorum. For example, in "Prayer Against Barrenness," with echoes of D. H. Lawrence, she celebrates the liberating phallus: "Let passion / come in the shape of a sword against winter and set me free."[52] In "Prothalamion" she declares the need to

> open the arms of the woman to him
> that he may take possession;
> open the body of the woman
> that his seed may be acceptable into her womb.[53]

This species of poetry suggests that Muriel Rukeyser's famous declaration in her 1935 *Theory of Flight*, "Not Sappho, Sacco," should not be affirmed too schematically as evidence of the displacement of individualistic, female, and sensual concerns by class politics in the 1930s.[54] Despite variations among the oeuvres of Genevieve Taggard, Ruth Lechlitner, and Joy Davidman, the sum total of their work suggests an axial tension – one that exists between their serrated expressions of feminist concerns and their steady loyalties to utopian visions of societies free of race and class oppression, visions usually suffused with natural beauty and often marked by untrammelled profes-sions of erotic passion. Genevieve Taggard expounded this tension, with an ultimate subordination of gender, in maintaining that her most mature poems "hold a wider consciousness than that colored by the feminine half of the race. I hope they are not written by a poetess, but by a poet. I think, I hope

I have written poetry that relates to general experience, and the realities of our time."[55]

The poems of these three women are conspicuous examples of texts by females that actively structure the meaning of sexual difference in their society, cognizant to varying degrees that gender is a categorizing contrived through cultural and social systems. Such writings cannot be assigned to any particular feminist canon, such as the decades-old view that female anger is the key that unlocks women's experience. Still, they afford historically critical materials for the analysis of the political implications of a number of possible intersections of feminist concerns and class loyalties in the mid-twentieth century. This achievement, however, took place under conditions where pro-Communist women writers were part of a political movement that devoted only limited theoretical attention to the origins and dynamics of women's oppression. The contrast was dramatic in comparison to the Communist Party's much more extensive analysis of the oppression of African Americans. Yet, despite the absence of a theory of gender oppression as compelling as that of national oppression, as well as the semi-autonomous organizational forms pioneered by Black Communists such as the League of Struggle for Negro Rights and the National Negro Congress, the aggregate of Left women writers within the cultural institutions led by the Communist movement was consequential and precursory.

## The Premature Socialist-Feminists

The term "feminism," prior to the "Second Wave" of the 1960s, primarily meant "bourgeois feminism"; that is, the battle for rights and equality for individual women within a capitalist framework. Such a standpoint was opposed by women in the Communist Party who believed that economic democracy, and the abolition of class and racial privilege, would be the context in which women would achieve liberation. The degree to which this perspective supported the autonomous struggle by women as women remained ambiguous, especially during the late 1930s when cross-class alliances against fascism were promoted. Certainly "the woman question" was recognized as a subject matter that raised consciousness about the differential treatment of women and the pervasive discrimination against them. "Male supremacy" was officially denounced, and occasionally efforts were made to advance women leaders as well as to institute organizations and publications that addressed women-specific matters. While it was accepted throughout the Communist movement that women's oppression was a pressing question, it was also determined secondary to the emancipation of the working class and fighting racism.[56] Within that framework, divers Communist women of note intermittently offered in the pages of the *New Masses* a range of critical analyses of the relationship of gender to class and revolution, including Grace Hutchins, Rebecca Pitts, Mary Inman, Ella Winter, Ruth McKenney, and Elizabeth Gurley Flynn.[57]

As was the case in the dominant culture, while some women creative writers aspired to adapt to patriarchal models, others found a range of ways of talking back to the masculinist paradigms. Regardless of the prevailing attempt to identify working-class life with the male experience, women invariably had an independent relation to work and the class struggle, and literary women forged their own portrayals and metaphors appropriate to their personalities and experiences. Meridel Le Sueur, for example, in her noted defense of Communist Party membership against Horace Gregory's plea for the right to stand "outside" the Party, does not present the same kind of expected, logical argument found in Mike Gold's ten-point manifesto in which he explained "why I am a Communist."[58] Instead, she pleads the case for a psychic break with the past and the need to strive for communal interaction. Using maternal and birth metaphors, she critiques bourgeois existence as impotent and infertile; if one can't act on a full belief, one doesn't "exude the warmth to hatch."[59]

It is unlikely that this particular form of gendered language was the mode of expression preferred by the *New Masses* editors since it nowhere else appears in other discussions of Communist Party commitment by males, such as the one by Edwin Seaver.[60] Indeed, the language used by Gregory was probably more in accordance with the magazine's style, despite his heterodox stance. But Le Sueur's *position* as the reliable defender of Communist Party commitment, against the stance of the vacillating Gregory, enabled her to employ language and ideas that might be seen as subversive to the masculinist gender-valorizing language normally published. As in the case of modernism, demonstrable political loyalty might earn one greater latitude in matters of literary style.

Thus women poets participated in shaping Left cultural practice from a variety of angles. Scholar Charlotte Nekola, for example, has identified three types of women's Left-wing poems in the 1930s. First, those that addressed the characteristic political issues of the day, which primarily afforded women an opportunity to write poems of larger scope than hitherto acceptable. Second, those that challenged moods of "ironic despair, aestheticism, and meaningless or elitist erudition" found in the works of such modernist poets as T. S. Eliot and Ezra Pound; these poems may have been implicitly feminist in the sense that males dominated the tradition under attack (female experimentalist poets such as Gertrude Stein were not indicted). The third and least constant type was "poems that dealt with issues of gender or celebrated specifically female traditions."[61] Of minimal significance, if written at all, were poems on women's work, factory or domestic, women in power relationships with men, women's community, and love relationships between women.

That male writers, overwhelmingly white and at least half of them Jewish, set the tone on the leading bodies of the official, New York–based publications of the Communist Left is indisputable. Within this framework, a dozen or so female poets and novelists have survived or else been revived as distinctive voices addressing the nexus between gender and class. What requires further illumination is the cultural practice of women among the rank and file of the Communist movement, the female counterparts of "Jimmie Higgins" – the Jenny Higginses of the Communist-inspired Literary Left.[62]

Of the twenty-nine poets included in *Proletarian Literature in the United States*, only Taggard and Muriel Rukeyser are female. The proceedings of *The American Writers Congress* (1935) published the speech of just one female participant, Meridel Le Sueur. Only Martha Gellhorn (1908–1998)[63] and Frances Winwar appear, alongside fifteen men, in the volume generated by the Second Congress, *The Writer in a Changing World* (1937). The third volume in the series, a compendium of remarks from the 1939 Congress assembled by Donald Ogden Stewart under the title *Fighting Words* (1940), includes only three women – Hope Hale (b. 1903), Dorothy Parker (1893–1967), and Sylvia Townsend Warner (1893–1978) – among the forty "Principal Contributors."[64]

The authority of the Soviet writers' organizations, which was inspirational rather than dictatorial, did little to promote women as a specific group within the cultural movement, although the contributions of female Soviet literary scholars were translated into English in *International Literature*, originally the organ of the International Union of Revolutionary Writers.[65] The International Conference of Revolutionary Writers and Artists held at Kharkov in the Soviet Union in November 1930 produced a six-point program that opposed white chauvinism and "middle-class ideas in the work of revolutionary writers and artists," but failed to mention the participation of females nor did it address the oppression of women.[66] At the same time, the seven-point program of the Midwest Workers' Cultural Federation, a broad umbrella group that included the John Reed Clubs, made a similar omission.[67] Moreover, when the International Union of Revolutionary Writers headquartered in the Soviet Union issued a scathing thirteen-point critique of the work of the *New Masses*, the matter of women's participation or contributions was not addressed.[68]

When the *New Masses* became a weekly in 1934, a publicity brochure with photographs, "Some Writers and Editors of the *New Masses*," was widely distributed. In the photograph were four women (Marguerite Young [dates unknown],[69] Josephine Herbst, Ella Winter, and Anna Rochester [1880–1966])[70] in contrast to sixteen men. Another group photograph of "five leading figures of the *New Masses*" only depicted men. The new editorial board was entirely male, and the four quotations endorsing the new weekly were by men.

Poetry collections of the 1930s and 1940s followed a similar pattern of gender representation, which was probably no worse than the record of mainstream publications. International Publisher's *Salud! Poems, Stories and Sketches of Spain by American Writers* (1938) contains exclusively the verse of thirteen males, although a brief essay at the end mentions that poems on Spain have also been written by Muriel Rukeyser, Genevieve Taggard, Edna St. Vincent Millay, and Joy Davidman. In the February 1937 issue of *Forum*, Horace Gregory presents "Fifteen New Poets," only four of whom were women. Only 10 percent of the fifty-five poets from the United States whose verse was included in Joy Davidman's *War Poems of the United Nations* (1943), sponsored by the League of American Writers, are female. *New Letters*, issued in 1938 under the editorship of Horace Gregory, with Eleanor Clark as associate editor, featured only eight women among the thirty-eight contributors. The 1939 volume, *This Generation*, edited by George K. Anderson and Eda Lou Walton, climaxed in a section of nearly 150 pages of mostly radical poems, entitled "American Revolutionists"; yet Muriel Rukeyser was the only female present.

Despite these depressing numbers, especially in light of the growing presence of women generally in modern literature of the previous decade (H.D., Gertrude Stein, Marianne Moore, Amy Lowell), there are indications that fortunes for women writers in terms of their visibility and prominence improved as the Communist-led cultural movement moved from the Third Period to the Popular Front. In part, this was due to a rhetorical shift from the vocabulary of militant class struggle where the "proletariat" was usually assigned archetypal male characteristics and where "work" almost always meant occupations that primarily employed males. However, the advent of the Popular Front also saw a growth in the number of participants in the Communist-influenced literary movement, less stringent political criteria for membership in cultural organizations, and a broader range of topics that were acceptable for publication. Hence, writers from upper-middle-

class economic circumstances, temperamentally unsuited to Communist
Party discipline, such as Lillian Hellman (1905–1984) and Dorothy Parker
(1893–1967), would become frequent headliners at Left-wing events, while
a popular humorist, Ruth McKenney (1911–1972), would be given a weekly
*New Masses* column with the highly un-Marxist title, "Strictly Personal."

In 1932, the only women listed as members of the League of Professional
Groups for Foster and Ford, the Communist candidates in the presiden-
tial election, were Leonie Adams (1899–1988), Fielding Burke (Olive Tilford
Dargan), Miriam Allen de Ford (1888–1975), Grace Lumpkin, and Ella Winter,
along with thirty-seven men.[71] During these years of the ultra-revolutionary
"Third Period," the *New Masses* set a poor example in its publication of
women poets, one little better than commercial and academic publications.
In 1929, five of the thirty-six poets represented in its pages were women
(Ellen Caye, M. A. de Ford, Helen Koppel, Lilith Lorraine, and Gale Wilhelm);
moreover, while several of the male poets were represented by as many as
nine contributions, women poets published only one poem each, a pattern
that would continue. In 1930 there were twenty-seven poets represented,
two of whom were female (Margaret Larkin and Regina Pedroso). In 1931
there were twenty poets, only one of whom was female (Dawn Lovelace). In
1932, there were eighteen poets, all male. In 1933, only three out of seventeen
poets whose verse appeared in the *New Masses* were female (Anne Bromberger, Lillian White Spencer, Rose Pastor Stokes).[72]

Leftist little magazines across the country, often affiliated with John Reed
Club chapters, carried some writing by women, most of whose names (possibly pseudonyms in some cases) are unknown today. To cite a few examples
from the first issues of such publications, volume 1, number 1 of *The Red
Spark: Bulletin of the John Reed Club of Cleveland* contains a long poem in the
voice of a woman worker by Jane Steele;[73] volume 1, number 1 of *The John
Reed Club Bulletin*, published by the John Reed Club of Detroit, contains a
poem, "Wage Slave," by Ethel Roland; volume 1, number 2 of *Revolt*, published monthly by the John Reed Club of Paterson, New Jersey, contains no
contributions by women; volume 1, number 1 of *Proletcult*, published by the
John Reed Clubs of the Northwest, contains three contributions by Dawn
Lovelace – a short story set in Portland, a prose poem about John Reed, and a
book review about a study of the Soviet Union; volume 1, number 1 (Spring
1931) of *The Left: A Quarterly Review of Radical and Experimental Art* (Davenport,
Iowa) includes the work of thirty-two contributors with Lola Ridge (1871–
1941, an independent socialist poet of the earlier generation) being the sole
female; Volume 1, Number 1 of *Red Boston* (Official Organ of the Boston John

Reed Club) contains only one contribution by a woman, a report on a public meeting by Rivka Ganz.

Among such proletarian little magazines and local John Reed Club organs, the *New Force* published in Detroit featured women more frequently, probably because the managing editor, Paula Golden (dates unknown), wrote much of the material. In the May 1932 issue, Anita Pavlov contributes two poems in which she alternately assumes the voice of two women in the South, one white and the other Black. In her first poem, "Ella May Wiggins Sings," Pavlov addresses the world from beneath the grave of Wiggins, the Gastonia strike martyr, transformed into a fertility symbol that will give birth to a new revolt:

All you workers,
don't think me dead.
But look to the rain
That soaks into my bed. . . .[74]

In "Black Woman's Lament" Pavlov becomes the voice of a Black woman who appears to have a perfect understanding of the Communist Party's view that only rich whites are responsible for the death of her son and husband, and that the organized interracial working class will set everything right.[75]

Golden herself contributed a satire of commercial literature to the January 1932 issue of *New Force*, "What the World Is Writing About for the World to Read." Depicting herself as paging through the Brentano's holiday catalogue, Golden interpolates actual advertising quotations into the social reality of the Depression as she initially considers how the adventure tales of pirates might strike the millions of unemployed. Next she muses about how the war memoirs of General John J. Pershing, said to be "gleaming with swift humor," will be received by maimed and crippled veterans. Finally, she relates a children's book about "The Singing Dog" to youngsters who are desperate for more bread and milk.

When women's issues receive special attention, they are almost always within the larger contexts of class war and the struggle against racism. In the same issue of *New Force* that carried Golden's satire, a poem by Freda Rigby, "Shoemaker's Children," acknowledges the specific yet common features of women's labor as she describes the work of fathers, daughters, and sons, all of whom toil to provide luxuries for the rich. The father builds tires for limousines all day, but to travel home he must hang exhaustedly from a strap "in a packed airless streetcar." The daughter goes blind while making fur coats, then shivers on the street corner in her cheap coat while waiting for a bus. The son shovels coal in the "bowels of a ship," while on deck the rich enjoy the sunlight as they drink and play cards.[76]

*New Writers*, which in Detroit succeeded *New Force* as a broader Left literary publication during the Popular Front, continued the earlier tradition of more extensive female representation. Typical of the publication's short run are the February 1936 issue, where three of the eight contributors are women, and the March 1936 issue where there are four women contributors out of eleven. Another example of the depiction of female experience in a broader context is "The Dead Corporal" by Marion Holden, a war story told from the point of view of a nurse.[77]

At the close of its first year, *The Partisan*, organ of the John Reed Club of the West, published a striking poem by Irene Kilbourne, "Today's Pioneer Women," treating gender in a class as well as antiracist context. After two stanzas describing how "our young grandmothers" and "Our young mothers" all "followed their men" to the Midwest and then the far West, she calls upon "my sisters" to collaborate with their men by moving into "another new land, an untried era." Reworking the images of conquest and colonization associated with the myth of the frontier, she declares a desire to

> ... break through the underbrush of ignorance,
> Cut away the thickets of greed. ...
>
> The hands that molded bullets for redskins
> Have begotten hands
> That can fight against the tomahawks of power
> And the war-whoops of profiteers;
> The slim arms that learned to use a musket
> Have begotten arms that shoulder placards
> On picket duty.
>
> Draw up our workers' unions
> Like a circle of covered wagons –
>
> Course, pioneer women![78]

Thus the tradition of worker-poetry, vivified by a female perspective, could become a site for a composting of perception that moved in the direction of turning the national mythology of Indian hating on its head.

The imbalance between male and female writers registered in magazines was duplicated in the composition of literary symposia organized by the Left during the Depression. "What Is Americanism? A Symposium on Marxism and the American Tradition," published by *Partisan Review and Anvil* during the brief fusion of these two magazines following the First American Writers' Congress, included Josephine Herbst and nine men.[79] The 1932 *New Masses* symposium "How I Came to Communism" solicited the recollections of six men.[80] Likewise, the *New Masses* request for statements by writers in response to Hitler's assumption of the German chancellorship in March 1933 resulted in another symposium, "Against the Fascist Terror in Germany," featuring the publication of statements by fourteen men.[81]

The growth of the League of American Writers was accompanied by a steady increase in the role women played as activists, even if they were not featured at the league's congresses. The Executive Committee elected at the First American Writers' Congress (1935) included only Josephine Herbst and Genevieve Taggard, together with fourteen men. Elected at the Second American Writers' Congress (1937) were Dorothy Brewster (1883-1979), Marjorie Fischer (1903-1961), Taggard, and Jean Starr Untermeyer, along with nine men.[82] The title Executive Committee was changed to "National Board" at the Third American Writers' Congress (1939), and the women elected included Nora Benjamin (1899-1988), Aline Bernstein (1881-1955), Brewster, Martha Dodd (1908-1990), Fischer, Lillian Hellman, Dawn Powell (1897-1965), Taggard, and Untermeyer, along with seventeen men (two of whom were African Americans – Sterling Brown and Richard Wright).[83]

Women elected to the National Board at the Fourth American Writers' Congress in 1941, well into the Hitler-Stalin Pact, which indicated in many cases a stronger loyalty to Communist Party positions, included Georgia Backus (dates unknown), Brewster, Joy Davidman, Dodd, Muriel Draper (1886-1952), Eleanor Flexner (1908-1995), Lillian Barnard Gilkes (1903-1977), Jean Karsavina, Ruth McKenney, Myra Page, Viola Brothers Shore, Tess Slesinger, Christina Stead, and Taggard, plus twenty-three men, one of whom was an African American, Ralph Ellison.[84] Nearly one-third of the teachers at the League of American Writers' New York Writers School were women. However, only four prominent males are listed as sponsors, while the school board consisted of two men and four women, one of whom, Lillian Gilkes, was the director. The National Board for all the schools (in places such Hollywood, California, and Monteagle, Tennessee) was led by a male president; one female and four male vice presidents, two of whom were African Americans; and a general membership of seven women and twenty-two men, including one African American. These statistics, while incomplete, offer a partial picture of how talented female cultural workers engaged in activities on behalf of a future world without war and bigotry. Moreover, as in the case of the mostly Communist volunteers in Spain, some of whom would be classified as "pre-mature anti-fascists" by U.S. intelligence agencies when they later signed up to fight in World War II, certain of these women writers were "premature socialist-feminists" – politically in advance of their time.

Indeed, recent feminist critics of the Communist-led cultural movement have argued compellingly that the rhetoric of the class struggle represented the proletarian fighter in masculinist ways, reproducing the dominant patriarchal constructions of gender. Such a rhetoric, of course, was hegemonic in the early 1930s, and remained present in Popular Front culture in a more muffled form, fusing with the antifascist rhetoric of World War II during the 1940s.[85] What is vexing is that class war texts of both periods tended to be texts that produce gender positions and valuations as well, with results that are not easily classifiable. Sometimes texts by women addressing women's issues are incapacitated by the contradictory messages they convey due to their failure to recognize differential group experiences between men and women; rarely do gendered themes suggest patriarchy as a primary vehicle of women's oppression. The insights of psychoanalysis, crucial to many writings of the Second Wave of feminism, in some instances are ridiculed as middle-class self-indulgence. Even when an author is a woman, her major focus might be on a male work experience (factory work, as opposed to domestic or service work), and the voice in a poem by a woman frequently might be gender neutral or even have masculine characteristics. An example of a such a gender-neutral text, in which the worker-protagonist's sex is not disclosed, is Ethel Roland's (dates unknown) "Wage Slave":

> Thirty cents an hour, just to be
> A bloody cog in a driving speedup wheel.
> Never to straighten tortured bones, or feel
> Beyond a senseless sweat of agony . . .

Clara Weatherwax's long poem in the February 1936 issue of *Partisan Review and Anvil*, "The Shape of the Sun," is narrated by a young woman on a farm, but from a perspective that appears conventionally subordinate to her father.[86]

Nevertheless, the Left culture generated by pro-Communist women writers does anticipate and prefigure radical feminist and especially socialist-feminist writings of the 1960s and later. These pro-Communist writings confirm the contemporary view that there was not a gap between the First and Second Waves of feminism but rather an ongoing tradition that persevered as a component of the Far Left. In order to identify this tradition, one must discern that such pre-1960s cultural work mostly operated in relation to the evolving Communist world outlook; it rarely approached the explicit feminist agendas promoted by Adrienne Rich, Alice Walker,

Marge Piercy, and other Second Wave writers who powerfully articulate as their primary concern the psychological, social, and cultural practices specific to women living in a patriarchal society. In the tradition between the two "waves," women's distinct forms of rage, the qualitatively distinctive characteristics of women's collective experience, and even the perspective of viewing women as trapped between the two coordinated systems of oppression (capitalism and patriarchy) are more frequently implicit than directly represented.

Yet women cultural workers who were attracted to a revolutionary, antiracist, and militantly antifascist movement gave voice to a treatment of conventional women's subjects such as courtship and marriage from new perspectives, took fresh stances on the development of women's consciousness, and devoted more attention to relations of female protagonists with other women, including characters from a variety of ethnic and racial backgrounds. A dispassionate assessment of women's Left culture during the mid-twentieth century can only occur if one concedes from the outset that it simply did not investigate the entire gamut of the female experience. Moreover, as the preponderance of their radical poems attest, in most cases a drive to reach a broad public with the message of opposition to class and race oppression tended to privilege realist narratives of a quest toward an integrated personality over modernist strategies organized around a fractured consciousness.

## CHAPTER 8

# Black Marxists in White America

## Transcending Narrow Nationalisms

Eugene Holmes and Eugene Gordon assembled the first discernible corpus of Black Marxist literary criticism, spanning the crucial divide between the early 1930s and the Popular Front.[1] In an unprecedented 1935 essay in *International Literature*, "The Negro and American Literature: An Estimate of American Negro Writers," Holmes (writing as Eugene Clay) inspected the achievements of revolutionary Black writers. He avowed that there were a dozen such writers, but only considered Langston Hughes, Sterling Brown, Richard Wright, and Countee Cullen in that category, with supplementary observations about the non-Left-wing Zora Neale Hurston's *Jonah's Gourd Vine* (1934) and a number of novels by white writers, including the Jewish American Guy Endore's revolutionary novel *Babouk*.

Holmes's essay offers a relatively unrefined correlation of texts to classes and class fractions, treating the Harlem Renaissance and its promotion of a "New Negro" as somewhat of a hoax concocted by white American capitalists seeking novel entertainments. Yet Holmes also shrewdly canvases specific texts and finds virtues in the work of nonrevolutionary southerners as well as weaknesses in pro-Communist Black writers. Especially telling is the estimate of his Howard University colleague Sterling Brown, praised for "forsak[ing] the purer English literary forms, not because of their ineffectiveness, but because his metier and format fit better in his earthy, 'down-home' dialect of the workers he knows so well."[2]

An abridged version of the essay was presented as a talk at the 1935 American Writers' Congress, and published in the congress's proceedings.[3] In this form, Holmes's piece was accompanied by a short speech by Langston Hughes, "To Negro Writers," which called on Black Communist cultural workers to use their art to reveal the vigor and undistorted character of the African American people, and to bare the shams of white philanthropy and false Black leadership: "Negro writers can seek to unite Blacks and whites in our country, not on the nebulous basis of an interracial meeting, or the shifting sands of religious brotherhood, but on the solid ground of the daily working-class struggle to wipe out, now and forever, all the old inequalities of the past."[4]

Eugene Gordon's contribution to the same 1935 American Writers' Congress proceedings, "Social and Political Problems of the Negro Writer," focused on the particularities of racial and national oppression beyond exclusively class exploitation:

> Closely linked up with the economic problem of earning a living, there are the social problems of where to live, with whom to associate, and of how to find recreation. These fundamental social problems are common to the Negro people as a whole, but they are the special problems of the Negro writer.

Gordon then traces the concentration of diverse kidnapped African peoples into a "Negro nation" centered in the Black Belt of the southern United States, and he polemicizes against "petty-bourgeois nationalist consciousness" reproduced in several works by W. E. B. Du Bois, Paul Laurence Dunbar, Charles W. Chestnut, Jessie Fauset, James Weldon Johnson, George Schuyler, and Nella Larsen. Other Black Communists addressed the Writers' Congress as well, including Angelo Herndon, who was out on bail after being sentenced in Georgia for eighteen to twenty years in prison for leading a demonstration demanding food, and Richard Wright, who broached from the floor the problem of "the isolation of the young Negro writer."[5]

At the Second American Writers' Congress in 1937, Holmes spoke on "A Writer's Social Obligations." His forceful oration opened with an outline of the burgeoning threat of fascism nationally and internationally, before concentrating on the dilemma of African Americans. In contrast to the situation in the Soviet Union, where Holmes believed that minority groups were being supported and encouraged, only a few voices of resistance were coming from the Black community in the United States at present—he cited Arna Bontemps's novel Black Thunder, and poetry by Langston Hughes, Sterling Brown, Richard Wright, Owen Dodson (1914-1983), and Frank Marshall Davis (1905-1987). After rehearsing the many obstacles faced by such writers, and scoring some of the errors made by those who choose to depict middle-class Black life or individualist solutions, Holmes concluded that the writer "must transcend narrow nationalisms, and insidious chauvinism, and realize that our tasks are international." Holmes postulated that the aftereffect will be writers who are "resolved to respect historic truth, and their knowledge of events and people will be more related to life as it is actually lived." Moreover, they will promulgate works that "will truly be the product of the social, intellectual and emotional activity of man, and an integral part of an expanding human culture." This will be the culture "which the artist is obligated to defend with his life."[6]

Richard Wright was busy as a chair and participant in the deliberations of the congress. As recorded in minutes taken by the pro-Communist novelist Leane Zugsmith, Wright, speaking in the novelists' commission, warned of

> the tendency of writers going into labor work and trying to escape their writer's personality. There is no backwardness on the part of trade unionists in accepting the writer as a writer. They realize his function, if the writer realizes it.[7]

In the debate that followed Holmes's paper, Robert Gessner[8] urged that the growing tensions between Blacks and Jews in Harlem be considered. Holmes rejoined:

> I don't think the average person realizes that anti-Semitism could flourish within an even more exploited and persecuted group. But I have seen it in Howard University where we have Jewish professors. That anti-Semitism exists among Negroes shows that the Negro misunderstands the entire minority set-up. Negroes look upon Jewish landlords and storekeepers as their immediate exploiters and don't try to get to the real facts accounting for their exploitation.

Holmes further averred that this was an issue that the congress needed to address: "It is tragic that Negroes should possess such thoughts about the Jews."[9]

Up until the mid- to late 1930s, including after the advent of the Popular Front, the attainments of the Harlem Renaissance – its literature as well as its jazz – were coded by the foremost pro-Communist Black writers as decadent. They usually claimed that Renaissance works were middle-class entertainments aimed at gratifying the psychological needs of white patrons. Such a "hard-line" approach can be found in Richard Wright's influential "Blue-Print for Negro Writing," published in the inaugural issue of *New Challenge* in 1937, which expressed the shared attitude of the members of the African American South Side Writers Club in Chicago. Harlem Renaissance writings are designated in Wright's manifesto as the accidental "fruits of that foul soil which was the result of a liaison between the inferiority-complexed Negro 'geniuses' and burnt-out white Bohemians with money."[10] Moreover, at the 1935 American Writers' Congress, all three pro-Communist Black speakers took swipes at the "New Negro" phenomenon, although Langston Hughes, who was one of the three, was cited as an illustration of a Left permutation, as was Sterling Brown.

Such a rejectionist view of the Harlem Renaissance, however, was not ubiquitous. For example, in his 1937 address to the second conference of the Communist-led National Negro Congress, longtime fellow-traveler Alain Locke, the main authority on the "New Negro," unambiguously stated his belief in "the considerable harmony . . . between the cultural racialism of the art philosophy of the 1920s and the class proletarian art creed of today's younger generation." His view is cogently argued by William Maxwell's 1999 study New Negro, Old Left, which provides evidence of a mutual indebtedness between the Harlem Renaissance and the early Communist Left.

The Third American Writers' Congress in 1939, which ensued prior to the Hitler-Stalin Pact, saw no further onslaughts against the Harlem Renaissance. It featured an address by Langston Hughes about the restricted market for Black writers. Another disquisition was by Jewish anthropologist Melville J. Herskovits of Northwestern University on "The Negro in American Literature – Past and Future," in which he pleaded that there existed a bounteous patrimony of African-based folk culture and of resistance to oppression. In the audience was Alain Locke, who took the floor and proclaimed a ringing endorsement of Herskovits's argument. In his remarks, Locke added that the accession of the "New Negro" movement in the mid-twenties had been based on the discernment that

> especially for the Negro writer and the Negro artist, one of the soundest possible developments was the development of an historical sense, a knowledge adequate and accurate, of the Negro's past, and we said definitely that the great cultural disability of the Negro as a minority group was the loss of this proud past which he would have to recapture.[11]

The Fourth American Writers' Congress opened on 6 June 1941, a few weeks prior to the German invasion of the Soviet Union, when the position of the Communist Party and those who shared its outlook converted from the isolationist "The Yanks Aren't Coming" to one of militant pro-interventionism in the war. The opening address of the congress was delivered by Richard Wright, who before an audience of 3,000 at the Manhattan Center agitated that the present war was an imperialist war in which African Americans had no stake. Moreover, he assailed the segregationist policy of the U.S. military, which he negatively counterpoised to the integrated International Brigades that had fought in the Spanish Civil War.[12] Although Langston Hughes was on the West Coast and could not be present at the congress, he sent a message of solidarity. Eugene Holmes and the Blues singer Leadbelly (Huddie Ledbetter) were among the participants, and Ralph Ellison was a pivotal organizer of the congress, chiefly engaged in the project of developing a national magazine to be sponsored by the League of American Writers.

Other than Richard Wright, no prominent African American writers were willing to risk the exposure of appearing in public as acknowledged members of the Communist Party. Yet sympathy for the Party was so prevalent that it is plausible to acknowledge African American Literary Communism as a major component of mid-twentieth-century culture, one that would grow even stronger during the late 1940s and early 1950s.[13] What is more memorable than formal membership in the Party is that, for Black writers, the publications, clubs, and committees that were at least in part created by Party members, and with Party support, constituted principal venues in which many Black writers came together to formulate ideas, share writings, make contacts, and develop perspectives that sustained their future creative work. A robust example of the positive contribution of Black Marxism prior to World War II can be found in the activities of the South Side Writers Club in Chicago, which performed a vital role in launching *New Challenge*.

## New Challenges

The South Side Writers Club was assembled in the wake of the Communist-led National Negro Congress that was held in Chicago in 1936. Richard Wright and Margaret Walker subsequently identified the following Black writers as among the originating members, in addition to themselves: Arna Bontemps, Frank Marshall Davis, Marian Minus, Edward Bland, Russell Marshall, and Robert Davis.[14] Of the last three, little biographical information has been preserved. Bland, close to poet Gwendolyn Brooks in Chicago, published literary criticism in journals such as *Poetry* and *Negro Quarterly*. One of his essays, "Racial Bias and Negro Verse," argued that the imposition by white racism of "pre-individualistic thinking" on Black writers resulted in "self-conscious 'race' values which impair and delimit the vision of the artist."[15] At the time of publication, Bland was a sergeant in the army stationed in New York City. Shortly afterward he was sent to Germany, where he volunteered for a dangerous mission and was killed.[16] Davis was a Communist Party member who was a poet working on the Federal Writers Project in Chicago; later he changed his name and moved to Hollywood, where he pursued a career in acting.[17]

Arna Bontemps (1902–1973), like Claude McKay and Langston Hughes, incarnated the links between the Harlem Renaissance and the revolutionary spirit of the Black Left in the 1930s.[18] Born in Louisiana, the son of a brickmason, Bontemps moved with his family to California to escape southern racism. There he fell under the sway of an uncle who was enthusiastic about minstrel shows, dialect stories, and signs and charms, much in contrast to Bontemps's father's assimilationist attitude. While earning a B.A. from Pacific Union College in 1923, Bontemps pledged himself to recount the bountiful legacy of African American folk culture and history in books and through the educational system. He migrated to New York to teach in private schools and launch his writing career, making his first mark as a poet. He had read Claude McKay's Harlem Shadows (1922), and was expressly taken with "If We Must Die" and "Harlem Dancer." In New York he became fast friends with Countee Cullen and Langston Hughes. His 1927 poem "The Return" resonates with many of the motifs of Cullen's and Hughes's early work. By the time of the Depression, Bontemps had become a family man, and he acquired a job at Oakwood Junior College in Huntsville, Alabama. There he was exceedingly appalled by the Scottsboro trial, and further incensed when he was subsequently told by the college authorities that his library of books was subversive and must be burned.

Bontemps in his maturity was a short, well-built man, extremely good looking with long wavy hair.[19] His first novel, God Sends Sunday (1931), was a picaresque tale about a black jockey in New Orleans who bears some likeness to Bontemps's favorite uncle. As an effect of his residence in Alabama, he wrote Black Thunder (1936), a revolutionary novel about the nineteenth-century slave rebellion led by Gabriel Prosser. This was succeeded by a novel about the Haitian Revolution, Drums at Dusk (1939), based on research Bontemps undertook in the Caribbean with the sustenance of a Julius Rosenwald Fellowship in creative writing. From 1935 to 1938 he taught at the Shiloh Academy in Chicago, where he made his contact with members of the largely pro-Communist South Side Writers Club. After that, he worked for the Federal Writers Project. He also acquired a second Rosenwald Fellowship to work on the "Negro in Illinois" project. Subsequently he earned an M.A. in library science at the University of Chicago in 1943. From that time until his retirement in 1965, he was the head librarian at Fisk University in Nashville.

In addition to composing numerous children's stories, Bontemps also wrote two plays, St. Louis Woman (with Countee Cullen), which was produced in 1946, and Free and Easy (1949). He also edited a number of major anthologies: Poetry of the Negro, 1746–1949, with Langston Hughes (1949); Book of Negro Folklore, with Langston Hughes (1958); American Negro Poetry (1963); Great Slave Narratives (1969); and The Harlem Renaissance Remembered: Essays (1972). His early poetry was collected in Personals (1963), and a volume of his short fiction and prose was posthumously published as The Old South (1973).

Bontemps's own statements attest that he was in the 1930s, and perhaps later, an independent Black revolutionary in private convictions, although reticent about public activities. While his trusted friends and collaborators included Communists and pro-Communists—such as Langston Hughes, Jack Conroy, and many members of the South Side Writers Club—there is less evidence of specific pro-Communist Party or pro-Soviet Union sympathy in his writings and letters. Still, he remained in regular contact with the Communist literary agent Maxim Lieber after Lieber fled the United States for Mexico and ultimately Poland, in the face of accusations by Whittaker Chambers that his literary agency was a front for espionage.[20] It is possible that Bontemps saw Communists much as he pictured the French characters in his novel *Black Thunder*, as sympathizers with a struggle that must be led by the targets of oppression themselves.

Bontemps's shy and retiring personality, and his reluctance to identify himself as a "Red," did not interfere with his appearing to share many dispositions of the Communist outlook of fellow-travelers such as Hughes and Conroy. Richard Wright's review of *Black Thunder* in *Partisan Review and Anvil* treated the text as an incomparable addition to the revolutionary tradition of proletarian literature, especially its folk component.[21] Moreover, in November 1942, Bontemps signed a call for a "Win-the-War Congress" sponsored by the League of American Writers to be held on the first anniversary of the Japanese attack on Pearl Harbor. By this time the politics of the league were more or less in line with official U.S. policy, but the organization was so closely associated with the turn-abouts of Soviet foreign policy that the list of other endorsers was politically narrower than in the past; for example, even Richard Wright, technically a Party member although increasingly disaffected, did not sign the call. Moreover, direct pressure from the U.S. government's Writers War Board, headed by Rex Stout (1886–1975), a prominent defector from the league, caused the cancellation of the congress and the loss of money contributed by Dashiell Hammett to support it.[22]

Frank Marshall Davis (1905–1987) was acclaimed as both a journalist and radical poet prior to the Cold War, and was near to the Communist Party and probably even a member in the 1940s. He had the physique of a football player and was an authority on jazz. Born in Kansas, he graduated from Kansas State before removing to Chicago. His collections of poetry seem to increasingly develop the Harlem Renaissance "New Negro" themes in a revolutionary fashion. Lynching, global war, and the class and race oppression that pervaded urban life are among his central poetic themes; the primary Euro-American influences on Davis appear to be the poetry of Carl Sandburg and Edgar Lee Masters.[23] The poems in his collections *Black Man's*

Verse (1935), *I Am the American Negro* (1937), *Through Sepia Eyes* (1938), and, finally, *47th Street: Poems* (1948) are in progression from a quasi–Black nationalist stance to a Marxist, proletarian outlook. The last book includes a commanding foreword by Davis castigating biological theories of race while espousing a subtle notion of cultural difference among ethnic groups. Davis concluded, however, that he writes not only as someone singled out for discrimination because an ancestor was a Black African, but as one of the common people divided from other common people "for continued domination by the economic rulers of the world." His poetry is therefore written on behalf "of all the common people, even though I know that many of another color and culture in their confusion consider me foe instead of friend."[24]

Davis was executive editor of the Associated Negro Press in Chicago from 1935 to 1947. He first met Richard Wright at the Conference of the National Negro Congress held in Chicago in 1936. In 1938 Davis became active in the League of American Writers, which had a concentrated impact on him: "Never before had I worked closely and voluntarily in equality with a number of whites."[25] In 1938 he was treasurer of the Chicago chapter and he signed the call for the 1941 Fourth American Writers' Congress. In the 1940s he lectured on jazz at the Communist Party-organized Abraham Lincoln School in Chicago, where he also assisted as a member of the board of directors. Davis additionally worked as a jazz radio disk jockey. He later recalled that his 1944 classes, "possibly the first regular courses ever given in the History of Jazz at a school," were "instigated primarily by Art Stern, a young Jewish intellectual, who realized the significance of this music in our continuing struggle for equality."[26]

During these years Davis participated in a writing circle with the pro-Communist Margaret Taylor-Goss (later Margaret Burroughs) as well as Gwendolyn Brooks, Henry Blakely, Gwendolyn Cunningham, Fern Gayden, and Mavis Mixon. He contributed to the *New Masses* and came to know and respect the Black Communists Benjamin Davis Jr., Angelo Herndon, and William L. Patterson. When Herbert Aptheker came to lecture in Chicago, Davis chaired many of the meetings at which he spoke.[27] Davis adhered to the view that the Soviet Union was being treated by world opinion in a manner similar to the handling of Blacks in the United States. As soon as the Young Communist League reorganized as the American Youth for Democracy during the war, Davis became a national sponsor of the organization and cooperated with it. When World War II began, Davis, who initially was confounded by Communist Party policy at the time of the Hitler-Stalin Pact, felt that Earl Browder's policy advocating cooperation with the war effort was far too conciliatory. In the postwar period Davis believed that the Communist Party was regaining its credibility in the Black community through its renewed struggle for civil rights, and he collaborated with Party leader Ben Davis in drawing up proposals for the Party leadership to fortify such work. During the McCarthy era, Davis's books were removed from libraries and schools, and in 1948 he moved once and for all to Hawaii, where he operated a wholesale paper business and wrote a regular weekly column for the *Honolulu Record*. After nearly a quarter of a century of silence, the poetry of Davis was revived by Detroit poet Dudley Randall and literary critic Stephen Henderson around 1973, and Davis undertook a triumphant tour of Black colleges in the United States. Still committed to the Left, he died in 1977.[28]

Marian Minus (1913–1973) was born as Mattie Marian Minus in South Carolina. She graduated from Fisk University with a major in sociology in 1935, and studied anthropology on a two-year Rosenwald Scholarship at the University of Chicago. She began publishing short stories in the 1930s and in 1937 became coeditor with her friend Dorothy West of *New Challenge*, the only time the two of them plainly demonstrated sympathy for Communism. From 1945 to 1952, Minus contributed numerous stories to *Women's Day* about middle-class white Americans, while her stories and essays about African American life appeared in *Opportunity*, *Black Life* and *The Crisis*. Later she worked as a clerk at Consumer's Union in Mount Vernon, New York.

Margaret Walker (1915–1998) pursued her search for poetic voice at the same time as she underwent an education in Marxism through her experiences in the Communist movement in Chicago. She was born in Birmingham, Alabama, and her family moved to New Orleans while she was still quite young. Her father was a scholarly minister educated at Northwestern University who cherished the classics, the Bible, and European philosophers. Her mother was a musician who habitually read Margaret poetry by Paul Laurence Dunbar, John Greenleaf Whittier, and Shakespeare. By the time she was eleven, Walker was reading Langston Hughes and Countee Cullen, and she was being immersed in family history by way of stories passed on to her by her maternal grandmother, the daughter of a former slave in Georgia. Walker graduated from Northwestern University in 1935. Having met Langston Hughes in 1932 and secured his encouragement, she published her first poem in the *Crisis* in 1934, at the beginning of her senior year at Northwestern. In the ensuing period she began an association with the Works Progress Administration (WPA), first as a volunteer at a recreation project. In March 1936 she became a full-time employee of the Federal Writers Project, working on the *Illinois Guide Book*. In 1937 her duties were reduced so that she could work on her novel, "Goose Island," about a social worker, which she completed in 1939 but never published.

In the later 1930s Walker developed relations with many cultural workers associated with the Communist movement, especially Black and Jewish writers. Some pro-Communist novelists were likewise connected with the Federal Writers Project, such as Nelson Algren (1909–1981) and Jack Conroy. She also sat in on the 1936 convention of the National Negro Congress in Chicago, where Richard Wright presided over the congress's writers' section. Her plan was to rendezvous with Langston Hughes, who was present at the congress, and give him copies of her poetry; but Hughes introduced her to Wright, and Wright acquainted her with Arna Bontemps and Sterling Brown. As a result Walker shared in the organization of the South Side Writers Club and played a principal role in soliciting writers to contribute to New Challenge, which was briefly to be the voice of the Black pro-Communist cultural Left.

Wright was already having conflicts with some of the local Black Communist Party leaders in Chicago, but at the time Walker was only cognizant that he was contemptuous of instructions from the Party that he not talk to certain writers and Party members who had been dubbed "Trotskyists." She felt Wright was justified. Otherwise she was persuaded by Wright's arguments that the political program of the Party was appropriate for a Black writer, that the Party would provide a political education, and that membership would also teach self-discipline. Thus she joined the Young Communist League in the spring of 1937, and, after Wright departed for New York, she also joined the Communist Party in the summer of 1937.[29] Although captivated by Party leaders such as Earl Browder and an enthusiastic student of Marxist doctrine in Party-led classes, Walker could also be sarcastic about the egoism and quirkiness of some of the aspiring writers around the movement. For most of 1938 Walker was a member of a loosely organized Writers Unit of the Party, so chaotic that it was frequently threatened with being disbanded and its members transferred to regular Party units. The main activity of the Writers Unit was building the Chicago League of American Writers chapter, although Walker requested that she be assigned by the Party to gather material for New Challenge.

In spite of the rejection of Walker's submissions to the New Masses, she published verse in Poetry, which had its office in Chicago and editors who were friendly to the Left. She also declared herself an impassioned admirer of the poetry of Sol Funaroff, and took on tasks for the journal New Anvil and the Negro People's Theater.[30] Among her poems that appeared in Poetry were "For My People" (1937), "We Have Been Believers" (1938), and "The Struggle Staggers Us" (1939). Both before and after Wright left Chicago, Walker collaborated with him; he gave her his opinions about the structure of her poems and advised her about books to read that would help provide her with a Marxist education, one that enabled her to write the historical novel *Jubilee* (1966). In return, Walker abetted Wright with the short story "Almos' a Man," *Lawd Today* (published posthumously in 1963), and *Native Son* (1940).

Unfortunately, Walker tended to be overzealous in her personal dealings with writers in Wright's circle, and Wright became suspicious that she was responsible for spreading gossip that poisoned some of his friendships. When Walker attended the Third Congress of the League of American Writers, she was stupefied at Wright's coldness and his announcement that he was breaking off all relations with her. There is no evidence that they were lovers, but Walker had developed an overly eager devotion to Wright as a genius, and had filled her numerous letters to him with anecdotes about mutual friends that tended to give the impression that they were disloyal while she was his main defender. When Wright thwarted Walker at the Third Congress in New York, she fell into despondency and trailed after him, trying to get a fuller explanation of his shift in attitude toward her. Finally, from Chicago she sent him a seven-page single-spaced self-criticism, in which she also reaffirmed her fidelity to the Party.[31] It was to no avail, and the only further communication between the two of them is a one-sentence formal note of congratulations from Walker on the publication of *Native Son*.[32]

Since her job at the Federal Writers Project was coming to an end, Walker enrolled in the University of Iowa's Writers Workshop in 1939, then directed by liberal poet Paul Engle (1908–1991). She received an M.A. from Iowa in 1942 for her collection of poetry *For My People*, winner of the Yale University Younger Poets Award. For most of the 1940s Walker taught college in the South and worked on *Jubilee*. In 1949 she moved to Jackson, Mississippi, to begin a long career teaching at Jackson State College. In 1962 she returned to the University of Iowa's Writers Workshop, once again working with Paul Engle, and finally completed *Jubilee*, which she submitted as her doctoral dissertation after three years. In 1970 she published a volume of poetry on the civil rights movement, *Prophets for a New Day*, followed by *October Journey* (1973) and *For Farish Street* (1986).

Once Wright had settled in New York, the Harlem Communist Party leader Benjamin Davis implored him to combine forces with Dorothy West to convert her magazine *Challenge* into a publication closer to the Communist Party, *New Challenge*, and to print a political-literary manifesto in the new magazine that the Party could use to sway sympathizers and recruit writers.[33] Wright was delighted to comply, and he drafted "Blue-Print for Negro Writing," which reflected perspectives on nationalism, the Harlem

Renaissance, and other matters discussed in the South Side Writers Club, for the inaugural issue.

*Challenge* was initiated in 1934, when West had returned to her hometown of Boston. Born in 1907, West was a single child, the daughter of an ice cream parlor owner. She secured private tutorials at a young age and went on to study philosophy and journalism at Columbia University in 1923. She commenced writing when she was seven, and her literary career began when *Opportunity* published her first story in 1926. West, who studied at Boston University as well as the Columbia University School of Journalism, associated with many participants in the Harlem Renaissance. Her stories were also published in Boston by Eugene Gordon, when he was editor of the *Saturday Evening Quill*. Due to a modicum of acting experience, she accompanied Langston Hughes to the Soviet Union in 1932 to bring about a film tackling anti-Black racism. When the film project collapsed, she tarried in the Soviet Union for another year with Hughes.

By launching *Challenge*, West aimed to unite the older generation of Black writers with the young radicals. A paradigmatic political evolution can be traced in its pages. James Weldon Johnson, Langston Hughes, Arna Bontemps, and Countee Cullen were among those featured in the first issue. In her editorial, West hinted at the view that would become stronger during the Popular Front years, that the Left literary movement among African Americans of the 1930s proposed to extend and transform the work of the Harlem Renaissance era: "It is our plan to bring out the prose and poetry of the newer Negroes. We who were the New Negroes challenge them to better our achievements. For we did not altogether live up to our fine promise."[34] A pro-Soviet tint was already visible through "Room in Red Square," an ardent memoir published under the name "Mary Christopher," which was "a pseudonym for a young woman who went to Russia a year ago with an acting company."[35]

In the second issue, Bontemps replied to the inaugural editorial in language suggesting that perhaps the original "New Negroes" were themselves going to make the journey to the fulfillment of the literary and political aspirations of the 1930s: "We're not washed up. Not by a jugful. . . . We left Egypt in the late twenties and presently crossed the Red Sea. . . . The promised land is ahead. Why Langston (Hughes) has just recently been spying it out for us, and the grapes are promising."[36] Indeed, in the fourth installment, West clarified that the reason why the magazine had not yet taken an explicit revolutionary coloration was due solely to the quality of the writing received: "Somebody asked us why *Challenge* was for the most part pale pink. We said because the few red articles we did receive were not literature. We care a lot about style." West spelled out her desire "to print more articles and stories of protest," and noted her sense of identification with the struggles of the "underprivileged." Yet in reproaching the relatively privileged younger Black students who lacked political consciousness, West implored them to become part of "the leadership of the literate," and made no mention of Marxist political parties or even unions.[37] Nevertheless, the formula for soliciting contributions mirrored the Communist policy toward Black leadership of interracial organizations such as the National Negro Congress: "*Challenge* is primarily interested in material by Negro writers. But all writers are invited to contribute to its pages."[38]

As *Challenge* evolved through six issues until the spring of 1937, Black radicals increased consistently among its contributors, including Claude McKay, Frank Yerby, William Attaway, and Owen Dodson. A position paper on Black writing crafted by Marian Minus in April 1937 seems to partake of many similarities with Richard Wright's approach. In it, Minus acclaims Arna Bontemps's *Black Thunder* as a major breakthrough for its use of folk material, and she declares that "The time is past when the patterns of veneer of a class which is foreign to the great bulk of Negro life shall guide creative work."[39] An editorial note in this issue of *Challenge* mentions that the magazine is on the threshold of cessation due to financial uncertainties, but that its one prospect for continuance is the aid of a group of Chicago writers, of which Minus was a member; this coterie had criticized the past practice of *Challenge*, and the editors responded by offering them space in a forthcoming issue.

Instead, the magazine appeared as *New Challenge* in the fall of 1937, under the editorship of West and Minus, whom Margaret Walker believed to be lesbian lovers.[40] Wright was associate editor, and there was a contributing editors list of mostly pro-Communist Black writers, including Sterling Brown, Robert Hayden, Eugene Holmes, Langston Hughes, Loren Miller, Arthur Randall (the brother of Detroit poet Dudley Randall), and Margaret Walker. The exact steps leading to the final transformation seem to have entailed a decision by West and Minus to take the publication on an explicit "leftward" trajectory, while Richard Wright interceded (when he came to New York in June of 1937 for the Second American Writers' Congress) to gain Communist Party assistance in the effort. In a letter to Langston Hughes, Wright recounted that he had the aid of Bontemps, and that the idea was to refrain from being "out and out red" but to place the emphasis "upon a social angle, at least for the time being." The strategy for gaining funds and a following would be borrowed from the *New Masses* (fund-raising balls) and *New Theater* (literary contests).[41]

The editorial in the revamped journal affirmed that the literary material of the new publication was to be based "in the proper perspective with regard to the life of the Negro masses," which specifically means "the great fertility of folk material as a source of creative material."[42] The magazine's object was to become the "organ of regional groups composed of writers opposed to fascism, war and general reactionary politics," of which the South Side Club was an exemplar, hence the inclusion of advisory editors from cities such as Detroit, Washington, and Baltimore. The editorial closed with the disclaimer that "The magazine, being non-political, is not subsidized by any political party."

The initial issue boasted an impressive poetry section with verse by Frank Marshall Davis, Sterling Brown, Robert Davis, Owen Dodson, and Margaret Walker; two critical pieces commenting on Wright's "Blueprint," Allyn Keith's "A Note on Negro Nationalism," and Eugene Holmes's "Problems Facing the Negro Writer Today"; and a review section that included critical comments about Claude McKay's *A Long Way from Home* by Alain Locke, a commentary on Zora Neale Hurston's *Their Eyes Were Watching God* by Marian Minus, a review of the WPA collection *American Stuff* that emphasized Black contributors, and Ralph Ellison's first published writing, a review of Waters Turpin's *These Low Grounds* (1937). Euro-American contributors included Norman MacLeod, Charles Henri Ford, and Benjamin Appel.

This was the only issue to occur, despite the considerable enthusiasm that was generated by its appearance. Margaret Walker was told that the money from newsstand sales never got back to the office, although there may have been friction between West and her coeditor Marian Minus. West was afterward employed as a welfare investigator in Harlem. She then worked for the Federal Writers Project until it ended in the 1940s, after which she became a regular contributor of short stories to the *New York Daily News*. In 1948 she published an autobiographical novel, *The Living Is Easy*, in 1994 *The Wedding*, and in 1995 *The Richer, the Poorer: Stories, Sketches and Reminiscences*. By 1997, the year before her death, she had achieved wide fame and was acclaimed by the First Lady, Hillary Rodham Clinton, as a "national treasure."[43]

## "New" and "Newer" Negroes

Among the Black cultural leaders closely associated with New York–based activities and publications, Alain Locke (1886–1954) is one of the most intricate and consequential. Locke came from Philadelphia and held degrees from Harvard and Oxford. After a ten-month tour of the American South in 1911, he became persuaded of the need for African American self-expression. Fifteen years later he produced a major contribution to this goal by becoming the champion of the Harlem Renaissance through the publication of his anthology, *The New Negro* (1925). Ensconced at Howard University as chair of the Philosophy Department when the Depression began, he was obviously affected by the radicalization of his colleagues, as well as friends from the Harlem Renaissance such as Langston Hughes.

Although his background was anchored in the elitism of the Niagara Movement and the Du Boisian philosophy of the "Talented Tenth," he was respectful of the new-sprung developments in proletarian and revolutionary literature throughout the 1930s.[44] He was active in the League of American Writers and the National Negro Congress, and, while there is no evidence that he considered himself a Communist, his cultural criticism of the 1940s and 1950s incorporated many Marxist themes. Often his judgments appeared to be richer, better informed and more complex classical Marxist correctives to the dogmatic perspectives emanating from the Communist Party. His writing appeared in the *New Masses* until the late 1940s.

His essay, "Sterling Brown: The New Negro Folk-Poet," written in 1934, traces the steps by which Black poetry had evolved and comments astutely on McKay, Hughes, and others; he proclaims that a new era had been launched by Brown's use of folk expression.[45] Two years later, in "Propaganda – or Poetry?," Locke appraised the verse of young poets such as Richard Wright, Frank Marshall Davis, and Sterling Brown who "show a gradually nearer approach to the poetry that can fuse class consciousness with racial protest, and express proletarian sentiment in the genuine Negro folk idiom." Locke offered intelligent discriminations in demarcating the poet's strengths and weaknesses. Locke was not opposed to politics or protest in poetry, but he sought poetic utterances "from the vital heart of the Negro experience"; he scorned derivative strophes that smacked of Moscow or Union Square origins. For him, Sterling Brown represented the pinnacle of the younger poets, for "Today it is the rise of this quieter, more indigenous radicalism that is significant and promising. Doubly so, because along with a Leftist turn of thought goes a real enlargement of native social consciousness and a more authentic folk spokesmanship." Locke concluded by respectfully counterpoising his views to those of "a recent writer, of doctrinaire Marxist leanings, [who] insists that . . . the proletarian poet should not be a racialist. . . . The art of our time is to be the 'class angle.' " Locke doesn't name this stand-in critic for the Party, but his assertion, in favor "of a high compatibility between race-conscious and class conscious thought," more scrupulously expresses the standpoint and mid-century cultural practice of Black Marxism.[46]

Another venue of Locke's Black Marxism in the 1930s may be located in his annual review of writings, "Literature of the Negro," which appeared in *Opportunity*. Locke cast his net widely, including not only all African American writers of fiction, sociology, drama, poetry, children's books, anthropology, and biography, but also Euro-American writers who treated Black Americans in these categories. Many such writers were pro-Communist, and Locke characteristically balanced criticisms of dogma and oversimplification with accolades for their apperception of crucial themes. In 1932 he praised the Jewish pro-Communist writer John Spivak's *Georgia Nigger* as "a pure propaganda novel, but with that strange power that propaganda takes on when it flames with righteous indignation."[47] In a survey of Black literature published in 1935, he greatly praised novels by the pro-Communist writers Erskine Caldwell and Grace Lumpkin.[48] In his 1936 review, he termed James Allen's *The Negro Question* "rigid" but "rigorous," lauding the book for portraying a "South . . . X-rayed to its economic bones." Locke then challenged anti-Communists to try to come up with a more appropriate alternative than Allen's to the "economic cancer" of the plantation system.[49]

His review of literature that appeared in 1937 likens Richard Wright's "Big Boy Leaves Home" to Jean Toomer's *Cane*, declaring Wright's story a portent of a whole exhilarating new era of "proletarian fiction." *New Challenge* was emphatically endorsed by Locke, especially the poetry of the Black Communist Robert Davis and the fellow-traveler Frank Marshall Davis. The Communist Angelo Herndon's *Let Me Live* is auspiciously compared to Claude McKay's *A Long Way from Home*. He acclaims Euro-American Communist Paul Peter's *Stevedore* as among the foremost plays to date on Black life. The collaborative work, *The Negro in Soviet America*, by James Ford and James Allen, was, as was Allen's earlier book, branded as too formulaic, but "that does not remove its realistic thrust as a contending alternative to the yet unsuccessful reformism of moral appeal and legislative guarantees."[50]

"The Negro: 'New' or Newer" was the title of Locke's review for 1938, and its primary focus was on Richard Wright, who had just published *Uncle Tom's Children*. Locke praised him for making use of "the novella with the sweep and power of epic tragedy" to launch "a major literary career."[51] When Wright's *Native Son* appeared, Locke unfalteringly placed himself in the Black Communist literary camp of Wright, Ellison, Walker, and Ward, and several Jewish Communist critics, against the more dogmatic Harlem political activists:

> There was artistic courage and integrity of the first order in his decision to ignore both the squeamishness of the Negro minority and the depre-

cating bias of the prejudiced majority, full knowing that one would like to ignore the fact that there are any Negroes like Bigger and the other like to think that Bigger is the prototype of all. . . . Wright's portrait of Bigger Thomas says more about America than it does about the Negro, for he is the native son of the black city ghetto, with its tensions, frustrations and resentments. The brunt of the action and the tragedy involves social forces rather than persons; it is the first instance of a Zolaesque "J'accuse" pointing to the danger symptoms of a self-frustrating democracy.[52]

For the next several years, Locke's literary criticism persevered in a comparable vein, always promoting pro-Communist writers and showing special sympathy for their objects of concern while never explicitly endorsing a revolutionary goal. Robert Hayden's first volume of poetry, published by an obscure press with Left-wing financial assistance, was admired mainly for its political poems which served as a showcase for his finer talents. Locke especially commended his poem "Coleman, Negro Veteran Murdered by the Black Legion."[53] At the time that *The Negro Caravan* appeared, edited by his friend and colleague Sterling Brown, Locke took exception to Brown's claim that "Negro writing" was an inappropriate term. While he was no doubt expressing his own opinion, Locke's admonition was only a softer version of the intemperate criticism of Brown's contention offered by Black Communist cultural leaders in the Communist press.[54] When International Publishers published the Communist Sidney Finkelstein's *Jazz: A People's Music* in 1949, Locke applauded it in *Phylon* for its unique ability to connect Black music and social history.[55] A year later he gave high acclamation to books by the pro-Communists Earl Conrad and Philip Foner.[56]

By 1952, however, Locke's writings registered a new and hostile tone regarding the Communist Left. The Euro-American scholar Wilson Record's mean-spirited *The Negro and the Communist Party* is complimented by Locke as "a fine example of an objectively factual study . . . a fair account of communist plans, tactics and results in the period 1919 to 1950."[57] Even more inexplicable, in his essay "From *Native Son* to *Invisible Man*," Locke introduced for the first time the reproach that *Native Son* "was marred only by Wright's overreliance on the Communist ideology with which he encumbered his powerful indictment of society."[58] This was his terminal column; two years later he died.

## Between Class and Nationality

Many other African American poets during the 1930s and 1940s also had associations with the Communist Left. The verse of Gwendolyn Bennett

(1902–1981) occurred mostly before 1935, which is when she first exhibited signs of pro-Communism. In the 1940s she became an administrator of two Communist-led educational centers, first the Jefferson School for Democracy in Manhattan and then the George Washington Carver School in Harlem. When the two institutions were investigated during the McCarthyite witch-hunt, Bennett retreated from public life and worked quietly as a secretary for the Consumer's Union, then retired to Pennsylvania where she became an antique collector.

Jessie Redmon Fauset (1882–1961) is another, less classifiable, radical writer whose achievements are principally related to the Harlem Renaissance period. As literary editor for the *Crisis* from 1919 to 1926, she promoted several authors who were then shifting to the Left, including Langston Hughes, Countee Cullen, and Claude McKay. She commenced publishing fiction and poetry in 1912, and two of her novels appeared in the early 1930s. *The Chinaberry Tree* (1931), set in a Black community in New Jersey, delineates a range of characters attracted to middle-class respectability in opposition to those exhibiting nonconformist behavior. *Comedy, American Style* (1933) portrays a self-hating Black woman. After the mid-1930s, when she was a member of the League of American Writers, her literary and political activity declined.

Sterling Brown (1901–1989) was championed by the Communist Party in the mid-1930s, and he demonstrated considerable sympathy for the Party's activities. Eugene Clay Holmes's "Sterling Brown: American People's Poet" appeared in the June 1934 issue of *International Literature*, two years after Brown's *Southern Road* was published. Holmes argued that Brown was a vanguard writer in a Black Marxist renaissance: "His poetry shows that he is conversant with the social, psychological, biological and economic arguments. And most important, he roots his work in the social soil of life he knows. This knowledge, derived from his varied experience has sharpened his poetic acumen, brought him nearer to his objective . . . and closer to our ranks."[59] The ensuing year Brown became a member of the National Council of the League of American Writers in the pre–Popular Front period, when the league was an organization of revolutionary writers. He remained on the council from 1936 through 1940. In 1936 Brown contributed to the Communist Party pamphlet *Get Organized!* It is likely that his sympathies led him at times close to joining the Party.

Brown was the son of a Howard University professor. He initiated writing poetry in high school in Washington, D.C. After receiving a B.A. from Williams College and an M.A. from Harvard, he taught in the South for six years, where he was profoundly affected by African American folklore. In developing his technique of dialect verse, however, he sought aid from the Left-wing Jewish folklorist Benjamin Botkin (1901–1975), who recommended that he drop the final "g" in verbs.[60] Brown inaugurated his own career at Howard University in 1929 and published *Southern Road* two years later. His closest ties were with members of the Left at Howard, including Eugene Holmes, E. Franklin Frazier, Abram Harris, and Ralph Bunche. From 1936 to 1939 Brown served as the editor on Negro Affairs of the Federal Writers Project, with Holmes as an assistant, and he contributed the section "The Negro in Washington" of the massive WPA guidebook, *Washington, City and Capital* (1937). In a 1978 interview, Brown described how the FBI had conducted an investigation of alleged Communist influence at Howard, interrogating himself and twenty other professors. He avowed that, in answer to the notorious question, he had responded: "Listen, son, any Negro who has been to the seventh grade and is against lynching is a Communist. I have been to the eighth grade and against a hell of a lot more than lynching." Brown believed that the Howard administration took no action against the accused faculty because "among our people it was a credit . . . a badge that you were a radical."[61]

William Attaway (1911–1986) was a committed Communist from the late 1930s well into the Cold War era. Attaway was born in Mississippi, the son of a schoolteacher and a physician, and moved at the age of five with his family to Chicago in the Great Migration. He rebelled early against his family's middle-class aspirations, and devoted himself to literature after reading Langston Hughes while in high school. He often skipped class and meandered out to Checkerboard Air Field to observe the planes, and eventually got a job washing the planes with the added benefit of going on free plane rides with the pilots. Attaway's parents coerced him to attend the University of Illinois Medical School, but he was determined to study law, then creative writing, and, finally, dropped out of school to hobo and work variously as a seaman, salesman, agricultural worker, and labor organizer during the early 1930s.[62] In late 1933 he re-enrolled at the University of Illinois and produced a play called *Carnival*.

When Richard Wright appeared on campus to speak about the union movement, they met and became friends; soon Attaway arranged for Wright to appear before the literary society, where he appalled the audience by reading his lynching story, "Big Boy Leaves Home." Attaway then joined the Federal Writers Project, where he again encountered Wright. Attaway's short story in the vein of a medieval romance, "Tale of the Blackamoor," appeared in Dorothy West's *Challenge* in June 1936, the same year he graduated from the University of Illinois. Attaway was briefly associated with the South Side Writers Club before moving to New York, where he worked at odd jobs and as a union organizer until he found employment acting in a traveling theater company.

He finished his first novel in Philadelphia. With mainly white characters and a plot that had some likeness to Steinbeck's *Of Mice and Men* (1937), *Let Me Breathe Thunder* (1939) was an "on-the-road" novel featuring two white migrants who befriend a nine-year-old Mexican American boy. When it appeared, the *Daily Worker* published an interview with Attaway, who announced that his next book would be "about the sharecroppers who were brought up to work in the Allegheny steel mills during the world war."[63]

With a two-year grant from the Julius Rosenwald Foundation, Attaway devoted himself during 1939 and 1940 to writing *Blood on the Forge* (1941), a magisterial novel about Southern Black workers in the 1919 steel strike in western Pennsylvania. The *Daily Worker* review, although amicable and laudatory of the novel's power, was firm in contending that the book "will not contribute . . . toward a sympathetic knowledge of the fate of the millions of Negro workers on Southern farmlands and in Northern industrial peonage." While the violent explosion of one of the main characters, Matt Moss, resembled the violence of Bigger Thomas in Richard Wright's *Native Son*, there was present no Mr. Max to sum up the situation, nor did Attaway "express hope for the final unity of black and white workers."[64] The mixed disposition of the Communist Party's institutional relation to Black literature is evident in these two pieces; on the one hand, the *Daily Worker* interview with Attaway gave recognition to a young and unknown writer; on the other, the review of *Blood on the Forge* revealed how shallow political criteria could be employed to negate the magnitude of a work judged as to whether it might be a potential "weapon in the class struggle."

Coming on the eve of the United States' entrance into World War II, *Blood on the Forge* had themes and perspectives that grated against the Communist Party's call to maintain national unity in the face of fascism. There is no doubt that Attaway wrote as a Black Marxist, one whose exertions were aimed in part at educating the white labor movement about the corrosive costs of continued racial chauvinism. Attaway remained a participant in the Party-led Harlem Writers Club and carried on other radical activities. His last published piece of fiction was the story "Death of a Rag Doll" in the literary journal *The Tiger's Eye* in 1947. It is a disclosure about the birth and death of art, but with a disturbing psychological focus. The story's central relation is between an older sister, dark and beautiful, and her younger brother, gray skinned with blue eyes. The brother remains mute except for playing an instrument, a Jew's harp, on which his sister teaches him to perform for her. On her wedding day, when the sister is about to marry without love into a wealthier family, the brother flees to the waterside and begins to play the Jew's harp to a rag doll surrogate for his sister. The sister, still ambivalent about the wedding and worried about her brother, hears the music. She rushes to her brother, rips up the rag doll, and returns to her wedding without looking back. The story is a likely metaphor of the death of Attaway's writing career; a biographical gloss might refer to his own sister, the actress Ruth Attaway, who had introduced him to art and then she moved on to a more successful commercial career. Whatever the totality of the forces at work in detaching Attaway from his original literary career – adverse economic circumstances would seem most obvious – "Death of a Ragdoll" may suggest some of the troubling issues at war within his psyche.

Attaway subsequently worked at odd jobs in Harlem. At the height of the Cold War he hid and transported Black Communist Party leaders who went underground.[65] His first novel was reissued as a mass market pulp thriller, *Tough Kid* (1952). Through his connections with Black Left-wing cultural leaders, he composed and arranged songs for Harry Belafonte and other singers. Attaway's only other published books were *Calypso Song Book* (1957) and *Hear America Singing* (1967). All his subsequent literary work was confined to writing scripts for radio, television, and films. From 1966 to 1976 he lived in Barbados, partly out of a desire to reside in a country with a Black government, Black police, and a Black professional class. He died of cancer in 1986 in Los Angeles.

In 1942 *The Negro Quarterly* was launched with strong Communist support. Angelo Herndon was the editor, and Black and white pro-Communists dominated the list of contributors in the first issue: Sterling Brown, Dorothy Brewster, Langston Hughes, Doxey Wilkerson, Millen Brand, Ralph Ellison, L. D. Reddick, Herbert Aptheker, and Augusta Jackson. The policy statement for this "review of thought and opinion" included a special emphasis on the relationship between political equality and the need for Blacks and whites to "share equally in the hardships of war, as well as in the victory to come."[66] With the second issue, Ralph Ellison became the managing editor, persevering to the end when he left to join the merchant marine.

Only four issues of *The Negro Quarterly* were published, but the sweep of topics addressed was extraordinary – history, international politics, current controversies in African American education, Black-Jewish relations, the situation in publishing, folk culture, and recent books of all types. The final editorial embodied a sustained commentary on World War II, which stylistically and thematically appears to be primarily the work of Ellison. Repudiated are the attitudes of passive subordination to the racist aspects of the military machine and wartime climate, as well as the opinion of those who express "unqualified rejection" of the war. While the latter arises out of a kind of "Negro nationalism" that admirably holds out for equal treatment, it also reflects "the attitude of one who, driven into a corner, *sees* no way of asserting his manhood except to choose his own manner of dying."

What is required is to recognize that African Americans "have their own stake in the defeat of fascism" and to see "the *peoples* aspect of the war." The alternative is "critical participation" in the war, which was seen as partly a nationalist expression in its recognition of "the Negro people's stake" in the antifascist struggle. The foundation for an potent intervention, then, is the outlook that "to fail to protest the wrongs done Negroes as we fight the war is to participate in a crime, not only against Negroes, but against all true anti-Fascists." Moreover, an effective fight means centralizing the "group unity" of African Americans of all classes. This is essential to guarantee the democratic role of the labor movement (which might be exploited for reactionary ends), as well as to prevent African Americans from playing the role of "sacrificial goat." To that end, African American leadership must "integrate" into the Black masses, urge the population to gain new mastery of technological skills available due to the war-time situation, and "learn the meaning of the myths and symbols which abound among the Negro masses." The zoot suit and Lindy-hop, for example, embody potential clues to effective slogans and tactics that might help "the Negro masses . . . to see the bright star of their own hopes through the fog of their daily experiences." This is a psychological issue "solved only by a Negro leadership that is aware of the psychological attitudes and incipient forms of action which the black masses reveal in their emotion-charged myths, symbols and wartime folklore." In effect, the use of words, although insufficient for social revolution, is absolutely necessary for a "skillful and wise manipulation of those centers of repressed social energy" to facilitate positive action.

Already pressing beyond the borders of acceptable Communist policy, the editorial went a step further in insisting upon Black autonomy and self-leadership as the only guarantor that African Americans would not simply become the instrument of "Labor" rather than "Capital." A final warning asserted that "leaders and organizations must be measured not by their words, but by their actions."[67] Retrospectively this was Ellison's declaration of Marxist independence from the Communist movement, a stance similar to that of Richard Wright. The proposition of an independent African American political movement intervening to keep the rest of Labor in line was certainly compatible with the original Leninist argument for self-determination adumbrated in the early 1930s. Yet its militant articulation at the height of Browderism and antifascist unity and in conjunction with

criticisms of the Party coming from other Black Leftists as well as Trotskyists for subordination of the Black struggle portended a potential political
break. Yet neither Ellison, nor Wright, who surely shared this perspective,
took that step in 1942.

By this time New York City had become the center of Black literary Marxism, much as it had become the headquarters of both the radical movement
in the United States as well as the publishing industry. The formation of
the League of American Writers in 1935, also headquartered in New York,
provided a new visibility for Black pro-Communist authors, and it brought
them into closer contact with each other as well as with like-minded Euro-
American writers. Langston Hughes and Richard Wright served as vice presidents of the league, and among its African American members were Arna
Bontemps, Countee Cullen, Frank Marshall Davis, Ralph Ellison, Arthur
Huff Fauset, Jessie Fauset, Eugene Gordon, Eugene Holmes, Alain Locke,
Loren Miller, Marian Minus, Margaret Walker, Theodore Ward, Dorothy
West, Frank Yerby, and Claude McKay.

Assuredly, Black Communists during the Depression lived and wrote in
other areas of the United States. Eluard Luchell McDaniel was born in 1912
in Lumberton, Mississippi. He resided on a small farm with his father, a
minister who was widowed three years after McDaniel was born. At the
age of ten he set out to see the world, working as a boot black, water boy,
news boy, bell hop, hotel porter, and automobile mechanic. While still in
his teens, he had visited most of the United States, hitchhiking and riding
the rails. By the time he was eighteen, he had settled in San Francisco and
in 1931 he began attending night school to learn short-story writing. Under
the title "2 or 3 Stories by Luchell," he published a group of anecdotes in *Story*
magazine in 1935, before volunteering to fight in Spain with the Abraham
Lincoln Brigade.[68] The *Crisis* reported on his exploits in 1938, describing how
he "drove back a whole company of Franco's troops by the use of hand gre-
nades, when the Loyalists were re-crossing the Ebro. He is now a black god
in Spain, with one explosive bullet in his left thigh." In remarking on the
absence of color prejudice among the Spanish Loyalist population, the *Crisis*
noted that "McDaniel is as black all over his body as a well-shined pair of
black shoes."[69] Following his return to San Francisco, McDaniel worked for
the Federal Writers Project and contributed to the collection *American Stuff*.

Ray Durem (1915–1963) was another African American Spanish Civil War
veteran who became a writer and a Communist. Born in Seattle, Durem ran
away from home at fourteen and served in the U.S. Navy before volunteering
for the International Brigades in Spain and joining the Communist Party. He
mainly supported himself by working in factories, shops, and warehouses

on the West Coast. Durem was sufficiently light-skinned that he could pass for white, and he was horrified by the discussions of Blacks by whites on which he eavesdropped. In the 1940s Durem commenced to write poems to express his anger and frustration; many of them were bitterly sarcastic and humorous. His work began appearing in Phylon and other magazines and drew the attention of Langston Hughes, who included his poetry in The Book of Negro Humor (1966) and Poetry of the American Negro (1970). During the Cold War, Durem took his family to Mexico. He died of cancer shortly after his return to Los Angeles in 1962. A posthumous collection of his poetry, Take No Prisoners, appeared in 1971.

Frank Yerby (1916–1992) was in the environs of the Communist movement in the late 1930s but quickly departed. He was born in Georgia, attended a private Black school, and graduated from Paine College in 1937. He received an M.A. in English from Fisk University in 1938.[70] In 1939 he enrolled in the Ph.D. program in English at University of Chicago and worked with the Federal Writers Project, where he made the acquaintance of Margaret Walker and other radicals. He had already published in Challenge and contributed a story to the New Anvil, Jack Conroy's sequel to The Anvil of the early 1930s. Yerby also joined the Chicago chapter of the League of American Writers. By 1940, financial problems caused Yerby to drop out of the university, and he spent some time teaching in the South before working from 1941 to 1944 in a defense plant in Dearborn, Michigan. In the 1940s he published a series of short stories treating racism, one of which, "Health Card," brought him offers from several publishers.[71] However, he resolved that writing about race was a dead-end and switched to producing what he called "The Costume Novel." His first such novel, The Foxes of Harrow, appeared in 1946, selling over a million copies in its first year; by the 1980s, it had sold nearly twelve million copies. This was followed by numerous other best-sellers, most of which were historical novels. After 1952, Yerby became an expatriate. He died in Madrid six years after publishing his last novel, which appeared in 1986.

Ralph Ellison (1914–1994) was among the most productive Black Communist critics during the late 1930s and very early 1940s. Born in Oklahoma in 1914, Ellison was only two when his father died. He became conscious of politics early on through his mother, a woman who supported the Socialist Party before World War I and remained an activist until her death in 1937. Ellison was precociously drawn to a range of cultural interests, including music, literature, sculpture, and theater. He won a scholarship to the Tuskegee Institute to study music, but left in his junior year to move to New York, where he lived from hand to mouth. Through Langston Hughes and Arna

Bontemps, he met Richard Wright just as *New Challenge* was appearing; at Wright's urging, Ellison published his first book review in the magazine, but it folded before his story, "Hymie's Bull," about a Jewish hobo who kills a policeman, appeared.

In 1938 Ellison joined the Federal Writers Project and was designated to gather folk material in Harlem. His writing began to appear in 1939 in the *New Masses* and then *Direction*, a pro-Communist publication associated with the League of American Writers. His literary criticism reflected a breadth of reading and concern with technical innovation that placed him squarely in the camp of Charles Humboldt and a world away from the "ask the worker" school of criticism. But his perspective indicated an impressive grasp of historical materialism as he theorized the evolution of Black literature from a folk consciousness to that of an urban proletariat. Many of his opinions were identical to those of Wright, especially his view of the centrality of combining national consciousness with an internationalist perspective of class unity. He even held up Wright's Communist affiliation as crucial to his artistic achievement. Speaking of Wright's period of leadership in the politically engaged John Reed Club, Ellison observed:

> Wright, through exercising his function as secretary of that organization, and, through his personal responsibility, forcing him to come to grips with those [social] issues and making decisions upon them, built up within himself tensions and disciplines which were impossible within the relaxed, semi-peasant environs of American Negro life. This mounted almost to the attainment of a new sensibility, of a rebirth.[72]

In addition to holding positions in the league, Ellison was active in Communist Party affairs. Information about his activities appeared in many issues of the *New Masses*, along with notices (sometimes with photographs) for speaking engagements such as one sponsored by the Council on African Affairs and at a *New Masses* series on Black writers with William Attaway. A. B. Magil and Howard Johnson (a Harlem Party leader in the 1940s) believe that Ellison held Party membership, while Ellen Wright (Wright's widow) denies this.[73] Ellison's personal correspondence with Richard Wright documents an intimate familiarity with Party life.[74] More important, Ellison's militant Communist convictions are consistently in evidence, rising to a fever pitch during the Hitler-Stalin Pact when former comrades such as Granville Hicks are denounced for their defection from the Soviet cause; Ellison even predicted that he and Wright would live to see a similar retreat by Black Party leaders such as Ben Davis, who lacked their true grasp of Marxist "necessity."[75]

For the most part, Ellison held that the Black leaders of the Party were far inferior in political acumen than the whites. Still, he was convinced of the revolutionary potential of the Black working class and underwent what he called a "mystical experience" when he attended the 1940 meeting of the National Negro Congress as a reporter for the *New Masses*. Along with Wright, he responded to the Communists' historic emphasis on Black folk culture and the psychological dimensions of oppression, and through wide reading and extraordinary intelligence approached the topics with an intense creativity that gradually began to be reflected in his essays and fiction. He was also convinced that writings by Wright and himself were pushing the Communist leadership toward more sophisticated and less formulaic approaches to the situation of African Americans, and in his new capacity on the *New Masses* editorial board in the early 1940s he dreamed of enlisting regular articles by Party supporters such as Franklin Frazier, Sterling Brown, Ralph Bunche, and Eugene Clay Holmes. Unfortunately, Ellison's devotion to mastering the full corpus of Marx and Hegel was also accompanied by oddball theories about female biological determinism.[76]

At the end of the 1930s Ellison passed through a first marriage to a woman named Rose, about whom he would subsequently remain immovably secretive, and also had an intense affair with the Communist writer Sanora Babb.[77] After serving as coeditor of the *Negro Quarterly* with the well-known Black Communist Angelo Herndon, and initiating a career as a short-story writer, Ellison joined the merchant marine as a second cook and baker from 1943 to 1945, seeing it as a means of contributing to the antifascist effort without serving in the segregated army. During this period, Wright, whom Ellison had declared to be his one and true "brother,"[78] evolved from dismay over the excesses of the Party's wartime policy to the more comprehensive critique that appeared in an essay excerpted from his autobiography, "I Tried to Be a Communist."[79] Ellison defended Wright's new position in arguments with William Attaway and others.[80] When the autobiography, originally called "American Hunger" and now entitled *Black Boy*, came out the following year, Ellison, back from the sea, similarly tangled with Eugene Clay Holmes, whom he now likened to a "Commissar."[81] At this point he was as disaffected as Wright from the Communist Party, but it was on the revolutionary Marxist grounds that the Party had sold out "our people" — meaning not only African Americans but the U.S. labor movement.[82] On the Left political spectrum, his views seem closer to the more orthodox William Z. Foster wing of the Party than to the more "Americanized" Browder wing, and at the time of Browder's expulsion Ellison even appeared skeptical that Foster was sincere about breaking from the earlier accommodationist policies. When Angelo Herndon, Ellison's former co-editor of *Negro Quarterly*, visited from Chicago and revealed himself to be a cynical businessman in the fields of insurance brokerage and women's clothing, Ellison and his new wife, Fanny, were taken aback.[83]

Ellison's insistence that he was to the Left of the Party, and repelled by its procapitalist policies, persisted for another year or two, but it is evident that he was not aggressive in expressing his opinions about the Party as emphatically in public as in private. In the summer of 1946 a representative of the *New Masses* approached him to ask if he might reestablish his former relationship.[84] Despite his tough talk to Wright about how he allegedly told off the Party comrades about their betrayals, his views must have been more ambiguously stated. When a section of *Invisible Man* appeared in *Horizon*, his old Party friend, Charles Humboldt, still a Communist, expressed his admiration to Ellison and proposed that they get together to talk about reprinting one of Ellison's *New Masses* stories in an anthology. Again, Ellison reported to Wright that he turned a cold shoulder and explained that he had completely changed literary direction in his new writing—although Humboldt claimed that he didn't see the difference.[85] In these years Ellison was working away at his early drafts of *Invisible Man*, a novel that emerged from the contradictions of his convoluted deradicalization process, as well as his complex relations to the Marxist work of Wright, Attaway, and others.

The achievement of the formative years of Black literary Marxism has yet to receive fitting recognition. Due to the widespread belief among publishers that only a limited audience existed for African American literature, many of the chief Black authors' texts—the poetry of Frank Marshall Davis; *Black Thunder*, by Arna Bontemps; and *Blood on the Forge*, by William Attaway—received only limited publicity and distribution. Richard Wright's first novel was rejected by publishers and appeared only after his death. Sterling Brown's second volume of poetry, "No Hiding Place," was also rejected, and several of his poems from the 1930s only emerged after the onset of the new Black radicalization of the 1960s. Robert Hayden's second collection, "The Black Spear," assembled in 1942, never found a publisher and was eventually abandoned.

In a way, Hayden's fate symbolized the situation of most radical Black writers. Relying heavily on research he had conducted while employed by the Detroit Federal Writers Project, Hayden hoped to pen a new epic interpretation of American culture that foregrounded the complexities of the African American condition. Toward this end, he aspired to draw upon every available literary technique, especially irony, montage, dramatic voices, and juxtaposition. Directly from this effort grew Hayden's "Middle Passage," one of the most admired poems in American literature, but one not generally recognized as a fruit of Black Marxism.

Despite the penchant of Claude McKay and Countee Cullen for more traditional verse forms, there is otherwise a remarkable coherence to Black Marxist verse of the formative period of the 1920s, 1930s, and 1940s. Early on, McKay inscribed the centrality of courageous resistance to racism even in the face of death in his "If We Must Die." McKay claimed to have initially written this poem to read to his crew of Black railway workers in response to the widespread lynchings that occurred in 1919. One trait of McKay's overall accomplishment is his giving a specificity to the tragedy of anti-Black racism while dialectically invoking universal themes, thus balancing class and nationality. For example, "If We Must Die" does not refer to African Americans as such, while another influential poem, "The Negro's Tragedy," insists that Black suffering can never be grasped by anyone other than a Black person.

Sterling Brown, on the other hand, relied more directly on the rich store of southern working-class and peasant folk culture to create humanized symbols of the Black nation in formation. Sometimes a trickster character, as in "Slim in Hell," will attack southern racism by exposing the absurdity of its racial codes. In other instances, a character like "Old Lem" will embody the fatigued resentment that came from witnessing decades of racist savagery. In Brown's "Strong Men," one senses his call for African American artists to fuse with the invincible spirit of southern folk resistance to economic and political exploitation by creating a new culture, and the new forms that give voice to it.

A complementary theme in Black poetry consists of satiric jibes at middle-class aspirations and delusions of African Americans who fail to affirm their class and national loyalties. Frank Marshall Davis's poetic creations "Robert Whitmore," "Arthur Ridgewood, M.D.," and "Giles Johnson, Ph.D.," are all doomed to early graves when their illusions are shattered. Langston Hughes canalizes a similar critique in the direction of northern liberals, especially in the "Dinner Guest: Me" section of *The Panther and the Lash,* a volume that thematically groups political poems written over four decades.

Among the most robust testaments of Black Marxism in poetry is Margaret Walker's 1942 collection *For My People.* This is work by a perfectionist equally immersed in African American culture and Popular Front Communism. The title poem, which opens the collection, blends personal biography and historical narrative to climax in a vision of phrases from "The Internationale": Walker's line "Let a new earth rise" is a variation of "the earth shall rise on new foundations" from "The Internationale"; and "Let another world be born" is a variation of "A better world's in birth." Her call to "Let a bloody peace be written in the sky" is a defense of violent revolution, and the concluding sentence expresses the Marxist demand for workers to seize the means of production: "Let a race of men now rise and take control."[86] The third poem, "We Have Been Believers," dramatizes the shift in consciousness from the alienation of religion to the moment of revolutionary action: "Now the needy no longer weep / and pray; the long-suffering arise, and our fists bleed / against the bars with a strange insistency."[87]

## From Banjo to Melody

The musicality of Walker's poems in form, references, and theme recall that Black music from its earliest literary depictions by African American radicals was understood by the Left, as well as others, to be a prime feature of the African American nationality as well as culture. Hence the political makeup of spirituals, blues, and jazz became contested terrain in cultural practice and criticism. For the Left, rural Black southern folk culture was coded as the authentic voice of the proletarianized peasantry; memories of resistance to slavery and signs of the subversion of Jim Crow racial capitalism were found lurking under every metaphor and simile. In 1934 the *New Masses* published a startling article by a white southerner writing under the pseudonym Richard Frank on "Negro Revolutionary Music." Frank argued that it was the music of Blacks that was Americanizing the ideology of Bolshevism and the working-class movement. Moreover, since whites were fascinated by Black music and often sang Black songs, Black music was truly the route to Communist politicization of the entire working class. As evidence, Frank gave a number of examples of spirituals in which revolutionary themes had been interpolated.[88]

Yet during the 1930s a shift occurred in the conception of the relation of Black music to revolutionary struggle, at least in terms of its literary representation, due to the impact of the events of the decade. This shift was felt in the excruciating intensification of class struggle nationally and internationally—the Depression, Scottsboro, Ethiopia, and Spain. The feeling grew among committed Black writers that every moment counted in life-and-death terms, which made cultural workers all the more susceptible to an increased strategic, almost military, approach to producing and judging writing. In terms of the depiction, dramatization, and assessment of the politics of music in novels, there is a paradigmatic shift from the 1920s to the 1930s that might be called "From Banjo to Melody."

Banjo is the main character in Claude McKay's 1929 novel of the same name, who plays the banjo in a rag-tag jazz band. Melody is a central figure in William Attaway's 1941 Black proletarian novel, *Blood on the Forge*, who plays a blues guitar. The correspondence between the two texts, published a decade apart, is noteworthy. Both stories are set in "exile" after World War I. McKay's Banjo is an escapee to Marseilles, France, from the Deep South, where he had seen his brother lynched. Attaway's Melody is also in flight, to the steel mills of Pennsylvania from rural Kentucky, to evade a potential lynch mob. Both characters are part of larger collectives. Banjo's is a jazz-band-in-formation of "beach boys" from diverse locales in the African Diaspora. Melody's is the close-knit family of the three Moss Brothers, each with an extravagantly different outlook on life. Finally, both musicians, characterized by fluidity and adaptability, are paired with an alter-ego of a more rigid temperament – Banjo with the Haitian intellectual, Ray; Melody, with his disciplined and fanatically religious brother, Matthew.

Otherwise, the novels tug in opposite directions, strongly indicative of the different moments they express in the evolution of the Left African American tradition of literary expressions of jazz and blues themes. The customary interpretation of *Banjo* is that it constitutes a middle stage in McKay's tripartite movement to a harmonious Black aesthetic. The first level was expressed in his novel *Home to Harlem*, and the third would come in *Banana Bottom*. In *Banjo*, McKay sought a fusion between the radical intellectual, depicted in the semi-autobiographical figure of Ray, and the instinctual spontaneity of Black creativity, represented by Banjo. The novel terminates with Ray's resolve to cut loose and "go vagabonding" with Banjo. Attaway, in disparity, was offering in his novel a direct challenge to the Left. In *Blood on the Forge*, he makes use of the role played by Blacks as scabs in the 1919 steel strike to dramatize how difficult it was actually going to be to build a culture of solidarity between Black and white workers.

*Banjo*, because it is basically an expression of the pre-Depression Black Left, can freely employ a European exile setting as the site for a healthy integration of serious commitment and vital art, symbolized by Black music. This is because Blacks living in France had increased agency and autonomy, due to the distance from the peculiarly virulent and constricting racism of the United States. *Blood on the Forge*, in contrast, coming at the end of the crisis-ridden 1930s, presents a more troubling and challenging vision because, although the novel's climax is horrifying, the novel's solution remains unstated.

Until the Moss brothers are literally broken by the new industrial system, Melody had been the most balanced of the three, using his blues guitar to assuage pain and communicate equanimity to those around him. His brother Chinatown had been a creature of immediate gratification who became blind due to an industrial accident. His older brother Matthew, a master of repression and controlled strength, explodes: first into sexual passion, then into violence as a tool of the police against the striking unionists, resulting in his death. The final scene has Melody, guitarless and with a self-inflicted broken hand, escorting the blind Chinatown off to new class battles in Pittsburgh. The contrast here with McKay's final scene of Banjo and Ray joyously departing Marseilles to vagabond together could hardly be more pointed.

Left critics responded to each novel similarly. Michael Gold, despite his earlier conflicts with McKay at the *Liberator*, warmly praised in the *New Masses* McKay's depictions of street life and his antibourgeois attitude in *Banjo*. Nevertheless, according to his political yardstick, Gold deemed the novel insufficiently "proletarian" in outlook and themes.[89] In parallel fashion thirteen years later, *Blood on the Forge* fell victim to the Party-line admonitions of Ralph Ellison in a six-page essay on Attaway in *The Negro Quarterly*. Attaway's novel was commended for its artistry, but also sharply assailed for its deviations from the Communist view of World War II, which had changed after the Soviet Union was invaded by Germany in June 1941. Ellison also upbraided Attaway for failing to include among his characters "the most conscious American Negro type, the black trade unionist." Concerning the treatment of Black music and culture, about which Ellison would later write so brilliantly, he formulaically condemns Attaway for exhibiting, in the fate of Melody, "the destruction of the folk," but not depicting "its rebirth on a higher level." By this, Ellison meant a class consciousness that grows out of folk elements but achieves an ability to distinguish between whites who are oppressors and white working-class allies.[90] Ironically, it was Ellison, in this instance the most severe administrator of the militarized strategic evaluation of the artistic use of Black music, who defected from the Left as the Cold War began. Attaway, whose artistic use of music evidenced a felicitous dramatization of a friendly but sharp political critique of Communism, continued loyal to his Left commitments. During the militant civil rights movement of the 1960s, Attaway marched in the South while Ellison remained aloof.[91]

Attaway was not the last pro-Communist writer to employ themes of Black music as a vehicle to understand the mutable and unfinished evolution of African American national culture in the context of race and class oppression. Indeed, the Communist Party would enjoy an equal if not greater success with African American cultural workers during the Cold War when such themes would be subject to further exploration, at times dogmatic and other times highly original. Moreover, the issues raised by Attaway in *Blood on the Forge* prefigured future developments. From the late 1940s through the late 1950s, the classical Black Marxist project – which delicately balanced the dialectical interplay of the class and national components of a struggle for liberation – became progressively disarticulated by a combination of economic, social, intellectual, cultural, and political challenges. Scarcely a major African American writer of the interwar years, and especially the poets, was unaffected by Marxism; after the war up to the present, few could avoid a rethinking and reformulation of the Black Marxist project, which occurred with widely varying results. Even for Richard Wright and Ralph Ellison, who separated from the Party in the mid-1940s, Marxism remained the touchstone for their political and creative thought for years thereafter.

From the outset, Black Marxists were compromised by faith placed in two allies. One was an illusion that the Soviet Union was a model for anti-racism and the fair treatment of national minorities. This fantasy was articulated very early by Black Communist leaders such as James Ford, who wrote in Nancy Cunard's famous 1933 anthology, *Negro*: "Soviet Russia's insistence upon absolute equality for all people . . . has led to the freedom of the nationalities formerly oppressed by the Tsarist regime in the same way that Negroes are oppressed in the United States."[92]

The other false friend was the utopian hope for white working-class allies. In Sterling Brown's "Sharecropper," published first in the *New Masses* and then in the Communist Party's 1939 pamphlet *Get Organized!*, Euro-American partners never appear in person as such. Yet the Black member of the sharecroppers union in Brown's poem refuses to identify Black or white union members as he is being tortured to death by white vigilantes, and he dies with a vision of a Black Oak and a White Oak growing side by side.[93] In Robert Hayden's "Speech," included in his 1940 collection *Heart-Shape in the Dust*, an African American worker pleads that the same hand, and the same voice, beat and divide Black and white workers; yet the poem is oratorical, not dramatic.[94] In the 1940 edition of Richard Wright's *Uncle Tom's Children*, the short story "Fire and Cloud" depicts unity in the form of the Black and white Communist buddies Hadley and Green; yet the two are barely sketched as characters, and their specific activities among Black and white workers are not revealed. In "Bright and Morning Star," the Black Communist Johnny-boy's fanatical belief in the primacy of class solidarity over racial division actually leads to his own death, which is avenged by his more nationalist-inclined mother, Aunt Sue.

The imbalance in artistic representations of the complex relationship of national oppression and class unity is partly explained by the relationship of art to experience. The experience of national and racial oppression was vivid, real, and overwhelming for Black writers. Full-blown interracial class solidarity was by comparison almost a leap forward to a quixotic chimera. This dream of a majority of Euro-American workers finding common ground with their darker sisters and brothers was limned primarily by a few admirable experiences in the Communist Left such as the instances of interracial collaboration in the Scottsboro case, the sharecroppers union, the struggles against evictions in Harlem, the camaraderie of the John Reed Clubs, and the integrated ranks of the International Brigades in Spain. It was present in literature in the Black political prisoner Angelo Herndon's 1934 pamphlet *You Cannot Kill the Working Class*, and especially in his narrative about a racist white worker in the South who joins a Black protest against unemployment because "an empty belly is a pretty punk exchange for the honor of being called a 'superior' race."[95] But an interracial utopia was not part of the day-to-day life experiences of ordinary African Americans in the segregated United States; and daily existence offers the raw materials of any sustained, rich, multifaceted, and fully textured artistic work in the realist vein.

Still and all, one might have expected Richard Wright to have gone further in elaborating the delicate balance between nationality and class at the very heart of pro-Communist Black Marxism. He was a public member of the Communist Party and active in several Party-related institutions. Further, in the circumstances of his time, he led an unusually interracial political, literary and personal life. Yet in 1940 it was Wright who shattered forever the trajectory that one might have expected to emerge from this crucible in light of his having published *Uncle Tom's Children*. In the pages of U.S. literature emerged Wright's unforgettable Bigger Thomas, and Black Marxist culture, African American culture, and American culture were shocked by a new sensibility. Here was a central character who had neither a positive Black national folk-religious culture, nor a hint of the utopian dream of international proletarian class unity. Bigger Thomas is depicted by Wright as the product of a commercially controlled mass culture, primarily manifested by the movies.

Ironically, Wright chose a mass-culture strategy as well—a *noir* murder mystery with a fake kidnapping plot and a citywide police manhunt—in which to cast his desperate plea for a profound revamping of the very terms of Black Marxism that he had once helped to formulate in his famous 1937 manifesto "Blueprint for Negro Writing." His choice of form is significant, for Wright was still very much within the Black Marxist tradition in 1940 and would remain so even after he left the Communist Party. Thus he subscribed to a Marxist orientation that regarded popular culture not as exclusively the site of indoctrination by commercial forces but as a vessel to be filled with multiple contents. His decision to write a novel that took the structure of a murder mystery and detective thriller would later be emulated by the radical African American novelists Chester Himes, Ann Petry, and Willard Motley, among others.

From the point of view of classical Black Marxism, Wright presented the rather terrifying vision that traditional Black culture cannot reach the Bigger Thomases, and that potential Euro-American working-class allies, symbolized by Jan, the Communist boyfriend of the murdered Mary Dalton, are simply part of a reified natural world of snowstorms and mountains against which Bigger must struggle to survive. Although Wright was defended in the Left press by the leading Jewish Communist writers, Mike Gold and Samuel Sillen, and the Black fellow-travelers, Chester Himes and Alain Locke, a number of African American political leaders and Communist Party activists in Harlem and elsewhere knew where the logic of his vision might lead; in private and internal discussions they denounced his novel harshly—no doubt because some of them had similar fears about the flaws inherent in the illusions of the traditional Black Marxist project.[96]

The legacy, then, of poetry and fiction written by pro-Communist African Americans of the pre-World War II era is more compelling in its use of Marxism to divulge the social and cultural bases and multiple levels of racial oppression rather than in articulating programmatic paths leading to liberation. Examples of texts exhibiting the fragile equilibrium between the writer's sure knowledge of racial oppression, leading to Black cultural resistance, and the same writer's tentative utopian hope of an interracial alliance against racism on the basis of common position, are scarcer. Such an equipoise can be found in several historically important Black Marxist poems by Langston Hughes, Sterling Brown, Richard Wright, and Robert Hayden. The dream of interracial unity appears as well in the concluding stories of Uncle Tom's Children and is represented by the characters Jan and Max in Richard Wright's Native Son, as well as by the French sympathizers of the Louisiana slave rebellion in Arna Bontemps's Black Thunder, and by the Jewish radical who leads the protest climaxing Theodore Ward's play Big White Fog (1938).

Conceivably the most poignant statement of that particular yearning for Black and white unity against racial and class oppression can be found in Ralph Ellison's "The Black Ball," an unpublished story from the late 1930s only recently discovered. The protagonist is a young Black father employed as a service worker in a hotel in the Southwest, who is approached by a white union organizer. The organizer's arguments about how unions have changed so that Black members are valued fall on deaf ears, until the Black man sees the burned hands of the organizer – hands scorched with a blowtorch because the organizer provided an alibi for a Black comrade falsely accused of rape. Still, the narrator disdains to take action at the time; but a series of subsequent incidents that humiliate him in front of his són cause him to accidentally cut his own hand, which in turn impels him to reach for the union card that the organizer had given him.[97] Ellison teaches us that experience can create the basis for an interracial alliance based on a working-class solidarity, but it is crucial that the extended hand of the white working class must be marked by some irrefutable evidence of its sincerity. Similarly, Richard Wright's Jan Erlone, in *Native Son*, earns his credibility with Bigger Thomas through his analogous ordeal of searing sacrifice in the loss of his beloved.

These are nonetheless rare moments in the literature composed by the pre-World War II Black literary Left. The poetry and fiction authored by the early Black Marxists provide an extensive amount of textual illustration of the Black proletarian experience, as well as satires of the Black middle class, which coexists with a few semi-utopian depictions of interracial partnership. The preponderance of the freshest and most compelling poetry and fiction of Sterling Brown, Margaret Walker, Langston Hughes, Richard Wright, and the other Black writers also dramatizes the dual consciousness of African Americans as a nationality with its own history and culture as well as a constituent of the working class. What transpired in the 1930s and early 1940s actualized a foundation for equally uncommon achievements to come. African American Marxist cultural practice thus responded to the tragic history of the intractability of racism in the United States that would, in the postwar era, yield, first, a recrudescence and then an extraordinary reconfiguration of the Black Marxist literary tradition.

# The Antinomies of a Proletarian Avant-garde

## Flights and Moorings

In the first years of the Depression, a young Vassar College student, tall and heavy-set, and ardently committed to the creative and intellectual life, felt increasingly distraught as she became mindful of the suffering of ordinary people. The disparity with the sheltered childhood she had enjoyed in her comfortable Manhattan West Side apartment in a Jewish middle-class neighborhood was unendurable. After completing two years, eighteen year-old Muriel Rukeyser left Vassar College in 1932, relocating to New York to write poetry while she resided at home. Already radicalized and attracted to the Young Communist League at Vassar, she attended a meeting of the Communist-led National Students League later that year where she encountered the *Student Review* editor Harry Magdoff and inquired of him whether she might write for the publication. Soon after, she borrowed her father's car and drove to Alabama with friends to attend the March–April 1933 trial of the Scottsboro defendants.

Arrested for fraternizing with African Americans, Rukeyser was jailed, during which time she contracted typhoid fever. Following her release, she and her friends were harassed by a racist posse as they made their way north. When they ran out of money, Rukeyser contacted her distressed parents, who paid her bills and transported her back home. The incident continued the escalation of Muriel's estrangement from her parents, which eventually led to frequent banishment from the family and continual threats of disinheritance.[1]

Once back in New York, Muriel found that the article on the Scottsboro trial that she had submitted to the *Student Review* had been well received by the editors and would be published.[2] Consequently, she joined the editorial board of the *Student Review* as literary editor, although the Communist student activists who ran the publication were too busy with exams and political work to hold editorial board meetings. Rukeyser asked Harry Magdoff if she might also submit her poetry to the *Student Review*. Despite a lack of confidence in his ability as a judge of poetry, Magdoff agreed and ran

"Scottsboro" in April 1933 and "The Trial" in January 1934.[3] Shortly afterward, Joseph Freeman of the *New Masses* contacted Magdoff and proposed that the two of them lunch together. The main topic of their discussion was Rukeyser's poetry; Freeman told Magdoff that her verse was outstanding. Freeman was unaware that Magdoff had been publishing her poems only because of his general respect for Rukeyser, not because of any literary expertise. Soon Rukeyser's poetry commenced to appear in the *New Masses*.[4] Thus one of the leading poets in the United States close to the canonical modernist tradition – a woman who was Jewish American and bisexual, as well as pro-Communist for nearly two decades – made her debut in the Left cultural milieu, which would provide her with a vision of sufficient vitality to sustain her artistic endeavor for the rest of her life.[5]

Rukeyser had been born in New York City in 1913. She attended the Ethical Culture and Riverdale Country Day Schools, where she was skipped ahead several grades so that she was always several years younger than most of her classmates. She also entered a childhood friendship with Robert and Frank Oppenheimer, the physicists who would endure victimization during the McCarthy era of the 1950s. Her father's family was descended from German-speaking Jews from Eastern Europe and had settled in Milwaukee in the nineteenth century. Starting in the gravel business in New York, Lawrence Rukeyser worked as a cement salesman in association in the 1920s with Generoso Pope, the publisher of *Il Progresso*, an Italian-language daily newspaper that defended Mussolini. Together they became the major purveyors of sand, mortar, and brick in New York City and eventually the leading developers on Manhattan's Upper West Side and the builders of most of the large apartment buildings on West End Avenue. Eventually Pope, who had Mafia connections, forced his partner Rukeyser to sell his portion of the business.

Muriel had a favorite routine with Robert Oppenheimer, who was a few years ahead of her in school; they would sneak up to the roofs of her father's nearly completed buildings on cold winter days. Lying on top of the water towers to feel the ambient heat from the water stored below, young Robert delivered minilectures on physics to her.

Muriel also roamed the neighborhood with packs of friends, carrying out pranks such as dropping bags of water from rooftops. But her relations with her parents became adversarial, and there were other childhood unhappinesses. Part of the difficulty was her father's demand for automatic obedience to parental and male authority. But her parents also mocked her weight by calling her "little elephant," and they disparaged her cultural interests. From the time her younger sister, Frances, appeared without warning, there was intense sibling rivalry. In later years Muriel's parents would torment her by comparing her unfavorably to her "good" sister, who settled down to a husband and children.

The family belonged to a reform synagogue and only superficially followed Jewish traditions. They appeared more engrossed in their summer home on Long Island, their country club, and their chauffeured limousine. Muriel was convinced that their allegiance to the upper classes made them insensitive to the plight of impoverished Jews and others; she even suspected that they might have been able to tolerate Hitler, had he not been so aggressive in his anti-Semitism. As a result she elected a positive stance of affirming her Jewish identity along with her radicalism, expressed in lines from her 1944 collection, *Beast in View*: "To be a Jew in the twentieth century / is to be offered a gift. If you refuse, / Wishing to be invisible, you choose / Death of the spirit, the stone insanity."[6] When she became a mother in the late 1940s, she decided to set up a Christmas tree, and even underwent a brief flirtation with Episcopalianism; but she also volunteered to teach Jewish Sunday school classes and remained in communication with her own rabbi from childhood. After the founding of Israel she emerged as a strong partisan, especially during the 1967 and 1973 wars when she feared the Jewish population would be decimated. During the 1970s, suffering from diabetes and other ailments, she finally realized her dream of visiting the Jewish state.

In her literary development, Rukeyser first read Shakespeare and the Bible at home. Then her parents bought for her sets of Dickens, Dumas, Hugo, de Maupassant, Balzac, *The Encyclopedia Britannica*, and *The Book of Knowledge*. After her adventures in Scottsboro, Rukeyser attended Roosevelt aviation school from 1933 to 1934. She ran out of money before obtaining her pilot's license and in later years would episodically launch other ventures to earn it, without success. Next she worked at Left-wing theater jobs (especially Theater Union) and for theater magazines; her fascination with drama had been kindled during her Vassar sojourn, during which time she met Hallie Flanagan (1890–1969), with whom she continued to be in touch. In the early summer of 1934 she was in residence at the Yaddo writers colony, and her *Theory of Flight* was published in the Yale Younger Poets Series in 1935.

In 1936 she traveled to Gauley Bridge, West Virginia, to witness the devastating effects of silicosis on the workers there. Then she went to England to meet T. S. Eliot and other writers, followed by a trip to Spain to report on the antifascist Olympics held during the summer of 1936 in Barcelona. Her sojourn in Spain coincided with the onset of the Spanish Civil War, and she formed a strong attachment to a German antifascist athlete, Otto Boch, who was later killed in the war and whom she would address in her poems decades afterward. Rukeyser next took jobs involving statistics, films, and photographs, publishing *U.S. 1* in 1938 and *A Turning Wind* in 1939. Throughout the Great Depression she indulged her large appetites for food, sex with a variety of male and female partners, and adventure. Even in her last decade, she took trips to North Vietnam (1972) and South Korea (1975) to protest the U.S. aggression against the former and state repression in the latter.

Rukeyser's relation to the Communist Party bore some similarity to that of Ella Winter (1898-1980), an intimate friend and occasional lover. Winter was first married to the muckraker Lincoln Steffens (1886-1935), assisting him toward pro-Communist views, and then to Donald Ogden Stewart (1894-1980), a comic playwright, novelist, and scenarist who also became pro-Communist and served as president of the League of American Writers from 1937 to 1940. Some Communist Party members, as well as various anti-Stalinists and anticommunists, believed Rukeyser and Winter to be "secret" Party members, and their activities and public positions tended to reinforce this belief. Robert Gorham Davis was convinced that Rukeyser held such a status because he claims to have seen her being bawled out by a Party functionary, Jack Stachel, for publishing a poem in a magazine thought to be anti-Party.[7] Rukeyser, however, who was far less active and prominent than Winter, was not especially interested in political factionalism; unlike Winter, she consorted with writers of diverse political persuasions, including the Trotskyists John Wheelwright and Sherry Mangan. Most likely she was a member of the Young Communist League in the early 1930s, but after 1940 she became increasingly independent.

In a 1980 interview, Rukeyser insisted that she had desired to be part of the Communist movement, but its political zig-zags made any stable relationship impossible. In particular, she was inspired by a pre-Popular Front vision of militant antifascist and anticapitalist collaboration by a range of radical tendencies she witnessed at the outset of the Spanish Civil War.[8] In the political biography she later imparted to her son, she said that she had come close to joining in the mid-1930s — to the point of taking out an application — but had pulled back at the last minute from a desire to protect her creative autonomy.[9] By 1940, however, she was adamant about her independence from the Communist Party in her correspondence, although there is no public record of her dissociating herself from the Party's slavish pro-Soviet policies during the next decade. In a June 1940 letter to Louis Untermeyer, she articulated the validity of a visionary, semimystical politics:

I believe in poetry. I believe that the life of people and the life of poetry must ultimately mean the same thing, in the different terms involved. I believe in the life of the spirit generally walking the earth, against war, against slavery, for the giving of all the processes and inventions and art and technique of living.

She insisted that her political views were consistent, namely that she was always personally ready and willing to fight fascism – whether in Spain or in France – but she opposed conscription and forcing others to fight. She concluded that "I do not belong to any party or organization, and that is why I say I am vulnerable from both sides."[10]

During the late 1930s Rukeyser moved to California where Robert Oppenheimer assisted her in finding work. There she met Harry Bridges, president of the International Longshoremen's and Warehousemen's Union (ILWU), and was active in causes supported by the Communist Party. As part of the Left-wing scientific community in Berkeley, including not only the Oppenheimer brothers but also the crystallographer Melba Phillips, Rukeyser pursued her literary and personal concerns without feeling much pressure to conform. She lived from hand to mouth, frequently borrowing apartments and small houses. During the war she resided in Oakland and afterward in San Francisco. In 1943 she took a job on the East Coast in the Graphics Division of the Office of War Information, but she was fired after a red-baiting campaign in the press which coincided with a disgraceful unsigned political and personal attack on her that appeared in the *Partisan Review*.[11] Returning to the San Francisco Bay Area in 1945, she taught a writing class at the Communist-led California Labor School. She also passed through a brief marriage in 1945 to the painter Glyn Collins (it was annulled), and in 1947 gave birth to a son by another man. She told the son, William, that his father had died, and to her parents she explained that the boy's father was Jewish and was killed fighting in Palestine. In the late 1950s, however, she acknowledged to William that his father was not Jewish and that he was still alive, although they had had no communication since the pregnancy. Among her affairs with women, two of the most intense were with Rebecca Pitts (1905–1983), a one-time Communist intellectual also close to novelist Josephine Herbst, and the writer May Sarton (1912–1995). Her last decades were spent in the companionship of her literary agent, Monica McCall.

When Rukeyser returned to the East Coast, she found a relatively safe haven at Sarah Lawrence College, during the presidency of Harold Taylor. She took a half-time position there in 1954, so that she could devote herself to raising her son as well as writing. Her works in the 1940s, 1950s, and 1960s included not only more volumes of poetry, but a biography of mathematical physicist Willard Gibbs, several volumes of criticism, some plays, a novel, and four children's books. Her teaching salary was a pittance, but the medical benefits were crucial. Occasionally she was red-baited by the local chapter of the American Legion, which demanded that the trustees get rid of her. Her situation was precarious – during the McCarthy era she lost a commission to write the script for the radio show "Omnibus" and a contract with Little, Brown publishing company. Nonetheless she maintained the job until her first stroke debilitated her in 1964. Among the students to whom she remained closest was the poet, and, later, novelist, Alice Walker.

In 1950, Ella Winter fled the McCarthyite witch-hunt by going to England with Donald Ogden Stewart. She and Rukeyser followed a similar political evolution: disillusionment with Stalin and his legacy, especially after the Khrushchev revelations of 1956, but also an attitude of refusing to explicitly renounce the Soviet Union in public because its policies provided a counterweight to the imperialist actions of the United States. Nevertheless, Rukeyser supported the Hungarians in their 1956 rebellion against Soviet domination and the Czechs in the "Prague Spring" of 1968. Rukeyser's later politics were also significantly influenced by Left-wing scientists she knew or had studied, such as the British Marxist J. D. Bernal (1901–71), famous for his view that science closely reflects economic development and should be used as a guide in formulating social policy. In particular, Rukeyser's optimism about revolutions in society was linked to the hopes and expectations arising from "revolutions" in physics and biology.

During her last years Rukeyser was embraced by feminist writers and activists, and her identification with the movement was wholehearted. Lines from her poems became the titles of two of the most influential volumes of women's verse, *No More Masks* (1973) and *The World Split Open* (1974). Yet Adrienne Rich described Rukeyser as "our Neruda," and there were ways in which Rukeyser probably felt more intellectually comfortable in the company of Frank Oppenheimer, who had by then become director of the San Francisco Exploratorium.[12] Increasingly she described her politics simply as "Left"; this was not due to an abandonment of socialism, but because, if she could not give a full and complicated answer, she preferred a term that did not lead to simple stereotyping. All her life she read voluminously, and she regarded herself as well versed in Marxism from her own point of view.

Throughout her literary career, Rukeyser rose to the challenge of developing techniques for communicating strong feelings about the lives of ordinary people. Oddly enough, while she regarded poetry as a gift with which people were born to enhance communication, she was scathing in her judgments about poets she considered lazy, and, as a teacher, she would make withering criticisms of her students' work. Like her friends Horace Gregory and Marya Zaturenska, she also scorned the politics of the literary establishment.

In a sense, her early association with *Dynamo*, where she was the only female contributor, placed her in appropriate company. As Herman Spector pointed out, in a plea to recruit financial support for the magazine, "Within the space limitations of a 38-page quarterly, we intend to show how the unity of revolutionary significance can illumine a multiplicity of techniques, temperaments, experiences."[13] Of all the Left poets of the interwar generation, Rukeyser was perhaps the most creative in carrying out her belief that a new age demanded new styles and subject matters if art were to be an effective agent of change. In her personal behavior, she was drawn to a romantic image of herself as living fast and dying young, and the health problems that started plaguing her after the age of fifty were a possible consequence.

Her own contributions to *Dynamo* were among her most direct statements of political commitment, including her stirring autobiographical testament, "Poem of Childhood."[14] In "Theory of Flight," which appeared in her book of the same title, she depicts the modern revolutionary leader as a pilot who must become the expression of "the people's" desire.[15] By the time she assembled "The Book of the Dead" section of her collection *U.S. 1,* comprising the first seventy-two pages, Rukeyser had blended her visionary approach with the documentary and reportage motifs of Depression culture to create a variant of the technique that Walter Benjamin theorized as "profane illumination."[16] The term refers to art capable of vivifying the common experiences of humankind with a religious glow, through the use of images from the nonsacred material world.

"The Book of the Dead," although structurally and thematically alluding to an Egyptian religious text treating life after death, is the rubric for a sequence of poems individually titled "The Road," "West Virginia," and variously by the names of American working men and women. The documentary raw material of this work is the court testimony, interviews with doctors, and speeches of dying men and their families in the context of an industrial catastrophe. The historical background on which she drew was the situation in the early 1930s when thousands of workers had been lured from throughout the United States by Union Carbide to dig a tunnel at a breakneck speed to maximize profits to divert a West Virginia river for a power station. As a result, hundreds breathed silica (a glass-like compound) into their lungs, which caused death.

Rukeyser's poetic sequence grounded in the circumstances proceeds on a complex journey during which the reader travels to West Virginia not only geographically, but historically; at the outset there are references to indentured servants from the colonial period (ancestors of the modern wage slaves) as well as to John Brown (prefiguring the rise of new abolitionists to destroy capitalism). This initiation is followed by the voices of members of the protest committee, led by the African American George Robinson; descriptions of the silicosis; interviews with doctors; and a tour of the power plant. The last poem in the collection offers an intimation of utopia in its depiction of a "fertilizing image" of "a tall woman."[17]

## A Social Poet's Progress

The progress of Rukeyser as a social poet was expertly traced by John Malcolm Brinnin (1916–1998) in his 1943 essay, "The Social Poet and the Problem of Communication." Brinnin argued that Rukeyser's three volumes of poetry published during the Depression were in miniature the literary-political record of the reshaping and transformation of a generation, instructive for others drawn to similar issues. Brinnin was well qualified to formulate this proposition, for he worked in the same tradition with many analogous concerns. Born in Nova Scotia, Brinnin was the son of a theater scenic artist from Boston. His family moved to Detroit when he was four. After an early education in Catholic schools, he entered Wayne University (later Wayne State University) already enthusiastic about Marcel Proust. He soon dropped out of school to begin a career of self-education in the public library as well as engage in the activities of the Detroit arts and Left-wing communities.

Supporting himself by working in bookstores, he quickly began to engage in publishing projects. In 1934 he established a magazine called *Prelude*, a miscellany of poetry and prose by Detroit writers. This publication merged with the Detroit John Reed Club's *New Force* to create *New Writers* in 1936, which published the work of radical as well as avant-garde poets and fiction authors. Later that year he launched *Signatures*, a larger and more impressive quarterly that featured sections of "work in progress" by a range of well-known contributors, mostly Left-wing, from the United States and England. Rukeyser was among the poets, along with Kenneth Patchen, Louis MacNeice, and Horace Gregory. Brinnin's own work in *Signatures* appeared under the name Isaac Gerneth.

The death of his father in 1936 prompted Brinnin to enroll at the University of Michigan to finish his education, where he supported himself by running a campus book shop, called "The Book Room," and winning

Hopwood prizes. A veteran of the Detroit John Reed Club and a member of the Young Communist League, Brinnin was active politically and culturally with other young writers and activists, some of whom were, like himself, gay. One of these was Kimon Friar (1911–1993), later a prominent translator of modern Greek literature.[18] In 1940 Brinnin moved to New York City. He then spent 1941 doing graduate work at Harvard, succeeded by five years of teaching at Vassar as an instructor. Following a period of travel and short-term jobs, Brinnin became director of the Poetry Center of the YM-YWHA in New York City, where he launched a sensational program of reading appearances by such major poets as T. S. Eliot, Robert Frost, Edith Sitwell, W. H. Auden, Wallace Stevens, Marianne Moore, E. E. Cummings, Stephen Spender, Dylan Thomas, and William Carlos Williams. While his first published works were volumes of poetry, including *The Garden Is Political* (1942), *The Lincoln Lyrics* (1942) and *No Arch, No Triumph* (1945), he eventually turned to scholarship, co-authoring with Friar the influential *Modern Poetry: American and British* (1951) and a series of studies of poets, the most well known being *Dylan Thomas in America: An Intimate Journal* (1956).

Several years into the Popular Front, Brinnin first began submitting verse to national Communist publications, and his work appeared on several occasions after 1937 in the *New Masses* under his pseudonym Isaac Gerneth. At the time, the poet, playwright, and, later, novelist, Norman Rosten (1914–1996) was helping to select poetry for publication in the *New Masses* and strongly encouraged Brinnin; from New York he communicated the enthusiasm about Brinnin's verse expressed by other young people working in the *New Masses* office such as Samuel Sillen and Joy Davidman.[19] Rosten also kept Brinnin informed of the economic constraints that threatened the regularity of the *New Masses* Literary Supplement, which encouraged an editorial policy of keeping poems to a maximum length of one page. Moreover, Rosten felt compelled to impress upon Brinnin that the magazine's priority for selecting verse was that the poems should "deal with acute 'social' material as much as possible." More specifically, Rosten told Brinnin that while his "lightning like diction and imagery" made him "a poet's poet," the *New Masses* editors, although "quick to recognize your ability," were still "a little wary of your lines." In particular, "The question of 'popular' understanding is very important for a revolutionary magazine." Thus the dilemma of a *New Masses* editor was to find poetry with "reading clarity" in an immediate sense. "You, being a fastidious worker of images and rhythms, are not too easy to grasp. A compliment, really. But the revolution must go on — even with lousy poetry."[20] Rosten's and Brinnin's verse appeared together in the Communist Party pamphlet *Salud! Poems, Stories, and Sketches of Spain by*

*American Writers* (1938), where they were identified as members of a "single literary group – the younger, social minded, 'proletarian' authors."[21] Brinnin's contribution, "For a Young Poet Dead in Spain," was well crafted and written from the heart – a good friend, Robert Campbell, had been killed in action in Spain – but was nonetheless a conventional tribute as well as a prediction of future promise.

A year later, the clash between immediate clarity and technique necessary for more complex creativity hit home when Brinnin's submission to a second Communist Party pamphlet, *Get Organized: Stories and Poems about Trade Union People* (1939), was rejected. The series editor, Alan Calmer, explained to Brinnin that his task in producing the volume paralleled that of a revolutionary poet's efforts in verse. It meant "catering a little to the demand for 'popular' poems and stories, while trying to feed it with good writing, even though to start with it has to be on a rather simple level." The Party's literary pamphlet series "must be on a central theme and of a direct character to reach a lay audience." If Brinnin could write a poem on the Flint sit-down strikes it would be usable. The work he had submitted, however, "Cadillac Square," "is fine but out of scope for the new collection."[22]

Thus in his 1943 essay on Muriel Rukeyser, Brinnin spoke from his own experiences as he explained her struggle to remain one of those poets who have their eyes on "the immediate issues of their time" while avoiding two temptations. The first of these was to succumb "so close to the partisanship of radical journalism that their verse is merely a kind of poetic commentary upon movements of the Party line"; the second was, in the face of "political stress and disillusion," to "retreat toward obscurantism, the withdrawal from the objective arena into the subjective room." Rukeyser, Brinnin argued, represents those who "have undergone the disappointments and tortured doubts of the last decade and yet succeeded in enlarging both their strength of purpose and the scope of their poetry."

Brinnin substantiates his contention by demonstrating Rukeyser's move from an emphasis on straightforward declarations, often in urban speech, toward the increasing use of images of a psychological and surrealist character, as well as a change in the use of symbols from those that were public and universal to those more "privately conceived and privately endowed." In her work one sees the classic – and insoluble in a formulaic sense – posing of the problem of "how" a poet should "sing" in the face of mass suffering. Brinnin puts it as follows: "Since the social poet is the one to whom communication is the first and necessary virtue, his attempts to be strong and clear without seeming banal, and his attempts to use the complex resources of the English language, are twin problems." He proposes considering Rukeyser's early career as a field in which to examine a variety of strategies: the equation of personal rebellion (against "father") with social rebellion (against the rulers of society); the "intellectual objectification" of her political views (her use of an airplane's flight to represent human aspiration); the Popular Front effort to appropriate popular heroes such as Lincoln; and the use of popular ballads for Marxist insights. While her focus tended to be on "the thing said" and "not the manner of expression," Brinnin locates a second movement under way in the later poems of U.S. 1, where he finds a "use of language so complex, and a compression of ideas so intense, that it is unquestionably removed from the grasp of the lay reader, not even to mention the proletarian."

Rukeyser, in fact, has come face to face with a familiar dilemma for the social poet:

> whether to insist upon first premises, even though that means a static repetition of familiar ideology, or to exercise full imagination and the resources of language in an endeavor to contribute a new dimension to poetry, though that attempt, in its inevitable intellectual concentration, must deny a social audience.

The genius of Rukeyser is that she refuses to fashion a definite choice, declining to break entirely with one aim or advance completely to another. Still, the trend in her work toward the latter choice is increasingly evident in A Turning Wind (1939); as Brinnin observes, in this work, "The problems of a generation, for instance, are no longer centered exclusively in the terms of the striker or the organizer, but in the larger concept of Death, who appears in many disguises."[23] Whereas Rukeyser's earlier books had been promoted by the New Masses, A Turning Wind was never reviewed in the magazine.

In reference to the achievement of poets such as Rukeyser, how, then, should the term modernism be used in illuminating the poetic practice of the pro-Communist literary Left? If it is to retain any meaningful coherence as a category typified by the Eliot-Pound revolution in poetic sensibility, the term must be employed with considerable specificity and caution. Most Left poets (Hughes, Hayes, etc.) have a relationship to modernism and might now and then produce a particular passage or poem that would be usefully treated under that rubric. But only a few (Rukeyser, Patchen) might convincingly be dubbed "modernist" in terms of the preponderance of their writing. This is partly because, as this book has documented, the weight of authoritative opinion within the Communist cultural leadership that cohered in the late 1920s was hostile to high modernism, and such opinion carried weight due to the nature of the time. Among the handful of exceptions was in regard to the adaptation of certain popular experimental techniques, especially cinematic and documentary, as evidenced in the work of Dos Passos, so long as the result did not appear to be too difficult or obscure. Of course, some voices of opinion did cry out that Left writers could learn from the moderns, but these tended to be of dissident and less official spokespersons.[24] Yet, in practice, while clearly opposed to the worldview of the "reactionary modernism" of Eliot and Pound, the modern Left writers certainly shared with many modernists a fondness for certain themes such as the city and technology. Moreover, there were assuredly calls for a fresh language, attention to craft, and technical innovations appropriate to a new kind of literature that were widespread on the Left and that provide solid evidence that much of the Left literary tradition has a crucial place in modern literature.

What is perhaps decisive is that, from the origins of the tradition of literary criticism produced by the mid-twentieth-century Communist cultural Left, while a few divergence can certainly be found, there is a steady steam of stern pronouncements against the "difficulty" that forms a prime feature of modernism. One can see this in statements such as the conclusion of a report issued by the Pen and Hammer research group (comprised of Communist academics in the early 1930s) that argued that "the revolutionary poet should, in general, so simplify his writing that it can be grasped by a mass audience."[25] Such a view was usually claimed as a political requirement, as stated in 1932 by the Midwest Worker's Cultural Federation demand of its members "to reject and deny all bourgeois culture as the culture of a dying class, and to build a revolutionary cultural tradition."[26] Another example is afforded by the leading Marxist critic Granville Hicks:

> Whereas the revolutionary novelist may, at least to a certain point, learn from the more critical of his bourgeois predecessors, the revolutionary poet has no earlier stage of revolt to which he can look for guidance. The result is that several of the younger poets who are in sympathy with Communism have tried to adapt to their purpose the forms and idioms of the experimental reactionary poets. Both Horace Gregory and S. Funaroff, for example, have been much influenced by T. S. Eliot. . . . Eliot and kindred reactionaries have evolved forms that express their own restlessness and futility. The attempt to use their technical devices for the expression of the revolutionary spirit inevitably involves a fundamental contradiction, and the resulting poems are confused and ineffective.

Hicks's conclusion is the familiar claim that poets like Gregory and Funaroff would "find much healthier nourishment" in the songs of such militant working-class poets as Joe Hill and Ella May Wiggins, rather "than in the elaborate elegies of T. S. Eliot and Ezra Pound."[27]

While many of these early 1930s formulations can be attributed to the "workerism" of the pre-Popular Front era, pressure on Left poets to simplify and write directly did not diminish in the late 1930s, although exceptions were sometimes made and latitude allowed for writers whom various Communist Party editors wished to court, especially in the *New Masses*. Exertion from certain editors as well as vocal readers to prioritize social immediacy and communicative lucidity is unmistakable in most publications associated with the Communist Party, such as *Sing Democracy* published by its Labor Poets of America and Young Labor Poets. Such concerns also shape the dominant character of submissions to poetry sessions of the conferences of the broader League of American Writers.

Instances of rebellion against the excesses of this pressure was, as one might expect, constant. A clear example of a dispute over issues related to modernism occurred when Joseph Freeman wrote a *Daily Worker* column in 1933 defending the work of poets whose poetry "is honestly describing the emotional world of those who have developed in bourgeois literature and are moving toward Communism." He emphatically concluded:

> I have asked our poets not to falsify this aspect of their development. It is only too common to find people who are Communists in thought and action and bourgeois in their feelings. Our emotions develop more slowly and painfully than our ideas. Some poets attempt to conceal or overcome this disparity by writing verse that represents only their ideas. In most cases the result is flat, stale and unprofitable.
>
> It is better to achieve genuine growth by following the evolution of our feelings naturally and honestly.[28]

Yet this was not the end of the matter. Private correspondence, as is often the case, enriches and complicates the published record.

In this instance, A. B. Magil responded to Freeman two days later in a personal communication saying that such remarks "repudiated almost all the literary criticism you have written during the past few years." Magil regarded such calls for "self-development" and "honesty to oneself" as a "laissez-faire" attitude in literature invoking nothing less than "venerable ghosts of the bourgeois twilight." Carried to its "logical conclusion," Magil continued, "this can only mean the substitution of bourgeois subjectivism and eclecticism in literature for Marxism." The task was not to judge literature by "honesty," but, rather, Marxist critics should guide poets toward Communism and "not allow them to shift for themselves, making a virtue of their stumblings and hesitations." He insisted that

> Proletarian literature is not achieved "naturally" (through spontaneous development) in a capitalist society any more than the proletarian dictatorship is achieved "naturally." [It] requires the conscious activity of those who have transcended the limitations of the bourgeois world-view, of the Marxist-Leninists.[29]

Magil wrote to Freeman as a comrade offering a sharp opinion, not as a higher official delivering a ukase. Over time Magil's cultural influence would increase while Freeman would be excommunicated.

One important variation is that the relative autonomy of the African American Literary Left allowed poets to develop in a manner that was free of accusations of crypto-modernist adaptations. The pro-Communist work of Robert Hayden and Sterling Brown clearly defended the autonomy and integrity of African-American culture while using a variety of linguistic and verse strategies, typified by Brown's "Scotty Has His Say." In this poem, Scotty, a poor southern Black proletarian, is disturbed about white employers overworking his lover. He makes threats of retaliation with African American "witchcraft" in a manner that mocks the whites' fear and ignorance of Black folk culture:

> ef yuh treats huh mean
> I gonna sprinkle goofy dus'
> In yo' soup tureen . . .
> I got me a Blackcat's wishbone,
> Got some Blackcat's ankle dus,'
> An' yuh crackers better watch out
> Ef I see yo' carcass fus' —[30]

Scotty's spirit of rebellion, which blended with Black-specific dialect, folk culture, and power relations of men and women to the dominant culture, falls within the realm of the Communists' view of class-based national oppression. Yet the poem also provides powerful confirmation of the need for a critical methodology such as Houston Baker's argument for a "racial poetics."[31]

Robert Hayden, in "Gabriel: Hanged for Leading a Slave Revolt," uses the rhythms and question-and-answer format of a nursery rhyme or ballad to inscribe the voice of a rebel-hero who even on his deathbed refuses to retreat one inch from his commitment to rebellion:

> Black Gabriel, riding
> To the gallows tree,

In this last hour
What do you see?

I see a thousand,
Thousand slaves
Rising up
From forgotten graves,
And their wounds drip flame
On slavery's ground,
And their chains shake Dixie
With a thunder sound.[32]

The use of such a mild and familiar form as the structure on which to hang a vision of horror and revenge is at once hypnotically spell-binding yet jarring to one's complacency.

These examples, while experimental, nevertheless remain rooted in a desire for comprehensibility, based in either a realist-naturalist recreation of a scene, or the familiar gothic features of Gabriel's apocalyptic vision. Notwithstanding, in additional verse by Brown, Hayden, and other radical Black writers, one can also discern more modernist tropes in the poetic treatment of Black culture, dialect, history, and worksongs. Fragmentation, a corrosive skepticism, and modern difficulty are evidenced in Brown's "Southern Road," in which it is almost impossible to understand the nature of the crime for which the African American speaker must serve a life sentence on a chain gang:

Burner tore his – hunh –
Black heart away;
Burner tore his – hunh –
Black heart away;
Get me life, bebby,
An' a day.[33]

There is intentional ambiguity here so that the reader, who struggles to make sense of the obscure references to Burner and the tearing away of his "Black heart," will eventually realize that the specific "crime" is not important; under the Jim Crow system a "crime" will eventually happen to a Black person. It is also difficult to pronounce the sound, "hunh," which seems to fuse the noise of the hammer striking stone with an exclamation of exertion made by the narrator (or the chain gang as a whole) with each swing.

The reader may grasp the necessity of enduring a chain gang in order to duplicate the authentic sound, once again reminding us of the distance between the poem's readers and subjects. In another example, Robert Hayden's "We Are the Hunted" is a poem that appears initially to simply recreate the fears of Black slaves escaping into the woods. Yet no one has satisfactorily explained the ambiguous metaphors of his closing lines:

> We shall find shelter from the black pursuit
> And doors against the tangled, multi-dark.[34]

This sort of writing, employing abstract although powerfully suggestive color-reversals, wrapped around an insubstantial center, was well-nigh atypical among the Black Marxist Left; too sparse in aggregate to be the basis of theorizing about forms. On the contrary, the consummate poet of the Left, for African Americans as well as Euro-Americans, was Langston Hughes, who made a virtue of his "simplicity" to the point that it becomes an aesthetic issue to be addressed.[35]

Indeed, Hughes's verse was an experiment in the complex simplicity Richard Wright advocated in his "Blueprint for Negro Writing."[36] Hughes's "Letter to the Academy," composed in formal diction and appearing in *International Literature* in 1933, observes belligerently that literature of the past, reflective of class peace, is incapable of responding to the new world situation. Moreover, a feature of the new era is the restoration of a sensuality where the "flesh," previously defeated by the "spirit," returns as an equal partner.[37] "Good Morning, Revolution," surfacing around the same time in *New Masses*, displays casual slang, colloquialisms, and irregular stanzaic patterns; Hughes whimsically domesticates "a guy named Revolution" into a superheroic proletarian buddy.[38] Ironically, Hughes pioneers a "familiarization" strategy, an odd parallel to the "defamiliarization" techniques of modernism.

"White Man," published in *New Masses* in 1936, is one of Hughes's most effective experiments in dereification. He starts on a personal note, speaking as a Black worker to a white man who takes "all the best jobs," lives in the finest housing, hobnobs with fascist powers, and reaps the profits from Black cultural production. Hitherto powerless in this situation, the Black worker has discovered, from reading Marx's writings ("something . . . that rich people don't like to read"), that this "White man" really spells his name "C-A-P-I-T-A-L-I-S-T" and may not even always be white.[39] The argument is expressed is a forthright manner, but its full absorption would turn the world on its head. Thus in a "simple" way the voice of Hughes's oral poem begins to tear down the current forms of language and thought so that new forms can emerge.

"Our Spring," from the same period, dramatizes the results of joining with the "buddy" Revolution and demystifying racism so as to disclose its true function as a legitimator of class power. With the speaker merged with Revolution as an international force, whose martyrs from Boston to Germany are replaced like "those rivers / That fill with the melted snow in spring," the standpoint has shifted from "I" to "we." Thus the seasons themselves will be returned to the people in a pastoral-utopian image where "the land will be fresh and clean again, / Denuded of the past—."[40]

Hughes's "Song of Revolution," from *The Negro Worker* in 1933, seems to fulfill the optimism so frequently demanded by readers and some editors of the Communist movement. It also posits a role for revolutionary verse, becoming "a song . . . Marching like fire over the world." The power of this song lies in its ability to work up its components from the material world, to become an instrument "drowning" the past, eliciting "youth and laughter," and banishing "doubt." Thus emboldened, the revolutionary force can surgically remove "fear" from the world, thereby allowing "the children of all creation" to emerge from a deep sleep into a new reality of "joy."[41] In contrast, "Revolution," appearing a year later in *New Masses*, surprisingly adulates the powers of "the Great Mob" for its numbers and singlemindedness that "knows no fear." A nameless leader directs this force against the exploiter made of "iron and steel and gold" whose "golden throat" must be split from "ear to ear."[42]

In 1928, Hughes asked the same question as did Alfred Kreymborg a few years later in "American Jeremiad." In three short couplets called "Johannesburg Mines," he described the situation of 240,000 natives working, and asked: "What kind of poem / Would you make out of that?"[43] The problem is repeated at the end, in order to engage the reader in the process of formulating a response, suggesting that an appropriate answer to this material fact requires a unity of poet and masses. Poems such as "Black Workers," printed five years later, are meant to represent Hughes's own answer to the question. In five lines he describes how the work of bees "is taken from them," then affirms that "We," the black workers, are "like the bees— / But it won't last / Forever."[44] Although he uses a condensed version of the traditional form of the fable (specifically alluding to Bernard Mandeville's eighteenth-century attack on idealism in "Fable of the Bees"), he shocks common sense by affirming that Black workers have such a status. This overstatement should cause the reader to seek out discrepancies, which of course lie principally in the area of human consciousness—the black worker's capacity to understand, theorize, and act to change circumstances. The decision to separate out the last word of the poem, "Forever," is a warning against an apocalyptic view of immediate gratification with the suggestion that the struggle may be long and hard.

## Poets and Criminals

In addition to such divisions on the cultural Left as that between Freeman and Magil over what constituted "laissez-faire" in literary policy, the obtainable documentation also implies that stock allegations, which often involved charges and of counter-charges about cultural opportunism on one side and vulgarity on the other, were habitually mixed up with jealousy, envy, and personality conflicts. While writers associated with the *Rebel Poet* and *Anvil* tended to see the *New Masses* after Walt Carmon's departure as increasingly elitist and unsympathetic to authentic worker culture, those drawn to establish *Dynamo* felt that the *New Masses* was too functionalist and unsympathetic to publishing a range of poetic sensibilities.

Edwin Rolfe, in particular, believed that he was under compulsion from older Party members, such as V. J. Jerome and Joseph North, to invoke criteria with which he felt uncomfortable. In letters to James T. Farrell between 1933 and 1936, he apologized for crudities in his own reviews, and for his inability to publish a story by Farrell in the "Features" section he was editing for the *Daily Worker* because one of the characters in the story makes a disparaging remark about "foreigners," which readers might construe as reflecting the author's own sentiments. One of Edwin Rolfe's poems, "Definition," while conceivably inspired by a conflict at the *Daily Worker*, embodied an indirect attack on the mentality of Communist Party leaders such as V. J. Jerome, whom he felt were manipulative in their dealings with young writers.[45]

Yet *Dynamo* poets detested not only Walt Carmon, seen as a publisher of "trash," but also his *New Masses* replacement, Stanley Burnshaw, regarded as a middle-class intellectual temporarily slumming at the time when proletarian literature appeared to be in a Bull Market.[46] It is conspicuous that various positionings on literary disputes do not fall into simple categories; they evolve within a force field of elements that are sometimes unique to little magazine production and other times peculiar to the political and cultural output of the U.S. Left. One can see in *Dynamo*, and even more aggressively in *Partisan Review*, a less dogmatic rejection of "difficulty." Yet the issue of "difficulty" in isolation hardly sums up the totality of the disputations that drove forward the Literary Left, debates addressing issues that render it still relevant to the contemporary transactions of those who continue to counterpoise their artistic visions and cultural critique to a world in which the haves methodically exploit the have-nots.

Prior to anxieties about "difficulty" were sentiments underpinning the choice to become a revolutionary artist in the first place, such as those exuded by the young Mike Gold, in his letters to Louis Untermeyer. Gold wrote during the World War I era where he dreamed of devoting literary publications to the goals of "vigor and recklessness." He expressed his pride in the magazine *Flame* for such qualities, dedicating it to be "the champion of all the lost causes – anarchism, vegetarianism, dynamite, obscenity, etc." Gold announced that he liked "fun, hellishness, beauty" and hated "righteousness and joylessness anywhere." Yet he wondered, "Why can't a lot of this stuff be made the starry hitching team for the wages of justice?" He was repelled by his discovery that so many writers ended up performing for the elite and failed "to stay with the masses." Hence he surrendered to the temptation to call "poets who only poeticize 'criminals,'" which he realized was "raw," but "I cannot help getting peeved at their eternal arrogances." His closing question is as applicable today as it was eighty years ago: "what sort of instincts can anyone have who is not seared and wounded by the sight of poverty, even when it does not hamper him personally? It is such an offense to the sense of beauty and love which the poet is supposed to have a monopoly on."[47]

What eventuated as such sentiments became allied to a specific political organization, its ideology, and its cultural institutions? It is seductive but ingenuous to assess the itinerary as merely the loss of innocence in which the writer forfeited self-reliant emotional response to ritualized political demands. Communist Party institutions were brimming with people who were as much affected by their unique cultural and personal backgrounds as by their miscalculations of all the contrarieties implicated in the Great Promise of the USSR. Writers were energized by their idealized view of this bold regime, and the U.S. Party's declaration of pro-Soviet ardor, as much as they may have been cowed or blinded by it. More personal factors such as one's self-assurance or the condition of one's intimate life might have much to do with his or her response to what the Party, its organization and ideology, had to offer. To understand a pro-Communist poet's relation to literary trends requires an investigation of formative aesthetic experiences, early literary models, networks of friends, and traumatic life experiences. As a generalization, one can only conclude that the Party had a moral authority that should be neither minimized nor exaggerated.

For most poets, their acquisition of an early aesthetic sensibility did not operate in terms of perceiving art in terms of "Left" and "Right" so much as simply responding to the literary texts available to them in light of their psychological state when encountering them. Very often a writer begins to produce verse under the inspiration of a favorite poet or two. In some cases there may be a political attraction, as in the instance of Walt Whitman's democratic views (although Whitman loathed political affiliations and ideology); other times the association was serendipitous. Edwin Rolfe, for example, encountered Hart Crane's work at a formative moment because his intimate friend, Leo Hurwitz, was the brother-in-law of a Crane enthusiast, Gorham Munson (1896–1969).[48] A poet's absorption of a Marxist viewpoint was frequently the result of strong emotions, observations, and experiences that caused a prior discontent with or opposition to the status quo; assimilated in this fashion, Marxism might clarify, but rarely created, one's radicalism.

There is empirical evidence, in cases such as Jerome, Trachtenberg, Gold, and Magil, that longevity as a Communist Party cultural leader or full-time editor seemed to require highly politicized approaches to culture. Yet one cannot fully understand the cultural unease that permeated the far more numerous rank-and-file of the cultural movement through simplistic binaries – such as positing modernist libertarians contra socialist-realist literary commissars. Some poets closest to modernist styles in their own work nevertheless made explicit non-literary "demands" on other writers, such as insisting that one could only improve one's poetry by becoming immersed in the working-class movement – too often a euphemism for carrying out Communist Party policies. Those who refrained from making such demands tended to be at arm's length from any organizational commitment to the Party, such as Kenneth Fearing (who may have been briefly a Party member) and Horace Gregory (who was mainly an ideological supporter), and to have had limited careers as committed revolutionaries engaged in organized Communist political practice. Thus their contribution to understanding the dilemma of the "committed" writer must be qualified.

Moreover, as the 1930s unfolded and the Popular Front policy was avowed, there was an comprehensible exertion on the part of broad layers of cultural workers, not just Communist Party cadre, to reach "the masses" in order to enlarge their political consciousness about the menace of fascism. There had always been pressure to be comprehensible but this was an unexpected new turn toward popularization. Oddly, it came in the same years when the more studied works of the British Left poets led by Auden were accruing celebrity. Thus the counter-orientation to move from being "proletarian" and "revolutionary" poets to becoming forthrightly popular "people's poets" cannot simply be construed as writers accepting orders from above to follow the line of the Popular Front; Left poets and their audiences were amenable to the Popular Front orientation because they personally felt a growing political urgency to fight against fascism. The Republican loss in the Spanish Civil War and the staggering advance of fascism in Germany impelled many to sound the alarm to the broader public. If literary history was merely a matter of a linear development of Left poetry from simple to more complex, it would seem that the kind of direct writing promoted in the late 1930s by the Labor Poets of America and Young Labor Poets should precede rather than follow the much more memorable achievement of the *Dynamo* poets of the early 1930s.

Perhaps the most imposing reason for applying the category of modernism to pro-Communist poets only with explicit qualifications, cognizant of the danger of obtruding a "theme" on the complexity of a writer's entire life, is that the basic framework for Left writers was the historical materialism of Marxism, which they assimilated in sundry ways and to variable degrees. Not only did such a philosophic perspective place poets in a special relation to all literary schools whose defining features were of a contrary *weltanschauung*; identification as a Marxist first, whatever its liabilities in terms of real or imagined political obligations, could liberate Left poets to utilize a variety of strategies to actualize their literary goals. A Marxist novelist might move among or blend the literary traditions of realism, naturalism, surrealism, hard-boiled fiction, and regionalism, to produce a *Judgment Day*, a *Yonnondio*, a *Day of the Locust*, or a *Native Son*. Many Left-wing poets had markedly hybrid styles, used varied strategies within or among poems, or employed a particular technique in order to comment satirically on it.

John Malcolm Brinnin was certainly astute in holding up Muriel Rukeyser's work as a model that brings the strains of the Communist literary tradition into bold relief: As a poet, she was promoted by a small group of Communist Party enthusiasts mainly for her more accessible writings; her more unequivocally modernist attributes were not broached or were implicitly criticized. Yet her growth as an artistic activist was largely self-determined by her choices and unusual freedom of movement; after the late 1930s she did not evolve as a participant in the collective projects of Communist Party-led publications and organizations. What she gained from the Communist tradition was, however, more than just a vision; the burden it placed on her to "popularize," to relate to common experience, drew her to new challenges and unique efforts. Fortunately, she rarely succumbed to the temptations of self-falsification or banality.

Her inner resources, and the autonomy of her personal life, kept Rukeyser at a distance from the one-dimensional anti-intellectualism and self-righteous "workerism" promulgated by Leftist militants who prided themselves on their real or alleged proletarian credentials, as well as by certain political activists who did not hesitate to proclaim knee-jerk edicts on cultural matters. The existence of such pressures sometimes motivated Left poets to disown or mute their real literary preferences, and in some instances undoubtedly caused them to modify their styles.

Notwithstanding, there was an acute "newness" of the emerging cultural vanguard around the Communist movement in the 1930s. The project of a culture consciously based on a newly rising class, especially one dispossessed of cultural heritage or a self-consciousness of its own worth, was a fresh if somewhat voluntaristic enterprise. But this voluntarism itself flows from an admixture of millenarianism of an uncommon kind; it was the customary belief in a distinctive destiny for the United States blended with the Marxist creed of a special destiny for the working class, and the Leninist view that the Russian Revolution had shattered the chain of capitalism at its weakest link, launching us into the unfamiliar. Incorporated into Left literature were older themes in U.S. culture, such as the mobility suggested in the "lighting out for the territory" of Mark Twain's Huck Finn, with the utilitarianism of Whitman. While there was a disapproval of self-emancipation through one's own imagination to create "a world elsewhere," the verity of a potential utopia in the United States also seemed distant from the concrete state of affairs of the 1930s. Such a disjuncture between craving for utopia and bleak immediate prospects may have induced a deeper dependence on imaginative resources than normally anticipated. In particular, there appeared a partial resuscitation on the part of certain U.S. Left writers, such as those promoted by Horace Gregory, of a reliance on symbolism and the use of the fable.

Still, the public character of most U.S. Left poetry, its goal of literary democratization, was a natural brake on the modernist tendencies to believe that one's unique sensibility can only be expressed through a private language, and to proclaim the self, as poet, an autonomous power in the world. If modernism is interpreted as a distinctive experimental tradition in postromantic art, characterized by the preeminence of cryptic speech and literary self-government, many Left poets assuredly had an ambivalent relationship to it. On the one hand, techniques such as Eliot's "objective correlative," using a set of objects to generate a feeling, or even Pound's "persona," the postulation of masks, were amiably employed by writers such as Spector and Fearing. Moreover, the imagist designs of classic hardness and exactitude, objectivity, parsimony of language, and autarchy of form were pervasive in learned writers such as Norman MacLeod, but also among the most "proletarian" of autodidacts such as Joseph Kalar. On the other hand, there was little fellow feeling for that aspect of modernism that looked back to the displaced aristocratic culture as incarnating the truly humanistic values.

Unquestionably there were those among the Left who felt it imperative to break aggressively with traditional art. Mike Gold's 1930 declaration of the tenets of proletarian realism and Richard Wright's 1937 "Blueprint for Negro Writing" are in the genre of revolutionary literary manifestos.[49] Further, to the extent that Enlightenment values might be seen as promoting "realistic" cultural forms and generating a presumed scientific rationality to legitimate the fortified powers of the status quo, there was certainly evident skepticism on the part of some on the Left. For example, Charles Humboldt's statement in the New Masses, supporting the "reworking" of reality through art, opposed the idea of practical cognition as a function of the instantaneous replication of appearance; rather, the emphasis was placed on the generative dynamism involved in reformation and elucidation.

Rukeyser, Spector, and others wished to articulate a vitality of spirit not rendered within any mode of representation given over to appearance. Yet Rukeyser was nearer to romanticism in perceiving a oneness of humanity and nature, something of a contrast to the recurrent modernist perspective of a fecund mind travailing in isolation in the face of a passive nature. Spector and Fearing surely tilted toward modernism in applying ironic strategies to cancel expectations evoked by representational art. Instead of imitating the external world, some of their verse, along with Rukeyser's, could be apprehended as executing an image, thereby becoming its own exceptional configuration of reality.

This is perhaps the design behind the collage technique employed by Rukeyser, Funaroff, and others—a means of heightening that sense of generative proximity. Collage signifies a poetic reasoning unimpeded by discursive coherence, and the movement of their work aspires to establish an ethos with the capacity to ameliorate society. However, for the pro-Communists, this strategy led beyond, not in the direction of, modernism; in fact, to them, modernism's demand for cultivated compact intelligence appears more suitable for curbing the catalytic potential of poetic reasoning than for making verse the bridge to mass action. Leftists like Rukeyser and Funaroff, in contrast, wished to affiliate the collage effect with the struggles of the working class and collective resistance to fascism.

Thus it seems plausible to theorize the pro-Communist proletarian and even some of the "people's culture" tendency as part of an avant-garde that grows out of modernism but holds distinct features. In this sense it evokes the revolutionary school of surrealism, frequently fathomed as a mode of interpreting modernism.[50] Until recent books by Cary Nelson,

Walter Kalaidjian, Michael Denning, and others, the Left avant-garde was perceived as pre-modernist, if not near-subliterary. This misunderstanding was a result of Left poetry's frequent tempering of experimental features to address class issues and achieve greater accessibility, and linking of individual voices to a collective protagonist; the appearance and content of pro-Communist poetry, fiction, and drama seemed to more aptly resemble realism and naturalism.

In sum, the narrative of the forging of a proletarian avant-garde is rooted in the life history of individuals brought into relationships with networks and institutions, expressed by clubs, magazines, political parties and organized cultural movements led by the Party directly or indirectly. From a ground-up examination one discovers that a semi-autonomy was fostered among Black writers, a proto-feminist consciousness arose naturally in the work of women writers, and other forms of ethnic consciousness varied more considerably depending on topic and period (Jewish consciousness becoming strong in the World War II era). While the rapprochement between the artist and Party institutions was never complete, the tendency was for institutions to try to progressively "tame" the writers in the name of the "state of emergency" mentality, thus rooting out certain kinds of ambiguity and difficulty that might lead to pessimism or hesitation. At the same time, there is a marked melancholy aura in the Left writing of Spector, Funaroff, Rolfe, Hayes, Rukeyser, and others; the same revolutionary romanticism that engendered utopian longings was also a personal refuge, a realm of privacy that unleashed doubts about the eventual realization of desire.

A precedent for investigating Left writers as an avant-garde was articulated by Charles Russell in his argument for the detachment of the "historically parallel" traditions of the avant-garde and modernism in *Poets, Prophets, and Revolutionaries* (1985). Russell reasons that archetypal modernists such as Proust and Pound cannot detect explanations in the "flow of modern history," so they fasten on a perception of "meaningless chaos" or "evident cultural decline." In contrast, the avant-garde, from Rimbaud and Apollinaire through the surrealists, futurists, and Brecht, yearn "to sustain a belief in the progressive union of writer and society acting within history." Such a view can be tracked to romanticism, but, unlike much romantic thought, the cause for optimism must be located in an entity beyond bourgeois society.

What stays is the "romantic belief in the prophetic and activist role of the writer," undertaken with "full awareness of the gulf that exists between them and the audience to whom they would speak." Thus modernists and the avant-garde have "a common awareness of the most problematic aspects of cultural modernity" but cleave to counter premises about the motives and rejoinders.[51] In the case of the Communist avant-garde, there are particular outgrowths such as the urge to blend the poet-seer with the class-conscious proletariat as agent of change, and assorted pressures to conjure up a pantheon of cultural heroes (Whitman, John Brown, Frederick Douglass). Moreover, like the rest of the avant-garde, the Left was always delimited in relation to modernism – not only because it shared many of the same interests but because modernism conquered as the paramount heritage in U.S. literary culture in the 1940s and after.

Russell claims that modernists "appeal to a presumed reality beyond mere society and its history," often premising aesthetics in racial fictions, mystical doctrines, or the realm of psychology, with aesthetic fealty surmounting social interests.[52] In contrast, the avant-garde, clasping the same social and aesthetic responsibilities, has battled to postulate the singularity "of activist aesthetic behavior against the threatening social realm."[53] Modernist and avant-garde writers partake of the hypothesis that they have to invent new forms and defenses for their art, which is why some theorists coalesce the two streams. Nevertheless, the avant-garde's turn to Left-wing activism customarily ends in a judgment of modernism as nihilism, and thus its inventiveness in form is perceived as nothing less than dissipated yet boisterous experimentalism.

From this perspective, there are ways in which Kenneth Fearing is a more emblematic example of an avant-garde political revolutionary than either Rukeyser, who is singularly experimental in form, or Gold, whose dramatic aesthetic posturing recalls the behavior of European cultural iconoclasts. What bonded the Left with the avant-garde was estrangement from the dominant culture and the social system it bolstered, a belief in joining with more powerful social forces to effect action, and a confidence that novelty in their art, in form as well as content, was an emissary in the revolutionary process. Yet Fearing's self-conscious experiments were solidly tempered by social necessity, such as a belief, like Brecht's,[54] that he should refrain from depicting characters whose political consciousness was in advance of the mass of the citizenry. Thus, like many avant-gardists, including the Futurists, Fearing's discernment of the imminent was constricted, a kind of obstructed utopianism. Equivalent to the dadists, Fearing guided his blows against society's vainglorious and shortsighted attachments. He recognized the pettiness and artlessness of his poetic characters' lives, and could be acrid and vindictive in his mockery.

Fearing and the other Left avant-gardists of the Depression era faded posthaste from public awareness during the Cold War years, albeit their names and writings were kept alive in the underground streams of the remnants of the Left tradition and Bohemia. This led to a speedy judgment in 1950s academe as to the fleeting quality of their attainments, and the careful reconstruction of the Great Depression as an aberrant time of misguided hopes. The moments of uncommon emotional power and creatively crafted political insights in poetry that I have tried to emphasize in this volume were lost to literary history; the traditional Communist vision of the artist exalted by commitment became transmogrified into a myth of poetry debased by politics.

Yet the dreams and commitments of the Communist avant-garde would quickly revive just a few years later in forms that were unanticipated, but recognizable nonetheless – as the latest and most novel installment of the ever-present longing to remake the world. Those who would live through the experience of the 1960s radicalization would see the bonds concealed within the incongruities, just as Joseph Freeman in 1955 thought he had discovered the young Mike Gold when he encountered Gregory Corso declaiming free verse into a telephone in a bar.

Signs of latent cross-generational linkage were even more apparent to Freeman in early mid-May 1959, when he and Charmion Von Weigand went to the McMillan Theater at Columbia University. The occasion was a symposium on the 1930s sponsored by *Partisan Review,* the one-time organ of the John Reed Clubs that Freeman had helped to launch, but which was now a voice of liberal anti-Communism. In the audience he noticed several former revolutionaries – Earl Browder, Max Eastman, Elliot Cohen (who founded *Commentary*). But he wrote to Daniel Aaron that he was principally enraptured by the youthfulness of the vast majority of the throng: "All over the USA young people have been reading about the Thirties and their curiosity about that decade is immense."[55]

The symposium itself was disheartening. Speaker after speaker dispensed what Freeman saw as self-serving remarks, muddling the factual history of the cultural Left in the 1930s, while he, who had been at the very core, sat mute and anonymous in the assemblage. "It was all dull and trivial except for two moments," due mainly to the novelist Norman Mailer. The first was when historian Arthur Schlesinger Jr., to Freeman's astonishment, denied that the Communist movement had strongly affected New Deal legislation; he was sharply disputed by Mailer. The second was when, in retort to a provocation by Mailer, the novelist Mary McCarthy denied that liberals had tacitly aided Joe McCarthy. Neither point, however, was pursued in the discussion that followed.

What Freeman felt, above all, was that the symposium's speakers wanted to "close the past." And yet he knew that at the heart of that paradoxical Great Depression decade was "the basic dream with the changing name" which is "like the phoenix" that "perished in the flames only to rise again out of its own ashes." Meditating on the young audience, rather than the speakers, Freeman observed:

> What the meeting . . . made clear was that there is a new generation . . . who have picked up the old dream and will soon find new ways of carrying it forward.
>
> Here's to them![56]

# Chronology of the Mid-Twentieth-Century Cultural Left

1911   The *Masses* magazine founded, lasting through 1917.

1918   *Liberator* founded in March. In 1924 it is united with *Labor Herald* and *Soviet Russia Pictorial*, becoming *Worker's Monthly*.

1919   Communists expelled from the Socialist Party.

1920   Journalist John Reed dies of typhus in Baku in the USSR.

1922   After an underground existence, various Communist parties unite to form the Workers Party of America as a legal party, which later becomes the Workers (Communist) Party and then the Communist Party, USA, in 1929.

1926   The *New Masses* founded, lasting until 1947.

1927   Execution of Sacco and Vanzetti in Boston. New Playwrights Theater launched.

1929   Stock market crash. In the spring and summer the workers at the Loray Mill in Gastonia, N.C., go on strike; this becomes the subject of a half dozen radical novels. In November, the editorial board of *New Masses* forms the first John Reed Club in New York. Workers Laboratory Theater founded (changing its name to Theater of Action in 1934). Publication of *Daughter of Earth*, by Agnes Smedley.

1930   The International Union of Revolutionary Writers meets in November in Kharkov in the USSR. Workers' Film and Photo League organized (components of which would evolve after 1935 into Nykino and Frontier Films). Publication of Michael Gold's *Jews without Money*.

1931   *Rebel Poet*, official organ of Rebel Poets, the Internationale of Song, founded in January, edited by B. C. Hagglund and Jack Conroy, and lasting until October 1932. Scottsboro Boys arrested and tried in Alabama. Group Theater offers its first production. *Workers Theater* is published, changing its name to *New Theater* in 1934.

1932   Theater Union organized. Workers' Dance League launched.

1933   The *Anvil* is founded by Jack Conroy and lasts until 1936.

1934   *Dynamo*, a journal of revolutionary poetry, is founded in January, lasting until December 1936. *New Masses* also relaunched in January 1934 as a weekly. *Partisan Review* is founded in February as a publication of the John Reed Club of New York. A national convention of thirty John Reed Clubs, representing more than 1,200 members, is held. San Francisco General Strike occurs.

1935   First American Writers Congress in New York City. Popular Front policy announced.

1936   Spanish Civil War begins. Moscow Trials begin. National Negro Congress held in Chicago. South Side Writers Group forms.

1937   Second American Writers Congress held. *Partisan Review* relaunched in December independent of the Communists. *New Challenge* publishes one issue as a pro-Communist Black literary publication.

1939   Hitler-Stalin Pact signed on August 24. *Black and White,* West Coast literary magazine led by Communist Party members, founded and lasts until 1940. Third American Writers Congress held.

1940   The Rapp-Coudert Committee of the New York State Legislature investigates Communist teachers at Queens, Hunter, Brooklyn and City College of New York. Dozens of teachers are fingered by informers and fired for being members of the Communist Party, or hiding their membership. Leon Trotsky assassinated in August. Negro Playwrights Company formed. *The Clipper* succeeds *Black and White,* lasting until 1941.

1941   Fourth American Writers Congress held. Germany invades the USSR on June 21.

1942   Communist Party membership hits peak of 85,000. Communist Party becomes Communist Political Association (CPA). Pro-Communist *Negro Quarterly* launched and lasts until 1944.

1943   Launching of Hollywood Writers Mobilization.

1944   *Negro Story* launched and lasts until 1946.

1945   Communist Party reformed; Earl Browder deposed and expelled in February 1946.

1946   *Jewish Life* is launched, renamed *Jewish Currents* in 1958. Founding of *Hollywood Quarterly.*

1947   House Committee on Un-American Activities (HUAC) investigates Hollywood, resulting in conviction of the "Hollywood Ten" for "contempt of Congress." *Mainstream,* a literary journal, launched by pro-Communist writers and lasts for one year. Organization of the Committee for the Negro in the Arts.

1948   In March, *Masses & Mainstream* (from merger with the *New Masses*) appears, lasting until 1956 when its name is changed to *Mainstream.* Henry Wallace's Progressive Party campaign is launched. Communist Party leaders arrested under the Smith Act.

1949   CIO expels all known Communists and Communist-led unions. *Harlem Quarterly* launched and lasts until 1950.

1950   Alger Hiss convicted of perjury. Hollywood Ten begin prison sentences. *Freedom* newspaper launched in Harlem and lasts until 1955.

1951   HUAC investigation in Hollywood creates blacklist of hundreds of screenwriters, actors, etc. Communist Party leaders sentenced to prison.

1952   Culmination of Prague Trials.

1953 Death of Stalin on 5 March. In June, Julius and Ethel Rosenberg executed for alleged espionage.

1954 Michael Wilson's *Salt of the Earth* and Kazan/Schulberg's *On the Waterfront* released. John O. Killens's *Youngblood* is published.

1955 Montgomery Bus Boycott begins.

1956 Nikita Khrushchev's 20th Congress speech in February admits Stalin's terror. USSR suppresses rebellion in Hungary in November. By 1958, Communist Party membership drops to a few thousand.

1959 Cuban Revolution. Lorraine Hansberry's *A Raisin in the Sun* performed.

1961 *Freedomways* launched and lasts until 1976.

1962 SDS issues the *Port Huron Statement.*

1963 Martin Luther King Jr. leads March on Washington. Betty Friedan publishes *The Feminine Mystique. Umbra* Black poetry journal launched and lasts until 1975.

1965 Death of Joseph Freeman.

1967 Death of Michael Gold.

1971 Publication of *Between the Hills and the Sea,* by Katya and Bert Gilden.

1976 Death of Walter Lowenfels.

1980 Death of Muriel Rukeyser.

1987 Death of John O. Killens.

1990 Death of Thomas McGrath.

1999 Death of Aaron Kramer.

2000 Death of Ring Lardner Jr., last of the "unfriendly witnesses" of the Hollywood Ten.

## Preface

1. For several opinions about the distinction between affiliations and forms, see Michael Denning, *The Cultural Front: The Laboring of American Culture in the Twentieth Century* (London: Verso, 1996), pp. xix–xx; and Alan Trachtenberg, "Introduction," in *Paul Strand*, ed. Maren Strange (New York: Aperture, 1990).

2. Because writers related to the Communist movement in various ways, and for longer or shorter amounts of time under differing circumstances, I have tried to be precise about each association. Still, there is no foolproof method of determining the depth or sincerity of one's commitment. Much depends on the reader's definitions and criteria; some assertions in my study will no doubt provoke legitimate disagreement. The term "Communist-led," when referring to organizations initiated and politically supported by the Communist Party, has a range of different meanings in regard to the precise role played by organized and unorganized Party members. When treating such organizations – the John Reed Clubs, League of American Writers, the Party's Cultural Commission, and so forth – I will try to provide more details about the institutional structure and culture.

3. Cited in Leo Ribuffo, "The Complexity of American Communism," *Right, Center, Left: Essays in American History* (New Brunswick, N.J.: Rutgers University Press, 1992), p. 136.

4. See the extensive discussion of Bourdieu's concept as a bridge between the objective and subjective in Richard Jenkins, *Pierre Bourdieu* (New York: Routledge, 1992), pp. 74–84.

5. The most helpful guide to this general subject is Paul Buhle and Dan Georgakas, eds., *The Immigrant Left in the United States* (Albany, N.Y.: State University of New York Press, 1996).

## Introduction

1. Guy Endore to the *New Republic*, 27 Feb. 1934. The 14 March 1934 issue carried a selection of letters about the event, but Endore's was not included. A copy of his letter is available in the Endore Papers at UCLA.

2. The letter continues: "That was a very fine period of grace. Secondly, it made sure that whatever might come of it would not be a universal crusade against Russia." Endore to Harry Braverman, 10 July 1941, Endore Papers. To another friend he wrote: "Only the Russians had a right to make a separate peace with the Nazis for they were able to protect themselves. So after offer-

ing collective action to all of those little countries who refused, they had a right to say 'go to hell' to all of them." Endore to Carl Drehier, 26 July 1941, Endore Papers. According to Ring Lardner Jr., the sole surviving member of the "Hollywood Ten," Endore and Samuel Ornitz were regarded as the "explainers" among Hollywood Communists, due to their role in justifying complicated or unexpected policy changes by the Party and Soviet Union. Wald interview with Lardner, Weston, Connecticut, October 1989. In the World War II period, Endore even corresponded with Comintern agent Otto Katz in Mexico about making a film about Stalin; see Endore to Katz, 22 Jan. 1943, Endore Papers.

3. Endore to Isidor Schneider, 9 July 1945, Endore Papers.

4. A favorable review by Charles Humboldt appeared in the issue of *New Masses* (11 Dec. 1945): 23-24; an enthusiastic letter appeared in the Readers' Forum in the *New Masses* issue of 8 Jan. 1946, p. 20.

5. The inquiry into Endore's Yoga is recalled in a letter from Sanora Babb to Guy Endore, 10 Nov. 1967, Endore Papers,

6. There are different recollections of the consistency of Endore's vegetarianism, as well as his motivations for it. In a 13 September 1989 interview, his older daughter, Marcia Endore Goodman, expressed the view that Endore was primarily concerned about his health, although episodically he returned to eating meat when his wife became annoyed with preparing different meals for family members.

7. The career of Endore will be revisited in a later volume, with special attention to his screen credits and post-Communist activities.

8. Daniel Aaron, *Writers on the Left: Episodes in American Literary Communism* (New York: Harcourt, Brace and World, 1961), p. 307.

9. Joseph Freeman to Daniel Aaron, 4 Apr. 1960, p. 11, Freeman Papers, Hoover Institute, Palo Alto, Calif.

10. Joseph Freeman to Daniel Aaron, 14 Sept. 1960, Freeman Papers.

11. Josephine Herbst to David Madden, quoted in the introduction to *Proletarian Writers of the Thirties*, ed. David Madden (Carbondale: Southern Illinois University Press, 1968), pp. xxi–xxii.

12. Maltz interview with Victor Navasky, 20 Feb. 1974, Maltz Collection, Library of Social History, Los Angeles, California.

13. The 1946 post-Browder cultural controversy is misdated 1943 in Aaron's discussion on pp. 386–90 in Aaron, *Writers on the Left*.

14. Walter Snow to Maurice Isserman, 24 Oct. 1972, University of Connecticut Library, Storrs, Conn. The collection of papers also includes Snow's letters from the 1930s, which are full of fascinating details and compelling interpretations of disputes within the cultural Left from Snow's perspective. In addition to his prolific career as journalist, editor, and author of mystery stories, Snow wrote poetry in the *Daily Worker* and elsewhere, much of which was collected in *The Glory and the Shame: Poems by Walter Snow* (Coventry, Conn.: Pequot Press, 1973).

Despite his hard line against "renegades" in his correspondence with Isserman, Snow's one novel, *The Golden Nightmare* (New York: Austen-Phelps, 1952), is an anti-Communist detective story; the book jacket boasts that Snow "was active in the long fight to oust Communists from control of the New York Newspaper Guild."

15. I have contributed to this critique myself in "The Legacy of Daniel Aaron," in Wald, *Writing from the Left: New Essays on Radical Culture and Politics* (London: Verso, 1994), pp. 13–27.

16. See "Revising the Barricades: Scholarship about the U.S. Cultural Left in the Post–Cold War Era," *Working Papers Series in Cultural Studies, Ethnicity, and Race Relations*, no. 11 (Pullman, Wash.: Department of Comparative American Cultures, Washington State University, 2000). This essay was originally intended to appear as a "literature review" in the Introduction to *Exiles from a Future Time*, but was cut due to its specialized academic character.

17. See my analysis of this novel and its context in "The Subaltern Speaks," in Wald, *Writing from the Left*, pp. 178–86.

18. See *Oral History of Guy Endore*, Endore Papers.

19. *Casanova: His Known and Unknown Life* (New York: John D. Company, 1929); *The Sword of God: The Life of Joan of Arc* (New York: Garden City Publishing Co., 1932); *King of Paris* (New York: Simon and Schuster, 1958); *Voltaire! Voltaire* (New York: Simon and Schuster, 1961); *Satan's Saint: A Novel about the Marquis de Sade* (New York: Crown, 1965).

20. Herbert Biberman to Guy Endore, 16 July 1965, Endore Papers.

21. The ancedote is reported in an undated page in the Endore Papers.

22. Kenneth Burke, "Literature and Science," in *The Writer in a Changing World*, ed. Henry Hart (New York: Equinox, 1937), p. 167.

23. Norman MacLeod to Jack Conroy, 2 Mar. 1969, MacLeod Papers, Yale University.

24. Josephine Herbst to Alfred Kazin, 8 Sept. 1965, Herbst Papers, Yale University.

25. Joseph Freeman to Josephine Herbst, 25 Oct. 1958, Herbst Papers.

26. In a letter of 4 August 1958, Freeman expressed his dismay when reading a manuscript (not by Aaron) prepared for the Fund for the Republic about the League of American Writers, depicting the league as a "conspiracy" hatched by a Communist leader rather than a response to the Great Depression and rise of fascism. The author had gone to three embittered ex-radicals who "naturally rattled off the jokes, anecdotes and spiteful pieces of gossip they have been telling for years, all of it enriched by fantasy and time, all of it told out of context without any attempt to check other people and sources."

27. "Part of Our Time, Too," *Nation*, 5–12 Apr. 1999, p. 63.

28. Leo Ribuffo, *Right, Center, Left: Essays in American History* (New Brunswick, N.J.: Rutgers University Press, 1992), p. 129.

## Chapter 1

1. Fearing and Gregory are among the best remembered of the Left poets. Two important volumes about Fearing appeared in the mid-1990s: *Kenneth Fearing: Complete Poems* (Orono, Maine: National Poetry Foundation, 1994), with superb editing, annotation, and an introduction by Robert M. Ryley; and the ingenious study *The Great Depression and the Culture of Abundance: Kenneth Fearing, Nathanael West and Mass Culture in the 1930s*, by Rita Barnard (New York: Cambridge University Press, 1995). A number of dissertations are devoted exclusively to Fearing: Andrew Anderson, " 'Fear Ruled Them All': Kenneth Fearing's Literature of Corporate Conspiracy" (Purdue University, 1989); James Perkins, "An American Rhapsody: The Poetry of Kenneth Fearing" (University of Tennessee, 1972); and Patricia Santora, "The Poetry and Prose of Kenneth Fearing" (University of Maryland, 1982). Both Fearing and Gregory were featured in the influential dissertation by Macha Louis Rosenthal, "Chief Poets of the American Depression" (New York University, 1949), and more recently in Cameron Bardrick, "Social Protest and Poetic Decorum in the Great Depression: A Reading of Kenneth Fearing, Horace Gregory, and Muriel Rukeyser" (Columbia University, 1984). The entire issue of *Modern Poetry Studies* 4, no. 1 (Spring 1973) is devoted to essays on Horace Gregory.

2. See my discussion of Fearing in "From Old Left to New in U.S. Literary Radicalism," in Wald, *Writing from the Left: New Essays on Radical Culture and Politics* (London: Verso, 1994), pp. 114–22.

3. Wald interview with Sanora Babb, Los Angeles, July 1989. In a 1989 interview in New York City, Annette T. Rubinstein stated her belief that this harassment had driven Taggard to suicide. To date, no evidence of her suicide has surfaced. Wald interview with Rubinstein, 10 Oct. 1989, New York City.

4. Horace Gregory to Charmion Von Wiegand, 13 Aug. 1965, Freeman Papers, Hoover Institute, Palo Alto, Calif.

5. Letter from Joseph Freeman to Horace Gregory, 28 June 1961, pp. 6–7, Gregory Papers, Syracuse University.

6. Joseph Freeman, *An American Testament: A Narrative of Rebels and Romantics* (New York: Farrar and Rhinehart, 1936), p. viii.

7. For an informative discussion of the use of Black dialect in canonical modernist poetry and fiction, see Michael North, *The Dialect of Modernism: Race, Language and Twentieth Century Literature* (New York: Oxford University Press, 1994).

8. Walter Snow, unpublished manuscript, "That Literary 'Shotgun Marriage,' " p. 8, Snow Papers, University of Connecticut.

9. A superior collection of primary source materials edited by Jon Christian Suggs shows the ways in which this shifting policy was manifest: Suggs, ed., *American Proletarian Culture: The Twenties and the Thirties* (Detroit: Gale Research, Inc., 1993).

10. Cary Nelson and Jefferson Hendricks, eds., *Edwin Rolfe: Collected Poems* (Chicago and Urbana: University of Illinois Press, 1993), p. 289.

11. On the other hand, the base for a specifically proletarian cultural movement was significantly eroded by the Popular Front, as Jack Conroy and Nelson Algren discovered when they tried to launch *New Anvil* in Chicago in March 1939; it lasted only until August 1940.

12. William Z. Foster to V. F. Calverton, 10 Aug. 1925, Calverton Papers, New York Public Library.

13. See "Historical Overview," in Suggs, *American Proletarian Culture*, pp. 3–16.

14. The 1925 prospectus for the *New Masses*, at that time called "Dynamo," states that the magazine intends to publish "Rhymed and free-verse poetry, favoring vigorous expression of positive ideas and ideals, and avoiding the ineffectual fatalism so prevalent in many aesthetic literary publications." See American Fund for the Republic Collection. An example of the Soviet preoccupation with fatalism occurs in Anne Elistratova's critique of the *New Masses* in *International Literature* no. 1 (1932): 107–14, where she takes Langston Hughes to task for his "distinctly decadent and passive mood" in his poem "Tired."

15. Published in Granville Hicks et al., eds., *Proletarian Literature in the United States* (New York: International Publishers, 1935), p. 171.

16. This was Daniel Aaron's apt phrase for Michael Gold's vision of working-class literature at the time Gold edited the *New Masses*. Aaron, *Writers on the Left*, p. 205.

17. See the minutes of the first national convention of the John Reed Clubs, May 1932, Chicago, where poet Kenneth Rexroth (1905–1982) starts an argument with the first question. Freeman Papers.

18. For evidence of continuities between poetry of the Old Left and New Left eras, see Dudley Randall, "The Black Aesthetic in the 1930s, 1940s and 1950s," in *Modern Black Poets*, ed. Donald B. Gibson (Englewood Cliffs, N.J.: Prentice-Hall, 1973), pp. 34–42; and Charlotte Nekola's essay, "Worlds Moving: Poetry and Literary Politics of the 1930s," in *Writing Red: An Anthology of American Women Writers, 1930–1940*, ed. Charlotte Nekola and Paula Rabinowitz (New York: Feminist Press, 1987), pp. 127–34. Walter Kalaidjian's *American Culture between the Wars: Revisionary Modernism and Postmodern Critique* (New York: Columbia University Press, 1993), brilliantly suggests such cross-generational connections as well.

19. The general characteristics of this rebellion are cogently described in the chapters "The New Paganism" and "Three Bohemias" in James Burkhart Gilbert's *Writers and Partisans: A History of Literary Radicalism in America* (New York: John Wiley and Sons, 1968), pp. 1–87.

20. Among the poetry and short story publications whose most visible contributors and often whose editors variously showed attraction to Communist ideas between 1929 and 1935 are *The Anvil, Blast, Blues, Challenge, Clay, Contempo, Contemporary Vision* (originally *Scepter*), *Direction, The Dubuque Dial, Dynamo, Folio,*

John Reed Review, The Hammer, Hinterland, Hub, The Left, Left Front, The Left Review, Leftward, Midland Left, The Morada, Nativity, The New Force, The New Quarterly, The New Tide, The Partisan, Partisan Review, Point, Pollen, Proletcult, The Rebel Poet, The Red, Red Pen, Revolt (New York), Revolt (Paterson, New Jersey), War, Western Poetry, and The Windsor Quarterly. In The Little Magazine: A History and Bibliography (Princeton, N.J.: Princeton University Press, 1946), Frederick J. Hoffman, Charles Allen, and Carolyn Ulrich observe that "The hold of revolutionary thinking and of the apparent necessity for social action upon the writers of the early thirties was so strong that it was difficult for any magazine to exclude it from its pages" (p. 316). This list conceivably could be expanded to include publications such as Pagany and even Hound and Horn. It's also important to note that many of the more explicit pro-Communist literary magazines, especially those associated with the John Reed Clubs, are not listed in the bibliography by Hoffman et al., which is widely regarded as definitive.

21. The most fully documented and discussed instance of such a dispute over the politics of literary judgment was the 1937 break between some of the leading editors of Partisan Review, organ of the John Reed Club of New York, and the Communist Party. I have discussed this development extensively in The New York Intellectuals, and I review subsequent literature on the topic in "The New York Literary Left," Michigan Quarterly Review 28, no. 1 (Winter 1989): 130–42, and "Learning from Adversaries," Boston Book Review 3, no. 6 (June 1996): 7–8. Many of the minor disputes between midwestern and New York-based writers are discussed in Douglas Wixson, Worker-Writer in America: Jack Conroy and the Tradition of Midwestern Literary Radicalism (Urbana and Chicago: University of Illinois Press, 1994).

22. Freeman began as a local-color storyteller in New England but produced works in many genres, including novels and plays. Markham was a schoolteacher on the West Coast who wrote several popular volumes of verse. Traubel was a journalist friend of Walt Whitman and a popularizer of socialism.

23. Chaplin was a journalist and artist as well as song-writer and poet. Giovannitti was born in Italy and also known as a lecturer and pamphleteer on behalf of the working class. Hill was a popular songwriter as well as cartoonist, executed after being framed on a murder charge in Utah.

24. Some of the background sources on the Left tradition in verse are summarized in the entry "Poetry, 1870–1930," by Paul Buhle in Mari Jo Buhle, Paul Buhle, and Dan Georgakas, eds., Encyclopedia of the American Left (New York: Oxford University Press, 1998), pp. 608–11.

25. See Charles Shipman, It Had to Be Revolution: Memoirs of an American Radical (Ithaca, N.Y.: Cornell University Press, 1993).

26. Manuel Gomez, ed., Poems for Workers (Chicago: Daily Worker Publishing, n.d.), p. 4. The selected poems were by the Chartist leader Ernest Jones; the United States journalist who witnessed the Paris Commune, Edward King;

the Irish nationalist martyr James Connolly; the English antiwar poet Siegfried Sassoon; and a variety of contemporary Left poets including Joseph Freeman, Arturo Giovannitti, Louis Untermeyer, Michael Gold, Langston Hughes, Claude McKay, James Oppenheim, Carl Sandburg, Donald Crocker, J. S. Wallace, Miriam Allen DeFord, Edward Connor, Francis W. L. Adams, Alice Corbin, John G. Neihardt, and Jim Waters.

27. For some of these observations, I am indebted to the excellent discussion of working-class literature by Martha Vicinus in *The Industrial Muse: A Study of Nineteenth Century British Working-Class Literature* (New York: Barnes and Noble, 1974), and the comments on politics and poetry by Barbara Harlow in *Resistance Literature* (New York: Metheun, 1987). For a rich study of the political poetry during World War I, see Mark Van Wienen, *Partisans and Poets: The Political Work of American Poetry in the Great War* (London: Cambridge University Press, 1997).

28. Papers of the Fourth American Writers' Congress, University of California, Berkeley.

29. Nelson and Hendricks, eds., *Edwin Rolfe: Collected Poems*, p. 212.

30. Allen Gutmann quotes a number of examples of this demand by *New Masses* writers in "The Brief, Embattled Course of Proletarian Poetry" in *Proletarian Writers of the Thirties*, ed. David Madden (Carbondale: Southern Illinois University Press, 1968), pp. 252–69.

31. Gomez, *Poems for Workers*, p. 7.

32. According to Aaron Kramer, who knew both Untermeyers well, Ms. Untermeyer was the more committed of the two to the Communist view. Wald interview with Kramer, Long Island, New York, 5 June 1994. The Untermeyers were first married in 1907, then divorced in 1925. Louis Untermeyer passed through two more marriages and divorces, then remarried and divorced Jean Untermeyer before his next and final marriage. Jean Untermeyer, who also attempted a career as a singer, published six volumes of verse. She was a member of the Executive Committee and National Council of the League of American Writers, but she withdrew during the Hitler-Stalin Pact.

33. See William L. O'Neill, *A Better World: The Great Schism: Stalinism and American Intellectuals* (New York: Simon and Schuster, 1982), p. 165.

34. Alden Whitman, "A Man of Many Talents," *New York Times*, 19 Dec. 1977, p. 42.

35. Gomez, *Poems for Workers*, p. 7.

36. Ibid., p. 39.

37. *Young Worker*, May 1922, p. 14.

38. Ibid., by W. E. E., May 1922, p. 18; C. Revilo, June–July 1922, p. 1; S. Max Kitzes, June–July 1922, p. 15; and Rena Deane, October 1922, p. 14.

39. Field was first a missionary in Burma, then a socialist and activist in the suffrage movement. Neihardt is best known for his poetry and prose about the Plains Indians, especially *Black Elk Speaks* (New York: William Morrow, 1932).

40. *Young Worker*, Aug.-Sept. 1922, p. 8.

41. Ibid.

42. The transit of literary radicalism in the United States during its first three decades has been traced in general terms in the major studies by Aaron, Gilbert, and Rideout, although none of them discuss poetry in any detail. The most thoughtful consideration of the evolution of radical poetry in the 1920s and 1930s can be found in Cary Nelson's remarkable *Repression and Recovery: Modern American Poetry and the Politics of Cultural Memory, 1910-1945* (Madison: University of Wisconsin Press, 1989). My assessment of the book appears in *The Responsibility of Intellectuals* (Atlantic Highlands, N.J.: Humanities Press, 1992), pp. 126-30. General insight into the currents shaping twentieth-century radical literary form and themes in its formative period are presented in Michael B. Folsom's "Literary Radicalism and the Genteel Tradition: A Study of the Principal Works of the American Socialist Movement before 1912," Ph.D. diss., University of California at Berkeley, 1972. A straightforward description of the *Masses* can be found in Thomas A. Maik, "A History of *The Masses* Magazine," Ph.D. diss., Bowling Green State University, 1968. A more contemporary analysis of the cultural, personal, psychoanalytical, and sexual dimensions of this milieu is offered in Leslie Fishbein's *Rebels in Bohemia: The Radicals of "The Masses," 1911-1917* (Chapel Hill: University of North Carolina Press, 1982). Two of the more recent studies of the Bohemian-Radical culture are Edward Abrahams, *The Lyrical Left: Randolph Bourne, Alfred Stieglitz and the Origins of Cultural Radicalism in America* (Charlottesville: University Press of Virginia, 1986); and Casey Nelson Blake, *Beloved Community: The Cultural Criticism of Randolph Bourne, Van Wyck Brooks, Waldo Frank, and Lewis Mumford* (Chapel Hill: University of North Carolina Press, 1990). The publication of Douglas Wixson's study of Jack Conroy and the Midwest radical cultural tradition, *Worker-Writer in America*, closes a serious gap in scholarship about this regional literary tradition.

43. Genevieve Taggard, ed., *May Days* (New York: Boni and Liveright, 1925), p. 13. Taggard bolstered her argument with a citation from Leon Trotsky's *Literature and Revolution* (1922) to the effect that those who hail the achievements of weak and colorless poetry on the grounds of the class origin of the poets, and who deny access to "the technique of bourgeois art," are themselves evidencing "contempt for the masses."

44. One piece of evidence for the link is the celebratory review of Hart Crane's *The Bridge* (1930), by Alan Calmer (a pseudonym for Abraham Klein, dates unknown), a young critic from Baltimore who was on the verge of becoming a leader of the John Reed Clubs and who subsequently became an employee of International Publishers. See *Modern Quarterly* 5, no. 4 (Winter 1930-31): 560-61.

45. See the thoughtful discussion of Gold's role in the *New Masses* in Marcus Klein's *Foreigners: The Making of American Literature, 1900-1940* (Chicago: University of Chicago Press, 1981), pp. 68-86. For an overview of the history of the

John Reed Clubs, see "Proletarian Literature and the John Reed Clubs" in Eric Homberger's *American Writers and Radical Politics, 1900–39: Equivocal Commitments* (New York: St. Martin's, 1986), pp. 119–40. In 1926 a group of pro-Communist intellectuals, in response to a communication from the All-Russian Association of Proletarian Writers, tried to launch a Proletarian Artist and Writers League in New York to coordinate various cultural activities, but it never got off the ground. See letter from Harry Freeman, 5 Oct. 1926, in the Calverton Papers.

46. *Rebel Poet* 1, no. 1 (January 1931): 1.

47. Ibid., p. 2.

48. Ibid., 1, nos. 6–7 (June–July 1931): 3–4.

49. Jack Conroy to Sterling Brown, 3 July 1932, Brown Papers, Howard University.

50. *Rebel Poet* 1, no. 5 (May 1931): 2.

51. Ibid., 1, nos. 8–9 (August–September 1931): 9.

52. The complete list of names appears in Aaron, *Writers on the Left*, p. 457 (n. 73).

53. This might explain why there were no follow-up volumes, which is surprising in light of the success of the first one. Likewise, the first and only competition for the best proletarian novel, a contest sponsored by the *New Masses* and John Day Company publishing house, also occurred in that fateful year.

54. Kalar's fugitive pieces were collected by his son, Richard Kalar, and privately published in 1985 as *Joseph A. Kalar: Poet of Protest* (Blaine, Minn.: RGK Publication, 1985).

55. H. H. Lewis proclaimed himself a devout Communist in four "Rebel Poets Booklets" published in Holt, Minnesota, by B. C. Hagglund: *Red Renaissance* (1930), *Thinking of Russia* (1932), *Salvation* (1934), and *Road to Russia: Poems Written by a Missouri Farmhand and Dedicated to Soviet Russia* (1935). After the 1940s, he lapsed into isolation and became increasingly eccentric. The most complete information available about Lewis appears in Wixson, *Worker-Writer in America*.

56. From the early 1930s through the civil rights movement, the Highlander Folk School in Monteagle, Tennessee, trained labor and civil rights activists. See John M. Glen, *Highlander: No Ordinary School, 1932–1962* (Lexington: University of Kentucky, 1988).

57. See the thoughtful discussion of Guthrie's promotion of his own legend in Bryan K. Carman, *A Race of Singers: Whitman's Working-Class Hero from Guthrie to Springsteen* (Chapel Hill: University of North Carolina Press, 2000). The definitive biography is Joe Klein, *Woody Guthrie: A Life* (New York: Knopf, 1980).

58. Don West to Langston Hughes, 19 Oct. 1943, Hughes Papers, Yale University.

59. Don West, *In a Land of Plenty: A Don West Reader* (Los Angeles: West End Press, 1982), p. 3.

60. Wald interview with Junius Scales, New York City, April 1991. Several of

West's sisters were also active in the Communist movement. While West may have dropped his Party membership after 1956, he continued his ties to the movement and expressed sympathy for the Soviet Union. As late as the mid-1980s West contributed to a Party-led journal about his favorable impressions of the Soviet Union; see "Appalachian Young People Visit the USSR," *New World Review* 52, no. 2 (March-April 1984): 27. Yet he also contributed to *Jewish Currents* in the years after its editors were castigated by the Party as renegades.

61. There is no reason to doubt the veracity of these claims. Two of the violent high points of his life as a Communist militant came in 1933, when West was beaten unconscious while serving as an organizer for the National Miners' Union in Harlan, Kentucky, and 1948, when the Ku Klux Klan torched his home. See the West Papers at the State Historical Society of Wisconsin. When West was active in the Scottsboro and Angelo Herndon defense efforts, the Gastonia Strike, and many other events in the history of southern radicalism, he was often forced to operate clandestinely and at great personal risk. In the 1950s he was hauled before Senate Internal Security investigating committees and vilified by the southern press.

62. West's project might be usefully discussed in light of the "romantic nationalism" that Jerrold Hirsch sees as a crucial component of the Popular Front. See his essay, "From Play-Party to Popular Front: B. A. Botkin, Folklore, and Proletarian Regionalism," *Intellectual History Newsletter* 19 (1997): 29–37. For a more critical view of West as one who romanticizes Appalachia, see Richard Marius, "Don West's Sermon on the Mount," *Appalachian Journal* 10, no. 4 (Summer 1983): 361–65.

63. West, *In a Land of Plenty*, p. 128.

64. Ibid., p. 94.

65. There was only one John Reed Club in the South, at Commonwealth College in Arkansas, and West never held membership in the League of American Writers nor signed any of its public statements. Only two of his poems, "Dark Winds" and "Southern Lullaby," were included in Hicks et al., *Proletarian Literature in the United States*, pp. 198–99.

66. See Georg Lukács, *The Meaning of Contemporary Realism* (London: Merlin, 1963).

67. Edwin Berry Burgum, "Three Radical English Poets," *New Masses* (3 July 1934): 33–36. For details about the "Auden School," see Samuel Hynes, *The Auden Generation* (Princeton, N.J.: Princeton University Press, 1972).

68. The theses are reprinted in Walter Benjamin, *Illuminations* (New York: Schocken, 1969).

69. Stanley J. Kunitz and Howard Haycraft, eds., *Twentieth Century Authors* (New York: H. H. Wilson, 1942), p. 1380.

70. Taggard's essay and the editors' comment appear in *New Masses* (25 Sept. 1934): 18–20. An additional essay was published on the topic, but this was mainly

a polemic against Max Eastman which did not take clear sides on the original dispute. See Granville Hicks, "The Vigorous Abandon of Max Eastman's Mind," *New Masses* (6 Nov. 1934): 22-23.

71. For comparison, see Leon Trotsky, *Literature and Revolution* (Ann Arbor: University of Michigan Press, 1975), pp.126-71.

72. The phrase is from Martin Buber in reference to the Russian populist Landauer.

73. Michael Löwy, "Marxism and Utopian Vision," *On Changing the World: Essays in Political Philosophy from Karl Marx to Walter Benjamin* (Atlantic Highlands, N.J.: Humanities Press, 1993), p. 22.

74. Max Blechman, "Preface," in Blechman, ed., *Revolutionary Romanticism* (San Francisco: City Lights Books, 1999), p. xvi.

75. Horace Gregory, *Poems, 1930-1940* (New York: Harcourt, Brace and World, 1941), p. 90.

76. An excellent discussion of Whitman's stature in Left poetry can be found in Alan Golding, *From Outlaw to Classic: Canons in American Poetry* (Madison: University of Wisconsin Press, 1995), especially pp. 94-100. A more recent discussion can be found in Carman, *A Race of Singers*, pp. 43-78.

77. Nelson Algren, "Strength and Beauty," *New Masses* (20 Aug. 1935): 25.

78. Hughes expressed this view in his introduction to the 1946 International Publishers edition of *I Hear the People Singing: Selected Poems of Walt Whitman*. The introduction was reprinted in *American Dialogue* 5, no. 3 (Spring-Summer 1969): 8.

79. Robert Hayden, "Vigil Strange I Kept on the Field One Night," in a 1942 unpublished manuscript, "The Black Spear," courtesy of Robert Chrisman.

80. Patchen, in fact, wrote disparagingly of Whitman at times, but the influence was nevertheless abundant. See Raymond Nelson, *Patchen and American Mysticism* (Chapel Hill: University of North Carolina Press, 1984).

81. This interpretation of Whitman can be found in Paul Zweig, *Walt Whitman: The Making of a Poet* (New York: Basic Books, 1984), pp. 3-8.

## Chapter 2

1. About half the books written by Gold identify him as "Michael" and the other half "Mike," and his *Daily Worker* column switches back and forth as well, so I follow suit and alternate between the two names.

2. "'The Red Decade' — a valuable study of America's literary Left of the 30s," by A. P. Towle (pseud. for Philip Stevenson), *Daily World*, 28 April 1962, p. 4. Actually, in the cartoon strip to which Stevenson refers, it was not Krazy Kat himself but a sidekick who specialized in bouncing rocks.

3. "Out of the Fascist Unconscious," *New Republic*, 26 July 1933, pp. 295-96.

4. Quoted in David Platt, "Mike Gold Is 60 – Tributes Pour In," *Daily Worker*, clipping in Gold Papers, University of Michigan.

5. Ed Falkowski to Kenneth Payne, 8 November 1971, Gold Papers.

6. Gold to Upton Sinclair, undated (probably mid-1920s), Sinclair Papers, Indiana University.

7. Dorothy Day, "Mike Gold," *Catholic Worker*, June 1967, p. 8.

8. This is reprinted in Michael Folsom, ed., *Mike Gold: A Literary Anthology* (New York: International Publishers, 1972), pp. 203–8.

9. Michael Gold, "May Days and Revolutionary Art," *Modern Quarterly* 3, no. 1 (February-April 1926): 161–64. Judging by the following passage from the review, Gold had at that time a critical distance from the organized Communist movement, whatever his membership status: "Why has the Workers' Party not been able to tap some of this rich literary material that is disclosed in an anthology like this? Despite the fact that American Communists have the narrowness of adolescence, and have shown a decided anti-literary bias, could they not have enlisted some of the splendid satirists and humorists who are included here?"

10. For one of several discussions of Gold's highly gendered treatment of revolutionary literature, see the section called "The Early 1930s: Proletarian Culture and Gender Ideology" in Charlotte Nekola and Paula Rabinowitz, eds., *Writing Red: An Anthology of American Women Writers, 1930–1940* (New York: Feminist Press, 1987), pp. 3–9. A harsher version of the same argument appears in Janet Galligani Casey, *Dos Passos and the Ideology of the Feminine* (Cambridge: Cambridge University Press, 1998), pp. 31–34.

11. The early manifesto is reprinted in Folsom, *Mike Gold*, pp. 62–70.

12. The history of the New Playwrights Theater will be discussed in a chapter about John Howard Lawson in a later volume, but it is worth noting here that one of the productions, Emjo Basshe's *The Centuries* (1927), was a likely influence on *Jews without Money*.

13. Steven Watson, *The Birth of the Beat Generation* (New York: Pantheon, 1995), p. 26.

14. Freeman to Mike Gold, 7 Jan. 1959, Gold Papers. The resumption of communication between the two men was jump-started by Daniel Aaron's research for *Writers on the Left*.

15. Linda Hamalian, *A Life of Kenneth Rexroth* (New York: Norton, 1991), p. 25.

16. Gold, "A Miscellany on Labor in the Sun and Modern Poetry," *People's World*, dated "1957," copy in Gold Papers.

17. Joseph Freeman, *An American Testament* (New York: Farrar and Rinehart, 1938), p. 368.

18. Gold interview with Michael Folsom, 13 Oct. 1966, Gold Papers.

19. Gold's reminiscences of Mayakovsky appear in three issues of the *Daily Worker* in 1940: 22 Aug., p. 7; 24 Aug., p. 7; and 27 Aug., p. 7.

20. Michael Gold, *David Burliuk: Artist-Scholar, Father of Russian Futurism; With*

*a Brief Sketch of Mayakovsky Whom Burliuk Discovered* (New York: A.C.A. Gallery, 1943).

21. In a letter from Elizabeth Granich to Folsom, 20 Apr. 1968, Gold's widow states that Gold's sister-in-law, who met Gold in 1921, believed that as early as his Boston pre–World War I years Gold was exhibiting the symptoms of diabetes attacks, including unconsciousness. After the illness was diagnosed in late 1939, Gold carried a note in his pocket that read: "I am a diabetic. . . . If I seem drunken, etc., it is a result of a diabetic attack. Please feed orange juice, milk, sugar water." Letter and a copy of the note are in the Gold Papers.

22. Dorothea Parrot to Michael Folsom, 27 Mar. 1975, Gold Papers. Ginsberg's nickname is given in Watson, *Birth of the Beat Generation*, p. 23.

23. Gold to Upton Sinclair, undated [1923], Sinclair Papers.

24. Al Richmond, "Some Recollections of Mike Gold," *People's World*, 7 May 1964, p. 6.

25. Gold has been the subject of a good deal of scholarship, although it is somewhat redundant and there remain periods of his life and texts that have not yet been fully explored. The best-known discussion of his life and work is in Aaron's *Writers on the Left*, and a more recent consideration appears in Marcus Klein's *Foreigners* (Chicago: University of Chicago Press, 1981). The foremost authority on Gold was Michael Brewster Folsom (1938–1990), who became Gold's personal friend and literary editor while attending graduate school in English at the University of California at Berkeley. Folsom spent long hours tape-recording conversations with Gold, and he believed that the original tapes were subsequently destroyed at Gold's request for fear that some of the information might be used to persecute radicals for their political beliefs and activities. Folsom published a landmark essay in the 28 February 1966 issue of the *Nation*, pp. 242–45, denouncing the corruption of the text of Gold's *Jews without Money* by the decision of Avon Books to delete the final, revolutionary paragraphs. Folsom's protest resulted in the restoration of these paragraphs in later editions. Another Folsom essay that same year, "The Education of Michael Gold," in *Proletarian Writers of the Thirties*, ed. David Madden (Carbondale: Southern Illinois University Press, 1966), became the primary source on Gold's early life for a generation of new scholars. Six years later, Folsom edited *Mike Gold: A Literary Anthology*, with an irreverent but affectionate introduction called "The Pariah of American Letters." This provoked an angry response in the Communist Party's *Political Affairs* from Gold's comrade, Art Shields, who felt that Folsom was too critical of the Communist Party and the Soviet Union ("Mike Gold, Our Joy and Pride," vol. 51, no. 7 [July 1972]: 41–52). Folsom's defense appeared in the December 1972 issue of that journal as "A Reply to Art Shields," vol. 51, no. 12, pp. 49–52, followed by Shields's "Differences with Folsom," pp. 52–56.

Doctoral dissertations in the United States on Gold include: John Brogna, "Michael Gold: Critic and Playwright," University of Georgia, 1982; Howard

Hertz, "Writer and Revolutionary: The Life and Works of Michael Gold, Father of Proletarian Literature in the United States," University of Texas at Austin, 1974; and Azar Naficy, "The Literary Wars of Mike Gold: A Study in the Background and Development of Mike Gold's Literary Ideas, 1920-1941," University of Oklahoma, 1979. John Pyros produced a privately published book called *Mike Gold: Dean of American Proletarian Writers* (New York: Dramatika Press, 1979); and James D. Bloom issued *Left Letters: The Culture Wars of Mike Gold and Joseph Freeman* (New York: Columbia University Press, 1992). A recent book with an excellent chapter on Gold is Rachel Lee Rubin, *Jewish Gangsters of Modern Literature* (Urbana: University of Illinois Press, 2000).

Some of the important essays on Gold include Paul Berman, "East Side Story: Mike Gold, the Communists and the Jews," *Village Voice* 15 (March 1983): 1, 9-11; Morris Dickstein, "Hallucinating the Past: *Jews without Money* Revisited," *Grand Street* 9 (Winter 1990): 155-68; Helge Norman Nilsen, "The Evils of Poverty," *Anglo-American Studies* 4 (April 1984): 45-60; Kenneth William Payne, "Naturalism and the Proletarians: The Case of Mike Gold," *Anglo-American Studies,* April 1983, pp. 21-37; Annette Rubinstein, "*Jews without Money* – Not *Jews without Love*," *Jewish Currents,* November 1960, pp. 7-10; and Richard Tuerk, "*Jews without Money* as a Work of Art," *Studies in American-Jewish Literature* 7, no. 1 (Spring 1988): 67-79. A moving and informative tribute is John Howard Lawson's "The Stature of Mike Gold," *Political Affairs* 46, no. 6 (June 1967): 11-14.

In addition to engaging in discussions and correspondence with me about Gold between 1973 and 1990, Folsom gave me a draft of his unpublished literary biography of Gold up to the year 1918, upon which I have relied for some details. I also examined FBI materials on Gold, released under the Freedom of Information Act, at the FBI Reading Room in 1992. However, most of the new biographical information that I obtained comes from personal interviews with Gold's widow, Elizabeth, and his son, Nick, in September 1995, as well as the collection of Gold Papers at the University of Michigan (which contains many items located by Folsom).

26. Gold, "Change the World," *Daily Worker,* 12 July 1959, Gold Papers.

27. Gold interview with Folsom, 16 Dec. 1965, Gold Papers.

28. Elizabeth Granich to Folsom, 6 Aug. 1970, Gold Papers.

29. Irwin Granich, "To One Dying," *New York Call Magazine,* 13 Aug. 1919, p. 10.

30. Gold, "A Great Deed Was Needed," *Workers Monthly,* September 1925, p. 496.

31. Interview with Michael Folsom, transcribed in "Mike Gold: A Literary Life" (unpublished manuscript), p. 14, Gold Papers.

32. Ibid., p. 15.

33. In an undated letter (probably 1926 or 1927) to Upton Sinclair, Sinclair Papers, Gold lists the possible titles as "An East Side Youth," "A Curse on Columbus," "The Proletarian Trap," "Poverty's Trap," "The Trap of Poverty," and "Poverty Is a Trap," indicating that the last is his favorite.

34. In a 3 June 1996 phone interview with Wald, Gold's sister-in-law, Gertrude Granich, confirmed that Waters worked as a house painter and died of lead poisoning from the paint fumes. Waters contributed four poems to Manuel Gomez, ed., *Poems for Workers* (Chicago: Daily Worker Publishing, n.d.). Gold contributed only one poem, his moving "John Reed's Body."

35. Quoted in Folsom, "Mike Gold: A Literary Life," p. 3.

36. Michael Gold, *Jews without Money* (New York: Liveright, 1930), p. 309.

37. Ibid., p. 274.

38. Wald interview with Nicholas Granich, September 1995, San Francisco. In a 15 January 1968 letter to Folsom, Elisabeth Granich recalled hearing descriptions of the speaker as wearing a plumed hat and other clothing that suggested Goldman would be the speaker but speculated that Gold may have met Flynn at the demonstration as well. Gold Papers.

39. See his "Change the World" columns in the *Daily Worker* for 3 Sept. 1946, p. 7; 7 Sept. 1946, p. 6; and 10 Sept. 1946, p. 7.

40. This is reprinted in Folsom, *Mike Gold*, p. 23.

41. Ibid., p. 14–15.

42. Manny Granich contributed poetry to the publication.

43. At the beginning of his 1928 short story, "Love on a Garbage Dump," Gold writes: "Certain enemies have spread the slander that I once attended Harvard College. That is a lie. I worked on the garbage dump in Boston. But that's all." The story is reprinted in Folsom, *Mike Gold*, pp. 177–85.

44. Folsom, unpublished manuscript, "Mike Gold: A Literary Life."

45. The plays are apparently lost, but a letter in the Gold Papers from Kenneth Payne to Folsom, 2 June 1972, provides brief descriptions from a Yale University doctoral dissertation by Robert Sarlos, "The Provincetown Players: Experiments in Style."

46. *M. N. Roy's Memoirs* (London: Allied Publishers, Private Ltd., 1964), pp. 117, 120.

47. The short story "Two Mexicos" is reprinted in *Mike Gold: A Literary Anthology*, pp. 49–61.

48. See Robert Leach, *Vsevolod Meyerhold* (New York: Cambridge University Press, 1989), especially pp. 30–49, 52–56.

49. Gold interview with Folsom, 13 Oct. 1966, Gold Papers.

50. Throughout his life, Gold wrote on art and even photography. See "The Jewish Artist in Search of a Subject," *Jewish Life* 2, no. 1 (November 1945): 7–10; and "The Face and Figure of Man," *Jewish Life* 10, no. 11 (September 1955): 9–10.

51. See the excellent discussion of the play in the context of a reconsideration of Gold's relations with Claude McKay and African American culture in William Maxwell, "The Proletarian as New Negro: Mike Gold's Harlem Renaissance," in *Radical Revisions: Rereading 1930s Culture*, ed. Bill Mullen and Sherry Linkon (Urbana and Chicago: University of Illinois Press, 1996), pp. 90–119.

52. Gold, "About *Hoboken Blues*," 19 Oct. 1966, Gold Papers.

53. It appears in the issue of 21 February 1928 under the title "Fun on Commerce St."

54. Michael Gold, *Life of John Brown* (New York: Roving Eye Press, n.d.), a reprint of the early biography by Bob Brown's press. Two scenes from the Cacchione play were published as "Councilman Pete" in *Looking Forward: Sections of Works in Progress by Authors of International Publishers on the Occasion of Its Thirtieth Anniversary* (New York: International Publishers, 1954), pp. 143–53.

55. Gold to Sinclair, n.d., Sinclair Papers.

56. However, for a compelling interpretation disclosing how Gold employs Jewish, Irish, and Chinese stereotypes as a matter of course in *Jews without Money*, see Eric Homberger, "Some Uses for Jewish Ambivalence: Abraham Cahan and Michael Gold," in *Between 'Race' and Culture: Representations of the Jew in English and American Literature*, ed. Bryan Cheyette (Stanford, Calif.: Stanford University Press, 1966), pp. 164–80. Also see Richard Tuerk, "Michael Gold's Hoboken Blues: A Experiment That Failed," *MELUS* 20, no. 4 (Winter 1995): 3–15.

57. See Gold, "Why U.S. Jews Should Study Story of His People," *Daily Worker*, 8 Apr. 1947, Gold Papers.

58. Gold also saw himself as dark-skinned and an outcast among whites. See "The East Side I Knew," *Jewish Life* 1, no. 1 (November 1954): 25–27.

59. "The Death of a Negro," *Liberator* 6, no. 10 (Oct. 1923): 20.

60. William Maxwell, *New Negro, Old Left*, p. 106.

61. "Claude McKay," manuscript by Michael Gold, Gold Papers.

62. "Change the World," *Daily Worker*, 6 Aug. 1943, Gold Papers.

63. *National Guardian*, 9 Apr. 1956, p. 7.

64. Gold, *David Burliuk: Artist-Scholar*, p. 10.

65. Ibid., p. 8.

66. Ibid., p. 10.

67. Although Gold's characters are poor, industrial work is not depicted, and the head of the protagonist's household has a middle-class consciousness. One of the most sectarian reviews, reflecting the charges against Gold made in the New York John Reed Club, was that of Melvin P. Levy, a young Communist novelist and playwright, in *New Republic* (26 Mar. 1930): 160–61. Levy criticizes Gold for his failure to show the systemically caused inevitability of the characters' poverty, to depict labor organizations and strikes, or to refer to the shirtwaist strike and triangle fire. The novel is compared unfavorably to Gold's play *Fiesta* in its ideological failures.

68. "Wilder: Prophet of the Genteel Christ" appeared in the 22 October 1930 issue of the *New Republic* and is reprinted in Folsom, *Mike Gold*, pp. 197–202; the correspondence, mostly protesting Gold's analysis but with a few supporting letters, extended to the issue of 17 December 1930. For Lewis, see James Bloom, *Left Letters*, p. 16.

69. See the excellent study by Richard Tuerk, "*Jews without Money* as a Work of Art."

70. See the story "The Password to Thought – to Culture," *Liberator*, 1922; this portrait is discussed, in light of the information that Gold rarely saw his mother in the 1920s, in a letter from Kenneth Payne to Michael Folsom, 12 May 1970, Gold Papers. In an interview with Folsom (transcription in the Gold Papers), Gold mentions that prior to leaving for Mexico he failed to tell his mother that he was leaving, and that he remained out of contact with her for a year, even though he knew that she was worried about him.

71. Paul Zweig, *Walt Whitman: The Making of a Poet* (New York: Basic Books, 1984), p. 39.

72. "Theater and Revolution," *Nation*, 11 Nov. 1925, 536.

73. Gold to Sinclair, 7 Jan. 1924 [probably 1925], Sinclair Papers.

74. Ibid.

75. Michael Gold, "Why I Am a Communist," *New Masses* (September 1932): 9.

76. This was the conclusion of the last of his February–March 1946 series of *Daily Worker* columns concerning Albert Maltz, which are reprinted in Folsom, *Mike Gold*, pp. 283–91.

77. "Horace Liveright and a Novel," unpublished manuscript, Gold Papers.

78. Maltz to Kenneth Payne, 18 Apr. 1972, Gold Papers.

79. Gold to Sinclair, marked "Early fall 1936," Sinclair Papers.

80. Wald interview with Garlin, Boulder, Colo., May 1990.

81. Gold to Walter Lowenfels, 12 July 1955, Lowenfels Papers, Yale University.

82. The poem first appeared in the *Liberator* in June 1924 and was reprinted many times (sometimes with "A Strange" changed to "The Strange"), and was set to music on several occasions, including one version composed by Aaron Copeland.

83. These three poems are reprinted in *Social Poetry of the 1930s*, ed. Jack Salzman and Leo Zanderer (New York: Burt Franklin Co., 1978), pp. 88–96.

84. Michael Gold, *Charlie Chaplin's Parade* (New York: Harcourt, Brace and Co., 1930), p. 26.

85. See the discussion in Aaron, *Writers on the Left*, pp. 237–43. Gold also referred to Jean Cocteau as a "feeble fairy" in "Six Open Letters," *New Masses* (September 1931): 3. For a critical survey of Gold's various statements on Whitman, see Richard Tuerk, "Mike Gold on Walt Whitman," *Walt Whitman Quarterly Review* 3 (Spring 1986): 16–23.

86. Gold, "Ode to Walt Whitman," *New Masses* (5 Nov. 1935): 21.

87. Letter to the *Daily Worker*, 1953, Lowenfels Papers.

88. Stanley Burnshaw to Wald, 10 Dec. 1990, in possession of Wald.

89. Wald interview with Nathan Adler, Mill Valley, Calif., September 1989.

90. Lester Rodney to Wald, 6 Aug. 1991, in possession of Wald.

91. Ibid., 30 May 1991.

92. Notes from Freedom of Information Act Files on Mike Gold, FBI Reading Room, Washington, D.C., July 1990.

93. Wald interview with Nicholas Granich, 16 Dec. 1992, San Francisco.

94. Notes from Freedom of Information Act Files.

95. Bernard Smith, *A World Remembered* (Atlantic Highlands, N.J.: Humanities Press, 1994), p. 21.

96. Aaron Kramer to Wald, 22 Feb. 1991, in possession of Wald.

97. Edward Dahlberg, *The Confessions of Edward Dahlberg* (New York: George Brazillier, 1971), p. 257.

98. Charles Yale Harrison, James T. Farrell, and S. J. Perelman also wrote fiction that employed Gold-like figures.

99. This identification was made by Hazel Rowley in her superbly researched *Christina Stead* (New York: Henry Holt and Company, 1993), p. 193. Rowley also points out that Gold's shipboard romance with his wife-to-be was reworked into the beginning of her novel, *I'm Dying Laughing* (1986).

100. Josephine Herbst to Genevieve Taggard, n.d., New York Public Library. In the late 1920s, Gold also had a significant relationship with Natalie Gomez, formerly the wife of Manny Gomez. See Joseph Freeman to Daniel Aaron, 6 June 1958, p. 8, Freeman Papers, Hoover Institute.

101. According to Nora Sayre, *Previous Convictions: A Journey through the 1950s* (New Brunswick, N.J.: Rutgers University Press, 1995), p. 349, "Black wouldn't marry him [Gold] because marriage was a bourgeois institution which might hamper him as an artist."

102. Irving Howe and Lewis Coser, *The American Communist Party: A Critical History* (Boston: Beacon, 1957), pp. 274–75.

103. Norman MacLeod to Jack Conroy, 2 Mar. 1969, MacLeod Papers, Yale University.

104. Dahlberg, *Confessions*, p. 286.

105. John Kobler, *Otto the Magnificent: The Life of Otto Kahn* (New York: Scribner's, 1988), 176.

106. *Daily Worker*, 29 Oct. 1934, p. 5.

107. Letter from A. B. Magil to Gold, n.d., Gold Papers.

108. Gold interview with Folsom, 11 Aug. 1966, Gold Papers.

109. Michael Folsom made a strong case for Gold's role in promoting the concept in "The Education of Michael Gold," in *Proletarian Writers of the Thirties*, ed. David Madden (Carbondale: Southern Illinois University Press, 1968), pp. 222–51.

110. Freeman to Daniel Aaron, 8 June 1958, p. 1, Freeman Papers.

111. Ibid., p. 7.

112. See Henry Stuart, *New York Times Book Review*, 29 Nov. 1925, pp. 5, 10; Sinclair Lewis, "Manhattan at Last!," *Saturday Review* 2 (5 Dec. 1925): 361; Michael Gold, *New Masses* (August 1926): 25–26; D. H. Lawrence, *Calendar of Modern Letters*,

April 1927, pp. 70–72; and Paul Elmore More, *The Demon of the Absolute* (Princeton, N.J.: Princeton University Press, 1928), p. 63.

113. Mike Gold, "The Education of John Dos Passos," *English Journal* 22 (February 1933): 95–97.

114. Mike Gold, "The Keynote to Dos Passos' Works," *Daily Worker*, 26 Feb. 1938, p. 7.

115. See Howe and Coser, *The American Communist Party*, p. 308.

116. *Daily Worker*, January 14, 1944, p. 6.

117. Gold to E. S. Wood and S. B. Field, n.d., Huntington Library.

118. Freeman to Aaron, July 5, 1958, p. 3, Freeman Papers.

119. Original in John Howard Lawson Papers, Southern Illinois University, Carbondale, Ill.

120. See Oral History of Albert Maltz, Oral History Collection, UCLA, p. 455.

121. Maltz to Kenneth Payne, 18 Apr. 1972, Gold Papers.

122. Nelson Algren to Richard Wright, 20 Mar. (year unknown), Wright Papers, Yale University.

123. Mike Gold, "Change the World," *Daily Worker*, 29 May 1944, p. 7.

124. "Eugene O'Neill's Early Days," *Daily Worker*, 26 Oct. 1946, p. 8.

125. Wright's biographer, however, believes that Gold hesitated in his ultimate pronouncement in order to get a sense of the Party leadership's final attitude. See Michel Fabre, *The Unfinished Quest of Richard Wright* (Urbana and Chicago: University of Illinois Press, 1993), pp. 184–85.

126. Lowenfels to Joseph North, n.d., Lowenfels Papers.

127. A discussion of the relationship of Gold to Amado appears in Thomas Colchie, "Jorge Amado: The Life of a Latin American Literary Giant Parallels the Story of a Tumultuous Century," *Washington Post Book World*, Sunday, 26 August 2001, p. 5. Freeman affirmed this judgment in a 3 July 1958 letter to Daniel Aaron, Freeman Papers, despite the fact that he and Gold had parted ways nearly two decades earlier.

## Chapter 3

1. Stanley Burnshaw, "Stevens' 'Mr. Burnshaw and the Statue,'" in *A Stanley Burnshaw Reader* (Athens: University of Georgia Press, 1990), p. 26. This originally appeared as "Wallace Stevens and the Statue," *Sewanee Review* 69 (Summer 1961): 355–66.

2. Horace Gregory to T. C. Wilson, 14 Nov. 1939, Gregory Papers, Syracuse University.

3. This notion of "elective affinity" is most fully elaborated in Michael Löwy, *Redemption and Utopia: Jewish Libertarian Thought in Central Europe* (Stanford, Calif.: Stanford University Press), 1988, p. 613.

4. The concept of the "force field" is refined in Pierre Bourdieu, *The Field of*

Cultural Production (New York: Columbia University Press, 1993), especially pp. 192–96. See also Richard Jenkins, Pierre Bourdieu (London: Routledge, 1992), pp. 84–91. George Hutchinson employs the concept of "force field" in relation to the Harlem Renaissance in The Harlem Renaissance in Black and White (Cambridge, Mass.: Harvard University Press, 1995), pp. 4–7.

5. See, for example, the extremely detailed and highly critical "Review of the New Masses" by Anne Elistrova, International Literature, no. 1 (1932): 107–14.

6. Freeman to Floyd Dell, 13 Apr. 1952, p. 12, Dell Papers, Newberry Library.

7. Barbara Foley presents an overview of this topic in "Soviet Influences on American Literary Radicalism" in Radical Representations: Politics and Form in U.S. Proletarian Fiction (Durham, N.C.: Duke University Press, 1993), pp. 63–85. In "The Wager of Benedict Bulmanis," the introduction to Phillip Bonosky's book Burning Valley (Urbana and Chicago: University of Illinois Press, 1997), pp. xiii–xiv, I discuss the influence of Soviet models on this U.S. Communist novelist.

8. The remark by Whitman was quoted in an article by Horace Traubel in Seven Arts 2 (September 1917): 35, and is cited in Daniel Aaron, Writers on the Left (New York: Harcourt, Brace and World, 1961), p. 7.

9. Joseph Freeman to Daniel Aaron, 17 June 1958.

10. In his "Theses on the Philosophy of History," Illuminations (New York: Schocken, 1969), p. 257, Benjamin writes: "The tradition of the oppressed teaches us that the 'state of emergency' in which we live is not the exception but the rule. We must attain to a conception of history that is in keeping with this insight."

11. Burnshaw, "Stevens' 'Mr. Burnshaw and the Statue,'" p. 24.

12. Moshe Nadir, "Poetry Out of Season," New Masses (18 June 1935): 25–26. Gregory could be a harsh critic from a Marxist perspective as well, but his analyses were usually more historical in framework and his argumentation more learned and subtle. See his review of work by Robinson Jeffers and Eugene O'Neill, "Suicide in the Jungle," New Masses (13 Feb. 1934): 18–19.

13. Much of this activity was monitored by the FBI, and I am grateful to Franklin Folsom for making available to me FBI files on the League of American Writers, which were first obtained by the historian Harvey Klehr. Files on numerous individuals associated with many of these Left literary organizations are discussed in studies such as Herbert Mitgang, Dangerous Dossiers (New York: Ballantine, 1989); and Natalie Robbins, Alien Ink: The FBI's War on Freedom of Expression (New York: William Morrow, 1992).

14. Max Eastman used that phrase as the title of his powerful indictment of Soviet cultural policy and practice under Stalin, Artists in Uniform: A Study of Literature and Bureaucratism (New York: Knopf, 1934). Subsequently the expression was sometimes used to attack the Communist cultural movement in the United States for an analogous enforced conformity.

15. The phrase "Communist-led" is meant as a generic term only to indicate

that Party supporters were centrally involved in establishing and maintaining the institution or publication under discussion. The degree of domination by such individuals as well as the extent to which collaboration with Party officials occurred varied considerably, and will be examined in several particular cases. The term "front group" is avoided because it typically implies consistent cynical manipulation and top-down control.

16. Moreover, the American Committee for Cultural Freedom (ACCF) did not significantly support human rights and free expression in the United States; whatever the virtues of its publicity about the repression of intellectual freedom in Soviet-bloc countries, its domestic role was to mobilize liberal arguments for maintaining the antiradical repression of the McCarthy era. One motivation for ex-radicals to join the ACCF was to get a clean bill of health; some who did this were disillusioned by the deceptiveness of the organization's leaders, at least one of whom was a CIA operative, and the hypocrisy of its domestic policy. See my review of some of the internal ACCF debates in *The New York Intellectuals: The Rise and Decline of the Anti-Stalinist Left from the 1930s to the 1980s* (Chapel Hill: University of North Carolina Press, 1987), pp. 270–80. A more comprehensive study of the activities of the CIA in this arena is Frances Stonor Saunders, *The Cultural Cold War: The CIA and the World of Arts and Letters* (New York: Free Press, 1999). For a sympathetic account of the ACCF, which lauds its refusal to defend the Martinsville Seven and other McCarthy-era civil rights victims, see the chapter "The 'Obnoxious' Americans" in Peter Coleman, *The Liberal Conspiracy: The Congress for Cultural Freedom and the Struggle for the Mind of Postwar Europe* (New York: Free Press, 1989), pp. 159–70.

17. Stanley Burnshaw reported to Granville Hicks on 5 July 1934 that an essay by E. A. Schachner in the spring 1934 *Windsor Quarterly* had even been examined by a representative of the Communist International. See Hicks Papers, Syracuse University. For Stevens, see Alan Filreis, *Modernism from Left to Right: Wallace Stevens, the Thirties and Literary Radicalism* (New York: Cambridge University Press, 1994); and Harvey Teres, "Notes toward the Supreme Soviet: Stevens and Doctrinaire Marxism," *Wallace Stevens Journal* 13, no. 2 (Fall 1989): 150–67.

18. In the early 1940s, for example, Langston Hughes was publicly denounced in an article in the Communist Party's *People's World*, even as he was strongly endorsed by Black Party leader William Patterson. See Arnold Rampersad, *The Life of Langston Hughes, Volume II: 1941–1967* (New York: Oxford University Press, 1998), pp. 5, 439.

19. See the informative discussion on this subject in Leah Levenson and Jerry Natterstad, *Granville Hicks: The Intellectual in Mass Society* (Philadelphia: Temple University Press, 1993), particularly on Hicks's refusal to alter his negative assessment of a novel by Albert Halper at the urging of *New Masses* managing editor Herman Michelson (p. 95), or to change sections of his biography of John Reed, at the suggestion of Earl Browder (p. 74).

20. Anne Elistrova criticizes the work of several leading Communist writers, including a piece by Gold as "light-weight," in her "Review of the *New Masses.*"

21. See the remarkable "Author's Field Day: A Symposium on Marxist Criticism," *New Masses* (3 July 1934): 27–32. In the 1940s, however, there were several instances where favorable reviews of novels were reversed in subsequent statements by the reviewers. Then, in the McCarthy era, writers who wished to illustrate anti-Communist credentials, or plead that they had been victimized by the Party, would cite hostile reviews of their literary work as evidence of official persecution. See, for example, the testimony of novelist Budd Schulberg in Eric Bentley, ed., *Thirty Years of Treason* (New York: Viking, 1971), pp. 434–57. Schulberg describes the shift in assessment of his work that appeared in *People's World.*

22. An important example is the declaration of the 1931 conference of the Workers Cultural Federation, which embraced all 130 Party-led organizations in the cultural field (allegedly representing 20,000 members). The "Program," published in *New Masses* (August 1931): 11–13, under the title "Art Is a Weapon!," cited statements by Stalin on culture as well as the resolutions of the Kharkov conference.

23. The poet Orrick Johns (1887–1946) gave the following description of *New Masses* editorial procedure during his tenure on the board in 1934: "Editorial authority was democratic. There was no arbitrary head, though Herman Michelson, former Sunday editor of the New York *World*, was our copy pusher and deadline boss. Once a week four or five of us spent the night at the printer's. It meant hard work every day including Sunday. I read more than 200 short stories a month, and double that amount of poems. The poems were all too much alike, factual material presented in realistic free verse, and few had much relation to poetry, but they showed an earnest search for vital themes. All these contributors required a personal reply, and some sort of criticism. Besides this work we wrote leaders, editorial paragraphs and special articles. The Central Committee of the Communist Party had its say in questions of policy, and even of specific pieces. The C.C. was usually represented by Joe North, whose style of reportage in reporting strikes became popular with our readers." See Orrick Johns, *Time of Our Lives: The Story of My Father and Myself* (New York: Stackpole Sons, 1937), p. 340.

24. The most substantial biographical account of Trachtenberg is Sender Garlin, "Publisher on Trial: The Lifework of Alexander Trachtenberg," *Masses & Mainstream* 5, no. 10 (October 1952): 17–27. Much of this information is repeated in the entry on "International Publishers Company" in *Dictionary of Literary Biography*, vol. 46: *American Literary Publishing Houses, 1900–1980* (Detroit: Gale, 1990), 196–98. See also the two obituaries, "A Tribune of the Printed Word," *Political Affairs* 46, no. 1 (January 1967): 13–14; and Robert W. Dunn, "Waiting for Trachty," *New World Review* 35, no. 2 (February 1967): 23–25. Some of this por-

trait is also based on the biographical sketch prepared by S. Luttrell for the descriptive inventory of the Trachtenberg Papers at the State Historical Society of Wisconsin.

25. Theodore Draper, *The Roots of American Communism* (New York: Viking, 1957), pp. 98–99.

26. In *The Soviet World of American Communism* (New Haven, Conn.: Yale University Press, 1998), p. 141, Harvey Klehr, John Earl Haynes, and Kyrill M. Anderson assert that Trachtenberg began receiving Soviet subsidies to assist publications in the early 1930s, although they provide no information as to the amount. In 1923, Trachtenberg had been elected a member of the Executive Committee of the Communist International.

27. Joseph North, *No Men Are Strangers* (New York: International Publishers, 1958), p. 102. The incident is discussed in Aaron's *Writers on the Left.* pp. 276–78, but neither Trachtenberg nor North is mentioned. Aaron reports that Dreiser at no time made a convincing retraction and was never called to account by the Party. North, however, writes that Dreiser made a satisfactory retraction of his statement. Communist writer Walter Snow claims that Dreiser was nevertheless punished for this indiscretion by not being proposed as chair of the League of American Writers in 1937. Instead, Donald Ogden Stewart was elected, and Dreiser refused to join the league. The record would seem to confirm this, since it indicates that Dreiser signed the calls issued by the American Writers' Congress only in 1935 and in 1941, and that he was elected honorary president only in 1941, during the last weeks of the Hitler-Stalin Pact. Snow to Maurice Isserman, 26 Oct. 1972, p. 2, Snow Papers, University of Connecticut.

28. Eric Homberger reviews some of the controversies wracking the clubs in *American Writers and Radical Politics, 1930–39: Equivocal Commitments* (New York: St. Martin's, 1986), pp. 119–40; as does Judy Kutulas in *The Long War: The Intellectual People's Front and Anti-Stalinism, 1930–1940* (Durham, N.C.: Duke University Press, 1995), pp. 52–58.

29. Aaron, *Writers on the Left*, pp. 281–82. In *Radical Representations*, p. 79, Barbara Foley argues that this development, culminating in the 1935 American Writers' Congress, should not be interpreted as an early turn to the Popular Front prompted by Moscow. Rather, it remained within the framework of the Kharkov Conference orientation, which was designed to win Left-leaning writers to Communism, and reflected a "mellowing" of the cultural Left from its earlier prescriptive excesses.

30. Quoted in "A Tribune of the Printed Word," *Political Affairs* 46, no. 1 (January 1967): 13.

31. Draft of memoir by Walter Snow, "That Literary 'Shotgun Marriage,'" p. 5, Snow Papers.

32. Matthew Josephson, *Infidel in the Temple* (New York: Knopf, 1967), p. 364.

33. Wald interview with Franklin Folsom, Boulder, Colo., May 1989.

34. Walter Snow to Jack Conroy, 12 Nov. 1971, Snow Papers.

35. Wald interview with Sender Garlin, Boulder, Colo., May 1989.

36. Freeman to Daniel Aaron, 1 July 1958, p. 10, Daniel Aaron Papers, Cambridge, Mass.

37. Wald interview with A. B. Magil, November 1990, New York City.

38. For the latter, see "Appendix: Bibliography of Radical Children's Books in the United States Published in English," in Paul Mishler, "The Littlest Proletariat," Ph.D. diss., Boston University, 1988, pp. 213–22.

39. Draft of memoir by Walter Snow, "That Literary 'Shotgun Marriage,'" Snow Papers, p. 5. Other examples of Trachtenberg's authority are given in Franklin Folsom, *Days of Anger, Days of Hope* (Niwot: University Press of Colorado, 1994), pp. 96–97. Folsom believed that, despite Trachtenberg's organizational talents, he showed poor judgment in dismissing the proposal that the Book Find Club, an organization that aimed to make inexpensive copies of radical books available to subscribers, become a project of the League of American Writers; forced to strike out on its own, the club turned out to be a major success.

40. Calmer was an extremely active participant in the Communist Cultural Left throughout the 1930s – a prolific author of essays and an activist in the John Reed Clubs and International Publishers – but he suddenly departed the movement in 1939. Originally from Baltimore, where he wrote as a critic, journalist, and aspiring author of hard-boiled novels, Calmer was associated with V. F. Calverton, but repudiated Calverton to side with the Communist Party in the early 1930s. For a brief period in the mid-1930s, he seemed to share the developing critique of the predominant Communist literary practice held by *Partisan Review* editors William Phillips and Philip Rahv, but he pulled back from their trajectory toward Trotskyism. After returning to Baltimore, he supported himself by working in his father's business and attempted to write a literary history of the early Republic. Wald telephone interview with Edward Newhouse, May 2000.

41. *Partisan Review* editor William Phillips does not refer to any proposal to affiliate with the league in his memoir *A Partisan View: Five Decades of the Literary Life* (New York: Stein and Day, 1983). He claims that the Communist Party tried to steal the magazine away from him and Philip Rahv by having Calmer put out an issue on his own, but that Calmer refused to do so.

42. Snow to Jack Conroy, 5 June 1973, Snow Papers. The same correspondence between Calmer and Freeman, treating a similar situation, shows Trachtenberg more as a strong-willed person around whom one had to maneuver. This dispute concerned the question of possibly fusing *Partisan Review* with the poetry magazine *Dynamo*, edited by Communists but lacking any official sponsorship. Calmer indicated that *Dynamo* editor Sol Funaroff's personal assent was necessary for such a fusion, even though Trachtenberg and the *Partisan* editors were all for the unification. However, Calmer expressed the view that, if Funaroff

opposed the merger, "the movement is not going to allow one person (Sol) to run the magazine as he has in the past." Moreover, Calmer conjectured, "I also know that if the two magazines continue separately, that the movement (thru Trachty) will push PR and continue to neglect *Dynamo* completely. . . ." Finally, Calmer noted that should the merger occur, Trachtenberg would oppose the addition of Nathan Adler, perceived as a troublemaker, to the editorial board. Calmer still thought the fusion could be finessed so that Adler would be involved. He felt that Adler was necessary to his (Calmer's) vision of a magazine "edited collectively by the eight or nine young Communist writers who had grown up in the movement." The failure of *Dynamo* and *Partisan Review* to fuse suggests that Trachtenberg had tremendous prestige and influence, but was not merely a dictator whose every command was obeyed by writers. Letter from Alan Calmer to Freeman, probably September 1935, Freeman Papers, Hoover Institute.

43. See Albert Kahn, *The Matusow Affair: Memoir of a National Scandal* (Mt. Kisco, N.Y.: Moyer Bell Limited, 1987).

44. See the superb study by Mark Solomon, *The Cry Was Unity: Communists and African Americans, 1917–1936* (Jackson: University Press of Mississippi, 1998). Also see the assessment by Wald, "African Americans, Culture and Communism," *Against the Current* 84 (January–February 2000): 23–29, and "The Black Cultural Front," *Against the Current* 86 (May–June 2000): 27–34.

45. During and after the Cold War, the term "cosmopolitan intellectual," along with associated notions such as "universalism," became transformed into terms associated with Eurocentric elite perspectives, especially as expressed through the evolution of the group that became known as "The New York Intellectuals." For a discussion of the "cosmopolitan ideal" as it operated among radicalizing young Jewish intellectuals, see my chapter "Jewish Internationalists" in *The New York Intellectuals: The Rise and Decline of the Anti-Stalinist Left from the 1930s to the 1980s* (Chapel Hill: University of North Carolina Press, 1987), pp. 27–45. For a recent discussion of African American intellectuals in relation to cosmopolitanism, see Ross Posnick, *Color and Culture: Black Writers and the Making of the Modern Intellectual* (Cambridge, Mass.: Harvard University Press, 1998).

46. One can also include the shorter reviews, poems, and sketches in pro-Communist newspapers in the South, such as the *Southern Worker* and *Cavalcade*, as well as publications of the League of Struggle for Negro Rights and the National Negro Congress, the *Daily Worker*, *People's World* (originally *Western Worker*) and even some contributions to Adam Clayton Powell Jr.'s *People's Voice* and the Left-liberal New York daily newspaper PM.

47. See Tyrone Tillery, *Claude McKay: A Black Poet's Struggle for Identity* (Amherst: University of Massachusetts Press, 1992), 58, 59; Geta LeSeur, "Claude McKay's Marxism," in *The Harlem Renaissance: Revaluations*, ed. Amritjit Singh et al. (New York: Garland, 1989), pp. 219–31; Claude McKay, *A Long Way from Home* (New York:

Harcourt, Brace and World, 1970), pp. 40–42; Claude McKay to Max Eastman, 19 Dec. 1932, McKay Papers, Indiana University. For a fascinating interpretation of McKay's writings about Marxism and African Americans, see William J. Maxwell, *New Negro, Old Left: African-American Writing and Communism between the Wars* (New York: Columbia University Press, 1999), pp. 63–94.

48. It was finally translated by Robert Winter and published as *Negroes in America* (Port Washington, N.Y.: Kennikat Press, 1972).

49. Wayne Cooper, *Claude McKay: Rebel Sojourner in the Harlem Renaissance* (Baton Rouge: Louisiana State University Press, 1987), pp. 329–30.

50. Alain Locke, "Spiritual Truancy," *New Challenge* 2, no. 2 (Fall 1937): 81–85.

51. Houston Baker makes a case for a more substantial connection of Cullen to the Black Aesthetic in *Afro-American Poetics* (Madison: University of Wisconsin Press, 1988), pp. 45–87.

52. See "In Memory of Eugene Gordon," *Political Affairs* 53, no. 4 (April 1974): 2. There is a small collection of his papers at the Schomburg Library in Harlem.

53. George S. Schuyler, "Views and Reviews," *Pittsburgh Courier*, 20 Mar. 1937, pp. 11, 15; *Opportunity* 11 (December 1933): 429.

54. Eugene Gordon, "Agenda," *Opportunity* 11, no. 12 (December 1933): 372–74, and 12, no. 1 (January 1934): 18–22.

55. *International Literature* 1, no. 7 (April 1934): 4.

56. "Jean Toomer: Apostle of Beauty," *Opportunity* 10, no. 8 (October 1932): 252–54.

57. Letter from Holmes to Hicks, 18 Jan. 1935, Hicks Papers.

58. John H. McClendon, "Dr. Holmes, the Philosophical Rebel," *Freedomways* 22, no. 1 (Winter 1983): 32–40.

59. See "The Main Philosphical Considerations of Space and Time," *American Journal of Physics* 18, no. 9 (December 1950). See also the work by Holmes's student Percy E. Johnston, *Phenomenology of Space and Time: An Examination of Eugene Clay Holmes' Studies in the Philosophy of Time and Space* (New York: Dasein Literary Society, 1976).

60. See the following essays by Holmes in *Freedomways*: "The Legacy of Alain Locke," 3, no. 3 (Summer 1963): 293–306; "W. E. B. Du Bois – Philosopher," 5, no. 1 (Winter 1965): 41–46.

61. J.R.C. *Bulletin* 1, no. 2 (April–May 1934): 9–10.

62. See the excellent discussion in "Afric's Sons with Banner Red" by Robin D. G. Kelley, in his collection of essays, *Race Rebels: Culture, Politics and the Black Working Class* (New York: The Free Press, 1994), pp. 103–21.

63. See Mark Naison, *Communists in Harlem during the Depression* (Urbana: University of Illinois Press, 1983), p. 68.

64. William L. Patterson, "Awake Negro Poets," *New Masses* (October 1928): 10.

65. Akiba Sullivan Harper, ed., *Langston Hughes: Short Stories* (New York: Hill and Wang, 1998), pp. 72–80.

66. For a meticulous chronicle of Hughes's relations with the Communist Party in this decade, see Rampersad, *The Life of Langston Hughes*, vol. 2.

67. Langston Hughes to Sterling Brown, 13 Oct. 1931, Brown Papers, Howard University.

68. Michael Gold, "Introduction," *A New Song* (New York: IWO, 1938), p. 8.

69. Hughes, "Let America Be America Again," in ibid., pp. 9–11.

70. For a discussion of Hughes's revisions of this poem during the Cold War, see Robert Shulman, *The Power of Political Art: The 1930s Literary Left Reconsidered* (Chapel Hill: University of North Carolina Press, 2000), pp. 302–3.

71. Brown recalls that Hughes regarded him as a Communist incapable of betrayal, but harbored a grudge against white Communists in Hollywood who had failed to introduce him into the business. Wald interview with Lloyd Brown, October 1990, New York City. See also Christopher C. De Santis, ed., *Langston Hughes and the Chicago Defender* (Urbana and Chicago: University of Illinois Press, 1995).

72. See the discussion of this episode in Faith Berry, *Langston Hughes: A Biography* (New York: Citadel, 1992), pp. 317–20.

73. Herbert Aptheker, ed., *The Correspondence of W. E. B. Du Bois*, vol. 3 (Amherst: University of Massachusetts Press, 1978), p. 387; Maxim Lieber to Josephine Herbst, 8 May 1953, Herbst Papers, Yale University.

74. Wald interview with Brown, New York City, October 1990; interview with Tiba Willner, Ojai, Calif., August 1989.

75. Langston Hughes to Charles Humboldt, c. 1958, Humboldt Papers, Yale University.

76. The definitive biography of Richard Wright to date is Michel Fabre, *The Unfinished Quest of Richard Wright*, 2d ed. (Urbana and Chicago: University of Illinois Press, 1993).

77. Abe Aaron to Jack Conroy, 13 Jan. 1934, Jack Conroy Papers, Newberry Library.

78. In a letter of 2 April 1938, Margaret Walker mentions Hughes's new name for Wright, and a month later, on 9 May 1938, she notes the resemblance of characters in "Bright and Morning Star" to those in Gorky's novel, *The Mother*. See Wright Papers. In his essay, Gold had argued: "In the last three years a great drift among thoughtful Negro workers and farmers has set in towards the Communist theory. These Negroes understand there is no hope in the bourgeois Uncle Toms who want everything to stand still, or to be done by lawyer-like diplomacy." Nancy Cunard, *Negro: An Anthology* (New York: Ungar, 1970; orig. 1933), p. 136. The arc of action in Wright's four, later five, novellas moves precisely in that direction.

79. See the 1937 correspondence between Farrell and Wright, Wright Papers. Among other things, Farrell prophetically warned Wright that a disadvantage

to his affiliation with the Communist Party was that he would be obligated to defend sudden and unanticipated shifts in policy that might interfere with the integrity of his creative work.

80. Richard Wright, "Not My People's War," *New Masses* (17 June 1941): 9.

81. Horace Cayton, *Long Old Road: An Autobiography* (Seattle: University of Washington Press, 1963), pp. 248–49. Ralph Ellison wrote Wright, who had left for Mexico, about attacks on the novel by Black Party leaders such as Abner Berry and Theodore Bassett, and its defense by the Jewish Communist Sender Garlin. Ellison's view was that Wright's Black Marxist critics were insufficiently "emancipated from bourgeois taboos." Ralph Ellison to Richard Wright, 14 Apr. 1940, Wright Papers.

82. See Gold's "Change the World" column in the *Sunday Worker*, 31 Mar. 1940, section 2, p. 7. See also the review of *Native Son* by Ben Burns (pseud. for Benjamin Bernstein), *People's World*, 2 Apr. 1940, p. 5. See also the range of responses to *Native Son* by Samuel Sillen, Chester Himes, Ben Davis, James Ford, Earl Browder, and others in *New Masses* between 23 April and 21 May 1941.

83. See Samuel Sillen, "Bigger Thomas on the Boards," *New Masses* (8 Apr. 1941): 27–28; and "12 Million Black Voices," *New Masses* (25 Nov. 1941): 22–24.

84. Samuel Sillen to Richard Wright, 7 May 1940, Wright Papers.

85. Sillen to Wright, 1 June 1940, Wright Papers.

86. Richard Wright to Ralph Ellison, 14 Apr. 1940, Wright Papers; Richard Wright to Lillian Gilkes, 30 Apr. 1940, Gilkes Papers, Syracuse University.

87. Melvin B. Tolson to Richard Wright, undated (probably 1938), Wright Papers.

88. Wright, "I Tried to Be a Communist," *Atlantic Monthly* 174 (August 1944): 61–70; and ibid. 174 (September 1944): 48–56. This essay became a classic of anti-Communist literature, later anthologized in Richard Crossman, ed., *The God That Failed* (New York: Bantam, 1965; orig. 1956). However, in *Richard Wright: Daemonic Genius* (New York: Warner Books, 1988), Margaret Walker disputes a number of Wright's claims, such as one at the climax of his memoir where he says that he was ejected from a May Day demonstration by Communist Party members.

89. James Ford, "A Disservice to the Negro People," *Daily Worker*, 5 Sept. 1944, p. 6.

90. Undated manuscript, Wright Papers.

91. One of his biographers concludes that he probably gave information about Communists in the United States in order to retain his passport. See James Campbell, *Exiled in Paris* (New York: Scribner, 1995), pp. 189–97.

92. His body was instantly cremated, without the consent of his family, so the exact cause of death was never verified. See Michel Fabre, *The Unfinished Quest of Richard Wright*, pp. 521–31.

93. Biographical information on Ward can be found in the entry by Faha-misha Patricia Brown, "Theodore Ward," *Dictionary of Literary Biography*, 76:182–76. He is also discussed in Doris Abramson, *Negro Playwrights in the American Theater, 1925–1959* (New York: Columbia University Press, 1969) and Rena Fraden, *Blueprints for a Black Federal Theater, 1935–1939* (New York: Cambridge University Press, 1994). I am especially grateful to Keneth Kinnamon for sharing a ten-page answer by Ward to inquiries sent to him on 4 April 1965.

94. The most detailed survey of Hayden's radical period can be found in Robert Chrisman, "Robert Hayden: Modernism and the Afro-American Epic Mission," Ph.D. diss., University of Michigan, 1999. Additional information comes from Wald interview with Robert Hayden, December 1976, Ann Arbor, Mich.

95. Interview with Hy Fireman, Detroit, November 1990. See also Paul Sporn, *Against Itself: The Federal Theater and Writers' Projects in the Midwest* (Detroit, Mich.: Wayne State University Press, 1995), p. 153.

96. "Brief Reviews," *New Masses* (21 Jan. 1941): 26.

97. See my "Belief and Ideology in the Work of Robert Hayden," in Wald, *Writing from the Left* (London: Verso, 1994), pp. 192–98.

98. The crucial study of the genre is Paula Rabinowitz, *Labor and Desire: Women's Revolutionary Fiction in Depression America* (Chapel Hill: University of North Carolina Press, 1991). See also Laura Hapke, *Women, Work and Fiction in the American 1930s* (Athens: University of Georgia Press, 1995).

99. Mary Ann Rasmussen, "Introduction," in Josephine Herbst, *Pity Is Not Enough* (Urbana and Chicago: University of Illinois Press, 1998), p. ix.

100. Janet Sharistanian, "Afterword," in Tess Slesinger, *The Unpossessed* (Old Westbury, N.Y.: Feminist Press, 1984), p. 381.

101. *People's Weekly World*, 21 Dec. 1996, p. 20.

102. *New York Times*, 24 Nov. 1996, p. 21.

103. *Nation*, 17 Feb. 1997, p. 34.

104. See the valuable collection of appreciations in *People's Culture*, n.s. 34 (1996).

105. This is reprinted in Le Sueur, *Ripening* (New York: Feminist Press, 1982), pp. 76–84.

106. The most helpful discussion of this phase of Le Sueur's writing is still Elaine Hedge's "Introduction" to *Ripening*, pp. 1–28.

107. "I Was Marching" was reprinted in *Ripening*, pp. 158–65.

108. "The Fetish of Being Outside," *New Masses* (26 Feb. 1935): 22–23.

109. See Constance Coiner, *Being Red* (New York: Oxford University Press, 1995), p. 94.

110. This has been reprinted as "Proletarian Literature and the Middle West," *Harvest Song: Collected Essays and Stories* (Albuquerque, N.Mex.: West End Press, 1990), pp. 204–7.

111. Alfred Knopf, the New York publisher with Left-wing sympathies, published more than half of these: *Chanticleer of Wilderness Road: A Story of Davy Crockett* (1951); *Little Brother of the Wilderness: The Story of Johnny Appleseed* (1947); *Nancy Hanks of Wilderness Road* (1949); *The River Road: A Story of Abraham Lincoln* (1954); and *Sparrow Hawk* (1950).

112. For a fuller discussion of scholarship about Le Sueur, see Wald, "The Many Lives of Meridel Le Sueur," *Monthly Review* 49, no. 4 (September 1997): 41–44.

113. Linda Ray Pratt, "Woman Writer in the CP," *Women's Studies* 14, no. 3 (February 1988): 247.

114. Ibid., p. 257.

115. Ibid., p. 258.

116. For example, see the cartoons in *New Masses* (16 Oct. 1934): 7, and ibid. (13 Nov. 1934): 7.

117. The most forceful example of the equation of successful writing with the male work experience can be found in Mike Gold's manifesto of "proletarian realism" in "Notes of the Month," *New Masses* (September 1930): 3–5.

118. The Proletarian Party was founded in 1920 after its members, formerly the leaders of the Michigan Socialist Party, refused to accept the underground orientation of the early Communist movement. It lasted until 1971 and produced a number of important leaders of the United Auto Workers, such as Emil Mazey and Frank Marquart.

119. H. H. Lewis, "The Man from Moscow," in *Thinking of Russia* (Holt, Minn.: B. B. Hanglund, 1932), p. 19.

120. Michael Gold, "The East Side I Knew," *Jewish Life* 9, no. 1 (November 1954): 27.

121. "A Communist Speaks at Faneuil Hall," *Red Boston* 1, no. 1 (September 1932): 8.

122. See Robert Shaffer, "Women and the Communist Party," *Socialist Review* 45 (May/June 1979): 105. In artistic circles, non-monogamous and bohemian sexual relations were more widely accepted, as well as a "don't ask, don't tell" posture toward homosexuality. However, one inveterate Bohemian Communist, Viola Brothers Shore, told her daughter that she married her third husband only because of Communist Party pressure, while gay Communist Harry Hay, recruited to the movement by another gay Communist, actor Will Geer, married and started a family due to pressure to present himself as a model Communist Party member. Wald interview with Wilma Shore, New York City, November 1992; see Harry Hay, *The Trouble with Harry Hay* (Boston: Alyson Publications, 1990), p. 97.

## Chapter 4

1. Carmon's literary credentials for the job were minimal, although he had a reputation for being self-sacrificing and sociable. He was a longtime radical out of the Midwest, was once a pitcher for the Cleveland Indians, and had spent time in Mexico with Mike Gold during World War I. Subsequent to leaving the *New Masses*, he went to the USSR from 1932 to 1936, where he was offered a job editing the English-language edition of the publication *International Literature*. After returning to the United States, he had some employment as a representative for Soviet publishing houses and then lived in obscurity with his wife, Rose, working as a bookkeeper in New Jersey at the time of his death. Information on Carmon is primarily based on notes from Rose Carmon's 25 April 1969 interview with William Reuben, Labadie Collection, University of Michigan. There are also passing references to Carmon in a number of books such as Douglas Wixson, *Worker-Writer in America* (Urbana and Chicago: University of Illinois Press, 1994), and Charles Shipman, *It Had to Be Revolution* (Ithaca, N.Y.: Cornell University Press, 1998).

2. See Wixson, *Worker-Writer in America*, p. 271.

3. Information on MacLeod is based on my correspondence with him from 1976 to 1985; the MacLeod Papers at Yale University (including an autobiographical manuscript, "Generation of Anger"); and notes from his 28 July 1969 interview with William Reuben, Labadie Collection, University of Michigan.

4. See my discussion of MacLeod's poetry in "Tethered to the Past," in *The Responsibility of Intellectuals: Selected Essays on Marxist Traditions in Cultural Commitment* (Atlantic Highlands, N.J.: Humanities Press, 1992), pp. 102–7.

5. For reactions to Chambers's writing, and a detailed review of Chambers's associations with the literary Left, see Sam Tannenhaus, *Whittaker Chambers* (New York: Random House, 1997).

6. This corresponds to A. B. Magil's recollections in an interview with Wald in New York City in October 1989. Magil believes that, in the early 1930s, Mike Gold didn't come to the *New Masses* office very often, thus it was Walt Carmon who really decided what went into the magazine.

7. Harrison was a leading figure in Left literary circles before that time. He had directed the Party's publicity campaign on behalf of Sacco and Vanzetti, served as a contributing editor of *New Masses*, and was a founder of the John Reed Clubs. A letter from Walter Snow to Jack Conroy on 24 January 1933 (in the Snow Papers, University of Connecticut) remarks on the article in the 23 January issue of the *Daily Worker* about Harrison's expulsion from the John Reed Clubs for protesting the Soviet Union's treatment of Trotsky's daughter. Snow observes that the article's claim that Harrison had driven his own wife to suicide was kind of "raw," but then goes on to make a number of personal charges against Harrison, claiming that he brought prostitutes to his home while his

wife was alive and "was always more or less of a racketeer." Harrison had his revenge when he pilloried Mike Gold and others in the Communist literary Left in his satirical novel Meet Me on the Barricades (1938). Harrison's relations with Trotskyism and his later evolution are described in Wald, The New York Intellectuals: The Rise and Decline of the Anti-Stalinist Left from the 1930s to the 1980s (Chapel Hill: University of North Carolina Press, 1987), p. 152.

8. MacLeod to William Ruben, 9 Apr. 1969, Labadie Collection, University of Michigan.

9. Norman MacLeod interview with William Ruben, 28 Mar. 1969, Labadie Collection, University of Michigan.

10. Rose Carmon interview with William Ruben, 25 Apr. 1969, Labadie Collection, University of Michigan.

11. This summary of the sectarian views in the New York John Reed Club was offered by Sender Garlin in a May 1989 interview with Wald in Boulder, Colorado, and by A. B. Magil in an interview in New York City in November 1990. Both men were at the time sympathetic to many of these criticisms of Gold.

12. At the conference Magil, on behalf of the trio, made a strenuous objection to the way the invitations had been handled. The complaint was referred to the Anglo-American Commission, which acted as if all those involved were loyal comrades, and everything was patched up. Magil stayed an additional seven weeks in Moscow, covering an early treason show trial of engineers for the Daily Worker. He shared a room with Gold, who was more upset about some criticisms that young Party activist Si Gerson had made of him in the Party youth paper than anything else. Magil later saw reports on the conference in International Literature and elsewhere that inaccurately covered the controversy and what he had said. Wald interview with A. B. Magil, New York City, November 1990.

13. Michael Gold, "Notes on Kharkov," New Masses (March 1931): 4–6.

14. Walt Carmon to Walter Snow, 22 April 1930, Snow Papers. The reference is to a review in New Masses (March 1930): 16, by Carlo Tresca of Escape, a novel by Frencesco Fausto Nitti. Since Tresca was an anarchist, Snow's letter of complaint, which has not survived, may have been as much about the reviewer as the content of the book. Carmon's reference to himself and the staff as "anarchists" may be a double entendre as well.

15. New Masses (1 Oct. 1935): 41–42.

16. Burnshaw, A Stanley Burnshaw Reader (Athens: University of Georgia Press, 1990), pp. 31–32.

17. Ibid., p. 22.

18. Ibid., p. 26.

19. Freeman to Daniel Aaron, 1 July 1958, p. 22, Daniel Aaron Papers, Cambridge, Mass. Sergei Mironovich Kirov was a trusted aide of Stalin and secretary of the Communist Party in Leningrad. In 1934 he was assassinated, an event that became the pretext for a purge of dissident Party members and their trials;

among those charged with and executed for the killing were Zinoviev, Kamenev, and Rykov. It is now widely believed that Stalin ordered the assassination himself.

20. Klehr, *The Heyday of American Communism* (New York: Basic Books, 1984), p. 350.

21. The history of disputes involving the *New Masses* that follows is limited to ones among personnel involved in literary matters, primarily poetry and fiction. The *New Masses* is worthy of a book-length study, one that would also give attention to its remarkable graphics and cartoons, its stunning reportage and eye-witness accounts, and its treatment of music, film, dance, drama, and the other arts.

22. Sam Tannenhaus, in his impressively researched *Whittaker Chambers*, p. 75, portrays Chambers's rise on the *New Masses* and in the John Reed Club rather melodramatically. Tannenhaus has Mike Gold, "the *New Masses'* ideological czar," appoint Chambers to "an important job" of ensuring that the magazine's "political message" remained undiluted while it continued to publish famous writers. The interpretation is faithful to Chambers's self-image as a sort of "mole" under Soviet command, but it paints a one-dimensional picture of the cultural movement in which Gold, like many others, was more of a loose cannon than a manipulator of foot soldiers and dupes.

23. Pass, born in Russia, had lived in Seattle, Washington, before coming to New York City in the 1920s. As a youth he had worked as a fireman on a river boat on the Yukon River in Alaska. During World War I he served a prison sentence for refusing to participate in the war and was later active in the 1919 Seattle General Strike. His literary ambitions had been fueled by reading Jack London and Upton Sinclair, but in the 1930s he became a journalist and editor for the International Labor Defense and the League against War and Fascism. Among his many pseudonyms, the one he used most frequently for book reviews was Gilbert Day. In 1932 Pass played a notable role when he was in charge of publicity for the Communist presidential ticket and he drew writers such as Theodore Dreiser, Matthew Josephson, and Robert Sherwood into supporting the campaign. At the end of his life, Pass had completed a book manuscript on Paul Bunyan and was researching a new one on Theodore Dreiser. See "Joseph Pass Dies at 85" in the *Daily World*, 24 May 1978, p. 7; and Art Shields, "Joe Pass, Working-Class Editor," *Daily World*, 5 Oct. 1978, p. 24.

24. North was an influential journalist who pioneered the Left-wing genre of "reportage." See David Peck, "Joseph North and Proletarian Reportage of the 1930s," *Zeitschrift fur Anglistik und Amerikanistik* 1985 33 (3): 210–20.

25. Committee members included William Gropper, Joseph Freeman, Joseph Pass, Walt Carmon, V. J. Jerome, Joseph North and Eugene Shachner; the text of the agreement fills twelve pages. I am grateful to James Lerner for providing me with a copy from his collection of Joseph Pass materials.

26. This is from a 5 August 1937 memo by Freeman, reviewing the earlier dispute; Freeman Papers, Hoover Institute.

27. "Problems of *New Masses*," unpublished manuscript, 1932, p. 4, Freeman Papers.

28. The organization Pen and Hammer was intended mainly for teachers, scientists, and researchers, but it attracted people who might otherwise have been drawn to the *New Masses* and duplicated the forums and publishing activities of the John Reed Clubs. Another organization that engaged in similar activities was the Revolutionary Writers Federation. This formation was supposed to coordinate the work of various writers groups who published in English as well as in foreign languages, but it, too, held debates and forums similar to those staged by the John Reed Clubs.

29. Rose Carmon interview with William Reuben, 25 Apr. 1969, Labadie Collection, University of Michigan.

30. Wald interview with A. B. Magil, New York City, November 1990.

31. Some of this information is based upon a 4 April 1941 letter from Freeman to Richardson Wood, Freeman Papers.

32. Burnshaw to Lee Baxandall, 6 April 1967, Burnshaw Papers, National Humanities Center, Austin, Texas.

33. Information on Burnshaw is based on Peter Revell, "Stanley Burnshaw," *Dictionary of Literary Biography* 48, pp. 63–69; Alan Filreis and Harvey Teres, "Interview with Stanley Burnshaw," *Wallace Stevens Journal* 13, no. 2 (Fall 1989): 109–26; Stanley Burnshaw, *Robert Frost Himself* (New York: George Brazillier, 1986), passim; Wald interview with Stanley Burnshaw, New York City, November 1992; the Burnshaw Papers; Stanley Burnshaw correspondence in the Granville Hicks Papers, Syracuse University; and Wald correspondence with Burnshaw between 1990 and 1998.

34. Alan Filreis and Harvey Teres, "Interview with Stanley Burnshaw," *Wallace Stevens Journal* 13, no. 2 (Fall 1989): 114.

35. See the thoughtful review by Communist English professor Morris U. Schappes in *Poetry* 44 (August–September 1934): 347–50.

36. Burnshaw's self-published prose poem, *The Wheel Age* (New York: Folio Press, 1929), was given a sympathetic review in the *New Masses* (July 1929): 18, by poet E. Merrill Root (1895–1973). Agreeing with Burnshaw that machines should not be uncritically embraced, Root urges that they be "tamed," not destroyed. Root's own political evolution diverged from that of Burnshaw. Although Root remained pro-Communist through the 1930s, he later turned sharply to the Right and became poetry editor of the John Birch Society's *American Opinion*. Root's poetry books include *Lost Eden* (1927), *Bow of Burning Gold* (1929), *Dawn Is Forever* (1938), and *Before the Swallow Dares* (1947).

37. Burnshaw, *Robert Frost Himself*, p. 40.

38. Burnshaw, "A Poet Takes His Stand," *New Masses* (August 1933): 27.

39. Christina Stead, "Some Deep Spell: A View of Stanley Burnshaw," *Agenda* 22, no. 1 (Winter–Spring 1983/84): 125.

40. Burnshaw, " 'Middle-Ground' Writers," *New Masses* (30 Apr. 1935): 19–21.

41. See "Stanley Burnshaw Protests," *Poetry* 44 (September 1934): 351–4.

42. Burnshaw, *Robert Frost Himself*, p. 60. The review appeared in the issue of 11 August 1936. Rolfe Humphries (1894–1969) worked as Latin teacher while he was a leading activist in League of American Writers and pro-Communist in the late 1930s. Having published a volume of poems in 1928, *Europa and Other Poems and Sonnets*, Humphries coedited the pro-Republican collection . . . *And Spain Sings* in 1937, translating about one-third of the poems in the volume from the Spanish. By 1940 he lost interest in Communism, although he translated Garcia Lorca's *Poet in New York* in 1940 and *Aragon, Poet of the French Resistance* in 1945. Later collections of his own verse include *Out of the Jewel* (1942), *The Summer Landscape* (1944), *Forbid Thy Ravens* (1947), *The Wind of Time* (1949), *Poems, Collected and New* (1954), and *Green Armour on Green Ground* (1956). Humphries's *Collected Poems* appeared in 1965. In *Poets, Poetics and Politics: America's Literary Community Viewed from the Letters of Rolfe Humphries, 1910–1969* (Lawrence: University of Kansas Press, 1992), p. 132, evidence is cited that Frost held a grudge against Humphries for the rest of his life due to the review.

43. The poet and pioneer filmmaker Willard Maas (1911–1971) held membership in the Communist Party for a short time. He was author of *Fire Testament* (1935) and *Concerning the Young* (1938). See Filreis, *Modernism from Left to Right*, passim.

44. Alan Filreis and Harvey Teres, "Interview with Stanley Burnshaw," *Wallace Stevens Journal*, p. 111. Burnshaw also discusses his *New Masses* experiences in *Robert Frost Himself*, pp. 50–53.

45. Burnshaw recalls that, even among those who were already in ideological agreement with the Communist Party, "A communist poet wouldn't have submitted [a manuscript] to us unless the poem's content – its subject matter and its attitude – had been congenial. If its subject matter and attitude were not congenial to the *New Masses* at that time we never would have considered it." See Alan Filreis and Harvey Teres, "Interview with Stanley Burnshaw," *Wallace Stevens Journal*, p. 117.

46. The poem was reprinted in *Social Poetry of the 1930s*, ed. Jack Salzman and Leo Zanderer (New York: Burt Franklin Co., 1978), pp. 1–4.

47. Burnshaw to Hicks, 7 Mar. 1940, Hicks Papers.

48. Burnshaw to Wald, 12 April 1992, in possession of Wald.

49. Burnshaw to Hicks, 27 February 1953, Hicks Papers.

50. Burnshaw, "The Bridge," *In the Terrified Radiance* (New York: George Brazillier, 1972).

51. Burnshaw, "Stevens' 'Mr. Burnshaw and the Statue,' " in *A Stanley Burnshaw Reader* (Athens: University of Georgia Press, 1990), p. 27.

52. Freeman, "Ivory Towers – Red and White," *New Masses* (11 Sept. 1934): 23.

53. According to Sender Garlin, Alfred Hayes told him that the reason that Hayes's poetry stopped appearing in the *New Masses* in the late 1930s was that it failed to meet the approval of the "Poetry Czarina," Joy Davidman. Whether Hayes and Davidman had feuded over personal or literary matters was not clear. Wald interview with Garlin, May 1989, Boulder, Colo.

54. Freeman to Browder, 5 Aug. 1937, Freeman Papers.

55. Miller, who was born in Nebraska, passed the bar there in 1928, practicing law briefly and then moving to California. From 1929 to 1933 he worked as a reporter, and eventually he became publisher of the *California Eagle* from 1954 to 1964. He also rose to become a prominent California attorney. In 1964 Gov. Edmund G. (Pat) Brown appointed Miller as a municipal court judge in Los Angeles.

56. Memo on *New Masses*, 5 Aug. 1937, Freeman Papers.

57. Freeman to Aaron, 2 Oct. 1960, p. 36 of letter, Aaron Papers, Cambridge, Mass.

58. Dupee's personal and political history is reviewed in Wald, *The New York Intellectuals*, pp. 85–88.

59. Freeman to Hicks, 6 May 1937, Freeman Papers.

60. "Between Ourselves," *New Masses* 24, no. 11 (7 Sept. 1937): 2.

61. Joseph Freeman, "Edmund Wilson's Globe of Glass," *New Masses Literary Supplement* (18 Apr. 1938): 74–79. A letter dated 6 December 1937 from *New Masses* editor Samuel Sillen to T. C. Wilson (T. C. Wilson Papers, Yale University) rejects a review of Edmund Wilson's book on the grounds that it is limited to a discussion of Wilson's attitude toward poetry. Sillen states that a more thoroughgoing criticism of Wilson was required by the editorial board. Freeman's essay fulfills that requirement and may have been suggested to him. In his published letters and diaries, Wilson left no record of a response to Freeman, although they had had personal associations.

62. "Introduction," in Horace Gregory, ed., *New Letters in America* (New York: W. W. Norton, 1937), p. 10.

63. Horace Gregory to T. C. Wilson, 17 Oct. 1937, Wilson Papers.

64. Leah Levenson and Jerry Natterstad, *Granville Hicks: The Intellectual in Mass Society* (Philadelphia: Temple University Press, 1993), p. 88.

65. Granville Hicks, "The Writer Faces the Future," in *The Writer in a Changing World*, ed. Henry Hart (New York: Equinox Press, 1937), pp. 193–94.

66. Earl Browder, "The Writer and Politics," ibid., p. 55.

67. Horace Gregory, ed., *New Letters in America*, p. 172.

68. Granville Hicks, "Those Who Quibble," *New Masses* (28 Sept. 1937): 22–23.

69. Horace Gregory, " 'Good News' in American Literature," *New Masses* (12 Oct. 1937): 17–18.

70. Muriel Rukeyser, Letter to the Editor, ibid., p. 18.

71. Marshall Schacht, Letter to the Editor, ibid., pp. 18–19.

72. Granville Hicks, Letter to the Editor, ibid., p. 19.

73. T. C. Wilson, Letter to the Editor, *New Masses* (2 Nov. 1937): 20–21.

74. Samuel Sillen, "By Way of Answer," ibid., p. 23. Selected from among a group of additional letters responding to the Hicks-Gregory debate was one by poet Rolfe Humphries defending lyric poetry (which had been disparaged in passing) as a manifestation of the human spirit, and also supporting Hicks's concern about the lack of musical quality in much modern verse, attributing this to technical incompetence. See Rolfe Humphries, "Discipline in Verse," ibid., p. 22.

75. See the review by Joseph Freeman in *New Masses* (June 1929): 14–15.

76. See Joshua Kunitz's long letter as "J. Q. Neets," in "Let Us Master Our Art!," *New Masses* (July 1930): 23.

77. Wald interviews with Franklin Folsom and Sender Garlin, Boulder, Colorado, May 1989. None of this attitude is indicated in Jessica Smith's highly laudatory tribute, "Joshua Kunitz: Legacy for Our Times," *New World Review*, July-August 1980, pp. 28–30.

78. "Is Poetry Dead?," *New Masses* (21 Dec. 1937): 9.

79. Lee Hays, "Wants Communist Poetry," and R. W. Lalley, "Good and Effective Poetry," *New Masses* (11 Jan. 1938).

80. Mike Gold, "Mike Replies," *New Masses* (25 Oct. 1937): 21.

81. Dorothy Van Ghent, "When Poets Stood Alone," *New Masses* (11 Jan. 1938): 41–47. For a biographical sketch of Van Ghent, including references to her Left associations at Berkeley, see L. R. Lind, "Dorothy Van Ghent: Teacher and Critic," *Classical and Modern Literature: A Quarterly* 16, no. 1 (Fall 1995): 7–18.

82. Martha Millet, "Is Poetry Dead?," *New Masses* (26 Jan. 1938): 20.

83. Robert Zachs, "A Slide Rule on Poetry," *New Masses* (1 Feb. 1938): 19.

84. Ira Benson, "Writers' and Readers' Writers," ibid., p. 20.

85. Robert Forsythe, "Wanted: Great Songs," *New Masses* (25 Jan. 1938): 12.

86. Granville Hicks, "Revolution in Bohemia," *New Masses* (12 Apr. 1938): 84–86.

87. Horace Gregory to T. C. Wilson, 14 Nov. 1937, Wilson Papers.

88. Ibid., 17 Oct. 1937.

89. Ibid., undated.

90. Ibid., undated.

91. Samuel Sillen to T. C. Wilson, undated, Wilson Papers.

92. Ibid., undated.

93. Sol Funaroff, "In Conclusion," *New Masses Literary Section* (10 May 1938): 127.

94. "Walt Whitman's Birthday," *New Masses Literary Section* (31 May 1938): 13.

95. Philip Stevenson, "Walt Whitman's Democracy," *New Masses Literary Section* (14 June 1938): 132–33.

96. Joshua Kunitz, "In Defense of a Term," *New Masses Literary Section* (12 July 1938): 145–47.

97. Clarence Weinstock, "Ivory Tower or Hole in the Ground," *New Masses Special Section* (24 May 1938): 21.

98. However, neither Gregory, in *The House on Jefferson Street* (New York: Holt, Rhinehart and Winston, 1971), nor Crichton, in *Total Recoil* (New York: Doubleday, 1960), is particularly candid about his experiences on the Left. Hicks, in *Part of the Truth* (New York: Harcourt, Brace and World, 1965), makes a more serious effort, but seems to lack insight into his own motivations as well as a memory adequate to providing a "thick" description of events.

## Chapter 5

1. For an entirely negative view of Jerome, see John Weber's *Communist Influence in Hollywood* (New York: Privately published, 1997), p. 2. The former Party educator of the Hollywood section describes Jerome as "a feckless pedant who simply parroted the Party line."

2. Biographical information on Jerome is based on letters from Jerry Warwin, the son from his first marriage; phone interview with Fred Jerome, a son from his marriage to Alice Jerome, August 1992; Jerome Papers, Yale University; Winwar Papers, Boston University; Wald interviews with Sender Garlin, Annette T. Rubinstein, and Franklin Folsom.

3. Jerome to Maxim Lieber, 1 Apr. 1964, Jerome Papers.

4. The son later used the name Jerry Warwin, his surname a reversal of his mother's maiden name. Frances Winwar seems to have gone to great lengths to obscure her first marriage and Jerome's paternity in all biographical references. Her son is referred to by a number of different first and last names, and he eventually turned Winwar into Warwin. Her marriage certificate is among the Winwar Papers at Boston University.

5. Jerry Warwin to Wald, 29 Mar. 1993.

6. Frances Vinci Roman, "Nazimova—Artist and Woman," *New Pearson's* 49 (March 1923): 44–46.

7. "Susan B. Anthony," *Woman Today*, July 1936, pp. 6–7.

8. Harold Norse, *Memoirs of a Bastard Angel: A Fifty-Year Literary and Erotic Odyssey* (New York: William Morrow, 1989), p. 44.

9. Information on Grebanier's testimony is provided in Ellen Schrecker, *No Ivory Tower: McCarthyism and the Universities* (New York: Oxford University Press, 1986), p. 78. In a letter of 22 August 1965, in the Hicks Papers (Syracuse University), Grebanier tells Granville Hicks that the negative reaction to his role in the hearings destroyed his marriage. However, Jerry Warwin, in his 29 March 1993 letter, states that reasons for the break-up were more complex. In his *Mem-*

*oirs of a Bastard Angel,* Norse describes being propositioned by Grebanier in a homosexual bath house (pp. 137-38).

10. For further details on her life, see *Fire and Grace: The Life of Rose Pastor Stokes* (Athens: University of Georgia Press, 1989), by Arthur Zipser and Pearl Zipser. Anzia Yezierska's 1923 novel, *Salome of the Tenements,* was partly inspired by the Stokes-Pastor marriage, as well as Yezierska's own relationship with John Dewey. See the introduction by Gay Wilentz to the 1995 edition, published by the University of Illinois Press.

11. Zipser and Zipser, *Fire and Grace,* p. 270.

12. Ibid., p. 299.

13. Jerome to Dargan, 26 June 1933, Jerome Papers.

14. Zipser and Zipser, *Fire and Grace,* p., 302.

15. It was finally published as *I Belong to the Working Class: The Unfinished Autobiography of Rose Pastor Stokes,* ed. Herbert Shapiro and David Sterling (Athens: University of Georgia Press, 1992).

16. Rose Pastor Stokes to Jerome, 27 Jan. 1932, Jerome Papers.

17. It was first published in the *Masses,* but the version Jerome read was in Genevieve Taggard, ed., *May Days: An Anthology of Verse from Masses-Liberator* (New York: Boni and Liveright, 1925), p. 258.

18. Jerome to Stokes, 11 June 1928.

19. The indispensable source for information about Hook's philosophical and political evolution is Christopher Phelps, *Young Sidney Hook: Marxist and Pragmatist* (Ithaca, N.Y.: Cornell University Press, 1997).

20. Jerome to Stokes, undated, Jerome Papers.

21. Jerome to Dargan, 6 Jan. 1933, Jerome Papers.

22. Andrei Aleksandrovich Zhdanov (1896-1948) was the Party boss of Leningrad who reorganized the postwar international Communist movement as the Cominform in 1947, and who advocated strict political control of intellectuals in the arts (called "Zhdanovism"). In Jerome's speech, delivered at the Stalin Memorial Meeting held at the Party's Jefferson School, he declared his admiration for Stalin's philosophical writings and stayed true to his mentor's style by frequently striking out against "revisionists" and traitors such as former Communist Party leader Earl Browder and the Czechoslovakian dissident Rudolf Slansky. See V. J. Jerome, "He Built the Future," in the special issue of *Political Affairs* devoted to Stalin's death, 32, no. 3 (April 1953).

23. Jerome to Dargan, 6 Jan. 1933, Jerome Papers.

24. "Newsboy" was adapted by Gregory Novikov (dates unknown) for the Workers Laboratory Theater; the text is reprinted in Albert Fried, ed., *Communism in America: A History in Documents* (New York: Columbia University Press, 1997), pp. 203-9.

25. *Rebel Poet* no. 15 (August 1931): 1. Appearing in the same issue, Jerome's "Communis' Blues" was just as artificial. However, a later poem, "To a Black

Man," at least imparts some dignity to the subject, largely due to his dropping the ersatz black dialect and speaking directly in his own voice (ibid., no. 17 [October 1932]: 6).

26. Jerome to Dargan, 6 Jan. 1933, Jerome Papers.

27. Jerome to Fast, 18 Dec. 1951. Rosalie McGee was the the wife of Black prisoner Willie McGee, who would be electrocuted on false rape charges; Amy Mallard was the widow of a lynch victim and active in support of the defense of Black Communist leader Benjamin Davis, who was imprisoned under the Smith Act; Elizabeth Gurley Flynn was another historic Communist leader indicted under the Smith Act.

28. Jerome's other publications include . . . *Stand Guard* (New York: Workers Music League, 1931), for which he wrote the text to accompany music by Lan Adomian; *Intellectuals and the War* (New York: Workers Library, 1940); *The Negro in Hollywood Films* (New York: Masses & Mainstream, 1950); and *The Treatment of Defeated Germany* (New York: New Century Publishers, 1945).

29. V. J. Jerome, "Toward a Proletarian Novel," *New Masses* (August 1933): 14–15.

30. V. J. Jerome, "Edmund Wilson: To the Munich Station," *New Masses* (9 Apr. 1939): 23–26.

31. Jerome's "A Letter to Howard Fast" was published in *Political Affairs* 39, no. 1 (January 1959): 60–65, to refute Fast's claim of mistreatment by the Communist Party. Daniel Aaron refers to the incident of Jerome criticizing an essay by Freeman for its treatment of Eastman in the 1920s in *Writers on the Left* (New York: Harcourt, Brace, and World, 1961), p. 370.

32. Franklin Folsom, *Days of Anger, Days of Hope* (Niwot: University Press of Colorado, 1994), p. 101. In his chapter "The Communist Party and the League," Folsom tells a number of anecdotes about Jerome and discusses his tendency to employ the method of "fiat" in both organizational and literary matters.

33. Victor Navasky, *Naming Names* (New York: Viking, 1980), p. 302.

34. A posthumous sequel was published as *The Paper Bridge* (New York: Citadel, 1966). See Joseph North's review essay of *A Lantern for Jeremy*, "And Then the Judges We Will Be," *Political Affairs* 31, no. 6 (June 1952): 58–64; and Sholem Stern, "How Jerome Saw the Shtetl," *Jewish Life* 9, no. 2 (December 1954): 18–19.

35. Wald interview with Sender Garlin, Boulder, Colo., May 1989.

36. Wald interview with Wilma Shore, New York City, November 1993.

37. Herbert Aptheker to Jerome, 2 July 1957, Jerome Papers. In a March 2000 interview with Wald, Aptheker reflected that he passed many hours working side by side with Jerome but learned little of Jerome's inner life or personal artistic concerns.

38. Text of Aronson talk, Jerome Papers.

39. Rockwell Kent to Jerome, 23 Jan. 1941, Jerome Papers; Kreymborg to Jerome, 15 Dec. 1940, Jerome Papers.

40. MacLeish to Jerome, 28 Jan. 1937, Jerome Papers.

41. V. J. Jerome, "Archibald MacLeish's *Panic*," *New Masses* (2 Apr. 1935): 43–44.

42. MacLeish to A. B. Magil, 22 April 1939, Jerome Papers.

43. Putnam to Jerome, 14 Jan. 1944, Putnam Papers; Bertram D. Wolfe, *Strange Communists I Have Known* (New York: Stein and Day, 1965), p. 60.

44. Quoted in Victor Navasky, *Naming Names* (New York: Viking, 1980), p. 288.

45. *The Communist* 16, no. 12 (December 1937): 1146–63.

46. Jerome to Dargan, 13 July 1944, Jerome Papers.

47. William Z. Foster to Jerome, 23 Dec. 1949, Jerome Papers.

48. Jerome to Administrative Committee, 6 Nov. 1953, 4 Jan. 1954, Jerome Papers.

49. See V. J. Jerome, "Remembering Dashiell Hammett," *Mainstream* 16, no. 5 (May 1963): 60–61.

50. Winwar's full intention in this analogy is not clear. The comparison seems especially apt in light of St. Augustine's reputation for vitriolic polemics and indefatigable exegesis of holy texts; he was also the scourge of anyone who doubted the church. Moreover, one might speculate as to whether she was also referring to St. Augustine's repentance of his dissolute youth. Reports from Winwar on meetings with the Department of Justice and FBI representatives, November 1952–February 1953, Jerome Papers.

51. There is a disputed account of an incident in prison in which Dashiell Hammet had to rescue Jerome from a knife-wielding inmate whom he had naively upbraided for cheating during a ping-pong game. Lillian Hellman claimed that the anecdote came from Hammet, and she recorded it in *Scoundrel Time* (Boston: Little, Brown, 1976), pp. 90–91. Frederick Vanderbilt Field refutes this version, which makes Jerome look idiotic, in *From Right to Left: An Autobiography* (Westport, Ct.: Lawrence Hill and Company, 1983), pp. 244–45.

52. V. J. Jerome to Alice Jerome, 26 June 1951, Jerome Papers.

53. Ibid., 25 Jan. 1953.

54. Alice Jerome to Albert Maltz, 25 Apr. 1955, Jerome Papers.

55. Wald interview with Annette Rubinstein, New York City, 10 Oct. 1990.

56. Brown to Jerome, 3 July 1952, Jerome Papers.

57. Finkelstein to Jerome, undated, Jerome Papers.

58. Ibid., 3 June 1953.

59. Ibid.

60. V. J. Jerome, "Caliban Speaks," *Masses & Mainstream* 6, no. 2 (February 1953): 21–25.

61. Jerome to Lowenfels, 6 Aug. 1963, Jerome Papers.

62. Lawson to Jerome, 10 Dec. 1957, Jerome Papers.

63. Wald interview with A. B. Magil, New York, October 1990.

64. Victor Navasky, *Naming Names* (New York: Viking, 1980), p. 302.

65. Jerome's 1963 critique of Sidney Finkelstein, "Towards the Marxist Theory

of Ideology," *Mainstream* 16, no. 8 (August 1963): 43–50, seems to feature the same old orthodox heresy hunting, albeit with less vigor and vitriol.

66. Jerome to Lowenfels, 1 Mar. 1963, Jerome Papers.

67. Jerome to Lieber, 19 May 1963, Jerome Papers.

68. Report of Alfred Rivkin, M.D., 6 Mar. 1965, Jerome Papers.

69. Alice Jerome to John Howard Lawson, 25 Feb. 1966, Jerome Papers.

70. Although Potamkin never held membership in the Communist Party, he was a founder of the John Reed Clubs, a club delegate to the 1930 Kharkov Conference of the International Union of Revolutionary Writers, and the secretary of the New York Club. He died of stomach ulcers in 1933. He contributed to a number of Communist publications, and International Publishers issued his pamphlet *The Eyes of the Movie* (New York: International Publishers, 1934). A collection of his film writings was edited by Lewis Jacobs, *The Compound Cinema: The Film Writings of Harry Alan Potamkin* (New York: Teachers College Press, 1977).

71. The poem appears in Marcus Graham, ed., *An Anthology of Revolutionary Poetry* (New York: Active Press, 1929), pp. 224–25.

72. Mike Gold, "My Generation," *The Worker*, 16 Oct. 1965, p. 6.

73. Bill Browder to Joseph Freeman, 14 Aug. 1933, Freeman Papers, Hoover Institute.

74. Ione Robinson, *A Wall to Paint On* (New York: E. P. Dutton, 1946), p. 196.

75. Conrad Komorowski to Freeman, 2 Nov. 1932, Freeman Papers.

76. Walter Snow to Isserman, 25 Oct. 1972, Snow Papers, University of Connecticut.

77. Freeman to Browder, 5 Aug. 1937, Freeman Papers.

78. Edward Dalhberg, *The Confessions of Edward Dahlberg* (New York: Brazillier, 1971), p. 236.

79. Albert Halper, *Good-Bye Union Square* (Chicago: Quadrangle, 1970), p. 269.

80. Wald interview with Tiba Willner, Ojai, Calif., July 1990.

81. Wald interview with Sender Garlin, Boulder, Colo., May 1989.

82. Ione Robinson, *A Wall to Paint On* (New York: E. P. Dutton, 1946), p. 98.

83. Wald interview with Robert Gorham Davis, who was subsequently Winter's lover, Cambridge, Mass., November 1991.

84. Wald interview with Tiba Willner, Ojai, Calif., July 1990.

85. Charmion to Freeman, 7 December 1941, Freeman Papers.

86. "What was particularly shocking was my realization that Max's animus was not really political; that he was using the mask of politics to release a purely personal spleen engendered by a rivalry for women. . . ." Freeman to Josephine Herbst, 16 June 1959, p. 37, Freeman Papers.

87. Wald interview with Sender Garlin, 2 May 1989.

88. Wald interview with Tiba Wilner, Ojai, Calif., July 1990.

89. Wald interview with Sender Garlin, 5 May 1989.

90. Halper, *Good-Bye Union Square*, p. 269.

91. See Freeman to Hindus, 19 May 1939; Hindus to Freeman, 21 May 1939; Freeman to Hindus, 24 May 1939, all in Freeman Papers.

92. Wald interview with Sender Garlin, 2 May 1989.

93. See Levenson and Natterstad, *Granville Hicks*, p. 76; and Hicks to Freeman, 26 Oct. 1936, Freeman Papers.

94. Freeman to Schneider, undated, Freeman Papers. For further details on the controversy regarding Farrell's book, see Wald, *James T. Farrell: The Revolutionary Socialist Years* (New York: New York University Press, 1978); and Wald, "The Athanasis of Union Square," introduction to *A Note on Literary Criticism* (New York: Columbia University Press, 1993).

95. Amter to Freeman, 29 May 1936. The specific accusations were that in his 6 June 1936 report in the *New Masses* on the convention of the Socialist Party, Freeman made the Socialist Party seem less right-wing than it really was, and that he was insufficiently derogatory in his references to Max Shachtman and Jay Lovestone.

96. Burnshaw to Wald, 20 October 1992, in possession of Wald.

97. Burnshaw to Hicks, 22 July 1936, Hicks Papers.

98. Undated correspondence with Christina Stead, Burnshaw Papers, National Humanities Center, Austin, Texas.

99. Christina Stead to Burnshaw, 2 Oct. 1936, Burnshaw Papers.

100. Freeman to Aaron, 3 July 1958, p. 23. In an interview with Wald in New York, in October 1992, Burnshaw confirmed that Freeman was subject to sudden voice loss for psychological reasons, a telling symptom inasmuch as his voice was his most attractive feature.

101. Freeman to Aaron, 16 June 1958, p. 8, Freeman Papers.

102. Ibid., 17 June 1958, p. 2.

103. Ibid., p. 3.

104. Ibid., 22 June 1958, p. 2.

105. The most careful consideration of issues in the debate appears in Homberger, *American Writers and Radical Politics*, pp. 134–38. This includes a discussion of Joseph Freeman's response to Eastman in his column in the *Daily Worker* issues of 22 November and 2 December 1933.

106. Freeman to Aaron, 2 Oct. 1960, p. 40, Freeman Papers.

107. Ibid., 1 Oct. 1960, p. 8.

108. Freeman to Cowley, 2 Mar. 1937, Freeman Papers.

109. Ibid.

110. Freeman to Aaron, 16 June 1958, Freeman Papers.

111. Freeman to Rolfe, 14 June 1937, p. 1, Freeman Papers. Between 1937 and 1939, Flores edited nine issues of the Marxist literary journal *Dialectics*, and he directed the production of a dozen pamphlets on literary subjects under the imprint of Critics Group Press.

112. Freeman to Rolfe, 14 June 1937, p. 2, Freeman Papers.

113. Freeman to Aaron, 9 Sept. 1960, Freeman Papers.

114. Freeman's version, basically from his point of view, is reported in Aaron, *Writers on the Left*, 365–75.

115. Freeman believed that when his political heresies in *An American Testament* were discussed at the Kremlin conference in 1937, only Browder defended Freeman against the drive to "crucify" him; and that Browder in 1939, according to a report from Mike Gold, stopped the *Daily Worker* from reprinting the "ukase of excommunication" which had appeared in the *Communist International*. Freeman to Aaron, 5 Aug. 1958, p. 11, Freeman Papers.

116. Freeman to Browder, 5 Aug. 1937, Freeman Papers.

117. Ibid., p. 2.

118. P. Dengal, "Book Reviewing Is a Serious Matter," *Communist International* 16, no. 8 (August 1939): 947–48.

119. See Freeman's introduction to Granville Hicks et al., eds., *Proletarian Literature in the United States* (New York: International Publishers, 1935).

120. Freeman to Jerome, 1 July 1939, Freeman Papers.

121. Wald interview with Tiba Wilner, Ojai, Calif., July 1990.

122. The first time was prior to the McCarthy era, during the Rapp-Coudert investigation of New York schoolteachers in 1940; this was because Freeman had mentioned the name of one of the accused teachers in *An American Testament*.

123. Wald interview with Tiba Willner, Ojai, Calif., July 1990.

124. Wald interview with Folsom, Boulder, Colo., May 1989. Harry Freeman was apparently an exceptionally able journalist. He had the capacity to collect a huge amount of information in his head and then produce a 10,000-word "round up" of events.

125. "The Poet Pure and Undefiled" was the title Freeman gave to a long sequence of autobiographical letters sent to Daniel Aaron in the 1950s.

126. Freeman to Dell, 1 Mar. 1951, p. 4, Dell Papers, Newberry Library.

127. Ibid., p. 5.

128. Ibid., p. 7.

## Chapter 6

1. Introduction by Gold to the poetry collection *We Gather Strength* (New York: The Liberal Press, 1933), p. 7.

2. The subject of Eliot and the Left warrants a book-length study. As examples of Eliot's impact, see the numerous references to him cited in the poetry of Horace Gregory, Kenneth Fearing, and Muriel Rukeyser in Macha Louis Rosenthal's landmark dissertation, "Chief Poets of the American Depression," New York University, 1949. Also see Jules Chametzsky's comments on Joy Davidman's relationship to Earl Browder and T. S. Eliot in the *Nation*, 8 Sept. 1979, p. 186.

3. Michael Gold, "Change the World!," *Daily Worker,* 5 June 1934, p. 6.

4. Spier published two volumes of poetry, *When the Siren Blows* (New York: B. B. Hagglund, 1933) and *You Own the Hills and Other Poems* (Philadelphia: Alpress Publishers, 1935). The first has an introduction by Jack Conroy, and the second is dedicated to Conroy. Spier is described as a worker whose verse appears mainly in publications of the John Reed Clubs and Communist Parties. Both volumes contain a number of translations of Hungarian poetry by Antel Hidas.

5. The letter is quoted in Michael Gold, "Change the World!," *Daily Worker,* 14 June 1934, p. 6.

6. Ibid.

7. Ibid.

8. See the collection of documents in *Aesthetics and Politics* (London: New Left Books, 1977).

9. Jeffrey Segall presents an overview of divers responses to Joyce by the U.S. Left in *Joyce in America: Cultural Politics and the Trials of "Ulysses"* (Berkeley: University of California Press, 1993).

10. T. S. Eliot, *The Waste Land and Other Poems* (New York: Harcourt, Brace and World, 1962), p. 19.

11. Bud Johns and Judith Clancy, *Bastard in the Ragged Suit: Writings of, with Drawings by Herman Spector* (San Francisco: Synergistic Press, 1977), p. 21.

12. Ibid., p. 33.

13. Ibid., p. 34.

14. Ibid., p. 57.

15. *New Masses* (February 1931): 23.

16. Harry Roskolenko, *When I Was Last on Cherry Street* (New York: Stein and Day, 1965), p. 109.

17. Spector, *Bastard in a Ragged Suit,* pp. 202–3.

18. Remarks of Judith Spector Clancy Johns at the funeral of Clara Spector, 11 Apr. 1988, San Francisco. Courtesy of Bud Johns.

19. Spector, *Bastard in the Ragged Suit,* p. 179.

20. Spector, "Harlem River," in Jack Salzman and Leo Zanderer, *Social Poetry of the 1930s* (New York: Burt Franklin and Co., 1978), p. 287.

21. Spector to Walter Snow, 17 Jan. 1933, Snow Papers, University of Connecticut.

22. Bud Johns to Wald, 20 Mar. 1991, in possession of Wald.

23. Spector, *Bastard in the Ragged Suit,* p. 142.

24. Alfred Hayes to Kenneth Fearing, dated only 1937, Fearing Papers, University of Wisconsin.

25. *Poetry* 58 (October 1938): 50–53.

26. Sol Funaroff, *Exile from a Future Time* (New York: Dynamo, 1943), p. 62.

27. *New York Times* obituary, 31 Oct. 1942, p. 6. See also Samuel Sillen, "No Wreath, But a Sword," *New Masses* (17 Oct. 1942): 22–23.

28. Guillaume Apollinaire, *Selected Writings* (New York: New Directions, 1971), p. 133. Funaroff's friend Nathan Adler first told me about the influence of Apollinaire on Funaroff.

29. Dahlberg, *The Confessions of Edward Dahlberg*, p. 283.

30. Wald interview with Leo Hurwitz, 11 Nov. 1989, New York City.

31. Wald interview with Gertrude Hayes, 8 Oct. 1989, New York City.

32. Adler did not pursue his writing beyond the early 1930s. He moved to the San Francisco Bay area, where he became an eminent clinical psychologist and taught at the University of California at Berkeley.

33. Wald interview with Nathan Adler, 12 Sept. 1989, Mill Valley, Calif.

34. *Dynamo* 1, no. 2 (March–April 1934): 21.

35. William Pillin (1910–1985), born in Russia, was a poet and ceramic craftsman who also developed a special interest in music. Influenced by Rilke, Lorca, and Neruda, he published *Poems* (1939), *Theory of Silence* (1949), *Dance without Shoes* (1956), *Passage after Midnight* (1958), *Pavanne for a Fading Memory* (1964), and *Everything Falling* (1971). Orginally active in the John Reed Club of Chicago, he moved to the Southwest and then to the West, increasingly attracted to anarchism.

36. *Dynamo* 1, no. 3 (Summer 1934): 20–25.

37. See Eric Homberger. "Communists and Objectivists," *American Writers and Radical Politics, 1900–1939*, pp. 163–86.

38. Williams was considered by Mike Gold, Granville Hicks, and others to be a participant in the proletarian literary movement although not an ideological Communist.

39. *Dynamo* 1, no. 3 (Summer 1934): 26–29.

40. Adler claimed that he and Funaroff wrote this together. Wald interview with Adler, Mill Valley, Calif., September 1989.

41. *Dynamo* 2, no. 1 (May–June 1935): 24–31.

42. *We Gather Strength*, p. 9.

43. Kenneth Fearing, "Historic Certainties," *Poetry* 58 (October 1938): 50–53.

44. James E. Breslin, ed., *Something to Say: William Carlos Williams on Younger Poets* (New York: New Directions, 1985), pp. 94–96. Originally published as "Image and Purpose" in the 16 August 1938 issue of the *New Masses*.

45. Funaroff, "Unemployed: 2 A.M.," *Social Poetry of the 1930s*, p. 49.

46. Funaroff, "Uprooted," ibid., p. 50.

47. Ibid., p. 50.

48. Ibid., p. 51.

49. Ibid., p. 53.

50. Ibid., p. 59.

51. Anita Tilkin, "A Worker – An Extraordinary Poet," *Daily Worker*, 1 Nov. 1938, p. 7.

52. Letter from Sol Funaroff to Nathan Adler, 10 Feb. 1940, in possession of Wald.

53. Varney graduated from Dartmouth and attended Yale Divinity School. From Harvard University he received a master of arts as well as a law degree. Following the Russian Revolution, Varney made several trips to the Soviet Union, spent a great deal of time in Europe in the 1920s, and was married for a brief time. He taught at New York University in the English Department from early 1930s to 1953, and thereafter wrote poetry and traveled. Varney published many books of his own verse: *First Wounds, A Story in Five Chapters of Verse* (1926), *Sketches of Soviet Russia* (1920), *Sparrow Hawks* (1950), *Stalingrad, New Years* (1943), *Star Men, U.S.A.* (1956), *Spun Sequence* (1960), and *Poems for a Prose Age* (1960).

54. Funaroff, *Exile from a Future Time*, p. 60.

55. Some of these details are from an undated letter from Hayes to Malcolm Cowley, Cowley Papers, Newberry Library; Wald interview with Nathan Adler, 12 Sept. 1989, Mill Valley, Calif.; and Wald telephone interview with Josephine Hayes Dean, 23 July 2001.

56. See the discussion in Archie Green, *Wobblies, Pile Butts, and Other Heroes* (Urbana and Chicago: University of Illinois Press, 1993), p. 87.

57. "I Dreamed I Saw Joe Hill Last Night," ibid., pp. 85-91.

58. Orrick Johns, "The John Reed Clubs Meet," *New Masses* (30 Oct. 1934): 25-26.

59. Wald interview with Gertrude Hayes, 8 Oct. 1989, New York City.

60. Sol Funaroff to Nathan Adler, 6 May 1937, in possession of Wald.

61. Wald interview with Nathan Adler, 12 Sept. 1989, Mill Valley, Calif.

62. Undated letter, probably written during the summer of 1937, from Hayes to Fearing, Fearing Papers.

63. Hayes to Granville Hicks, 28 Dec. 1934, Hicks Papers, Syracuse University.

64. Hicks et al., *Proletarian Literature in the United States*, p. 166.

65. Alfred Hayes, "Singleman," in Salzman and Zanderer, *Social Poetry of the 1930s*, pp. 109-11.

66. Hicks et al., *Proletarian Literature in the United States*, p. 166.

67. Hayes, "In a Home Relief Bureau," Salzman and Zanderer, *Social Poetry of the 1930s*, pp. 117-88.

68. Gold, "Change the World," *Daily Worker*, 5 June 1934, p. 6.

69. Alfred Hayes, "As a Young Man," *Welcome to the Castle* (New York: Harper and Brothers, 1950), pp. 42-44.

70. Ibid., p. 48.

71. Alfred Hayes, *Just before the Divorce* (New York: Atheneum, 1968), pp. 3-4.

72. Ibid., p. 17.

73. Hayes, "The Café G," in ibid., p. 26.

74. The story appears in Hayes, *The Temptation of Don Volpi* (New York: Atheneum, 1960).

75. Wald interview with Nathan Adler, 12 Sept. 1989.

## Chapter 7

1. Statement on back flap of the book jacket of *Genevieve Taggard: Collected Poems, 1918–1938* (New York: Harper, 1938).

2. These are reprinted in *Writing Red: An Anthology of American Women Writers, 1930–1940*, ed. Charlotte Nekola and Paula Rabinowitz (New York: Feminist Press, 1987), pp. 149, 152.

3. Statement on the back flap of the book jacket of *Genevieve Taggard*.

4. Biographical information on Taggard is based on the Genevieve Taggard Papers at the New York Public Library; correspondence with her daughter, Marcia Durant Liles; interviews by Wald with Sanora Babb and Franklin Folsom; Barbara Antonina Clarke Mossberg, "Genevieve Taggard," *American Women Writers*, 4:199–201; "Genevieve Taggard," *Dictionary of Literary Biography* (Detroit: Gale Research, 1986), 45:376–81; Taggard, "Poet Out of Pioneer," in *These Modern Women: Autobiographical Essays from the Twenties*, ed. Elaine Showalter (New York: Feminist Press, 1978), pp. 62–68. Two other studies that discuss Taggard's life and work are Mary Lefkowitz, *Experimental Lives: Women and Literature, 1900–1945* (New York: Twayne, 1992); and Nina Miller, *Making Love Modern* (New York: Oxford, 1999).

5. Genevieve Taggard, "Hawaii, Washington, Vermont," *Calling Western Union* (New York: Harper and Brothers, 1936), pp. xi–xxxii.

6. Letter from Leonard Bacon, 25 Mar. 1949, Taggard Papers.

7. "Married by Contract," *New York Times*, 15 Apr. 1916, p. 13.

8. Genevieve Taggard to Herbst, 16 Oct. 1923, Taggard Papers.

9. Ibid.

10. See *After Disillusion* (New York: Thomas Seltz, 1935); *Deux Contes* (New York: Isthmus Press, 1928); and "Literature and Revolution" in *New Masses* (January 1929): 19.

11. Taggard to Sara Bard Field, undated, Taggard Papers.

12. Taggard, "USSR, 1917–1937," *Falcon* (New York: Harper and Brothers, 1943), p. 8.

13. Taggard to Hicks, undated, Hicks Papers, Syracuse University.

14. Taggart, "Lark," *Collected Poems*, p. 164.

15. *Partisan Review* 2 (April–May 1935): 50–51.

16. Ruth Lechlitner, ". . . anti-war and anti-fascism," *Carleton Miscellany* 6, no. 1 (Winter 1965):77–81. In this memoir, Lechlitner claims that she was only associated with the League of American Writers from 1935 to 1937; however, the records of the LAW show her teaching at the league's New York Writers School in 1939. See Franklin Folsom, *Days of Anger, Days of Hope* (Niwot: University Press of Colorado, 1994), p. 301.

17. See Paul Corey, "Lurching toward Liberalism," *Books at Iowa* 100, no. 5 (December 1995): 35–71.

18. *Tomorrow's Phoenix* (New York: Alcestis Press, 1937), p. 62.

19. *New Masses* (13 June 1939): 24.

20. "This Body Politic," *Tomorrow's Phoenix*, pp. 13–22.

21. Ibid., p. 33.

22. T. S. Eliot, "Tradition and the Individual Talent," *The Sacred Wood* (London: Metheun and Company, 1920), pp. 47–59.

23. Ruth Lechlitner, "Garland for Spring, 1937," *Tomorrow's Phoenix*, p. 46.

24. Information on Joy Davidman was assembled from the following sources: the papers of Joy Davidman at Wheaton College, Wheaton, Illinois; Paul Leopold's two-part study in *The Bulletin of the New York C. S. Lewis Society*, "The Writings of Joy Davidman," 14, nos. 4, 5 (February and March 1983):1–10 and 1–9; Lyle W. Dorsett's *And God Came In* (New York: Macmillan, 1983), and "The Search for Joy Davidman," *The Bulletin of the New York C. S. Lewis Society* 14, no. 2 (December 1983): 1–7; interview with Dorsett in Wheaton, Illinois, September 1992; Wald interviews with Franklin Folsom, June 1990; Mary Elting, June 1990; Aaron Kramer, September 1994; and Sender Garlin, 1990; Davidman's essay "The Longest Way Round" in *We Found the Way*, ed. David Wesley Soper (Philadelphia: Westminster Press, 1951); the six-part *New York Post* series on "Girl Communist," 31 Oct.–30 Nov. 1949; correspondence with V. J. Jerome, Jerome Papers, Yale University; and correspondence with Granville Hicks, Hicks Papers.

25. A score of 140 or above was then considered to be the genius level.

26. Joy Davidman, ed., *War Poems of the United Nations* (New York: Dial, 1943), pp. 299–300.

27. Dorsett, *And God Came In*, p. 16.

28. Joy Davidman, *Letter to a Comrade* (New Haven, Conn.: Yale University Press, 1938), pp. 86–87.

29. Joy Davidman, "The Apostate," *Hunter College Echo*, November 1934, pp. 17–26.

30. Joy Davidman, *Anya* (New York: Macmillan, 1940), p. 123.

31. See Alfred Kazin, *New York Herald Tribune Books*, 14 July 1940, p. 2; John Cournos, *New York Times Sunday Book Review*, 14 July 1940, p. 7; and N. L. Rothman, *Saturday Review of Literature*, 13 July 1940, p. 10.

32. *Those Who Found the Way* (Philadelphia: Westminster Press, 1951), p. 20.

33. Robert Frost was named co-recipient for that year.

34. Dorsett, *And God Came In*, p. 37.

35. Ibid., p. 43.

36. Biographical information on William Lindsay Gresham is assembled from the following sources: the papers of Joy Davidman and the papers of William Lindsay Gresham at Wheaton College, Wheaton, Illinois; Leopold, "The Writings of Joy Davidman"; Dorsett's *And God Came In*, "The Search for Joy Davidman," and a personal interview with Dorsett in Wheaton, Illinois, September 1992; Wald interviews with Folsom, Elting, Kramer, and Garlin; and Gresham's essay

"From Communist to Christian," in *We Found the Way*, ed. David Wesley Soper, (Philadelphia: Westminster Press, 1951).

37. Jean Karsavina contributed regularly to the pulps even as she published two Left-wing books for young people with International Publishers, *Reunion in Poland* (1945) and *Tree by the Waters* (1948). Later she translated Tolstoy and wrote opera librettos while she edited *Soviet Review* and *Problems of Soviet Literature* (from 1958 to 1965) and *Reprints from the Soviet Press* (from 1965 until her death). In 1974 she published a major novel of her childhood, *White Eagle, Dark Skies*, which received a prize from the Jewish Book Council.

38. William Lindsay Gresham to Davy [David Gresham], 20 Jan. 1960, Gresham Papers, Wheaton College, Wheaton, Ill.

39. Dorsett interview with Douglas Gresham, 4 June 1984, Gresham Papers.

40. *New Masses* (31 July 1945): 4. The poem is called "Quisling at Twilight," and the personal references are obscure.

41. Dorsett, *And God Came In*, p. 62.

42. The novel became the 1947 film *Nightmare Alley*, directed by Edmund Goulding and starring Tyrone Power.

43. Bel Kaufman, "A Joy Observed," *Commonweal*, 25 Mar. 1994, p. 7.

44. Dorsett, *And God Came In*, p. 85.

45. Gresham to Davidman, 3 Feb. 1955, Davidman Papers.

46. This claim occurs throughout the six-part *New York Post* series "Girl Communist," 31 Oct.–30 Nov. 1949.

47. The marriage with Lewis was consummated, despite disclaimers by those acolytes of Lewis unable bear the thought of their cultured Christian idol in bed with the outspoken and occasionally vulgar New York Jew. See Leopold, "The Writings of Joy Davidman."

48. Davidman, *Letter to a Comrade*, p. 31.

49. Ibid., p. 94.

50. Ibid., p. 57.

51. Ibid., p. 91.

52. Ibid., p. 61.

53. Ibid., p. 64.

54. The passage is discussed as a movement from abstraction to historical necessity in Louise Kertesz, *The Poetic Vision of Muriel Rukeyser* (Baton Rouge: Louisiana State University Press, 1980), pp. 4–5.

55. Taggard, statement on back flap of the book jacket of *Collected Poems*.

56. See the excellent discussion in Robert Shaffer, "Women and the Communist Party USA, 1930–1940," *Socialist Review* 45 (May 1975): 73–118.

57. For the first three, see the selections in Nekola and Rabinowitz, *Writing Red*. See also Grace Hutchins, "Feminists and the Left Wing," *New Masses* (20 Nov. 1934): 14–15; and Ella Winter, "Love in Two Worlds," *New Masses* (16 July 1935): 17–19. For a series of exchanges on women's domestic work involving McKenney

and Flynn, see *New Masses* (11 Feb. 1941): 10–11; and *New Masses* (21 Mar. 1941): 10–11.

58. See Michael Folsom, ed., *Mike Gold: A Literary Anthology* (New York: International Publishers, 1972), pp. 211–14.

59. Meridel Le Sueur, "The Fetish of Being Outside," *New Masses* (26 Feb. 1935): 23.

60. See Edwin Seaver, "Another Writer's Position," *New Masses* (19 Feb. 1935): 21–22.

61. Nekola and Rabinowitz, *Writing Red*, p. 131.

62. "Jimmie Higgins" is a popular term for the ordinary, everyday activist in the socialist movement, who keeps the organization going without the glory enjoyed by the top leaders. It gained widespread currency from Upton Sinclair's novel, *Jimmie Higgins* (Racine, Wisc.: Western Printing and Lithographing Company, 1918).

63. Gellhorn, author of many works of fiction and reportage, was a longtime personal friend of Eleanor Roosevelt and the third wife of Ernest Hemingway. Like Hemingway's, her political views sometimes coincided with those of the Communist Party, especially at the time of the Spanish Civil War. See Carl Rollyson, *Nothing Ever Happens to the Brave: The Story of Martha Gellhorn* (New York: St. Martin's Press, 1990).

64. Hope Hale was a Communist Party member and pulp fiction writer who had married the British Communist journalist Claude Cockburn in the early 1930s; at the end of the decade she would marry the American Communist literary critic Robert Gorham Davis, although both became disaffected from Communism at the time of the Hitler-Stalin Pact. In the 1960s, a collection of her short fiction about the "darker regions of the civilized female psyche" appeared as *The Dark Way to the Plaza* (New York: Doubleday, 1968), and twenty-five years later she published her autobiographical *Great Day Coming: A Memoir of the 1930s* (South Royalton, Vt.: Steerforth Press, 1994). Dorothy Parker was a Jewish-American humorist sympathetic to the Communist Party during the 1930s and loyal to the Left afterward. She is the subject of two biographies, John Keats, *You Might as Well Live: The Life and Times of Dorothy Parker* (New York: Simon and Schuster, 1970); and Marion Meade, *Dorothy Parker: What Fresh Hell Is This?* (New York: Villard Books, 1988). Sylvia Townsend Warner was a British Communist novelist. For a discussion of her work, see Andy Croft, *Red Letter Days: British Fiction in the 1930s* (London: Lawrence and Wishart, 1990). One novel of the Depression era, *Summer Will Show* (1936), is considered a classic of "lesbian fiction." Terry Castle, "Sylvia Townsend Warner and Lesbian Fiction," *Sexual Sameness: Textual Differences in Lesbian and Gay Writing*, ed. Joseph Bristow (New York: Routledge, 1992), pp. 128–47.

65. See, for example, the essay "Political Poetry," by Elena Usiyevich in *International Literature* 9 (1937): 92–102. Her argument is surprisingly ungendered,

insisting primarily that all poetry is political. However, a preoccupation with Soviet affairs led to the publication of articles that examined the status of women in changing societies; see, for example, the two-part series by Joshua Kunitz, "New Women in Old Asia," in *New Masses* (2 Oct. 1934): 23–27, and (9 Oct. 1934): 15–19.

66. This program was adopted by the various John Reed Clubs, as explained in *New Force* 1, no. 5 (July–August 1932): 2.

67. *New Force*, ibid., p. 4.

68. "Resolution on the Work of *New Masses* for 1931," *New Masses* (September 1932): 21–22.

69. Marguerite Young is identified as the Washington Bureau correspondent of the *Daily Worker* in 1934. Around 1936 she is reported to have moved to New York, where she served on the *New Masses* editorial board for a time. According to a June 1998 telephone interview by Wald with A. B. Magil, she was married to another bureau correspondent. Due to the widespread secrecy about Party affiliations caused by fear of political persecution, one cannot entirely rule out the possibility that this Marguerite Young is the same well-known Marguerite Young (1908–1994) who authored *Miss MacIntosh, My Darling* (1965) and who also wrote on utopian socialism and Eugene V. Debs. However, all available biographical material for the latter places her in Chicago from 1933 to 1936 and in Indianapolis from 1937 to 1941. See Miriam Fuchs, ed., *Marguerite Young, Our Darling* (Normal, Ill.: Dalkey Archives Press, 1994).

70. Rochester was a Communist Party member who worked for the Party-led Labor Research Association and for a time represented the Party on the board of the American Civil Liberties Union. She wrote a number of pamphlets published by International Publishers on capitalism, including *Capitalism and Progress* (1945), *The Nature of Capitalism* (1946), and *American Capitalism* (1949).

71. Adams was a poet who had published several volumes of her own work as well as translations of François Villon. In the early Depression she taught at New York University, where she met and married the critic William Troy in 1933. The two then taught at Bennington College until 1944, after which she worked at Columbia University and was consultant for poetry at the Library of Congress. She participated in the 1935 American Writers' Congress but in later years described herself as a Left-wing Democrat. De Ford, who lived in San Francisco after 1920, produced biographies and mystery stories and contributed journalism to the Left-wing Federated Press. There is no evidence of her support for the League of American Writers. Lumpkin was a pro-Communist novelist who later became an anti-Communist religious crusader.

72. In addition to women previously identified, Gale Wilhelm (1908–1991) is known as a pioneering lesbian novelist; although she receives a few insightful paragraphs in Rabinowitz's *Labor and Desire*, available biographical material does not refer to her having Left-wing commitments, and her *New Masses* con-

tributions are not cited. Margaret Larkin (1900–1967) came from the western United States to New York City in the 1920s, where she began her writing career as a poet and was also a folksinger. In 1926 she published the one-act drama *El Cristo*, and in 1929 she published articles in both the *Nation* and *New Masses* about the songs of Ella May Wiggins, the martyred balladeer of the Gastonia Textile strikers. In 1931 she published *Singing Cowboy: A Book of Western Songs*. When she began working for the Theater Union, she met the writer Albert Maltz, to whom she was married from 1937 to 1964. Anne Bromberger is listed as a member of the League of American Writers in 1937.

73. This is possibly a pseudonym for Janet Metzger, married to the Cleveland-based proletarian novelist Robert Cruden, who wrote under the pseudonym James Steele.

74. *New Force* 1, no. 4 (May 1932): 4.

75. Ibid., p. 13.

76. *New Force* 1, no. 1 (January 1932): p. 13.

77. Marion Holden, "The Dead Corporal," *New Writers* 11, no. 3 (March 1936): 12–16.

78. *The Partisan* 1, no. 6 (September–October 1934): 9.

79. *Partisan Review and Anvil* 3, no. 3 (April 1936): 3–16.

80. *New Masses* (September 1932): 6–10.

81. Ibid. (April 1933): 10–13.

82. Brewster was a critic and short fiction writer, and Fischer a mystery writer.

83. Nora Benjamin was the pseudonym of Eleanor Gottheil Kubie, the award-winning author of nonfiction and fiction books for children. Aline Bernstein was a stage designer and the lover of novelist Thomas Wolfe. Martha Dodd was a novelist who would be accused of espionage during the McCarthy era. Dawn Powell, the novelist, was a close friend of Communist playwright and screenwriter John Howard Lawson. Brown and Wright will be discussed in chapter 8.

84. Backus was active in Hollywood, but no other information is available about her. Draper was known mainly as a feminist and supporter of liberal causes. Flexner was a Marxist drama critic and later a feminist historian.

85. Among the best resources on the history of the Communist Party and women are Rosalyn Baxandall, "The Question Seldom Asked: Women in the CPUSA," in *New Studies in the Politics and Culture of U.S. Communism*, ed. Michael Brown et al. (New York: Monthly Review, 1993); Elsa Dixler, "The Woman Question: Women and the American Communist Party, 1929–1941," Ph.D. diss., Yale University, 1974; Jayne Loader, "Women in the Left, 1906–1941: A Bibliography of Primary Sources," *University of Michigan Papers in Women's Studies* 2 (September 1975): 9–82; Robert Shaffer, "Women and the Communist Party USA, 1930–1940," *Socialist Review* 45 (May 1975): 73–118; and Kathleen Wiegand, "Vanguards

of Women's Liberation: The Old Left and the Continuity of the Women's Movement in the United States, 1945–1970s," Ph.D. diss., Ohio State University 1995.

86. Clara Weatherwax, "The Shape of the Sun," *Partisan Review and Anvil* 31, no. 1 (February 1936): 26.

## Chapter 8

1. In 1923, Claude McKay published a book in Russian that was translated five decades later as *The Negroes in America* (Port Washington, N.Y.: Kennikat Press, 1979). This contains short chapters titled "Negroes in Art and Music" and "Negroes in Literature," but it was not available in the United States to become part of the evolving Black Marxist tradition.

2. *International Literature* 6 (1935): 82.

3. Eugene Clay, "The Negro in Recent American Literature," in *American Writers' Congress*, ed. Henry Hart (New York: International Publishers, 1935), pp. 145–52.

4. Hart, *American Writers' Congress*, p. 129.

5. Ibid., p. 178.

6. Henry Hart, ed., *The Writer in a Changing World* (New York: Equinox, 1937), p. 179.

7. Ibid., 226–27.

8. Robert Gessner (1907–1968) was a Jewish American author of two books about Native American Indians, a nonfiction work called *Massacre* (1931) and the novel *Broken Arrow* (1933), as well as a book about anti-Semitism, *Some of My Best Friends Are Jews*. He had published a thirty-page poetic paean to international revolution called *Upsurge* (1933) and episodically contributed poems to the *New Masses* throughout the 1930s. In the 1940s, Gessner turned increasingly to fiction and then launched a successful career as a teacher and scholar in film studies at New York University.

9. Ibid., 233–34.

10. Richard Wright, "Blue-Print for Negro Writing," *New Challenge* 2, no. 2 (Fall 1937): 53–65.

11. Donald Ogden Stewart, ed., *Fighting Words* (New York: Harcourt, Brace and Company, 1940), p. 75.

12. The speech is reproduced in Franklin Folsom, *Days of Anger, Days of Hope* (Niwot: University Press of Colorado, 1994), pp. 197–200.

13. The most judicious assessment to date appears in James Smethurst, *The New Red Negro: The Literary Left and African American Poetry, 1930–1946* (New York: Oxford University Press, 1999).

14. This list is quoted from a *Daily Worker* article by Wright in Margaret Walker's *Richard Wright: Daemonic Genius* (New York: Warner Books, 1988), p. 110–12, and she offers no corrections in what is otherwise a highly critical book.

15. Edward Bland, "Racial Bias and Negro Poetry," *Poetry* 63, no. 6 (March 1944): 328–33.

16. Gwendolyn Brooks memorialized him in her lead poem of the 1949 collection *Annie Allen* (New York: Harper, 1949).

17. Wald telephone interview with Mrs. Richard Durham, sister of Robert Davis, 10 June 1999.

18. See Sandra Carlton Alexander, "The Achievement of Arna Bontemps," Ph.D. diss. University of Pittsburgh, 1976.

19. Horace Cayton, *Long Old Road: An Autobiography* (Seattle: University of Washington Press, 1964), p. 247.

20. See 1950s correspondence between Arna Bontemps and Maxim Lieber, Bontemps Papers, Syracuse University.

21. See "A Tale of Folk Courage," *Partisan Review and Anvil* 3 (April 1936): 31.

22. Folsom, *Days of Anger, Days of Hope*, p. 229.

23. John Edgar Tidwell is the authority on Davis. See his entry in *Dictionary of Literary Biography* and the introduction to his edition of Davis's autobiography, *Livin' the Blues: Memoirs of a Black Journalist and Poet* (Madison: University of Wisconsin Press, 1992).

24. Frank Marshall Davis, *47th Street* (Prairie City, Ill.: Dicker Press, 1948), iv–v.

25. Davis, *Livin' the Blues*, p. 248.

26. Ibid., p. 284.

27. Herbert Aptheker (b. 1915) came from a wealthy Jewish family in Brooklyn. He received a B.A. from Columbia University in 1936 and wrote a master's thesis, "Nat Turner's Revolt: The Environment, the Event, the Effects." In 1937 he published a two-part essay, "American Negro Slave Revolts" in *Science and Society*. In 1939, after a period spent in the South as an educational worker for the Food and Tobacco Workers Union, Aptheker joined the Communist Party, where he published under the pseudonym H. Biel. From then on, his work regularly appeared in the *Journal of Negro History*, *Opportunity*, and pamphlets published by International Publishers. In 1943, while training as an army officer, his Ph.D. dissertation was accepted and published by Columbia University Press as *American Negro Slave Revolts*, which marked a significant turning point in the historiography of the subject.

28. Wald telephone interview, March 1993, with Howard "Stretch" Johnson, a former Communist Party leader in Harlem who lived in Hawaii and worked alongside Davis.

29. Margaret Walker to Wright, 1 June 1938, Wright Papers, Yale University.

30. Ibid., 30 June 1938.

31. Ibid., 7 June 1939.

32. Ibid., undated.

33. Constance Webb, *Richard Wright* (New York: G. P. Putnam, 1968), pp. 143–44.

34. *Challenge* 1, no. 1 (March 1934): 39.

35. Ibid., p. 40.

36. Ibid., no. 2 (September 1934): 29.

37. Ibid., no. 4 (January 1936): 38.

38. Ibid., no. 5 (June 1936): 49.

39. Marian Minus, "Present Trends of Negro Literature," *Challenge* 2, no. 1 (April 1937): 10.

40. Walker to Wright, 19 Apr. 1938, p. 4, Wright Papers.

41. Wright to Langston Hughes, 29 May 1937, Hughes Papers, Yale University.

42. "Editorial," *New Challenge* 2, no. 2 (Fall 1937): 3.

43. Walker to Wright, November 1938, Wright Papers. Andrew Yarrow, "Dorothy West, a Harlem Renaissance Writer, Dies at 91," *New York Times*, 19 Aug. 1998, p. C23.

44. See A. Gilbert Belles, "The Politics of Alain Locke," in *Alain Locke: Reflections on a Renaissance Man*, ed. Russell J. Linnerman (Baton Rouge: Louisiana State University Press, 1982), pp. 50–62.

45. This appears in the reprint of Nancy Cunard, ed., *Negro Anthology* (New York: Negro University Press, 1969), pp. 111–15.

46. This appeared in *Race* 1 (Summer 1936): 70–76, 87.

47. *Opportunity* 11 (January 1933): 14–18.

48. Ibid. 14 (January and February 1936): 6–10; 42–43, 61.

49. Ibid. 15 (January and February 1937): 8–13; 40–44. James Allen (1906–1990, born Sol Auerbach) was the son of Left-wing Russian Jewish immigrants and a Ph.D. candidate in philosophy at the University of Pennsylvania until he was expelled for his radical activities. He joined the Communist Party in 1928 and in 1930 traveled to the South to become the first editor of the underground *Southern Worker*. With a background of organizing Alabama sharecroppers and working on the Scottsboro case, Allen later published major books on African American history and politics, including *Reconstruction: The Battle for Democracy* (1937) and *Negro Liberation* (1938), both with International Publishers.

50. *Opportunity* 1 (January and February 1938): 7–11, 27, 39–42.

51. Ibid. 17 (January and February 1939): 4–10, 36–42.

52. Ibid., 19 (January and February 1941): 4–9, 48–52.

53. Ibid., p. 52.

54. Ibid., 20 (February and March 1942): 36–41, 83–87; *Masses & Mainstream* 2, no. 8 (August 1949): 4–5.

55. *Phylon* 10 (First and Second Quarters, 1949): 5–14, 167–72.

56. Ibid. 12 (First and Second Quarters, 1951): 5–12, 185–90.

57. Ibid. 13 (1952): 7–18.

58. Ibid. 14 (1953): 33–34.

59. *International Literature* 8 (June 1934): 122.

60. Sterling Brown to Benjamin Botkin, 22 May 1932, Brown Papers, Howard University.

61. Joann V. Gabin, *Sterling Brown: Building the Black Aesthetic Tradition* (Westport, Conn.: Greenwood Press, 1985), p. 51. The interview cited was conducted with Brown by James Early and Ethelbert Miller on 19 May 1978 at Howard University. There is no evidence that Brown's recollection was ever independently corroborated. On the contrary, the written record suggests that Brown grew completely silent during the McCarthy era.

62. See Samuel B. Garren, "William Attaway," *Dictionary of Literary Biography*, 76:3–6, and Richard Yarborough, "Afterword," *Blood on the Forge* (New York: Monthly Review, 1987), pp. 295–310.

63. Milton Meltzer, "William Attaway, Negro Novelist," *Daily Worker*, 26 June 1939, p. 7.

64. Ralph Warner, "*Blood on the Forge* Is Story of Negro Brothers," *Daily Worker*, 8 Nov. 1941, p. 7.

65. Wald telephone interview with Howard "Stretch" Johnson, March 1993.

66. *Negro Quarterly* 1, no. 1 (Spring 1942): 3.

67. "Editorial Comment," *Negro Quarterly* 1, no. 4 (Winter–Spring 1943): 295–302.

68. See *Story* 6, no. 31 (1935): 30–34. Biographical information based on an undated letter to the editors of *Story*, "My Twenty-Two Years," Princeton University.

69. "Wounded," *Crisis* 10 (1938): 321.

70. Jeffrey D. Parker, "Frank Yerby," *Dictionary of Literary Biography*, 76:222–31.

71. *Harper's* 188 (May 1944): 448–53.

72. Ralph Ellison, "Recent Negro Fiction," *New Masses* (5 Aug. 1941): 25.

73. In a letter from A. B. Magil to Wald, 7 Apr. 1976, Magil states: "My impression is that Ellison was not only close to the CP, but for a time a member." In a phone interview by Wald with Howard Johnson, March 1995, Johnson said: "I think that Ralph was in the Party, just about the same time that Richard Wright was." Lloyd Brown recalls Charles Humboldt telling him that Ellison was a member of the Communist Party's Writers Unit in New York. Wald interview with Lloyd Brown, October 1990, New York City.

74. This view is also presented in Barbara Foley, "Ralph Ellison: Proletarian Journalist," *Science & Society* 62, no. 4 (Winter 1998–1999): 537–56.

75. Ellison to Wright, 22 Apr. 1940, Wright Papers.

76. Ibid., 11 May 1940.

77. Wald interview with Sanora Babb, Hollywood, July 1989.

78. Ellison to Wright, Nov. 3, 1941, Wright Papers.

79. This essay, originally intended to be the conclusion of Wright's autobiographical *Black Boy*, appeared in *Atlantic Monthly* 174 (August 1940): 61–70, and (September 1944): 48–56.

80. Ellison to Wright, 5 Sept. 1944, Wright Papers.

81. Ibid., 5 Aug. 1945.

82. Ibid.

83. Ibid., 23 Sept. 1946.

84. Ibid., 24 Aug. 1946.

85. Ibid., 1 Feb. 1948.

86. Walker, *For My People* (New Haven, Conn.: Yale University Press, 1942), p. 14.

87. Ibid., p. 16.

88. "Negro Revolutionary Music," *New Masses* (15 May 1934): 29–30.

89. Mike Gold, "Dark with Sunlight," *New Masses* (July 1929): 17.

90. Ralph Ellison, "Transition," *Negro Quarterly* 1 (Spring 1942): 87–92.

91. Wald interviews with Howard Johnson, July 1995, and Lloyd Brown, September 1996.

92. Nancy Cunard, ed. *Negro: An Anthology* (New York: Ungar, 1970; orig. 1933), p. 151.

93. Alan Calmer, ed. *Get Organized!* (New York: International Publishers, 1939), p. 12.

94. Robert Hayden, *Heart-Shape in the Dust* (Detroit: Falcon Press, 1940), p. 27.

95. Angelo Herndon, *You Cannot Kill the Working Class* (New York: International Labor Defense and the League of Struggle for Negro Rights, n.d. [ca.1934]), p. 25.

96. A 23 May 1940 letter from Theodore Ward to Wright, in the Wright Papers, reports on the turmoil, including a meeting of the Harlem branch of the Party where some members proposed the establishment of a bureau to which novelists such as Wright would have to submit manuscripts before publishing them.

97. "The Black Ball" in Ralph Ellison's *Flying Home and Other Stories* (New York: Random House, 1996), pp. 110–122.

## Conclusion

1. There are several versions of Rukeyser's Scottsboro adventures in circulation, but the above is based on a 28 December 1998 interview by Wald with her son, William Rukeyser, in Davis, California. Additional biographical material is based on the Rukeyser Papers at the Library of Congress, and a personal interview with Rukeyser in September 1980 in New York City.

2. "From Scottsboro to Decatur," *Student Review* 1, no. 6 (April 1933): 12–15.

3. See ibid., pp. 12–15, and vol. 2, no. 3 (January 1934): 20.

4. Letter from Harry Magdoff to Wald, 29 Oct. 1991.

5. Rukeyer's poetry is the subject of a substantial book-length study by Louise Kertesz, *The Poetic Vision of Muriel Rukeyser* (Baton Rouge: Louisiana State University Press, 1980). Among the most useful published studies of Rukeyser's work are John Malcolm Brinnin, "Muriel Rukeyser: The Social Poet and the Problem of Communication," *Poetry* 61 (January 1943): 554–75; Laurence Goldstein, "Muriel Rukeyser's 'Theory of Flight,'" in *The Flying Machine and Modern*

*Literature* (Bloomington: Indiana University Press, 1986), pp. 117–23; and M. L. Rosenthal, "Muriel Rukeyser: The Longer Poems," in *New Directions in Prose and Poetry*, no. 14 (New York: New Directions, 1953), pp. 201–29. A doctoral dissertation that attempts to place Rukeyser's entire career in perspective is Anne Frances Herzog, " 'Faith and Resistance': Politics and the Poetry of Muriel Rukeyser," Ph.D. diss., Rutgers University, 1993.

6. Jan Heller Levi, ed., *A Muriel Rukeyser Reader* (New York: W. W. Norton, 1944), p. 104.

7. Letter from Robert Gorham Davis, 13 June 1986. An examination of Davis's correspondence with Ella Winter, however, indicates that he did not actually see the incident but only heard about it. Davis felt that Stachel would not have taken such liberty with anyone not considered a member.

8. Wald interview with Muriel Rukeyser, New York City, September 1980.

9. Wald interview, 28 Dec.1998, with her son, William Rukeyser, in Davis, California.

10. Muriel Rukeyser to Louis Untermeyer, 25 June 1940, Untermeyer Papers, University of Delaware.

11. See "Grandeur and Mystery of a Poster Girl," *Partisan Review* 10 (September–October 1943): 471–73. The purported satire not only accuses Rukeyser of literary and political opportunism, but pokes fun at her weight and sexual appetites. She was defended by Rebecca Pitts in "The Rukeyser Imbroglio," *Partisan Review* 11 (Winter 1944): 125–29; and F. O. Mathiessen in "The Rukeyser Imbroglio Continued," *Partisan Review* 11 (Spring 1944): 217–18.

12. Adrienne Rich, "Beginners," *Kenyon Review* 15 (1993): 16. Wald interview with John Simon, Rukeyser's publisher and first literary executor, 6 July 1996.

13. Herman Spector to Walter Snow, 17 Jan. 1933, Snow Papers, University of Connecticut.

14. *Dynamo* 2, no. 1 (May–June 1935): 23.

15. Ibid. 1, no. 2 (March–April 1934): 8–9.

16. See Walter Benjamin, "Surrealism," in *Marxist Literary Theory*, ed. Terry Eagleton and Drew Milne (Oxford: Blackwell Publishers, 1996), pp. 70–80.

17. Muriel Rukeyser, *U.S. 1* (New York: Covici Friede, 1938). p. 69.

18. Wald interview with Hy Fireman, November 1990, Detroit, Mich.

19. Norman Rosten to John Malcolm Brinnin, 9 June 1937, Brinnin Papers, University of Delaware.

20. Rosten to Brinnin, 15 Sept. (1938?), Brinnin Papers.

21. Alan Calmer, ed., *Salud! Poems, Stories, and Sketches of Spain by American Writers* (New York: International Publishers, 1938), p. 46.

22. Calmer to Brinnin, 25 Apr. 1939, Brinnin Papers, University of Delaware. "Cadillac Square," together with his Spanish Civil War poem slightly retitled, lead off Brinnin's 1942 collection dedicated to Kimon Friar, *The Garden Is Political* (New York: Macmillan, 1942).

23. John Brinnin, "Muriel Rukeyser: The Social Poet and the Problem of Communication," *Poetry* 61 (January 1943): 554–75.

24. An example of a major statement that explicitly urges aspiring proletarian writers to take a "stiff dose of modern fiction – Hemingway and Faulkner, Joyce and Proust," is Alan Calmer's "Reader's Report," a summary of the results of a contest for the best novel on a proletarian theme. See *New Masses* (10 Sept. 1935): 23–35.

25. "Revolutionary Verse," *Pen & Hammer Bulletin* 2 (12 July 1934): 137–40.

26. *New Force* 1, no. 5 (July–August 1932): 4.

27. Granville Hicks, "Problems of American Fellow Travelers: Notes on American Novelists, Poets and Critics," *International Literature* 3 (1933): 108–9.

28. Joseph Freeman, *Daily Worker*, 17 Nov. 1933, p. 4.

29. A. B. Magil to Freeman, 9 Nov. 1933, Freeman Papers, Hoover Institute.

30. Sterling Brown, "Scotty Has His Say," *Southern Road* (Boston: Beacon Press, 1974), p. 23.

31. See Houston A. Baker Jr., *Afro-American Poetics: Revisions of Harlem and the Black Aesthetic* (Chicago: University of Chicago Press, 1988), p. 5.

32. Robert Hayden, "Gabriel," *Heart-Shape in the Dust* (Detroit: Falcon Press, 1940), p. 23.

33. Sterling Brown, *Southern Road* (Boston: Beacon Press, 1974), p. 46.

34. Hayden, "We Are the Hunted," in *Heart-Shape in the Dust*, p. 46.

35. See the discussion of this aspect of Hughes's writing in Donna Akiba Sullivan Harper, *Not So Simple: The "Simple" Stories, by Langston Hughes* (Columbia: University of Missouri Press, 1995).

36. Wright warns: "A vulgarized simplicity constitutes the greatest danger in tracing the reciprocal interplay between the writer and his environment." *New Challenge* 2, no. 2 (Fall 1937): 63–64.

37. Reprinted in Faith Berry, ed., *Good Morning Revolution* (New York: Citadel, 1993), pp. 1–2.

38. Ibid., pp. 2–4.

39. Ibid., pp. 4–5.

40. Ibid., pp. 5–6.

41. Ibid., pp. 6–7.

42. Ibid., p. 7.

43. Ibid., p. 13.

44. Ibid., p. 14.

45. Wald interview with Leo Hurwitz, 11 Nov. 1989, New York City.

46. See Sol Funaroff to James T. Farrell, 19 Mar. 1934, Farrell Papers. In a 1989 interview Gertrude Hayes recalled that the *Dynamo* poets "called Burnshaw 'Birdshit' and saw his going Left as being fashionable. He came from the world of the middle class and was ensconced as an editor." Wald interview with Hayes, 8 Oct. 1989, New York City.

47. Michael Gold to Louis Untermeyer, undated, sent from Boston, Untermeyer Papers.

48. Wald interview with Leo Hurwitz, November 1989, New York City.

49. For characteristics of the genre, see Janet Lyon, *Manifestoes: Provocations of the Modern* (Ithaca, N.Y.: Cornell University Press, 1999).

50. For a recent discussion of Marxist perspectives on surrealism, see E. San Juan Jr., "Surrealism and Revolution: Perspectives from Antonio Gramsci, Walter Benjamin, Aimé Césaire," in *Working Papers Series in Cultural Studies, Ethnicity, and Race Relations* (Pullman, Wash.: Department of Comparative American Cultures, Washington State University, 2000).

51. Charles Russell, *Poets, Prophets and Revolutionaries: The Literary Avant-Garde from Rimbaud through Postmodernism* (New York: Oxford University Press, 1985), p. 7.

52. Ibid., p. 11.

53. Ibid., p. 14.

54. Ibid, p. 225.

55. Joseph Freeman to Daniel Aaron, 19 May 1959, p. 2, Aaron Papers, Cambridge, Mass.

56. Freeman to Aaron, 19 May 1959.

## ACKNOWLEDGMENTS AND SOURCES

While it is not possible to list all their names, my first debt is to the graduate and undergraduate students in my seminars and lecture courses at the University of Michigan, including "Marxism and Cultural Studies," "Writers on the Left," "Resistance to Racism in U.S. Literature," "The Radical Novel," "The African-American Literary Left," "Radical Culture Reconsidered," "The 'Other' Thirties," and "The 'Other' Fifties." Several of my graduate students in the field of U.S. literary radicalism have launched their own academic careers, publishing impressive books and essays from which I have learned much, and have thus in turn become my teachers. These include Howard Brick, Robbie Lieberman, Tim Libretti, Brian Lloyd, Mark Pittenger, Paula Rabinowitz, and Zaragosa Vargas.

Another spur to my undertaking has been the appearance of a new, post-1960s generation of scholars who creatively engage the categories of race, ethnicity, and gender; accord serious treatment to mass, folk, and popular culture; and who have rethought the concepts of class and ideology on a more sophisticated plane than had radicals of earlier decades. Numerous debts to earlier, contemporary, and younger scholars will be evident in references throughout this book. Space limitations have obligated me to publish my review of recent scholarship in the field as a separate essay.*

In addition, it is no secret that the ability to carry out primary research on the scale employed in this book requires not only enormous amounts of time, but significant amounts of money to pay for travel, living expenses on the road, photographic reproduction of materials, and myriad other costs that accrue collaterally in carrying out a major research project. Therefore, I could not have completed the research for this book without generous financial support from the limited resources of my mother, Ruth Jacobs Wald, who underwrote several emergency domestic expenses that threatened to halt my work; and without the extraordinary personal assistance in family care matters provided by Dorothy and Quentin Stodola. Equally important was the willingness of my late wife, Celia, and my children, Sarah and Hannah, to give up most of our vacation time for many years. I am grateful to the American Philosophical Society for a travel grant; the Yip

* See "Revising the Barricades: Scholarship about the U.S. Cultural Left in the Post-Cold War Era," *Working Papers Series in Cultural Studies, Ethnicity, and Race Relations*, no. 11 (2000), published by the Department of Comparative American Cultures, Washington State University, Pullman, Washington.

Harburg Foundation for research funds to study blacklisted writers; the F. O. Matthiessen Room at Harvard University for a week's free lodging; Yale University for a one-month visiting fellowship at the Beinecke Library; the Michigan Humanities Fellowship Program for one term of release time in the winter of 1996; the University of Michigan Institute for the Humanities for a faculty fellowship in 1997–98; the John Simon Guggenheim Foundation for a fellowship in 1999–2000; and several units of the University of Michigan for funds which allowed me to augment attendance at scholarly conferences with a few additional days of research. The University of Michigan English Department, Undergraduate Research Opportunity Program, and Institute for the Humanities variously provided support for student assistants to help with library errands and the transcription of tape-recorded interviews and handwritten letters. The office of the Vice President for Research (OVPR) at the University of Michigan provided a grant to assist with the cost of obtaining photographs and permission to quote published work.

As I indicated in the acknowledgments of earlier books, my political views are tempered by my activities in a variety of social movements, and through a fifteen-year association with the journal *Against the Current* and its sponsoring organization, Solidarity. The grievous loss of renowned Marxist Ernest Mandel, who died in 1995, deprived me of challenging criticism from the individual who taught me the most about contemporary socialist theory and practice. Fortunately, the pages of *International Viewpoint, New Left Review, Monthly Review, Z Magazine, New Politics, Science & Society,* and many other similar publications continue to keep alive the spirit of creative, liberatory, and combative socialism.

In *Exiles from a Future Time,* I cite materials from the following libraries and institutional collections, and I am grateful for assistance and in some instances for permission to quote from letters and manuscripts: George Arents Research Library, Syracuse University; Homer Babbidge Library, Storrs, Connecticut; Beinecke Library, Yale University; Butler Library, Columbia University; FBI Reading Room (for the FBI files of Nelson Algren, Michael Gold, Kenneth Fearing, Josephine Herbst, John Herrmann, F. O. Matthiessen, Irwin Shaw, and Richard Wright); Hoover Institution, Stanford University; Huntington Library, Huntington Beach, California; Labadie Collection, University of Michigan; Library of Social History, Los Angeles; Moorland-Spingarn Research Center, Howard University; Newberry Library, Chicago; New York Public Library; Northwestern University Library; Oral History Collection (for the oral histories of Guy Endore and Albert Maltz), University of California, Los Angeles; University of Oregon Library; Harry Ransom Research Center, University of Texas; Research Library, University of

California, Los Angeles; Research Library, Indiana University, Bloomington; Research Library, Southern Illinois University; Research Library, University of Wisconsin; the Schomburg Center for the Study of Black Culture;
the State Historical Society of Wisconsin; Sterling Library, Yale University;
Tamiment Library, New York University; Charles Patterson Van Pelt Library,
University of Pennsylvania; and the Marion E. Wade Collection, Wheaton
College. The following individuals gave me access to material from their
private collections: Daniel Aaron, Cambridge, Massachusetts; Nathan Adler,
Marin County, California; Robert Gorham Davis and Hope Hale Davis, Cambridge, Massachusetts; Franklin Folsom, Boulder, Colorado; Maurice Isser-
man, Clinton, New York; and Aaron Kramer, Long Island, New York.

For material used in this volume, the following people participated in
personal interviews of varying degrees of formality, some of them tape-
recorded: Nathan Adler, Herbert Aptheker, Sanora Babb, Michael Blankfort,
Philip Bonosky, Lloyd Brown, Stanley Burnshaw, Malcolm Cowley, Hope
Hale Davis, Robert Gorham Davis, Josephine Hayes Dean, Mary Elting,
Hy Fireman, Angel Flores, Franklin Folsom, Marcia Folsom, Sender Garlin,
Marcia Endore Goodman, Elizabeth Granich, Gert Granich, Nick Granich,
Horace Gregory, Gil Green, Louis Harap, Gertrude Hayes, Dorothy Healey,
Rose Hoffman, Leo Hurwitz, Esther Jackson, James Jackson, Paul Jarrico,
Howard Johnson, Matthew Josephson, Aaron Kramer, Bobby Lees, Meridel
Le Sueur, Alice McGrath, A. B. Magil, Jerre Mangione, David Montgomery,
Edward Newhouse, Tillie Olsen, Carl Rakosi, Annette Rubinstein, Muriel
Rukeyser, William Rukeyser, Eva Russo, John Sanford, Morris U. Schappes,
Wilma Shore, Janet Sillen, Adelaide Walker, Saul Wellman, Tiba Willner, and
Marya Zaturenska.

The following people shared information with me, usually through cor-
respondence (including email) and phone conversations: Bill Bailey, Lee
Baxandall, Dan Bessie, James Bloom, Melba Boyd, Ernie Brill, Alex Buchman,
Paul Buhle, Art Casciato, Larry Ceplair, Robert Chrisman, Constance Coiner,
Jack Conroy, Bill Costley, John Crawford, Robert Cruden, Sam D'Arcy, Peggy
Dennis, Ben Dobbs, Bill Doyle, Dorothy Doyle, Joe Doyle, Michel Fabre,
Milt Felsen, Henry Ferreni, Alan Filreis, Fred Fine, Barbara Foley, Eric Foner,
Moe Foner, Marvin Gettleman, Dan Georgakas, Alan Golding, Max Gordon,
Reuben Granich, Frances Gray, Archie Green, Trevor Griffiths, Albert Halper,
Elaine Harger, Granville Hicks, Eric Homberger, Peter Hyun, Edith Jenkins,
Chris Johnson, Richard Kalar, Robin Kelley, Harvey Klehr, Herb Kline, Elinor
Langer, Andrew Lee, Robbie Leiberman, Jerry Lembke, James Lerner, Elsie
Levitan, Minna Lieber, Townsend Luddington, Esther McCoy, John McDon-
ald, Ben Maddow, Harry Mahoney, Anouar Majid, Bill Maxwell, James

*Acknowledgments and Sources*

Miller, Charles Miller, Paul Mishler, Jessica Mitford, Herbert Mitgang, Cary Nelson, Steve Nelson, Mark Nichols, Victor Paananen, Carl Padover, Howard Parsons, David Peck, Ruth Pinkson, Patrick M. Quinn, William Reuben, Mary Ann Rasmussen, Dolly Rauh, Abe Ravitz, T. V. Reed, Sam Roberts, Lester Rodney, M. L. Rosenthal, John Schultz, Mimi Schwartz, Pete Seeger, Sol Segal, Per Seyersted, Harry Shachter, Myron Sharpe, Mike Sharple, Alice Shugars, Paul Siegal, Layle Silbert, Dave Smith, Judith Smith, Morton Sobel, Clare Spark, Beverly Spector, Judy Spector, Jacquilene Steiner, Fred Stern, Jon Christian Suggs, Claude Summers, Loretta Szeliga, Shelley Tenzer, Vic Teich, Toby Terrar, Rachel Tilsen, Helen Travis, Joseph Vogel, Jerry Warwin, Seama Weatherwax, Tom Weatherwax, Susan Weissman, Hilda Wenner, Fred Whitehead, David Williams, Leon Wofsy, Ella Wolfe, Richard Wormser, Richard Yarborough, and Arthur Zipser.

The following provided various kinds of technical assistance and offered suggestions about the content of the book: Daniel Aaron, Marvin Gettleman, Doris Gold, Murray Goldberg, John Gonzalez, Ernie Goodman, Tim Hall, Glenn Jenkins, Carol Jochowitz, Walter Kalaidjian, Elissa Karg, Sharon Krauss, Elinor Langor, Mike Parker, Paula Rabinowitz, Robert Ryley, Ellen Schrecker, Justin Schwartz, Zaragosa Vargas, Edward Weber, and Douglas Wixson.

This is the third book that I have published with the University of North Carolina Press. The fact that I keep returning to UNC Press is evidence of the high esteem I have for the competency of its entire staff. I am grateful, also, to the two anonymous readers for the Press and to proofreader Jessica K. Printz.

Portions of the manuscript-in-progress were presented orally before several meetings of the American Studies Association, the Modern Languages Association, and the Institute for the Study of Culture and Society of the Marxist Literary Group. They were also presented at the 1993 National Poetry Foundation conference on "Poets of the Thirties"; the 1996 Paris Conference on "African-American Music in Europe"; the 1996 Tag Lecture at East Carolina University; the English Department and Program in Jewish Studies at UCLA; the Institute for the Study of Ideas and Society at the University of California at Riverside; and the 1993 Liverpool Conference on "Africa in the Americas." I appreciate the critical comments and suggestions from fellow panelists and audience participants on those occasions. In addition, a section of chapter 3 appeared in a different form as "The Many Lives of Meridel Le Sueur" in *Monthly Review* 49, no. 4 (September 1977); I am grateful to *Monthly Review* for permission to republish.

Draft sections of the manuscript were critically read by Howard Brick,

Laurence Goldstein, Jean Hauptman, A. B. Magil, Patrick M. Quinn, Christopher Phelps, and Paula Rabinowitz. My friend Arlene Keizer, a devoted scholar and poet in her own right, endured nearly two years of my talking incessantly about numerous issues in the research, writing, and editorial preparation of the book. None of these individuals, nor anyone else who was interviewed or who rendered assistance, is in any way liable for the opinions or judgments expressed in this book.

# INDEX

# Index

*Index*